Where Blind

Finding Meaning Behind Every Creed
Song & Light Beyond the Story

Men See

Trey Ulrich

Columbia Biography Press

CONTENTS

To my wife and our two M&M's –
I love you!

PREFACE

This book is a journey through Creed's music and the story behind it. It's a walk through the highs and lows of a band that wasn't afraid to delve into the shadows, to confront their own brokenness, and to seek something greater than themselves. Each chapter explores the themes of their songs, the struggles they faced, and the insights they gained. It's an invitation to reflect on your own journey, to explore the questions you may carry, and to find a new perspective on faith, redemption, and the human spirit.

In writing this book, my hope is that it will be more than just a history of Creed or an analysis of their music. I want it to be a conversation, one that takes place within the pages but resonates within your own heart. Creed's music is about more than entertainment—it's a spiritual journey, an exploration of what it means to be fully human and to seek something beyond this life.

As we dive into their lyrics and story, let us remember that Creed's journey, like our own, is not about arriving at a final answer. It's about discovering a deeper understanding, finding grace in our struggles, and realizing that no matter how lost we may feel, there is always hope. This is not a book of easy answers but of honest reflections, an attempt to connect with that sacred longing within us all.

May this book serve as a companion to Creed's music, a guide to the themes of redemption, struggle, and hope that have defined their journey. And may it remind you that you are not alone—that, in the end, there is always a place for you in a story greater than any one of us could write alone.

Welcome to the journey.

INTRODUCTION

The world felt different in the late 90's—somehow peaceful, yet more uncertain. We were on the cusp of a new millennium, filled with equal parts excitement and anxiety, and music was our refuge, our way to make sense of the world. Amidst it all, Creed emerged, a band that didn't just play songs but seemed to reach into the deeper places of our souls, tapping into questions of purpose, longing, and the divine. For so many, their music wasn't just something to turn up loud; it was a hand reaching out, something that felt almost sacred in a world that often felt anything but.

I remember the first time I heard them—it was like something in me that had been sleeping for years finally woke up. My teenage years were a mess of emotions and questions, as they are for many. Growing up, I hadn't known much about God or religion. My dad was a Communist-turned-Capitalist, a man of extremes, rooted in earthly beliefs, who seemed to have no space in his life for spirituality. My mom, on the other hand, was a gentle soul. Though we never went to church, I'll never forget the day I asked her about our faith. It was a random question for a nine-year-old, maybe spurred by a friend at school who had mentioned going to Sunday school. I asked, "Mom, what religion are we?"

She paused, and then softly said, "Well, Jesus is God, so we're Christians."

In that brief exchange, something planted itself in my heart. I didn't know what it meant or what to do with it, but I felt as if I'd been given a key to a door I didn't yet know how to open. From that day forward, an unspoken quest began. I wanted to know more about who Jesus was, this figure who apparently held the key to understanding life, purpose, everything. But without guidance or a community of faith, I wandered through those formative years searching for answers in places I didn't know were empty.

Then, at nineteen, during a restless summer, music became my sanctuary. One afternoon, I ran into a neighbor who had just come across a bootleg copy of Creed's *Human Clay*. She was buzzing with excitement, insisting I come over and listen. I had my own prized possession—an album by the Red Hot Chili Peppers that I had just bought and was eager to share—but something about her energy drew me in. We sat in her small living room, the worn-out speaker crackling to life as the opening chords played.

I wasn't prepared for what I heard. Scott Stapp's voice, raw and yearning, cut through the noise in my head, while Mark Tremonti's guitar riffs seemed to have this mystical pull, as if each note was carefully strumming a part of my soul. The lyrics were powerful, full of searching, pain, and hope, resonating with emotions I didn't fully understand but felt deeply. It was as if the music was speaking to a part of me I hadn't acknowledged in years. We sat there, song after song, as if in some unspoken agreement not to talk, just listen.

Afterward, I couldn't stop thinking about those lyrics, those melodies. I felt this strange mixture of peace and a profound ache. I knew I couldn't leave empty-handed, so I asked if we could trade albums. That night, I took *Human Clay* home, and in the quiet of my room, I dissected each song, each lyric. It was more than music; it was a dialogue, a confrontation with questions I hadn't had the courage to ask aloud.

In those songs, I began to feel closer to God—not in a fully understood or doctrinal sense, but in the raw, stumbling way that only someone who's still finding their way can understand. There was a vulnerability to Stapp's lyrics that made me feel like I wasn't alone in my own journey. They echoed my own fears, doubts, and fragile hopes. For the first time, I felt like my search for God wasn't this isolated, secret endeavor. I was part of a larger story, a story that Creed somehow gave voice to.

I remember saving up my paychecks from my summer job that year and going out to buy *My Own Prison* and *Human Clay*. Each song became a chapter in my personal journey, each lyric a map guiding me closer to what I yearned to understand. Songs like "One Last Breath" and "With Arms Wide Open" weren't just tunes to play on repeat; they were spiritual anthems, reminders that maybe, just maybe, there was a greater love, a deeper truth, and perhaps even redemption waiting for me on the other side of my questions.

Creed wasn't just a band; they were a bridge. They took all the fragments of my spiritual longing and wove them together, pointing me towards something beyond the music, something I hadn't been able to name. As I look back now, I see that this was one of the pivotal moments in my faith journey, a moment when I began to realize that my story was intersecting with something far greater than I had imagined. It would be years before I fully embraced my faith in Christ, but this was a piece of the puzzle, a whisper that would eventually grow into a voice calling me home.

Writing this book is a way for me to retrace those steps, to share that journey with others who may feel as lost as I once did. Creed's story, from their humble beginnings to their meteoric rise, their heartbreak, and reunions, is a testament to resilience, faith, and the human need for connection. Their music is more than just a soundtrack for road trips or background noise; it's a lifeline for those of us searching for something bigger than ourselves.

As we walk through their story together, we'll explore the layers of meaning in each song, the personal struggles that birthed them, and the impact they continue to have on listeners around the world. I want this journey to be more than just a history lesson on the band. I want it to be a path you can walk alongside, one that helps you confront your own questions, doubts, and, perhaps, your own faith.

In the pages that follow, you'll hear about the quiet strength of Tremonti's guitar work, the tortured poetry of Stapp's lyrics, and the unsung heroes behind their success. You'll see the cracks that fame exposed and the moments of grace that mended them. And maybe, as we journey through their music and their struggles, you'll find a bit of yourself in these stories—a reminder that you are not alone, that others have walked this path before, seeking meaning, healing, and hope.

This book isn't just about Creed or even just about music. It's about the power of art to speak to our souls, to remind us that our questions matter, and that sometimes, in the searching, we find the beginnings of an answer. Creed's songs have shaped my life, pointing me towards a faith that continues to grow and deepen, and my hope is that, by sharing their journey, you'll find inspiration for your own.

So, as we dive into each song, each story, let this be a guide—not to tell you what to believe but to encourage you to listen, to feel, and perhaps to encounter the same presence that has been quietly calling you all along. May this journey bring you closer to the Savior through repentant faith in Him, as it has for me, and may it be a step in the direction of your own discovery of what it truly means to believe. For this story is just beginning.

PART I
The Journey of Four Men

CHAPTER I
Court Is In Session

C reed's story begins like a murmur in the deep Floridian night, where four young men found each other amidst the waves of angst, a restless energy surging through Tallahassee's small music scene. It was 1994, and rock was at a crossroads—a time when the weight of grunge was starting to dissipate, leaving a void where the raw edge of alternative rock was eager to carve its new niche. There, in those college-town bars and cramped garage sessions, Scott Stapp, Mark Tremonti, Scott Phillips, and Brian Marshall came together, driven by a common desire to speak to something deeper, something universal. Creed wasn't just about music; it was a search for meaning, a way to channel both faith and doubt, glory and grit.

Their debut album, *My Own Prison*, was born from these conflicting ideals, each track like an anthem of existential reckoning. There was nothing easy or clean about it, yet it struck a nerve. This was music about struggle, not just personal, but cosmic—a raw, powerful dive into the idea that perhaps salvation could be found in the tension between redemption and despair. The critics were cold at first, dismissing them as another post-grunge act; the bands that were supposed to fill the shoes of Nirvana, Alice in Chains, and Soundgarden had come and gone. But the audience was listening. Creed's music, with Stapp's yearning vocals, Tremonti's soulful guitar, and the grounding force of Phillips' drums and Marshall's bass, felt as though it was calling people back from the brink. They weren't giving answers, just allowing people to feel, to confront their own questions—and for that, fans embraced them.

My Own Prison was soon followed by *Human Clay*, an album that would solidify Creed's place in rock history. With *Human Clay*, Creed reached for something more ambitious, pushing past the boundaries of what was expected. Here, they blended a sense of grandeur with deeply personal storytelling. It wasn't just an album; it was a dec-laration—a belief that in our frail, human hands, we hold both de-struction and creation. The diamond-certified success of *Human Clay* reflected more than record sales; it was the sound of millions finding themselves within those songs, carried along by the soaring riffs and earnest lyricism. And then there was "With Arms Wide Open," a track that stood apart, a song about fatherhood and the weight of bringing life into a world both beautiful and broken. When it climbed to number one and won a Grammy, it wasn't simply a victory for Creed. It was a triumph for everyone who understood the complexity of love, loss, and the hope of starting anew.

Despite their success, Creed's path was anything but straightfor-ward. The band was a paradox—a group who, despite the light they cast outward, seemed to wrestle with shadows that were just as pow-erful. Brian Marshall's departure in 2000 hinted at deeper cracks, fractures beneath the surface that fame couldn't conceal. Fame it-self became a pressure cooker, with expectations from every angle threatening to split them apart. Yet they pushed forward, carrying on without Marshall and pouring everything into their next project, *Weathered*. By the time *Weathered* was released in 2001, the band was battered yet unyielding. They carried the weight of fame like a cross, bearing the scars of criticism that were both personal and artistic. But they stood their ground. The album was their last cry of defiance, a testament to resilience even as they strained against the inner turmoil threatening to tear them apart.

And tear apart, they did. By 2004, Creed disbanded. Scott Stapp, the frontman whose voice had become synonymous with Creed's introspective style, went his own way, embarking on a solo career filled with its own highs and lows. Meanwhile, Tremonti, Phillips, and Marshall found new purpose in Alter Bridge, a project that allowed them to explore their musicality without the weight of Creed's history. The three of them, along with vocalist Myles Kennedy, created something raw and fresh, an evolution of their sound that took them into different, though familiar, waters. The split was not without pain, but there was growth in it. For some, it felt like closure, a bittersweet end to a band that had captured so much of what it meant to be searching for something in the dark.

But Creed's story, like any tale rooted in transformation, wasn't over. In 2009, they surprised fans with a reunion, releasing *Full Circle*, an album that was both a nod to their past and a step into something new. The title was telling—these were men who had traveled through their own personal crucibles and come back around. The years had tempered them; there was a maturity in their sound, an understanding that the world they had left behind had changed, and so had they. The reunion tours that followed were charged with nostalgia, yet there was also a sense of unfinished business, a feeling that the story of Creed had always been about more than just a few albums and a handful of hits. It was about redemption, about finding a way to reconcile who they had become with who they had been.

After another break in 2012, Creed seemed to fade again into memory, as though they had once more receded into the places from which they'd come. Each member pursued his own journey, growing, evolving, redefining himself beyond Creed's shadow. The music they created, however, never quite left the public consciousness. Creed had become more than just a band; they were a kind of mirror, a reflection of the struggles, the victories, and the quiet, unspoken questions of a generation.

In July 2023, a whisper began to circulate among fans—a hint that Creed might be coming back. And then it was confirmed: Creed would once again take the stage for a headlining tour in 2024. It was a reunion forged not by necessity, but by choice. This time, they weren't young men grappling with fame or struggling to define themselves. They were seasoned, a group who had walked through fire and come out the other side, carrying the wisdom of both their triumphs and their failures. Creed wasn't looking to relive the past; they were here to share what they had learned, to create once again for a new generation who, perhaps, would see themselves in those songs just as their parents had.

As the world prepared for Creed's return, there was a feeling that this tour would be different. It wasn't simply a comeback; it was a reawakening, a continuation of a journey that had always been about more than fame or success. Creed's music had carried with it a kind of healing, an invitation to look inward, to confront the parts of ourselves we often ignore. This reunion felt like another chapter in a larger story—one about finding purpose, about growth and resilience, and about facing the darkness with hope, with arms wide open.

Creed's legacy wasn't just built on records sold or awards won. It was carved from the vulnerability of four musicians willing to explore the duality of human nature, the constant tension between fear and faith, doubt and belief. Their story, still unfolding, remains a testament to transformation—to the idea that even the most broken among us can find strength in the journey, that every fall carries within it the potential for rebirth. And as they prepare to step back into the light, Creed reminds us that sometimes, even when you think the story is over, it's just beginning.

History

The seed of Creed's journey was planted on humid Tallahassee nights, where two young men—Scott Stapp and Mark Tremonti—began their quiet rebellion, each lyric and riff a statement against the world around them. They were just college students then, bound by the unspoken rules of the South, by small-town pressures, by the weight of expectations that come from family and faith. But amid all of this, there was an undeniable restlessness, a hunger for something greater, and a shared love for music that felt as vital as breath.

It was 1994, and the dream of grunge had begun to fade. The world was still reeling from Kurt Cobain's death, and for those who understood the agony and rawness he had channeled, it was a wound that ran deep. But for Stapp and Tremonti, that very rawness was a kind of fuel. They didn't want to replicate what had already been done; they wanted to find their own voice, one that might resonate with anyone grappling with faith, fear, and self-doubt. Music was a way to pull back the curtains on their own internal struggles, particularly for Stapp, who wrestled with a complicated upbringing under the shadow of a Pentecostal minister stepfather. There was a relentless ache within him—a need to reconcile his personal beliefs with the musical path he wanted to tread.

Their first attempts at songwriting were intimate, hesitant explorations into the depths of their own lives. They found themselves writing about themes of redemption, forgiveness, and inner conflict—words that felt less like lyrics and more like prayers, confessions whispered into the universe. The pairing of Tremonti's deep, melodic riffs and Stapp's brooding, baritone voice gave life to these themes in a way that felt both sacred and raw. It was as if the music allowed them to reach toward something divine while remaining rooted in the harsh truths of their own human experiences.

After countless late-night discussions and scribbled lines, they reached a decision: this music needed to reach others. They held auditions, hoping to find musicians who could understand the gravity of what they were trying to create. And there, in a small room filled with thick, buzzing anticipation, they met Brian Marshall and Scott Phillips, two musicians who not only complemented their sound but brought it to life. Together, they felt electric—a force that, if given the chance, could be as relentless and unapologetic as the lyrics they were crafting.

With their newfound members, the band took to Tallahassee's small venues and dives, playing anywhere that would welcome them. Those early performances were raw and unpolished, but it didn't matter. They were cutting their teeth, discovering the way the music moved through them, how it could draw out emotion and reach into the lives of those who watched them play. The crowds weren't always large, and the responses were often mixed, but there was always someone, somewhere in the room, who understood—who connected. And for those moments, as the music reverberated through cramped spaces with walls pulsing to the beat, it was all worth it.

One of those performances stood out in their memory, not for the songs they played, but for the name they had chosen for that night: Naked Toddler. Tremonti had seen the phrase on a newspaper headline that morning and had found a strange, almost humorous allure in its rawness. But as they took the stage that night, the reaction from the crowd was swift and merciless. The name had missed the mark—spectacularly. People sneered, others laughed, and a few simply looked confused. As the last notes of their set faded, Stapp and the rest of the band knew they needed to find a name that would better reflect the gravity of their music.

In the days that followed, they tossed around ideas, but none seemed right. Then, during a late-night conversation, Brian Marshall mentioned an old band he had been part of called Mattox Creed. The word "Creed" struck a chord with Stapp, who saw it as a powerful encapsulation of what they were trying to express—a statement of beliefs, a testament to the values they held. It was a name that spoke to the themes of faith, resilience, and introspection that had already woven themselves into their music. In a single word, they found their identity. They were Creed.

With this newfound sense of self, they pressed forward, refining songs that would soon become the bedrock of their debut album, *My Own Prison*. These weren't just songs; they were emotional narratives, stories of wrestling with inner demons, pleas for absolution, and confrontations with the darkest corners of the soul. Tracks like "Torn" and "What's This Life For" became expressions of deeply personal pain and longing, shaped by the influences of Stapp's childhood and the strict religious teachings he had both clung to and fought against. For Tremonti, each chord progression was a chance to add depth to the narrative, crafting a sound that felt as tortured and reflective as the lyrics themselves.

The quartet channeled this momentum into local performances, with every show slowly building their reputation. The crowds began to grow, and the whispers of Creed's sound spread like a secret among those who were searching for something genuine, something that felt as if it was born from the same aching questions they themselves held. They were young, unpolished, but fiercely determined to find something beyond the ordinary.

The music, however, was only the beginning. Their journey was about more than just fame or success; it was about finding answers to the questions that had haunted them since childhood, questions that lay at the intersection of faith and doubt, hope and despair. Creed wasn't just a band; it was a quest, a means of exploring what it meant to believe, to struggle, to fall and, ultimately, to rise again. And while they had no idea what lay ahead, each song felt like another step toward something larger than themselves—an anthem not just for them but for anyone who had ever felt lost, for anyone who had ever cried out in the darkness searching for meaning.

This was just the start of their journey, and already, it was clear: Creed was becoming more than a name, more than a band. It was becoming a voice for those who yearned for truth and for those who believed, deep down, that even in the shadows, light could be found.

My Own Prison

The smoky, dim-lit bar in Tallahassee hummed with the low murmur of conversation and the clinking of glasses. The air was thick with anticipation and a sense of raw, unpredictable energy. Jeff Hanson, a seasoned manager with a keen ear, scanned the crowd and took in the scene. He had taken a risk by booking an unknown band, a group that had somehow convinced him that they could pack the house with their friends and word-of-mouth promises. They were local, gritty, and most of all, hungry for a break. Tonight, that hunger was palpable, and Hanson found himself uncharacteristically drawn in.

As the band took the stage, the audience surged forward, filling the space in front of the small stage. Scott Stapp stood at the mic, gripping it with both hands, his gaze intense and almost haunted. There was something different in his eyes—a quiet rage, a longing, as if he was on the edge of something both profound and destructive. He opened his mouth, and the first chords of "My Own Prison" reverberated through the room. Tremonti's guitar riffs sliced through the noise with a unique sound, raw yet meticulously crafted, embodying a deep-seated pain and a spark of defiance.

For the first time, Hanson saw what the crowd had likely known all along. Creed wasn't just another bar band. The songs carried an emotional weight, a reflection of inner battles, isolation, and the deep human desire to find meaning amidst the chaos. Hanson was mesmerized. These weren't just lyrics; they were a guttural expression of something many people in that room could relate to but had never found the words for.

Without hesitation, Hanson made a decision that would change everything. He pulled Stapp aside after the show, his voice brimming with excitement, and said, "I don't know where you're headed, but I want to be a part of it." The next few days moved with a blur of conversations, paperwork, and plans as Hanson signed Creed to his management company. Together, they would build something that could extend far beyond this bar, this city, or even Florida itself.

For their debut album, Hanson connected the band with John Kurzweg, a producer who had an instinctive feel for the kind of sound that would bring Creed's raw energy to life. With barely enough money to rent studio time and equipment, they scraped together $6,000—funded by Hanson, whose faith in the band was unwavering. In a rented studio, Creed poured their hearts into their music, recording what would soon become *My Own Prison*. They didn't have the luxury of time or an endless budget; they recorded fast, pushing through long hours and imperfect takes. But those imperfections added grit, lending the album a distinctively unpolished, authentic edge that resonated with listeners.

When *My Own Prison* was released on their own label, Blue Collar Records, it spread like wildfire across Florida, finding a devoted fanbase that connected with the themes of struggle and redemption woven into each track. They had managed to sell 6,000 copies without any major label backing, a testament to the potency of their music. It was as if the band had tapped into a collective angst, a shared sense of alienation, and transformed it into something listeners could both escape into and feel empowered by.

It was around this time that *My Own Prison* landed in the hands of Diana Meltzer from Wind-Up Records. Meltzer, known for her instinctual talent scouting, felt an immediate connection to Creed's music. When she first heard the album, she described feeling a chill—a sensation of stumbling onto something with the potential to be monumental. She didn't just hear songs; she envisioned arenas packed with thousands, each person echoing back the lyrics in a cathartic release. Creed was different from the polished, image-centric bands that had saturated the airwaves. They felt real, and that was something she couldn't ignore.

Within a week, Meltzer, alongside Wind-Up's president Steve Lerner and CEO Alan Meltzer, flew down to Tallahassee to see Creed perform live. By now, the band was in their element, confident yet grounded, still stunned by how quickly their music was gaining traction. As they took the stage, the room crackled with electricity. Stapp's voice filled the space with an intensity that bordered on spiritual. Tremonti's guitar riffs swelled and roared, creating an anthemic wall of sound that seemed larger than the small venue could contain. This wasn't just a show; it was a visceral, almost religious experience. The Wind-Up team didn't need any more convincing. That night, they extended an offer, solidifying Creed's future.

Signing with Wind-Up Records marked a turning point. The label saw in *My Own Prison* something extraordinary, but they also saw the need to make it accessible to a wider audience. They remixed the album, crafting a sound that was more polished yet still retained the band's raw emotional core. In August 1997, *My Own Prison* was re-released, this time with Wind-Up's backing. As if ignited by the label's push, the album catapulted onto the Billboard charts, where its singles quickly began climbing. Each one—"My Own Prison," "Torn," "What's This Life For," and "One"—resonated deeply, echoing the pain and hope that countless listeners felt but couldn't quite articulate.

Creed had accomplished something unheard of for a debut album: four singles at number one on the Billboard Hot Mainstream Rock Tracks chart. The album's success defied industry norms. They hadn't relied on heavy MTV rotation or an oversaturated media blitz. Instead, the music found its way into the hearts of listeners through word of mouth, the growing internet buzz, and sheer grit. With little industry fanfare, *My Own Prison* went platinum six times over. In a world that seemed increasingly obsessed with surface-level appeal, Creed's raw honesty was a revelation.

In a span of mere months, they had gone from playing in crowded bars and recording on a shoestring budget to receiving accolades as Billboard's Rock Artist of the Year in 1998. They dominated the charts, not with manufactured pop anthems, but with songs that asked real, often uncomfortable questions. What does it mean to find yourself in a world that often feels like a prison? How does one wrestle with faith, purpose, and the inner demons that linger, even in the face of success?

For Stapp, these themes were deeply personal, drawn from his own struggles with identity and faith. There was no separation between the man and his music. Each song was an open wound, a confession that he laid bare for the world to hear. He didn't sing to entertain; he sang because he had to, because there were things inside him that could only be exorcised through music.

And Tremonti, with his intricate guitar work, became the perfect counterpoint. His riffs added a haunting, almost ethereal quality to Stapp's introspective lyrics, grounding them while giving them wings. Together, they created a sound that was both heavy and hopeful, a testament to the complexity of human experience.

As they entered the mainstream consciousness, Creed's influence began to spread. Their song "My Own Prison" became an anthem, not just for the fans in packed arenas but also for listeners who felt trapped in their own lives.

Human Clay

The night felt endless in the small apartment where Creed's early dreams had taken root. With the unexpected success of *My Own Prison*, the band found themselves riding a wave of achievement few had anticipated. What started as a raw exploration of personal pain and searching had resonated, giving them a taste of validation that both thrilled and terrified. As the royalties began to accumulate, they realized they now had the freedom—and the pressure—to create something new. They could go beyond survival, beyond just playing for small crowds, beyond wondering if the next gig would pay enough to cover their rent. They could reach further, risk more.

The conversations that followed were intense and filled with creative tension, yet there was a shared sense of purpose among them. Scott Stapp's voice, weathered by experience and introspection, carried an urgency that resonated with Mark Tremonti's relentless drive to push their sound further. Together, they began to draft the vision for *Human Clay*, an album that would go beyond the self-reflection of *My Own Prison* and grapple with the wider human experience—fatherhood, dreams, regret, resilience. This was an album born out of freedom but tempered by the scars of their journey so far.

The release of *Human Clay* was nothing short of a seismic shift. The album's first single, "Higher," was an anthem—uplifting, gritty, and strangely redemptive. It was the kind of song that felt like a sonic prayer, resonating with listeners who had their own visions of "higher" places, dreams that transcended everyday struggles. It spent a record-breaking 17 weeks at the top of the rock radio charts, a testament to how deeply it connected with people. The entire album debuted at No. 1 on the Billboard 200, selling 315,000 copies in its first week alone, a figure that stunned the band and reinforced that they were on a path no one had anticipated. As the sales surged, *Human Clay* eventually achieved diamond status, a rare accomplishment for any rock album, let alone one as introspective and unpolished as Creed's second record.

As *Human Clay* dominated the airwaves, Creed found themselves thrust into an arena where they were both worshipped and criticized. Success was a double-edged sword, magnifying every tension within the band. The praise was validating, yet the pressure weighed heavily on them. "Higher" had opened doors they hadn't even dared to knock on, but those doors led to uncharted territory. They were no longer just a group of guys with guitars and amps; they were an international phenomenon.

But fame, as it often does, brought with it fractures. Bassist Brian Marshall was slipping into a dark spiral of alcoholism. The tension between band members, especially between Marshall and Stapp, escalated. Scott and Mark Tremonti, driven by their loyalty to their friend and bandmate, organized a meeting with management to discuss Marshall's future. They wanted to support him, offering to stand by him if he would take the difficult step of going to rehab. It was a hard conversation, one marked by both love and frustration, but Marshall rejected their pleas, his pride holding him back from seeking help.

As they wrestled with Marshall's struggles, a public controversy erupted. In a radio interview with KNDD in June 2000, Marshall made disparaging comments about Pearl Jam's lead singer, Eddie Vedder. He claimed that Scott Stapp was a superior songwriter and that Pearl Jam's recent albums were "songs without hooks." It wasn't just criticism—it was a clear separation, an act of defiance that drew a line between Creed and a band many had admired for years. When Stapp learned of the interview, he was dismayed. He understood Marshall's frustration with the frequent Pearl Jam comparisons, but he also recognized the arrogance and, perhaps, the bitterness in his bandmate's words.

"People think they know us," Stapp confided to Tremonti one night. "But they don't know what it took to get here, what we're trying to say." He felt an urge to protect the integrity of their music, to let fans know that the words Marshall spoke weren't representative of Creed as a whole. As tensions rose, Stapp released a statement distancing the band from Marshall's comments, acknowledging how hurtful those words could be to the fans who had supported them. "I ask you all not to judge Creed as a band, because the statements made were not the band's feelings, they were Brian's."

It was a painful step, one that tore at the heart of their friendships and pushed the band to the edge of fracture. Stapp and Tremonti's pleas for unity fell on deaf ears, and Marshall's refusal to seek help strained their relationship to the breaking point. Soon after, Marshall parted ways with Creed. He joined a new band, Grand Luxx, with some of his former bandmates from Mattox Creed. To the public, his departure seemed abrupt, even shocking, but for the band, it felt like a slow unraveling of the bond that had held them together through the early years.

In Marshall's absence, Creed brought in Brett Hestla from Virgos Merlot as a touring bassist. The void left by Marshall was felt, yet the band pushed forward. With each new single from *Human Clay*—"What If," "With Arms Wide Open," "Are You Ready?"—they solidified their status as a powerhouse in the rock world. The songs themselves were deeply reflective, each one revealing a new layer of their journey. "With Arms Wide Open," a song Stapp wrote about becoming a father, became a heartwarming anthem about embracing life's changes with open arms. Its success was undeniable, and in 2001, it earned the band a Grammy Award for Best Rock Song.

The journey of *Human Clay* was one of growth, introspection, and, inevitably, sacrifice. As they toured and basked in their newfound fame, they were also forced to confront the personal costs of their success. It was a time of soaring triumphs and painful reckonings, a time when they were both celebrated and criticized, praised and scrutinized.

Weathered

The year 2001 was supposed to be Creed's time. Riding high on the success of *Human Clay*, the band was teetering on the edge of something vast—a space reserved for those who had cracked the code of stadium rock. Yet, even as they began crafting *Weathered*, there was an almost imperceptible heaviness, a tension threading through their work and relationships.

In the studio, Mark Tremonti picked up the bass with a clear purpose. For him, it wasn't merely about preserving the sound they'd built, but preserving the brotherhood, the essence of Creed itself. Each note, each riff, was meticulously layered to reflect that initial spark the band had ignited years ago. Despite the creative closeness,

Tremonti's decision to assume the role left Brett Hestla—a bassist and their touring member—observing from the sidelines. For Hestla, being part of the touring lineup, yet held at arm's length in the studio, reflected Creed's struggle with internal cohesion, an early sign of the storm brewing.

When *Weathered* released on November 20, 2001, the album felt prophetic, carrying both the ache and aspiration of the band's journey. The songs reflected stories of pain, endurance, and an almost desperate desire for redemption. Singles like "My Sacrifice" and "One Last Breath" struck a universal chord, reaching fans not merely as songs but as shared experiences. They spoke of vulnerability, of holding on by a thread, echoing the band's quiet unraveling. *Weathered* took the world by storm, debuting at No. 1 on the Billboard Top 200 and staying there for eight weeks—a feat matched by few. Yet as the singles charted and the awards buzzed, the music's success masked an internal fracture, an imperceptible line of strain that would soon split open.

Scott Stapp, the band's iconic frontman, was facing battles unseen by the public eye. A car crash in early 2002 left him with a concussion and damaged vertebrae—a physical blow that would become intertwined with his mental and emotional descent. In pain and increasingly dependent on both alcohol and painkillers, Stapp was fighting wars on multiple fronts. The medication and self-medication began to cloud the edges of reality, pushing him further into a spiral that would eventually threaten not only his life but the unity of the band he helped build. As Creed launched into their tour to promote *Weathered*, Stapp's inner turmoil became harder to contain, like a tightly wound coil beginning to snap.

The tour, however, wasn't without its electric moments. There were nights when the audience would roar, hands raised, voices merging with Stapp's in a crescendo of shared emotion. But these highs

were growing fewer. Tremonti and Phillips could feel the disconnect widening, their bandmate slipping through their fingers, even
as the music continued. Their eyes often caught each other during
the shows, sharing an unspoken worry, a silent question that hung
in the air with every riff. As each city passed, the intensity of Stapp's
pain—and his dependence—became a shadow that trailed them.

The breaking point came on December 29, 2002, at the Allstate
Arena in Rosemont, Illinois. Fans who had followed the band's journey from the days of *My Own Prison* and *Human Clay* were there,
packed tightly into the venue, expecting another night of the raw,
soul-baring performance that had defined Creed. But what they witnessed was a different scene altogether. Stapp staggered on stage, vis-
ibly affected. His voice, once a force of guttural power and precision,
was faltering, scattered. Each attempt to sing seemed like a struggle, a
distant echo of the man they'd come to know. The fans were bewil-
dered, hurt, their disappointment tangible as murmurs of confusion
turned to vocal discontent.

When four concertgoers filed a lawsuit against the band, claiming
Stapp had been "so intoxicated and/or medicated that he was unable
to sing the lyrics of a single Creed song," it was a wake-up call the band
couldn't ignore. The lawsuit became a public spectacle, a raw exposure
of the cracks in Creed's foundation. The band issued an apology, a
formal statement acknowledging the disappointment, though Stapp
himself seemed torn—caught between denial and acceptance. In quieter moments, he would later admit that he had been intoxicated,
though he insisted he wasn't incoherent. Still, the fans' memory of that
night lingered, a reminder of the fallibility hidden beneath the rock
star veneer.

By 2003, the tour was over, and so was the sense of unity. Stapp's
growing battles were isolating him not only from the fans but from

the very men who had once stood beside him as brothers. The studio, once a sanctuary where they'd forged their dreams, had become a place of tension, of words unspoken and frustrations unvented. While Tremonti, Phillips, and Marshall wrestled with the disappointment, Stapp had isolated himself, spiraling further in Maui, an island paradise juxtaposed against his inner chaos.

In June 2004, Creed officially disbanded. The announcement, though inevitable, felt surreal. For Tremonti, it was like saying goodbye not only to a friend but to a vision they'd all once shared. It wasn't just a band breaking up—it was the end of a dream they'd built together. Tremonti would later reveal that the creative flow had ceased, a result of the mounting tension and the growing distance between them and Stapp. The friendship had become strained beyond repair, and the creative synergy that once bound them felt more like a memory than a reality.

As the dust settled on Creed's era, a new beginning took shape for Tremonti and Phillips. Almost immediately after the announcement of Creed's break-up, the duo joined forces with Marshall and found a new voice—Myles Kennedy. Together, they would form Alter Bridge, a phoenix rising from Creed's ashes.

Full Circle

The return of Creed in 2009 felt less like a comeback and more like an overdue chapter finally unfolding. For Mark Tremonti, Scott Stapp, Scott Phillips, and Brian Marshall, it was as though they were drawn by an unspoken need to revisit what they'd left behind years before. This wasn't simply a nostalgic reunion; it was a reconnection, a reawakening that struck chords both personal and profound for each member.

Seven years had passed since they'd last taken the stage together, years filled with uncertainty, solo pursuits, and the quiet realization of how deeply intertwined their lives had become through Creed's music. Tremonti, who once declared the band "officially in our past," found himself face-to-face with emotions and memories he thought he'd buried. Yet, as the idea of a reunion took shape, the hesitation gave way to something unexpected—excitement. "We're all very excited to reconnect with our fans and each other after seven long years," Tremonti admitted, almost surprised by his own words. The sentiment was echoed by Phillips, who, reflecting on the band's sudden disbandment, saw the opportunity not merely to revive Creed but to take their bond to new depths, both musically and personally.

In interviews, Stapp voiced a feeling that transcended words like "reunion" or "reformation." For him, this was a rebirth, a chance to reshape Creed's legacy. "We never felt like we weren't together," he shared with quiet intensity, "It's more of a rebirth." Stapp wasn't just talking about the band's return to music but about the shared journey, the kind of journey that only those who have endured the highs and lows of fame together can truly understand. The audience sensed it, too. When the announcement of the 2009 tour and new album spread, anticipation grew. Fans, many who had grown up with Creed's anthemic sound, were ready to witness the band's evolution.

The first show in Salt Lake City on August 6, 2009, was electrifying. The energy in the venue was palpable, a mix of nostalgia and raw intensity, as if every chord struck and every lyric sung was part of a collective release. Standing under the lights, they were not just musicians—they were four friends reclaiming something they had lost, something vital. Tremonti's riffs roared through the crowd with newfound power, Phillips' drumming felt more precise, more resonant, and Marshall's bass lines seemed to pulse with a deeper sense of connection. And Stapp, with that unmistakable, gravelly voice, became the anchor, the voice of longing, resilience, and rebirth.

Creed's first album in eight years, *Full Circle*, released on October 27, 2009, bore a title that mirrored the band's own journey. As Stapp explained, "It really defines and articulates, melody-wise and lyrically, what's happened with us." The name captured the essence of where they had come from and where they hoped to go. Songs like "Overcome" and "Rain" encapsulated not just their personal trials but a collective resilience that resonated with fans who had weathered their own storms since Creed's last days on the charts. The album was met with mixed reviews, but for those in the audience and for the band themselves, *Full Circle* was more than a record—it was a testament to survival, forgiveness, and the unbreakable bond that only time and trial could forge.

In Houston, Texas, the band's Creed Live concert in 2009 marked a historical moment. Using an unprecedented 239 cameras, they captured the night in a way that had never been done before, breaking multiple world records and achieving what few thought possible—immortalizing a moment in which the band wasn't just reliving past glories but redefining themselves in real-time. The performance, captured in stunning clarity, allowed viewers to feel the raw energy of the night, and the groundbreaking "big freeze" technology brought an element of surrealism to an already unforgettable experience.

Yet, the rebirth wasn't without its challenges. Despite the grand vision of the *20-10 Tour*, which offered affordable tickets to make concerts accessible, not every show sold out. The critical reviews ranged widely, reflecting both the intense devotion of longtime fans and the shifting tastes of new listeners who had grown up in Creed's absence. And still, night after night, Creed played with the same passion, the same urgency, driven by something deeper than commercial success. This was about reconnecting with their roots, the fans who had stood by them, and the spirit of Creed itself. With Skillet joining the tour,

Creed's sound took on an added intensity, fueling their own renewed
fire as they traversed cities, pouring themselves into each performance,
reaffirming their commitment to the journey they had begun so many
years ago.

In late 2011, whispers of a new project surfaced. The band came
together, this time with an ambitious idea—to revisit the albums that
had defined them, *My Own Prison* and *Human Clay*, playing them
front to back on a dedicated tour. For the fans, this wasn't just a
chance to hear favorite tracks; it was an invitation to relive a musical era
that had shaped a generation. In a time when technology and culture
had rapidly transformed, Creed's music was a reminder of a different
world, a bridge between the past and the present.

When the tour kicked off in April 2012 at the Chicago Theatre,
it felt like a pilgrimage. The first night, devoted entirely to *My Own
Prison*, brought fans back to the raw, uncompromising sound that had
first catapulted Creed into fame. Every note echoed with the unfiltered
angst and aspiration of their beginnings, a musical reflection of the
world they inhabited in those early days. On the second night, as they
moved through *Human Clay*, they invoked memories of *Higher* and
With Arms Wide Open, songs that had once dominated airwaves and
had become anthems of resilience and hope for fans worldwide. The
crowd sang along, their voices swelling in unison, their connection
with the band almost tangible. In that theater, Creed wasn't just per-
forming—they were sharing an experience, a mutual recognition of
the highs and lows they had all endured since those songs had first hit
the airwaves.

Following their U.S. performances, the tour took Creed across
oceans, through South America and into the vibrant musical landscapes of Indonesia. Each stage, each city, was a reminder of how far
they had come and of how universal their journey was. They found

themselves re-energized by the international fans who welcomed them with open arms, as if time had never passed, as if *My Own Prison* and *Human Clay* were released yesterday. The connection was immediate and visceral, proof that their music transcended borders and language.

In the quieter moments between shows, Creed's members found themselves reflecting on what this new chapter meant. Away from the stage lights and the roar of the crowd, they were just four people who had weathered the storms of success, separation, and self-discovery.

The Great Divide

The hiatus for Creed was more than just a break in the music. It was a slow unraveling, the kind that happens almost imperceptibly, like the silent shifting of tectonic plates. Years stretched between the last chords they played together and their future plans, if any could still be called that. It's as if the bond that once tied them—the blood, sweat, and unyielding ambition of younger days—had dissolved into an ocean of time, distance, and bruised egos. This wasn't the story of a band falling apart in a cataclysmic explosion but rather one of erosion, one grain of sand at a time.

In October 2013, Scott Stapp reflected on the road they'd traveled, noting how close they'd come to creating something new. They had spent months in 2011 and 2012 putting pieces together for a fifth album, crafting, experimenting, perhaps rekindling some of that old fire. Yet the project, almost like a ghost, had vanished before it ever saw the light of day. To Stapp, Creed was "still a band," an entity alive in his mind and heart, a bond that perhaps only he seemed to feel so strongly after all the dust had settled.

Mark Tremonti, in his own way, had walked away years before anyone made it official. By 2015, while Stapp remained hopeful, Tremonti acknowledged, almost dispassionately, that he and Stapp hadn't truly been friends for close to a decade. The memories of shared stages, nights on the road, and the incredible journey from obscurity to stardom seemed to lie under layers of resentment and fractured communication. Tremonti's attention was elsewhere, channeling his energy into Alter Bridge, where Myles Kennedy offered a creative counterpart unburdened by the weight of their shared history. Creed's past lingered like a shadow, but it was Alter Bridge that provided him a new life, one not dependent on the raw, turbulent energy that had once fueled Creed's rise.

In September 2015, Stapp's hope for a reunion seemed undiminished. Sitting down on *The Dr. Oz Show*, he publicly extended a hand to his former bandmates: "Come on, guys, let's make a record." It was a plea more than a proposition, a moment where he laid himself bare, holding out for the chance to reclaim something he thought they had lost together. In his voice, there was a sincerity that hadn't been dulled by the years or by personal struggles that had played out in the public eye. But while Stapp was ready to revive Creed, Tremonti's solo projects and his commitments with Alter Bridge were moving forward with relentless momentum, like a train he couldn't—or wouldn't—stop. The worlds they now inhabited were miles apart, held together by threads that seemed too thin to bear the weight of a full reunion.

November 20, 2015, saw the release of *With Arms Wide Open: A Retrospective*, a boxed set that gathered up pieces of Creed's legacy: their hits, some rarities, and acoustic versions of their most iconic songs. For fans, it was a reminder of what once was—a glimpse into a world they'd once inhabited with the band, songs that had been soundtracks to countless lives, carrying memories of a time when Creed had been a force that no one could ignore. Yet even this release, a beautifully packaged remembrance, felt almost like a farewell. The exclusivity of its release at Walmart gave it the air of something final, a memory you could hold onto, not a promise of something more.

The years that followed saw each member take their separate paths with even greater conviction. Stapp joined Art of Anarchy in 2016, a venture that let him pour his turbulent energy into a new project, away from the weight of Creed's name. With them, he released *The Madness* in 2017, his voice raw and unfiltered, as if trying to push through layers of pain, anger, and hope. Tremonti's solo career flourished as he released album after album with a relentless drive, albums like *Dust* in 2016 and *A Dying Machine* in 2018, where he seemed to channel all the complexity and darkness that he might never have fully unleashed in Creed's early years.

Scott Phillips, too, found his own creative outlet in Projected, where he laid down tracks for *Ignite My Insanity* in 2017, a project that let him stretch beyond the boundaries of Creed's style. It was a world away from the mainstream success of Creed's early days, but perhaps it was this distance that allowed each member to find an unburdened sense of creative freedom.

Meanwhile, Stapp continued to redefine himself, moving further into solo territory with *The Space Between the Shadows* in 2019. It was an album born of struggle and transformation, his voice bearing the scars of battles fought both on stage and in his own mind. The album was perhaps as much a declaration of survival as it was a musical endeavor, a testament to his own resilience. While he had always been the heart of Creed, in his solo work, he was something more vulnerable and fierce, the layers stripped back, revealing the man beneath the myth of the rockstar.

And yet, as the years stretched on, Creed's story wasn't over. In November 2020, a small ripple stirred the quiet waters of their legacy. Drummer Scott Phillips suggested that a reunion was "a possibility." It was a simple statement, understated and almost easily overlooked, yet it hinted at the chance that the thread holding them together hadn't frayed entirely. Phillips' words reignited a faint glimmer of hope, as if somewhere beneath the surface, something still bound them together, though what that was remained unseen, like a relic buried under years of silence and change.

This was more than just music; it was a story of redemption, of forgiveness that had yet to happen, of years that could never be undone but might yet be understood. Creed's silence held its own music, the echo of a time when they had been unstoppable, when their songs had been anthems of defiance and pain, faith and doubt. If they came back together, it wouldn't be a revival of the band they once were—it would be the formation of something new, something shaped by all they had endured in the years apart. The reunion, if it ever happened, would be an alchemy of time, sorrow, joy, and a hard-won understanding of who they each had become.

In this moment, there was no certainty, only a lingering sense of unfinished business, an unwritten chapter waiting for its first words. And as they each continued on their separate paths, the thought of Creed lingered, like a heartbeat just beneath the surface, waiting for the right moment to rise again.

Reconciliation

It was the kind of resurgence that felt like fate finally found its rhythm—a rhythm forged by years of silence, internal battles, and raw memories lingering in the chords of their greatest hits. Creed's reunion in 2023 wasn't just about getting the band back together. For each member, it was a return to the origins of their journey, a journey that had seen their songs rise to dizzying heights and plunge into the depths of personal turmoil. But this time, it was different. The world was different, and maybe, so were they.

On July 19, 2023, a simple announcement shattered nearly a decade of quiet. Creed was back. And they wouldn't just tiptoe onto the stage—they would dive headlong into it, headlining the Summer of '99 cruise in April 2024. It was an unexpected launch pad, a symbolic return to the era that had defined them and a nostalgic invitation to a generation that had grown up with their music pulsing through the boomboxes of their youth. Fans across the world felt an electric surge, a ripple of anticipation as news of their return exploded across social media.

For the band, it wasn't just another gig or even a reunion—it was a reckoning with the past, a chance to step back into the spotlight with scars now stitched into strength, wounds slowly healing into stories. They knew what was at stake, the weight of expectations both theirs and their fans. They were no longer young men finding their way through the labyrinth of fame and fortune; they were seasoned musicians who'd experienced their own rises and falls. And this time, they seemed ready to confront it all with a fierce honesty.

As October 30, 2023, approached, the whispers grew louder. Fans wondered if the cruise was a one-time event or a hint of more to come. Then, the second bombshell dropped—the announcement of *The Summer of '99 Tour*, a nod to the era that had been both their pinnacle and crucible. This would be their first full-fledged tour since 2012, a tour designed not just to rekindle their connection with old fans but to spark a new connection with younger ones who might only know their music as echoes from another era.

The tour wouldn't be a solitary journey. It was a lineup that felt like a reunion of long-lost friends, with fellow rockers like 3 Doors Down, Finger Eleven, Daughtry, Switchfoot, Tonic, and Big Wreck joining them on select dates. Each band brought its own story, a shared tapestry of the struggles and resilience that defined rock music in the late '90s and early 2000s. There was a palpable sense of camaraderie and shared history in this lineup, a gathering of musicians who had ridden the same waves, who had endured the cyclical rise and fall of rock in mainstream culture.

There was an unspoken agreement, almost sacred, among them. This tour wasn't about outshining one another; it was about relighting a fire, a celebration of a sound and spirit that had once defined a generation's sense of rebellion, longing, and introspection. They were together in this, not as competitors but as storytellers revisiting their most potent chapters.

The road to this moment hadn't been easy for Creed. Their music had always walked a tightrope between introspective spirituality and raw, unfiltered emotion. Behind those lyrics of self-discovery and hope, of searching for identity in a tumultuous world, were real struggles and deeply personal battles. Their journey from skyrocketing fame to the painful unraveling in the years that followed had left scars on each of them—scars that now, with time, had softened, transformed, and deepened their resilience.

Then came the announcement on February 6, 2024, of yet another tour—the *Are You Ready? Tour* set for November, signaling that Creed's return wasn't a mere fleeting moment. They were here to stay, once again embracing the unsteady world of live performances and fan expectations. With supporting acts like 3 Doors Down, Mammoth WVH, and Finger Eleven, the tour was building up to be more than just a comeback—it was an anthem of endurance, a testament to the power of music to survive even the darkest nights.

By June 2024, the impact of their return was undeniable. Creed's name started to appear again on Billboard charts, with their songs echoing across playlists, radio stations, and stages in a way that seemed to bridge the years between past and present. It wasn't just nostalgia that was drawing fans back; there was something fresh, something raw, in the way Creed's music connected to the struggles and resilience that defined the modern age. The world had changed, but the themes of identity, redemption, and hope that pulsed through their lyrics remained universal, perhaps now more relevant than ever.

Creed's sound had always been steeped in a sense of searching, a yearning for something beyond the surface. It was a sound that resonated deeply in the human psyche, drawing on themes of personal redemption and spiritual exploration that seemed timeless. And now, as the lights dimmed and the first chords rang out on stages across the country, it was as though time itself had folded, bringing the energy of 1999 into 2024, with the same intensity, yet tempered by the wisdom of experience.

The anticipation grew with every tour stop announcement, every cryptic post and teaser dropped online. Fans shared their stories of what Creed's music had meant to them—stories of survival, of heartbreak and healing, of faith found and lost and found again. They were stories that spanned generations now, from those who had been there in the beginning to those discovering Creed's music for the first time.

For Creed, this resurgence wasn't about reclaiming fame or fortune. It was a revival of purpose, an affirmation of the power of music to heal, to connect, to bridge the gaps between past and present. In every note, every lyric, there was an invitation for fans to join them on a journey of introspection, to confront the shadows and emerge with a renewed sense of self.

At the time of this writing, as they prepare for their "Are You Ready? Tour", Creed seemed to stand not just as a band but as a symbol of transformation, a testament to the resilience of four guys who are true friends and brothers.

PART II
Created My Own Prison

CHAPTER 2

"Torn"

To expand on the song "Torn" and delve into its layers, we need to understand how Creed crafts not just a song but an immersive experience of conflict, struggle, and longing. "Torn" is a piece that transports listeners into the heart of an internal battle—a place where ideals of peace, self-worth, and love are under siege by betrayal, deception, and emotional disarray. Creed, both through lyrics and instrumentation, creates an environment that allows the listener to feel the tension and weight of this inner turmoil.

At the core of "Torn" lies a battle for the soul—a conflict where ideals clash violently with the harsher realities of life. The lyrics serve as a visceral account of someone ensnared by their own misgivings and doubts. It's a raw portrayal of a person caught in the middle of an identity crisis, where the allure of peace seems far removed, replaced by confusion and anger. In lines like "Peace is dead in my soul," we witness the narrator's despair and recognition of an internal loss that words barely capture.

Creed uses blunt language to paint this bleak psychological landscape. By stating his "intentions poor," the narrator isn't merely confessing but, in a sense, exorcising the parts of himself that have contributed to his fractured state. It's almost as if he's laying himself bare, acknowledging the missteps that led him here, not to gain sympathy, but to face the reality of his choices.

This sense of inner conflict between self-condemnation and the yearning for peace taps into a deeply universal experience. The language oscillates between clarity and confusion—sometimes blaming himself, other times projecting frustration outward. The narrator's struggle becomes an anthem for anyone who has felt lost within themselves, yearning for peace but unsure how to reach it. Creed, through these words, offers a mirror to our own moments of self-doubt and inner conflict, creating a cathartic, shared experience of vulnerability and self-reflection.

The instrumentation in "Torn" is a masterclass in sonic storytelling. It begins with a solitary guitar riff that feels almost like an open wound, creating a sense of exposure and rawness from the very first note. This haunting sound carries an emotional weight, suggesting vulnerability and setting a somber tone for what's to follow. It's not just the notes themselves, but the way they're played—restrained yet wounded, soft yet insistent, capturing the tentative nature of someone on the edge, unsure of their own footing.

As the song builds, the bass and drums add a layer of depth that amplifies this sense of conflict. The rhythmic intensity reflects an escalation, as if the narrator's internal world is caving in on him. The steady, driving beat gives the song a gritty, almost relentless energy, underscoring the feeling that there's no easy escape from this emotional turmoil.

The guitars shift from a restrained tone to something explosive, mirroring the internal journey of the narrator. There's a sense of catharsis in the music itself, as if each progression is a struggle to reclaim a lost part of oneself. The power chords, with their minor progression, create a feeling of restlessness, an unresolved tension that speaks to the narrator's inability to find peace. It's not just music;

it's a dialogue between restraint and release, vulnerability and rage—a musical manifestation of the internal war tearing the narrator apart.

In "Torn," the narrator is caught in a cycle of resentment, longing, and self-examination. Lines like "Born in my own misery" and "Peace is dead in my soul" suggest a soul that's been fragmented by both internal and external forces. There's an acknowledgment that the torment he feels is, in part, self-inflicted. This sense of self-awareness deepens the song's impact, presenting a complex individual who is both victim and perpetrator of his own suffering.

The refrain, "Yes, I'm the one who / The only one who / Would carry on this far," suggests a weary acceptance. It's as if the narrator realizes that he alone has brought himself to this breaking point. There's an isolation here, a recognition that no one else can truly understand the depths of his struggle or bear the weight of his choices. In this, he's both liberated and imprisoned—free to define his own path but burdened by the consequences of his own decisions.

The narrator's inner monologue reveals a person who is, at his core, yearning for peace and redemption. Yet, he's trapped in a world where those ideals feel unattainable, obscured by layers of resentment and bitterness. The lyrics convey a sense of duality: a man who wants to rise above but is constantly pulled down by the very chains he has forged. This dichotomy between self-improvement and self-destruction is a powerful motif, resonating with anyone who has struggled with their own limitations and desires for change.

The musical structure of "Torn" parallels the narrator's internal struggle, capturing the oscillation between moments of introspection and bursts of rage. The verses are subdued, almost whisper-like, as if the narrator is confessing his darkest thoughts in solitude. These quieter sections invite listeners into a personal space, a realm of unspoken fears and regrets.

As the chorus erupts, the band's intensity swells, creating a wave of sound that feels almost primal in its release. The distorted guitars, pounding drums, and heightened tempo capture the essence of a soul unleashing its pent-up rage. This shift in dynamics not only underscores the song's emotional turbulence but also mirrors the human tendency to swing between self-blame and defiance. The music becomes a vehicle for both confession and catharsis, allowing the narrator to confront his demons in a way that words alone cannot.

Each return to the chorus is a reminder of the unending nature of this battle. There's no easy resolution, no neat ending. Instead, the song leaves us in a state of flux, as if the struggle will continue indefinitely. This sense of unresolved tension is part of what makes "Torn" so impactful—it mirrors the cyclical nature of human struggle, the endless dance between peace and chaos, acceptance and defiance.

At its heart, "Torn" is a meditation on the loss of innocence and the scars left by betrayal. The recurring imagery of lies infiltrating the narrator's mind suggests that his battle is not only against external forces but also against his own internalized fears and doubts. These lies, these seeds of self-doubt, have taken root, poisoning his sense of self and making it difficult to find solid ground.

The song speaks to anyone who has experienced betrayal, particularly the betrayal of trust or self-belief. It captures the way such experiences can shatter one's sense of identity, leaving behind a fragmented soul struggling to make sense of what remains. In this light, "Torn" is not just a song about personal struggle but a universal anthem for those who have grappled with their own inner fractures.

While "Torn" is steeped in themes of anguish and despair, there's an underlying current of hope—a hope that, despite the pain, redemption is possible. The lyrics may not offer a clear path to healing, but they do hint at the possibility of self-forgiveness and peace. By confronting his own failures and missteps, the narrator begins a journey of self-acceptance, a step toward reclaiming his own sense of worth.

In lines like "Peace is dead in my soul," there's an implicit recognition that peace is not lost forever—it's simply dormant, waiting to be revived. The narrator's journey is one of confrontation, of facing his own inner demons with brutal honesty. This act of self-examination is itself a step toward healing, a way of acknowledging that, while he may be "torn," he's not beyond repair.

To fully understand the depth of "Torn," it's helpful to examine it through a historical and grammatical lens, focusing on the mindset and emotional landscape of the songwriter. Creed's lyrics here are not mere poetic expressions—they're a direct outpouring of personal anguish, a way of grappling with the harsh realities of life. This approach helps us see "Torn" not as an abstract song, but as a deeply personal narrative, a self-reflection written not for an audience but for the songwriter himself.

This historical perspective gives the song a new dimension, allowing us to view it as a snapshot of a person at their breaking point. The narrator's voice is that of someone who has been forced to confront their own fallibility, who has seen the limits of their own strength and is left with a choice: to give in or to fight on. In this sense, "Torn" becomes a story of transformation, of a soul that has been battered but remains resilient, striving to find meaning in the midst of despair.

"Torn" is not merely a song—it's an emotional experience, a cathartic journey that invites listeners to confront their own inner struggles. Through powerful lyrics, haunting instrumentation, and dynamic shifts between restraint and release, Creed crafts a visceral portrayal of a soul wrestling with itself. The song resonates because it speaks to the universal experience of inner conflict, of the desire to find peace amidst chaos, and of the painful but transformative process of confronting one's own flaws.

In the end, "Torn" leaves us with a sense of unresolved tension, a reminder that life's struggles are rarely neatly concluded. Yet, within that tension, there is also a glimmer of hope—a suggestion that, while peace may feel elusive, it's not beyond reach. The song becomes both a confession and a declaration, a reminder of the strength that can emerge from facing one's own limitations. Through "Torn," Creed offers a raw, unfiltered look at the human experience, inviting us to join in the search for redemption and self-acceptance.

Application

Through the song *Torn*, we find a raw expression of struggle and emotional conflict—a journey that mirrors the Christian walk through valleys of doubt, brokenness, and ultimately, transformation. *Torn* speaks to the human condition, to the tug-of-war between our desire for peace and the inner turmoil that so often shadows it. Yet, within these struggles lies the potential for deep spiritual growth. In honesty, vulnerability, and humility before God, we come to understand the essence of Christian resilience and the path to transformation.

The narrator's acknowledgment of pain—"born in my own misery"—expresses the universal human experience of feeling trapped within ourselves, confronting past decisions, and recognizing the brokenness that lies within. This transparency is where transformation begins. True change is born not in self-righteousness but in self-awareness, which Scripture calls believers to cultivate, confronting our inner darkness and acknowledging our dependence on God.

The path of self-honesty leads us into Scripture, where verses such as Proverbs 28:13 remind us, "Whoever conceals their sins does not prosper, but the one who confesses and renounces them finds mercy."

This powerful truth underscores that concealing sin only compounds our misery, keeping us in bondage to guilt and shame. But in confession and renunciation, we are freed and find mercy—a mercy that does not come from human effort but from the grace of God. This release is the starting point of transformation, as it opens us up to God's work in our lives.

Similarly, Jesus' words in the Sermon on the Mount—"Blessed are the poor in spirit, for theirs is the kingdom of heaven" (Matthew 5:3)—echo this call to humility. Being "poor in spirit" requires a recognition of our own insufficiency. When the narrator admits, "my intentions poor," they are voicing this poverty of spirit. It is an admission that is foundational to Christian growth, as it places us in a posture to receive grace, leaning on God's righteousness rather than our own.

One cannot embark on a journey of transformation without confronting pride. Proverbs 16:18 warns, "Pride goes before destruction, a haughty spirit before a fall." Pride blinds us to our flaws, convincing us that we are above the need for change. It creates a barrier that obstructs our spiritual growth. The Bible, however, offers self-honesty as the antidote to pride. The painful process of looking within, acknowledging our poor intentions, our blame-shifting tendencies, and our faults, is a humbling act that aligns us with God's truth and opens us to the Spirit's refining work.

In the act of self-honesty, we encounter not only our flaws but also the profound grace of God. Psalm 139:23-24 captures this with David's prayer: "Search me, God, and know my heart; test me and know my anxious thoughts. See if there is any offensive way in me, and lead me in the way everlasting." David's prayer is one of vulnerability, inviting God to uncover the hidden places within him that need transformation. Like David, we are called to invite God into the depths of our hearts, allowing Him to reveal the areas that require His grace and healing.

This inner work is a continuous journey, as the Apostle Paul reminds us in 2 Corinthians 13:5, "Examine yourselves to see whether you are in the faith." Paul's call for self-examination is a reminder that growth in faith requires regular introspection. It's not enough to merely profess belief; we are called to look inward, measuring our lives against Scripture and acknowledging our need for grace.

While self-honesty and introspection are necessary, they also confront us with a difficult truth: transformation requires responsibility. Galatians 6:5 instructs, "For each one should carry their own load." While community and support are integral to the Christian life, we are ultimately responsible for our spiritual growth. Blaming external factors or others for our struggles may provide temporary relief from guilt, but it hinders our progress. True transformation begins when we take ownership of our role in our struggles and place our lives in God's hands for guidance and redemption.

Scripture calls us to a higher standard of accountability, one that transcends cultural norms. While the world may offer sympathy for our hardships, it often encourages a victim mentality that leaves us stagnant. The Bible, however, calls us to see our trials as opportunities for growth, trusting that God can bring about something good from every hardship. Taking responsibility means recognizing our own role in our challenges while also believing that God is working in us for a greater purpose.

In Jesus' call to self-denial—"Whoever wants to be my disciple must deny themselves and take up their cross and follow me" (Matthew 16:24)—we find the heart of transformation. Self-honesty leads us to this place of surrender, where we acknowledge our insufficiency and look to Christ for strength. True transformation cannot occur without dying to ourselves, for it is only in surrendering our pride, desires, and agendas that we find new life in Christ.

The act of confession, as described in 1 John 1:9, "If we confess our sins, he is faithful and just and will forgive us our sins and purify us from all unrighteousness," is central to the journey of transformation. Confession realigns us with God's truth, reminding us that our sins do not define us; rather, we are defined by God's grace and mercy. This process is not merely an intellectual acknowledgment of wrongdoing but a deep, heartfelt turning back to God—a movement away from self-reliance and into reliance on His love.

In our self-honesty, we face the uncomfortable truth of our own brokenness, but we are met with God's unwavering faithfulness. The desire for peace—expressed in the song as a yearning for relief from inner turmoil—is fulfilled not through human efforts but through the peace that Christ offers. The narrator's lament, "peace is dead in my soul," resonates deeply, as it reflects a state of spiritual exhaustion, one that many believers encounter. Yet, Scripture offers us a peace that transcends understanding, one that anchors our hearts in God's promises, even amidst life's storms (Philippians 4:6-7).

True peace is not the absence of conflict but the presence of God in our lives. It is a gift, as seen in Isaiah 26:3, "You will keep him in perfect peace, whose mind is stayed on You, because he trusts in You." This peace is unshakable, rooted in trust, and sustained by our relationship with God. Yet, like the narrator, we often lose sight of this peace, focusing instead on our circumstances. But even in the darkest moments, God calls us to lift our gaze, to remember His faithfulness, and to trust in His provision.

In Philippians 4:6-7, Paul instructs believers to bring their anxieties before God in prayer, promising that "the peace of God, which surpasses all understanding, will guard your hearts and minds through

Christ Jesus." This peace is not a passive state but a protective force, a divine guard over our hearts that strengthens us for the journey ahead. As we lean into God's peace, we are empowered to move forward, trusting that He will sustain us.

In surrender, we find the freedom to release our tight grip on control. Proverbs 3:5-6 reminds us, "Trust in the Lord with all your heart and lean not on your own understanding; in all your ways acknowledge Him, and He shall direct your paths." Surrendering control to God is not an act of passivity but of trust, an acknowledgment that His wisdom far surpasses our limited understanding.

As we embrace self-honesty, take responsibility for our growth, pursue peace, and surrender control, we find ourselves on a transformative journey. This path does not promise the absence of struggle; rather, it assures us of God's presence in every trial. Our resilience, as believers, is not born of human strength but of divine grace, a grace that carries us forward even when we feel weak.

In moments when we feel "torn," we can look to the Apostle Paul's words in 2 Corinthians 12:9-10: "My grace is sufficient for you, for my power is made perfect in weakness." Through this acknowledgment of our limitations, we find the strength to carry on, not in our own might, but in God's enduring faithfulness.

The journey of transformation is a lifelong process, a sanctifying work that draws us closer to Christ's image. Our struggles, rather than breaking us, become the instruments through which God refines us. And as we press on, we find that our faith, resilience, and trust in God grow deeper, shaping us into vessels of His love and grace. The call to transformation, while challenging, is also a call to draw nearer to God, to discover the depths of His love, and to become more fully who He has created us to be.

Through Torn, we're reminded that the path through pain and conflict is not only one of survival but of sanctification. It is a journey that
deepens our dependence on God, strengthens our faith, and conforms
us more closely to the image of Christ. We may be *torn*, but in God's
hands, our brokenness becomes a means of grace, a path to glory.

In embracing our struggles with an open heart and a surrendered
spirit, we become living testimonies of God's faithfulness. And as we
walk this path, we can rest assured that He who began a good work in
us will bring it to completion at the day of Jesus Christ (Philippians
1:6).

CHAPTER 3
"Ode"

The lyrics of Creed's "Ode" venture into a haunting landscape of vulnerability, desperation, and the relentless yearning for affirmation in a world marked by hostility and indifference. It's a song that resonates with the human desire to be seen and understood, even when reaching out feels as though it leads only to disappointment. This plea for acknowledgment is painted in stark, agonizing imagery: "Hang me, watch awhile," and "Take me, as my body burns." Such phrases evoke a powerful scene of suffering, as if the speaker stands at the edge of life and death, suspended in a moment that demands the listener's attention. The listener's role here is complex—rather than offering comfort or empathy, they become almost voyeuristic, a passive observer to the speaker's suffering.

The opening lines establish an atmosphere that is dark and oppressive, drawing the listener into the speaker's psychological anguish. The music itself mirrors this tone, with heavy, distorted guitar riffs and a relentless beat that creates a sense of inevitability. This isn't merely background noise; the music becomes a powerful tool, conveying the raw emotion of the lyrics. In the realm of music theory, Creed's choice of aggressive chords and tension-building progressions adds layers to the experience, capturing the restless, cyclical nature of the speaker's pain. The notes often linger without resolution, leaving the listener hanging, mirroring the unresolved inner turmoil of the speaker. The structure of the music thus enhances the message, shaping a space where anger and desperation blend into something both cathartic and suffocating.

As the song progresses, the speaker's defiance surfaces. This isn't a passive acceptance of suffering but rather a last stand against the indifference that surrounds them. They demand recognition from someone who remains "too proud" and oblivious to the devastation their disregard has caused. Creed paints a vivid picture of pride and detachment—a person whose "head is in the clouds," utterly removed from the impact of their indifference. The speaker's cry for acknowledgment becomes sharper, more desperate, as they reach out to someone who refuses to see, almost as if the lack of connection is a choice.

In a moment of poignant irony, the lyrics introduce the idea of "one light to the blind." This phrase hints at the possibility of revelation, a glimmer of hope that the speaker might break through the blindness and pride of those around them. It's a delicate balance—on one hand, there's an unmistakable bitterness that others cannot see or feel their pain. On the other, there remains a fragile belief that maybe, just maybe, something could change. The idea of "one light" suggests a yearning for validation, for a moment of understanding that could transcend all the alienation and suffering the speaker has endured. In this way, the song reaches beyond anger, touching on a universal human desire for connection and acknowledgment.

The refrain, "One touch on the head, and we believe," introduces a different layer to the song's exploration of recognition. Here, the speaker reflects on how easily people can be moved, even manipulated, by a simple gesture of acknowledgment. It's a bittersweet sentiment—the speaker knows that even a small act, a nod, a word, or a touch, could validate everything they feel. This line speaks to the power of human connection, but it also underscores the fragility of that need. There's a haunting suggestion that, despite their anger and defiance, the speaker still yearns for that brief moment of affirmation. It's a paradox, a simultaneous recognition of both the depth of their own pain and the potential for a single gesture to make it all feel worthwhile.

The song's tone captures this paradox by blending aggression with a subtle undercurrent of heartbreak. The plea for recognition becomes ritualistic, almost like a sacrificial offering. In calling out to someone who remains unmoved, the speaker's suffering takes on a ceremonial quality, as if they are being martyred by those who should have cared. The reference to people "walking all over others" speaks to a broader societal indifference—a world where individuals prioritize themselves, stepping over those who might need them most. The speaker's pain becomes emblematic of a universal struggle for validation in a world that often seems cold and unfeeling.

As the song reaches its crescendo, the repetition of the refrain amplifies this ritualistic quality, intensifying the sense of an unanswered cry. This cyclical repetition suggests a painful reality—the speaker's plea may never be heard, their suffering forever unseen. Yet, there's a paradoxical strength in this unending cycle. By repeating, "We believe," the speaker affirms something that transcends the need for external validation. Amidst the crushing weight of dismissal, they discover a kernel of self-awareness, a resilience born from within. This refrain becomes an anchor, a quiet declaration that, regardless of who sees or acknowledges them, they hold onto a belief, a truth, that is theirs alone.

In this sense, the song's journey is not just about suffering and rejection; it's a path toward self-worth that doesn't rely on external recognition. The song speaks to the struggle of finding one's value amidst a world that may never offer it. It's a journey marked by confrontation and a profound need for transformation. The speaker confronts their need for validation, and in doing so, glimpses the possibility of finding strength within themselves. This is not an easy realization—it's a hard-won insight that comes from facing the depths of rejection and despair. The speaker's vulnerability becomes a source of power, an inner light that guides them even when the world seems dark and indifferent.

Creed's "Ode" thus transforms from a song of suffering into a testament to the resilience of the human spirit. It becomes a call to anyone who has ever felt unseen, urging them to look within for the acknowledgment they seek. In the darkness, there is a kind of clarity—a recognition that self-worth is not dependent on the affirmation of others but can be found in the depths of one's own experience. The speaker's journey mirrors this transformation, evolving from a cry for external validation into a discovery of inner strength. By the end of the song, the refrain takes on a new meaning; "We believe" is no longer just a plea but a declaration of self-belief, a commitment to hold onto what is true, regardless of who sees it.

In its exploration of suffering and recognition, "Ode" invites listeners to confront their own need for validation. It asks difficult questions about the nature of worth and the human desire for connection. The song suggests that while the acknowledgment of others can be meaningful, it is not the only path to self-worth. This message is particularly powerful in a world that often equates value with visibility, where being seen by others can feel like the ultimate measure of worth. Creed's lyrics challenge this notion, offering a different perspective—one that sees value as something intrinsic, something that can exist even in the face of indifference.

The song's impact lies not only in its words but also in its musical composition. The tension in the chords, the unresolved progressions, and the distortion of the guitar all contribute to a soundscape that mirrors the speaker's emotional turmoil. This interplay between music and lyrics creates an immersive experience, drawing the listener into the speaker's world. It's as if the music itself is a cry for acknowledgment, a raw, unfiltered expression of the pain and defiance that define the speaker's journey. The music becomes a voice, speaking alongside the lyrics, reinforcing the song's message of vulnerability, suffering, and resilience.

In conclusion, Creed's "Ode" is a powerful exploration of the human desire for acknowledgment in a world that often seems blind to suffering. The song's lyrics and music create a landscape of raw emotion, where vulnerability meets defiance and hope is tempered by despair. Through vivid imagery and haunting melodies, the song captures the tension between the need for external validation and the discovery of inner strength. The speaker's journey is one of transformation, a movement from dependence on others' recognition to a realization of self-worth that transcends their suffering. In this way, "Ode" becomes more than just a song; it's a meditation on the nature of worth, resilience, and the power of belief in the face of rejection. It invites listeners to find strength within themselves, to hold onto what is true even when the world seems indifferent, and to believe that their worth is not defined by others but by the courage to keep going amidst the darkness.

Ultimately, Creed's "Ode" resonates as a timeless anthem for those who have felt unseen, a reminder that even in the absence of acknowledgment, there is a strength that comes from within—a strength that no amount of rejection can diminish. This message of resilience and self-discovery is both universal and deeply personal, a testament to the enduring human spirit and the transformative power of inner belief. In the end, it's not about finding validation in others; it's about discovering the light within, a light that shines even in the darkest of moments.

Application

Applying the themes from "Ode" to one's own life requires us to look deeply at the dual desires for validation and self-worth. The song speaks to a universal tension: wanting recognition from others while learning to recognize our own value, regardless of others' acknowledgment. Here are some ways to channel this insight into positive personal growth:

The speaker's yearning to be seen—to have others acknowledge their suffering and worth—strikes at something deep within all of us. It's as if they're crying out from the depths of their soul, searching for validation that their pain matters, that their story is worthy of someone's attention. This desire isn't merely a fleeting wish; it's a reflection of a universal longing, one that traces back to the very core of our humanity. We all desire to be known, understood, seen for who we truly are. There's something profoundly human in wanting someone to look at us—not just our outward actions or words but into our hearts, to recognize the struggles we bear and the battles we face in the hidden places of our lives.

This yearning, however, can become a trap if we let it consume us. The need to be affirmed can evolve into a quest for worthiness measured solely by the attention or admiration of others. And when this happens, we allow others' perceptions to define us, to determine our value, to validate our existence. But Scripture speaks to a different approach—a higher, truer understanding of self-worth that doesn't rely on the approval of others. Proverbs 29:25 says, "The fear of man brings a snare, but whoever trusts in the Lord shall be safe." Here, we're reminded that depending on people's opinions to measure our worth will only ensnare us. The alternative, the liberation we seek, lies in finding security in something unchanging and reliable—in God Himself.

If we pause to examine this desire to be seen, we may uncover an even deeper truth: we want others to validate our existence, yes, but at the root, we long for a kind of love and understanding that won't waver, that won't disappear when circumstances change. In Psalm 139, David writes, "O Lord, You have searched me and known me." He speaks of a God who sees all, who understands not only what we show the world but what we hide. The yearning to be known, to be affirmed, is met fully by this reality—that God has already seen us. He knows our inmost thoughts, our hidden fears, our unspoken dreams. We are fully known and fully loved in His sight.

But knowing this truth intellectually doesn't always transform our emotional reality overnight. It's a journey to move from understanding our worth in theory to truly living from that place of assurance. For many, this journey involves unlearning the patterns we've built over years, where self-worth was chained to external validation. In John 2:24-25, it says, "But Jesus did not commit Himself to them, because He knew all men, and had no need that anyone should testify of man, for He knew what was in man." Jesus Himself didn't hinge His identity on others' approval. He knew the heart of man, and because of that, He didn't allow their praise or criticism to alter His purpose or identity. This example teaches us to ground ourselves in God's approval, which is constant and unmoved by human whims.

Practically, this shift in mindset starts with small, deliberate steps. Recognize and affirm your efforts, your accomplishments, your faithfulness in the day-to-day, even if no one else does. This isn't about arrogance or self-praise; it's about honoring the unique journey God has placed you on and acknowledging His work within you. When you step into a challenging task, overcome a personal struggle, or display kindness in a moment of frustration, take a moment to recognize that these actions hold worth, even if they go unseen by others.

When Jesus was baptized, before He performed any miracles or preached to the multitudes, a voice from heaven declared, "This is my beloved Son, in whom I am well pleased" (Matthew 3:17). Notice that God's affirmation of Jesus' worth wasn't based on public approval or achievement—it was rooted in relationship, in identity. In the same way, our worth in God's eyes isn't something we earn or prove; it's something we receive, a gift of grace given by a loving Father.

However, letting go of the need for human approval doesn't mean isolating ourselves emotionally or becoming indifferent to the people around us. Instead, it means finding an inner balance, a place where we can welcome affirmation when it comes but don't depend on it. When we anchor ourselves in God's affirmation, we can interact with others from a place of fullness rather than emptiness, seeking to serve and love rather than to gain approval.

This stability becomes especially crucial when we face criticism or rejection. The more we depend on others for validation, the more fragile we become in the face of disapproval. A critical remark or a dismissive glance can shake us to our core. But when we've built an identity founded on God's unchanging love and value, we gain resilience. We begin to see others' opinions for what they are—human perspectives, often incomplete, sometimes flawed. We don't have to ignore or resent criticism, but we also don't have to let it define us.

Scripture often points us toward humility, not in a way that undermines our worth but in a way that strengthens it. Humility, in the biblical sense, isn't about thinking less of ourselves; it's about thinking of ourselves less, placing our identity and worth in God's hands. In this way, humility becomes a pathway to freedom—freedom from the endless chase for validation, freedom to walk confidently in our

God-given purpose without being swayed by the changing tides of human approval.

For those who struggle with feelings of unworthiness or invisibility, remember that God Himself is near to the brokenhearted (Psalm 34:18). He is not distant or indifferent. In Isaiah 43:1, God speaks tenderly, saying, "Fear not, for I have redeemed you; I have called you by your name; you are mine." There is something profoundly intimate and affirming in these words. The Creator of the universe not only sees us but claims us as His own. This truth offers a security that no human praise or affirmation could ever match.

Learning to internalize this truth may require time and intentionality, but each step toward it builds a foundation of inner stability. Practice speaking truth to yourself, reminding yourself of God's promises and the worth He has placed on you. In Romans 8:16, we're reminded that "the Spirit Himself bears witness with our spirit that we are children of God." There is a witness within us, a constant reminder of our identity that transcends human opinions.

When you find yourself yearning for someone to notice your struggles, your hard work, or your pain, pause for a moment and turn your gaze upward. Ask yourself if you're seeking in others what only God can provide. This shift in focus doesn't negate our human desire for connection or affirmation, but it reorients it, aligning our hearts with a love that is unconditional and everlasting.

Over time, as we build this inner stability, we may find that our relationships change, too. We approach people with openness and empathy, no longer weighed down by a need for affirmation. We can appreciate compliments and constructive feedback without letting them become the foundation of our identity. This freedom brings joy because it allows us to celebrate others and support them genuinely, without the shadow of comparison or insecurity.

Embracing this biblical perspective on self-worth transforms how we interact with the world. We no longer depend on others to feel whole; instead, we bring a wholeness that is rooted in Christ. And in that freedom, we become witnesses to a love that isn't contingent on achievement, a worth that isn't dependent on external validation. This is the kind of love Jesus showed—one that sought to serve, uplift, and heal, drawing strength from His identity as the beloved Son of God.

So, as you reflect on the lyrics that speak of a yearning to be seen, let them serve as a reminder of the deeper truth: you are already seen, fully known, and deeply loved by the One who matters most. Let this knowledge be a steady anchor for your soul, a foundation that remains unshaken by the shifting opinions of people. And as you practice affirming yourself in light of this divine affirmation, may you grow in confidence, knowing that your worth is secure, held firmly in the hands of a loving God.

CHAPTER 4
"My Own Prison"

To expand on the evocative narrative and the layered emotions in Creed's "My Own Prison," let's delve even deeper into each element—unpacking the nuances that lie within the lyrics, the composition, and the themes of existential anguish and a yearning for redemption. Each stanza, each note, and each pause in the song resonates with a depth that reveals a profound exploration of the self, accountability, and a glimmer of hope. This is a song of contrasts—darkness and light, guilt and grace, punishment and liberation—and each tension adds to the song's haunting power.

The title itself, "My Own Prison," is a powerful metaphor that serves as the foundation of the song's narrative. It's not a prison built by others or a punishment inflicted by an external force; rather, it's a self-imposed confinement. This notion of being one's own jailer introduces a theme of personal responsibility and introspection. The narrator is not merely suffering under circumstances but is acutely aware that his choices, actions, and failures have led him to this desolate place. This internal conflict drives the song, making it a universal exploration of human frailty and the weight of our past decisions.

As the song opens, we're thrust into a stark, dimly lit courtroom—a place of judgment and reckoning. This is not an ordinary courtroom with the structure and order of legal justice; rather, it's an abstract, haunting space within the narrator's mind. The court scene is more symbolic than literal, representing an inescapable confrontation with oneself. In this realm, he is both the accused and the judge, bound by a law that he cannot escape. The "cold and pale walls" suggest an unyielding environment, devoid of warmth or mercy—a place where every misstep is magnified, and the weight of guilt is palpable. This imagery sets the tone, evoking a bleak and relentless setting where accountability cannot be avoided.

The song's instrumentation enhances this scene, creating an atmosphere that feels claustrophobic and unyielding. The guitar, grinding and layered, reinforces a feeling of confinement. Its distorted, resonant sound reflects the narrator's turmoil, amplifying the sense of entrapment and hopelessness. Each chord progression is heavy, as though mirroring the weight of guilt that sits on his shoulders. The soundscape is deliberate, as if to remind the listener that, within these walls of regret, there's no easy escape. It's a sonic representation of a soul ensnared by its own history, unable to break free from the echoes of past mistakes.

Scott Stapp's lyrics paint this scene with striking imagery that calls to mind both isolation and judgment. Words like "cage made of steel" speak to the permanence of this prison, a structure that feels impenetrable. Here, the prison isn't just physical—it's spiritual and emotional, a place that holds his deepest regrets and mistakes. The use of a cage rather than walls emphasizes a sense of transparency; his sins and flaws are visible, laid bare for judgment. In this realm, the walls don't just enclose; they expose. This is a place where he cannot hide from himself, where every failing and misstep is displayed in stark detail.

As the song continues, the lyrics deepen in their exploration of internal suffering. The silence within the prison becomes almost tangible, a haunting stillness that reflects both the narrator's isolation and the weight of his conscience. This silence is broken only by the sound of his own breathing, emphasizing a solitude that borders on despair. There's a sense of being trapped in one's mind, unable to escape the thoughts that continually replay the past. The muted shades and shadows create a mental image of a space that's dimly lit, as though the only light comes from slivers slipping through prison bars. It's a place of perpetual twilight, suspended between the extremes of light and dark, freedom and captivity.

The demons that "clutter around" suggest both an inner haunting and the unresolved conflicts that linger. These are not literal demons but manifestations of his fears, regrets, and unresolved traumas. They crowd around him, taunting him with reminders of every failure, every hurt caused, and every opportunity missed. It's a suffocating presence, these "demons" that hover just beyond reach, yet close enough to make their influence felt. In this prison, he's haunted not only by what he's done but by the shadows of what might have been—a reminder of paths he didn't take and dreams he didn't pursue.

In the raw refrain of "Ohh," the song allows the narrator a moment of catharsis. This is not a melodic line but an unfiltered exhalation, a visceral release from the torment that festers within. It's a sound that transcends words, capturing the raw ache of a soul that's burdened by self-condemnation. The repetition amplifies this release, as though each exclamation digs deeper into the pain, offering a momentary respite before the walls of guilt close in again. This refrain becomes a ritual of expression, a way to confront and externalize the pain that's otherwise confined within him.

The intensity of the narrator's struggle escalates as he grapples with the absence of absolution. In this prison of the soul, there's no opportunity for penance or redemption. He recognizes his sins, feels their weight, but there's no way to atone, no chance for forgiveness. His "skin burning" is a powerful image, a visceral manifestation of guilt that consumes him from within. It's both the searing heat of regret and the smoldering anger he feels toward himself and those who judge him. This burning is relentless, a reminder of his moral decay and the shame that lingers just beneath the surface.

The line "Hiding hate that burns inside, which only fuels their selfish pride" reveals a duality in his heart—a resentment toward those who judge him, yet an awareness of his role in perpetuating this judgment. This anger isn't directed solely at others but also at himself, at the weaknesses that have led him to this place. It's a cycle of self-reproach and defiance, where he both resents and embraces the prison he has created. In this internal struggle, he finds no peace, only an endless loop of recrimination and regret.

The chorus, with its poignant line about "a sun that shines on only some," reflects on the inequity of grace. Why, he wonders, do some find forgiveness and freedom while he remains trapped in his self-made prison? This sun, symbolic of hope and redemption, feels inaccessible, reserved for others while he languishes in shadows. It's a deeply human sentiment, the longing for grace and the resentment that it seems to shine only on others. In this moment, the narrator confronts the mystery of grace and the feeling of being overlooked, of waiting for a light that never reaches him.

As he envisions the cross, there's a shift in the narrative—a glimpse of hope mixed with despair. The cross, a symbol of both suffering and salvation, is a reminder of the sacrifice made for humanity. He recognizes the pain "given on that sad day of loss," a profound acknowledgment of Christ's sacrifice. Yet, this symbol of forgiveness feels achingly distant, as though it's something he can see but not touch. This longing for salvation is a thread that runs through the song, a yearning for redemption that seems forever out of reach.

The roaring lion that emerges in the darkness adds another layer to the song's imagery. Often associated with both judgment and protection, the lion symbolizes power and the potential for liberation. There's a sense that this figure holds the key to his freedom, the hope of being freed from the burden he carries. Yet, the lion remains distant, its roar a reminder of a power that he cannot access. This duality—the potential for salvation and the reality of confinement—creates a tension that's both hopeful and tragic.

In the refrain "Should have been dead on a Sunday morning, banging my head," the narrator confronts a moment of reckoning. Sunday, traditionally a day of rest and resurrection, becomes a day of turmoil and regret for him. This line speaks to the missed opportunities for peace and the restless anguish that fills his soul. There's no time for mourning, only a ceaseless cycle of regret. He's bound to this prison of his own making, unable to find closure or peace. It's a reminder that even in moments meant for rest, he's plagued by the choices that led him here.

The final verse reaches a crescendo of introspection, as the narrator calls out to God, seeking only His decision. This plea is not for freedom but for understanding—a need to know where he stands. When Gabriel, the archangel associated with revelation and truth, confirms, "I've created my own prison," it's a moment of raw self-discovery. He's forced to confront the reality that this confinement is his own doing, the result of his actions, his regrets, and his unresolved guilt. It's a painful revelation, yet there's a hint of empowerment in this acknowledgment. He understands that his imprisonment is not imposed by fate or others but is a consequence of his own choices.

Ultimately, "My Own Prison" is a journey into the darkest recesses of the human soul. It's a reflection on the consequences of our actions and the weight of guilt that we carry. The song's structure, with its echoing chords and relentless percussion, reinforces the feeling of being trapped in time, each loop of melody mirroring the cycle of regret and introspection. This is not simply a song of despair but a plea for transformation—a hope, however faint, for a way out of the shadows.

As the song draws to a close, there's no easy resolution, only the lingering hope that, somehow, grace might reach even those who feel undeserving. "My Own Prison" is more than a lamentation; it's an invitation to confront our deepest flaws and to find within ourselves

Application

In "My Own Prison," we are drawn into an intimate, haunting exploration of personal responsibility and redemption. Through poetic lyrics and a raw, vulnerable narrative, the song confronts the painful reality of self-made confinement, where the choices we make entangle us in a spiritual and emotional prison. Yet, amid the stark depictions of guilt and isolation, a glimmer of hope emerges, signaling that transformation, though challenging, is always within reach. The journey depicted in these lyrics becomes a mirror, urging listeners to consider their own lives and the paths they have tread, and it does so with an almost cinematic intensity, inviting us to enter deeply into the world of the narrator's struggle and hope for something greater.

The song's foundation is self-reflection—a raw, unfiltered examination of one's life and choices. This is no casual introspection; it's a plunge into the heart of regret, forcing us to confront the inner walls we've constructed, the wounds we may have ignored, and the failures that haunt us. The narrator speaks of a prison "created" by his own hand, evoking a sense of a place that didn't merely exist but was actively built through specific choices. The idea here is profoundly biblical; it reminds us of the verse, "For as he thinketh in his heart, so is he" (Proverbs 23:7). Here, our inner life—our thoughts, intentions, and motives—lays the groundwork for the outward realities we encounter. This prison, then, is not just a place of physical confinement but a spiritual exile, a self-imposed punishment stemming from the narrator's own heart.

In recognizing his contribution to his own suffering, the narrator opens the door to something life-changing: the possibility of transformation. This moment of realization, painful as it is, serves as a catalyst for growth, a first step toward breaking free from the chains of destructive behavior. It reminds us that true growth comes not from denying our mistakes but from acknowledging them. This invitation to self-reflection challenges us to think about our own lives. In what ways have we erected barriers, closed ourselves off from others, or isolated ourselves through choices we regret? Self-reflection, then, becomes a form of spiritual humility, a willingness to see ourselves as we truly are—a step that ultimately leads us closer to God and His redemptive power.

"My Own Prison" doesn't just speak to self-awareness but moves us into the realm of accountability. To say "I created my own prison" is a monumental admission, one that requires honesty and courage. Scripture often emphasizes the importance of personal responsibility, encouraging us to "examine ourselves" (2 Corinthians 13:5) and to "work out [our] own salvation with fear and trembling" (Philippians 2:12). This call to take ownership of our actions is a critical part of spiritual growth and maturity, pushing us to stop blaming external circumstances and instead recognize our agency in shaping our lives.

The realization of personal responsibility is not meant to lead us into despair or self-condemnation; rather, it offers us freedom by reminding us that, if we had the power to create our own prison, we also have the power, with God's help, to dismantle it. This idea is empowering—it gives us the ability to choose differently, to seek forgiveness, and to begin anew. In a world that often promotes victimhood, where people are encouraged to place blame on everyone but themselves, this narrative speaks to a deeper truth. Yes, there are external forces and pressures, but within the crucible of those challenges, we have the agency to respond in ways that either bring us closer to or further away from God's intended path for us. This moment of accountability, then, is an invitation to personal empowerment through surrender to God's guidance.

The narrator's honesty about his struggles and guilt is what gives the song its poignancy. Vulnerability, often perceived as weakness, is presented here as a conduit for healing. This openness to one's brokenness aligns closely with the biblical notion that "His strength is made perfect in weakness" (2 Corinthians 12:9). Admitting failure is not a sign of defeat; rather, it's a courageous act that opens us to the possibility of transformation and community. By confessing his guilt, the narrator reveals that he is not hiding behind excuses or justifications—he is raw and exposed, standing in the ruins of his decisions, searching for grace.

In this moment of vulnerability, there's a powerful lesson: by sharing our struggles, we allow others to enter into our pain and offer us compassion, understanding, and perhaps even healing. When we are vulnerable, we create spaces where others can connect with us on a deep level, transcending surface judgments and fostering authentic relationships. It is this kind of vulnerability that has the power to bring people together, reminding us that our humanity is shared, and that none of us is beyond the need for redemption. This vulnerability also aligns with the biblical idea of confessing our sins to one another, creating a community that bears each other's burdens.

The song offers glimpses of hope, using symbols like the cross and the lion's roar to point toward redemption. Here, we find a powerful image of light that "grants life eternally," a clear nod to the promise of salvation found in Christ. This image reflects the truth of John 8:12, where Jesus says, "I am the light of the world. Whoever follows me will never walk in darkness, but will have the light of life." The cross, a symbol of ultimate sacrifice and love, represents the bridge between human sinfulness and divine forgiveness. The lion's roar, a powerful, almost primal sound, echoes the majesty and authority of God—a reminder that He is both willing and able to save those who call upon Him.

This is a reminder that no matter how dark our personal prison may seem, there is always the possibility of redemption through Christ. The hope offered here is not mere wishful thinking; it is a steadfast assurance grounded in God's promises. This path to redemption, however, requires surrender, a recognition that we cannot break free from our prison by our own strength. We must come to the cross, acknowledge our need for God's grace, and trust that He alone can transform our hearts. This is the hope that the song ultimately gestures toward—a hope that promises liberation, not just from guilt, but from the bondage of sin itself. It invites us to lay down our burdens and find freedom in Christ.

The refrain "We the meek are all in one" speaks to the collective nature of human struggle. It is a reminder that suffering and guilt are not unique to any one person; they are universal experiences. In the Sermon on the Mount, Jesus calls the meek "blessed," promising that they "shall inherit the earth" (Matthew 5:5). Here, the meek are those who recognize their own limitations and are humble enough to seek help. They are not self-sufficient; they are dependent on God's grace, and it is precisely this dependence that brings healing.

This shared experience of struggle creates a bond between us, allowing us to draw strength from the knowledge that others, too, wrestle with regret, fear, and longing for something more. In realizing that we are not alone, we can open ourselves to community, support, and the healing that comes from walking alongside others who understand our pain. It is this communal aspect of redemption that gives hope, as we see that we do not have to bear our burdens in isolation. Instead, we can find comfort in knowing that there is a community of fellow believers who, like us, are journeying toward freedom.

The song thus becomes a testament to the power of shared experiences. When we share our stories, our vulnerabilities, and our moments of doubt, we extend a hand to others who may feel trapped in their own prisons. We remind them that they are not alone, and we create a space where healing can flourish.

Each of these elements—self-reflection, accountability, vulnerability, redemption, and shared struggle—builds upon the song's core message of hope and transformation. It reminds us that, though we may create our own prisons, there is a path forward, a way to break free. As we journey with the narrator through his pain, his realizations, and his moments of hope, we are invited to reflect on our own lives, to seek God's forgiveness, and to trust in the redemptive power of Christ.

This journey, however, is not a swift or simple one. It demands courage, humility, and faith. It requires us to confront the darkness within, to lay down our pride, and to seek the light that offers life eternally. But in this journey lies the promise of a freedom that is not just the absence of guilt, but the presence of God's transformative love, a love that can turn even the deepest prison into a place of hope.

Overall, *My Own Prison* shows us that while facing our own mistakes and regrets may be painful, it's a crucial step toward healing and growth. The song doesn't provide easy answers, but it offers hope that, through self-reflection, accountability, and faith, we can begin to free ourselves from the mental and emotional prisons we sometimes construct. It teaches that true liberation comes from within, and with honesty, vulnerability, and the courage to seek redemption, we can transform our lives for the better.

CHAPTER 5
"Pity For A Dime"

As "Pity for a Dime" unfurls, Creed immerses us in an intro-spective tableau, one where the scenery is more than a mere backdrop—it's a metaphorical mirror reflecting the turmoil within. The lyrics evoke an image of a shadow-drenched street scene seen through a rain-spattered window. It's an almost cinematic view, where rain doesn't simply cascade down but creates an illusion of fresh beginnings. Yet, the "summer rain" Creed references here is not one that refreshes or cleanses. Instead, it masks, cloaking the character's inner despondency under the guise of a season that usually symbolizes vitality. Creed invokes an "artificial season," a period where emotions are held hostage by something that should revive yet somehow stifles, stagnates, and obscures.

This rain, symbolic of the speaker's burden, transforms the familiar into something distant and isolating. The paradox of rain—typically viewed as a natural renewal—is subverted here, taking on a claustro-phobic quality. In this artificial season, where nature and life itself feel suspended, the character is left to grapple with the discord between appearance and reality. It's as though he's living behind a mask, one that simulates normalcy but hides the fractures beneath. This is a place where one's emotions are left raw, hanging in the air like humidity after a storm, pervasive yet inescapable.

The music that accompanies these lyrics reinforces this heavy introspection. Minor chords ground the piece, anchoring it in an oppressive atmosphere that weighs on the listener as much as it does on
the protagonist. The rhythm is deliberate, almost hesitant, echoing the
feeling of being trapped within a stasis—of forward movement sacrificed for introspection. Each note is weighted, deliberate, as though
each one is a step deeper into the speaker's disillusionment. It's not a
progression but a descent, a reluctance to move forward that mirrors
the existential paralysis the lyrics reveal. This musical backdrop is not
merely passive; it actively draws the listener into the speaker's internal
labyrinth, each refrain cycling through self-doubt and bitter reflection.

The lyrics "Shadows paint the sidewalk / A living picture in a frame"
evoke an image of a street where life itself has lost its luster, where
colors have dimmed, and faces blur together into indistinct shadows.
This world feels bleak, stripped of vibrancy, its inhabitants not as
individuals but as interchangeable silhouettes in a somber setting.
The speaker's alienation is almost palpable; he looks upon the people
around him not with connection but with a sense of estrangement.
In his world, individuality has lost meaning, and each passerby is no
different from the next—a reminder that he, too, may be fading into
the same monochrome anonymity. This haunting imagery points to a
deeper malaise, where life's moments repeat in an endless loop, devoid
of substance or satisfaction.

The chorus, with its stark line "sell my pity for a dime," introduces
a grim irony. "Pity" here is a strange currency, a commodity, yet it's
almost worthless—a dime. It's as though the speaker's sorrow has
become so pervasive, so overwhelming, that he'd willingly part with
it for a trivial price. But beneath this transaction lies a deeper cost. To
exchange pity, even at such a small price, is to part with fragments of

oneself, each interaction taking something vital away. This offering of pity becomes a surrender of identity, a piece of his soul parceled off for mere survival. The line "another man take my soul" reveals the ultimate cost of these exchanges—a loss of self-worth, as though each act of devaluing his sorrow erodes the core of his being, leaving him hollow and worn.

As the song progresses, the sense of emptiness grows, accentuated by the repetition of "plain talk can be the easy way / signs of losing my faith." There's an erosion of belief here, not necessarily in a spiritual sense, but in life's intrinsic value and in his own authenticity. Plain talk, in this context, is a facade—a way to avoid confronting deeper, uncomfortable truths. It's a shield, but one that distances him further from his true self. There's a loss of faith not only in external ideals but also in his own voice and the legitimacy of his experience. His own expression feels hollow, like a forced smile or a practiced response, all serving to mask an inner void that no amount of superficial interaction can truly fill.

The desperation in these lines builds as the song crescendos, reaching a point where the tension is nearly unbearable. Creed's instrumentation is not merely background—it's an intensifying force that mirrors and amplifies the speaker's torment. The layered guitars, distorted and mournful, act as an extension of the character's struggle, each note a heartbeat echoing his desire to escape the darkness but being pulled back time and again into despair. The instruments reflect this inner chaos, capturing the pull of hope and the weight of resignation in each chord. The music swells and recedes like waves against a shore, illustrating the ebb and flow of a soul caught between surrender and survival.

"Pity for a Dime" ultimately delves into the essence of a soul wrestling with its value in a world that feels devoid of individual meaning. The lyrics close without resolution, leaving the listener suspended alongside the speaker, entrapped within the same liminal space of uncertainty. There's no clear path to freedom, no moment of catharsis or redemption. Instead, there's a lingering question: can one's hidden pain, obscured behind feigned expressions and polite lies, ever truly be worth the sacrifice of one's peace? The song's conclusion hangs in the air, unresolved, as if the listener, too, is left to grapple with the implications of this quiet tragedy, this understated and unrelenting surrender.

Through "Pity for a Dime," Creed captures an emotional landscape that resonates with anyone who has felt the weight of existential disillusionment. This song doesn't offer solutions or relief; it provides a mirror, a reflection of the moments we hesitate to voice. It dares to confront the ache of masked sorrow, of lost individuality, of a soul questioning its worth in a world quick to dismiss it. There's no tidy resolution, no comforting closure. Instead, Creed leaves us with an open wound—a reminder of the human condition's fragility and the resilience needed to endure it.

In this song, Creed allows us to witness, to feel, and to inhabit a world that's both intimately familiar and profoundly isolating. The artificial season, the shadows on the sidewalk, and the bartering of pity for a mere dime are not just images—they're symbols of the quiet despair many carry, often without others noticing. Creed's introspective approach gives voice to that silent struggle, an ode to the unseen battles within. And though the song ends without resolution, there's a subtle invitation—to recognize, if not to overcome, the parts of ourselves we often ignore, to confront the masks we wear, and perhaps to find worth in our own sorrow, no matter how small the world may deem it.

As we sit with these lyrics, it becomes clear that "Pity for a Dime" is a meditation on the cost of hiding pain, of treating one's sorrow as something expendable, a commodity to be traded for survival. It's about the slow erosion of faith—not just in ideals or others, but in oneself. And in this, Creed doesn't just describe despair; they reveal the price of carrying it alone, of letting one's soul be chipped away, piece by piece. This quiet tragedy, woven into the song's fabric, becomes a shared experience between the speaker and the listener—a momentary alignment of brokenness and understanding.

Ultimately, "Pity for a Dime" is not just a song but a haunting exploration of a soul's value, a question of what it means to retain humanity in a world that often trivializes the depth of individual suffering. There's an implied question left for each listener to ponder: In a world so quick to put a price on pain, how much of ourselves are we willing to lose? Creed may leave us without answers, but in their refusal to provide a tidy resolution, they grant us the space to find our own meaning in the shadows, the rain, and the fragmented reflections they lay before us.

Application

As we peel back the layers of "Pity for a Dime," it's as though we're stepping into a raw, unguarded space—a realm where a profound, almost tangible tension between despair and hope comes alive. The song doesn't merely recount a struggle; it brings us directly into the mind of someone grappling with feelings of alienation and worthlessness. By doing so, it invites us to confront the uncomfortable reality that many of us mask behind daily routines and polished smiles. What emerges is a portrayal of the human heart caught between two worlds: the reality of despair and the possibility of healing—a journey from numbness to resilience that speaks to anyone who's felt alone, unworthy, or disconnected.

Authenticity over Masks

The protagonist of "Pity for a Dime" is someone we've all been, or perhaps still are: one who learns to hide pain so well that even they almost forget it's there. Each forced smile, each dismissal of sorrow as unimportant, constructs a façade that conceals the wounds underneath. But pretending doesn't bring peace; it only amplifies the inner void, distancing us further from ourselves and from others. In moments of brutal honesty, however, we begin to see that true peace only follows authenticity.

Scripture often encourages truthfulness in our inward parts. The Psalms echo this, capturing David's anguished cries in moments of raw vulnerability. David did not hide his pain from God or others; he poured it out, exposing his heart with an honesty that might seem uncomfortable but was, in truth, freeing. This authenticity becomes a bridge—one that connects us to God and invites Him into our struggles, as we see in Psalm 34:18, where it says, "The Lord is near to the brokenhearted and saves the crushed in spirit."

In acknowledging our pain instead of pretending it away, we step into the healing light of truth. We open a door to genuine relationships and the kind of inner healing that God desires for us. The courage to be honest, especially about our struggles, is where redemption often begins. When we let down our masks, even in sorrow, we extend an invitation to God and to others to see us fully and love us completely.

The phrase "selling my pity for a dime" is haunting, as it illustrates a profound crisis of self-worth. The metaphor suggests that the protagonist feels their pain and struggles are worth almost nothing—something that could be traded for the smallest coin. This concept echoes the lie that many believe: that they are somehow worth less because they struggle, that their value diminishes with each failure, each broken dream.

However, the biblical perspective offers a completely different narrative. Psalm 139 speaks of being "fearfully and wonderfully made," a testament to the inherent worth of each soul, crafted with purpose and significance by the Creator Himself. Our worth is not something that can be sold, nor is it subject to our emotional highs and lows. Instead, it's rooted in the reality that we are made in the image of God, carrying an eternal value that no coin can quantify.

Recognizing this truth leads to a profound shift: we begin to see ourselves not as beings of momentary worth, but as individuals with intrinsic value and purpose. Embracing this truth means protecting what we hold dear—compassion, resilience, faith—and guarding it against the corrosive effects of self-deprecation and neglect. Rather than trivializing our struggles, we learn to honor them as part of a larger journey, one that points us back to the One who gives us worth.

The lyrics speak of seeing "a sea of people" with indistinguishable faces, a vivid image of the isolation that so often haunts those who feel disconnected. This alienation is not uncommon; many experience it while standing in a crowd, wondering if they're truly known or loved by anyone around them. Yet, instead of numbing these feelings, "Pity for a Dime" encourages confronting them—leaning into that ache instead of turning away from it.

This openness to vulnerability can be transformative. By facing these feelings, we can start to understand that isolation, while painful, is also part of the human condition and a reminder of our need for connection. Scripture reveals a way forward in this—Jesus Himself experienced the depths of isolation, particularly on the cross when He cried, "My God, my God, why have you forsaken me?" (Matthew 27:46). This was the ultimate experience of alienation, one that He bore so that we would never have to feel truly alone.

When we recognize our shared vulnerabilities and fears, we begin to empathize more deeply with others. Our pain can soften our hearts, helping us reach out to others who might be struggling in similar ways. In this way, our own alienation transforms into a bridge of empathy, a path toward a community grounded in mutual understanding and compassion.

The lyric "signs of losing my faith" is a poignant reminder of the moments when we feel as if we're drifting, when the guiding light of purpose seems dim. Such times of doubt are universal, and they can either lead us to despair or prompt us to a deeper reflection on what we truly believe and why. Rather than signaling an end, these moments of questioning can become opportunities for rediscovery.

In 2 Corinthians 13:5, Paul encourages believers to "examine your-selves, to see whether you are in the faith." This self-reflection isn't about doubt for its own sake; it's about refining and reaffirming our beliefs, rediscovering what genuinely holds us up. Sometimes, a crisis of faith strips away superficial beliefs, revealing the core truths we cling to even in the darkest times.

The positive takeaway here is the chance to re-evaluate what drives us. What values, convictions, and hopes do we still hold, even when life feels bleak? For the Christian, this can mean a return to the foundation of faith—a reminder that, no matter how lost we feel, God remains unchanging, a solid rock amid shifting sands. In moments of doubt, we are invited to press deeper, allowing the crisis to draw us closer to the One who is always faithful, even when we falter.

Finally, "Pity for a Dime" honors the act of enduring, of con-fronting the darkest places within ourselves and emerging stronger. It doesn't promise a quick fix or a magical escape from pain. Instead, it suggests that by facing our darkness head-on, we can eventually transcend it.

Resilience, in the biblical sense, is more than just getting through a tough time; it's about growing through it. James 1:2-4 speaks to this, saying, "Count it all joy, my brothers, when you meet trials of various kinds, for you know that the testing of your faith produces steadfastness." Our trials are not meant to crush us but to strengthen us, to develop a steadfastness that goes beyond mere survival.

Resilience is not born from denying pain or pretending it doesn't exist. It comes from acknowledging it, wrestling with it, and, ultimately, growing through it. When we allow ourselves to confront and work through our struggles, we gain a depth of character and a sense of compassion that only those who have known pain can truly understand. This resilience doesn't just help us survive; it allows us to thrive, to live with a sense of purpose and strength that glorifies God even in our darkest hours.

In embracing resilience, we learn that despair doesn't have to have the final word. God's promises remain true through every valley, and His presence is constant, even when our circumstances are bleak. It's in the heart of suffering that we often find a strength we didn't know we had—a strength rooted not in ourselves but in the One who sustains us.

As we journey through the themes in "Pity for a Dime," we see a powerful narrative emerging—a story of transformation and self-discovery. It's a story that encourages us not to flee from pain but to confront it, to let it refine us, and to discover the beauty of God's grace in the process. This journey is ongoing, a continual invitation to draw closer to God, to grow through our struggles, and to emerge more resilient, more compassionate, and more whole.

Though this reflection ends here, the journey is far from over. As we press forward, there is more to uncover, more depths to explore, and more truth to embrace. In our darkest hours, we are never alone, for the One who knows us best is with us, leading us toward healing, purpose, and hope.

In essence, the positive application from "Pity for a Dime" lies in allowing ourselves to feel deeply, accept discomfort, and find a path forward through authentic self-reflection and connection with others. The song reminds us that transformation isn't always found in immediate answers or solutions, but in the willingness to confront our innermost struggles and discover a way to reclaim our worth and purpose.

CHAPTER 6
"In America"

C reed's haunting tone becomes a vehicle for introspection, taking us into the soul of a narrator who confronts the idealism of American identity, questioning the values, promises, and contradictions that permeate modern life. In the process, we find that Creed isn't merely pointing fingers; they are searching, searching for truth, for belonging, for the America they once believed in.

Creed opens with a statement that is simultaneously ironic and profoundly troubling: "Only in America we're slaves to be free." This paradox invites us to confront the limitations of a cherished national ideal—freedom. The concept of freedom in America has often been romanticized, painted as an ultimate good, yet Creed turns this notion on its head by suggesting that the very pursuit of freedom may lead to new forms of bondage. The word "slaves" conjures images of entrapment and loss, a sense that while people chase autonomy, they find themselves chained in other ways.

What are these chains? They are not the tangible, historical chains of physical enslavement but rather the invisible, internalized shackles of modern existence. In the song, freedom isn't merely about escaping external forces; it becomes complicated by consumerism, societal expectations, and self-inflicted pressures. In America, where every person has the right to carve their path, people find themselves paradoxically imprisoned by the very choices they make in their quest for freedom. Perhaps it's the relentless pursuit of success, the pressure to conform to a certain lifestyle, or the need to belong in an increasingly fragmented society.

Creed's lyrics bring to mind the idea that in the pursuit of individualism, people may lose their sense of connection and community. The freedom celebrated here becomes an isolating force, leading individuals into a maze where they feel unmoored and disconnected. The band doesn't vilify America but instead asks: Has freedom lost its way in a world where the promises of autonomy and prosperity have turned hollow?

As we journey further into the song, Creed moves to an even more painful theme: "Only in America we kill the unborn to make ends meet." Here, Creed touches on the harsh realities faced by many in the struggle to survive. This line isn't an accusation but rather an observation of the difficult choices people confront. In its haunting simplicity, it speaks of sacrifice, of human life lost in the balancing act between survival and idealism.

This lyric embodies a collective ache, a recognition of the emotional and moral toll that economic hardship can inflict. It's not a condemnation of individuals but rather an exploration of systemic issues, where the cost of "making ends meet" can force people into choices that weigh heavily on the soul. The heartbeat-like rhythm of the song here mirrors the vulnerability of this line—an acknowledgment of how fragile human existence can be when caught in the tug-of-war between moral ideals and economic demands.

Creed's approach to this topic is layered and complex. They are not making a definitive statement on moral issues but are inviting listeners to feel the weight of societal pressures. This choice, this sacrifice, becomes a haunting symbol for a society where survival sometimes comes at a profound cost. The music underscores this tension, almost

as though each note is a heartbeat, each beat a reminder of the pre-
ciousness of life and the heavy burdens many bear.

The line "sexuality is democracy" almost unfolds like a question,
drawing the listener into a nuanced exploration of identity in the
public sphere. In America, where democracy is often synonymous
with freedom and equality, Creed raises a thought-provoking point:
has this concept of democracy been trivialized or commodified? Has
it become a spectacle rather than a genuine expression of personal
freedom?

The intertwining of sexuality and democracy here implies an unsettling dynamic—one in which personal identity, rather than being a
sacred aspect of self, is tangled up with societal expectations and public
discourse. By equating sexuality with democracy, Creed is highlighting
how deeply personal aspects of life have become subjects of debate
and politicization. What should be an intimate, individual experience
becomes instead a matter of public scrutiny, leading to a sense of
alienation.

The dissonance in the music here reflects this theme. With minor
intervals and haunting undertones, Creed creates a feeling of internal
conflict and estrangement. The listener is pulled into a space where
personal identity feels exposed, scrutinized, and at odds with public perception. The song's melody shifts, giving voice to the tension
between the public and the private, between autonomy and external
judgment.

When Creed reaches the refrain, "What is right or wrong? I don't
know who to believe in. My soul sings a different song in America," it's
as though we've arrived at the heart of the disillusionment. These lines
capture a profound sense of abandonment, a feeling that the moral
compass has spun wildly, leaving no clear sense of direction. Creed's

confession becomes a universal one—a plea for clarity in a world where certainty is elusive, and truth feels malleable.

The refrain is not a question with an answer but rather a cry of frustration and sorrow. It's as if Creed is articulating a collective discontent, a sense that the structures once meant to guide and support have instead led to confusion and disorientation. This disconnect is expressed not only in the lyrics but in the almost primal delivery of the vocals, where each word feels like a howl, a raw release of pent-up anguish.

The music swells in intensity here, amplifying the theme of a soul adrift. There is no resolution, no peace in these lines; instead, the listener is left with a lingering sense of emptiness, as though the foundations that once held society together have crumbled, leaving only uncertainty in their wake. Creed's haunting delivery underscores the emotional weight of this revelation, making it clear that the journey is one of unresolved tension, of yearning for truth amidst chaos.

In the next verse, Creed turns their gaze to institutionalized faith, painting a somber picture of a church where "their leader falls to the ground." This image is powerful in its simplicity, a symbol of hypocrisy and corruption. For those who looked to religious leaders for guidance and hope, this moment represents a deep betrayal—a collapse not only of a person but of an ideal, of the trust placed in institutions meant to provide moral clarity.

The music shifts to a solemn tone, almost a dirge, reflecting the mourning for a lost sense of integrity. Creed's critique here is not directed at faith itself but at the flawed individuals who represent it, those who have fallen short of the responsibility to lead and inspire. The song laments not only the leader's fall but also the disillusionment of those who followed, who now find themselves questioning the authenticity of their beliefs.

This verse resonates with a sense of profound loss, a grieving for the innocence and faith that have been tarnished by corruption. It is a reminder that even institutions meant to provide solace and guidance can falter, leaving individuals to grapple with faith in a world where trust has been shattered.

As the song draws to its close, Creed reaches a poignant realization: "I am right and you are wrong. No one's right and no one's wrong." Here lies the essence of the song's discontent—a world where absolute truths seem to have vanished, leaving only shades of gray. This moment of reckoning is both liberating and deeply unsettling, as the speaker acknowledges the futility of rigid judgments in a polarized society.

This final stanza feels like a surrender, an admission that the search for an absolute "right" or "wrong" may be an illusion. And yet, in this realization, there is no peace—only a sense of profound emptiness, a void left by the collapse of once-unshakable beliefs. The music reaches a crescendo, reinforcing this unresolved tension, as if the song itself is left hanging in the air, incomplete, yearning for a resolution that never comes.

Ultimately, "In America" is not a rejection of the country or its ideals. Rather, it's a lament—a yearning for something truer, more genuine. Creed's lyrics, music, and voice combine to express a kind of disillusionment born from love. This is a love that aches for what has been lost, that remembers the ideals once cherished, and that hopes, somehow, for redemption. The song is a soul's cry, a plea for a return to something real, something that resonates with the speaker's deepest values.

Creed doesn't offer answers in "In America"; instead, they create a space for reflection, for questioning, and for hope. The song invites listeners to sit with their discontent, to confront the fractures in their beliefs, and perhaps, to find in those broken pieces a path toward healing. It's a reminder that even in disillusionment, there is room for love—a love that, though disappointed, still holds out hope for what America could become.

In the end, "In America" is a song of reflection, of lament, but also of possibility. It asks us to look honestly at the contradictions and sacrifices that define modern life and to search, despite the fractures, for something whole.

Application

When we encounter the themes in this song—the disillusionment with culture, the struggle to discern right from wrong, and the feeling of isolation in one's values—there's a real opportunity to reflect on where we find our grounding. Scripture shows us that when society feels chaotic and values appear contradictory, there is still an anchor available, one that doesn't waver. That anchor is God's truth, and it remains steadfast, even when everything else feels uncertain.

In an age marked by shifting values, the song's lyrical search for truth reflects a common, often painful struggle. It paints a picture of disorientation, of people drifting, of standards that are fragile and change with the currents. This captures the exact plight we face when we place our hope in the opinions of others or in society's fluid definitions of morality. The Word of God, however, provides an anchor—steady, unwavering, and eternal. Psalm 119:105 reminds us, "Your word is a lamp to my feet and a light to my path." It's not just a guide; it's a lifeline, illuminating a path through the dim fog of cultural confusion and offering an enduring standard when everything else crumbles.

We live in a society that glorifies personal experience, often elevating it as the ultimate gauge of right and wrong. Yet, feelings can lead us astray. Cultural trends shift, telling us one day that something is acceptable and the next that it's reprehensible. They lure us into a mirage of stability and autonomy only to leave us feeling adrift and lost when our own experiences fail to provide clear answers. When we allow ourselves to be swayed by what feels right in the moment, we're like ships tossed about in a storm. Scripture stands in stark contrast to this. The Word doesn't just adapt to suit human preferences; it transcends them, grounding us in truth that is steadfast and unwavering, pointing us to the nature of God Himself, His righteousness, and His holy design for life.

The song's lyrics also voice disappointment with leaders—especially religious ones—who have fallen short or abused their authority. It's a theme that resonates painfully in today's world, where scandals and failures among trusted figures have eroded trust in institutions and left people feeling abandoned. Jeremiah 17:5-7 cautions us against placing our confidence in human beings, even well-meaning ones, lest we invite disillusionment. It's true that people, no matter how faithful or devoted, are prone to error, sometimes gravely so. They are flawed vessels, fragile as we are. Our hope, therefore, cannot rest in individuals or institutions; rather, it must be rooted in Christ, who is steadfast and unfailing. He is the Good Shepherd, the one who sacrifices Himself for His sheep, and the only one who will never abandon us.

When we place our hope in Christ, we find security and peace that transcend human flaws. Leaders may fall, mentors may disappoint, and institutions may crumble, but Christ remains faithful. By fixing our gaze on Him, we protect our hearts from the bitterness of disillusionment and the despair that arises when we feel betrayed by those we once trusted. Jesus is not only the standard of leadership but the ultimate example of steadfast love. He models humility, compassion, and unwavering commitment, traits that should inspire, not replace, our faith. Our confidence in Him helps us to move forward, free from the wounds of disillusionment, strengthened by a hope that is eternal and unshakeable.

The song's expression of feeling "enslaved to be free" echoes a profound truth. Society's version of freedom—absolute autonomy, unrestricted choice—often leads to enslavement of a different kind. We are promised liberty, yet we find ourselves chained to our own desires, expectations, and the pressure to define our own path. In stark contrast, the freedom Christ offers comes through surrender. "You shall know the truth, and the truth shall make you free," Jesus declares in John 8:32. This freedom is not the freedom to do whatever we want, but the freedom to live as we were created to live, in alignment with God's design. It is the liberation from sin, from self-centeredness, and from the futile attempt to find meaning in our own authority. In submitting to God's will, we paradoxically find true autonomy—the kind that no external force can steal, rooted in a peace that surpasses all understanding.

In a culture preoccupied with defining personal identity, the song's lyrics reflect a struggle to find solid ground. The search for identity has become a journey of constant change, with new labels emerging daily, each claiming to offer answers. This ceaseless quest, however, often results in greater confusion. Yet, Scripture offers us a stable identity rooted in Christ Himself. Galatians 2:20 tells us, "I have been crucified with Christ; it is no longer I who live, but Christ lives in me." When our identity is in Him, we are freed from the pressure to define ourselves by cultural or social standards. We are no longer beholden to the expectations of others or to the ever-shifting values of society. In Christ, we find a security that no label can offer. We are His, loved and chosen, and this identity gives us clarity and purpose, even when the world around us seems to be in a constant state of flux.

The call for discernment in the song's refrain, "What is right or wrong? I don't know who to believe in," resonates in a world that seems increasingly gray. The Bible's wisdom literature, particularly Proverbs, frequently calls us to seek understanding and discernment. James 1:5 further promises that God will give wisdom generously to all who ask. True discernment doesn't come from intellectual prowess or self-assurance; it is a gift from God to those with hearts surrendered to His will. To navigate life's complexities, we need more than knowledge; we need spiritual wisdom. It's an invitation to approach every decision prayerfully, seeking the guidance of the Holy Spirit and the wisdom embedded in God's Word. In doing so, we align our hearts with God's purposes, making choices that honor Him rather than capitulating to social pressures.

At times, the world can seem chaotic and alien, and the song captures this sense of being out of place. It's an experience familiar to many believers—feeling as though we don't quite belong. The Bible reminds us that this feeling isn't a mistake; in fact, it's a consequence of our citizenship in another kingdom. Acts 17:26-27 reveals that God has determined our time and place, situating us here with intention and purpose. In the midst of societal upheaval, we are called to rest in God's sovereignty, trusting that He has placed us here for a reason. We are called to be salt and light, bringing His truth and love into a world that desperately needs it. When the world feels chaotic, we remember that God is in control, working all things according to His plan. Our lives have a purpose that transcends the transient nature of the cultural moment.

If you are feeling lost, adrift in a world of competing voices and shifting standards, know that God offers a path of clarity and purpose. His Word stands firm, a foundation that cannot be shaken. His promises are true, enduring through every generation. Our hope lies not in the approval of society, but in the faithfulness of Christ, who offers us life, identity, and freedom. In a world that celebrates self-reliance and autonomy, we are invited into a relationship with a Savior who knows us fully, loves us deeply, and guides us gently. Let these truths be a reminder that, even in moments of uncertainty, you are not alone. The Lord is your rock, your refuge, and your firm foundation, leading you on a path of transformation that goes beyond the limitations of human wisdom and the instability of cultural trends.

Our journey is far from over. Transformation in Christ is not a one-time event; it's a daily walk, an ongoing sanctification as we lean into His truth and allow His Spirit to work in us. There is much more to explore in this journey of faith, more insights to uncover, and more depth to grasp. As we navigate the trials and triumphs of life, may we continually turn to God's Word for guidance, allowing it to shape our minds, comfort our hearts, and direct our steps. In doing so, we embrace a life not bound by shifting cultural currents but anchored in the timeless truths of Scripture and the unchanging character of our Savior.

CHAPTER 7

"Illusion"

In "Illusion," Creed crafts a haunting exploration of inner turmoil and the fragile human psyche, unveiling a tapestry of quiet desperation that resonates on a deeply personal level. Woven with the threads of self-doubt, questions of purpose, and a relentless search for identity, each lyric whispers of a life suspended between hope and resignation. This is a song of introspection, a search for meaning that is neither grand nor overtly heroic. Instead, it is foundational—a quest for the reassurance that life is not merely a mirage but holds something real beneath the surface.

The opening line, "The sun rises to another day," serves as more than just an observation. It's an acknowledgment of time's inevitable march, each dawn marking the return of familiar routines and cycles. But there's a heaviness in that return, a suggestion that the protagonist is struggling to find meaning in this endless cycle. Watching the sun rise day after day, he senses that his "constitution keeps changing, 'til it slips away." Here, "constitution" represents his very essence—his values, his beliefs, the core of who he is. That sense of self feels fragile, eroding a little more with each passing day. This notion of slipping away calls forth an image of something once strong and whole, now gradually wearing down like stone facing the unyielding force of water over time. It's a subtle process but one that carries profound implications, as if each sunrise pulls him further from a version of himself that he once knew.

This struggle is one of subtlety and nuance, not the loud, fiery battles often associated with quests for identity. As the protagonist lies awake, pondering questions like "Should I stay or go? Should I sleep or stay awake?" there's an unsettling depth to his indecision. These are not simple choices about rest or activity; they hint at existential questions about his purpose and place in the world. There's an implicit wondering about whether his existence matters or if his actions have any significance. The repetition of questions hints at a mind that cannot settle, trapped in a loop of reflection and doubt. When he wonders, "Am I really happy, or is it all just an illusion?" a faint yet potent sense of fear creeps in. The very concept of happiness itself is called into question, casting doubt on whether his experiences are genuine or mere constructs—a defense mechanism to keep him trudging forward, despite an underlying emptiness.

Musically, "Illusion" mirrors this existential unease. The song's somber, steady guitar riffs build tension without ever reaching a climactic release. There is no grand resolution, no satisfying conclusion, mirroring the unresolved questions plaguing the protagonist. The tone of the guitar is neither bright nor dark but rather suspended in a kind of emotional gray space, resonating with a restrained intensity that echoes the protagonist's own quiet despair. Each chord hums with a feeling of anticipation, like a sigh held just before release, a breath never fully exhaled. The music hovers in this unresolved state, oscillating between minor and major keys—a delicate shift that represents the protagonist's fluctuating outlook, caught somewhere between melancholy and a faint, unreachable optimism. The tension lies in this back-and-forth, with each minor chord pulling him into darker introspection, while each major chord hints at a flicker of hope that never fully takes hold.

From a theoretical perspective, the oscillation between minor and major chords reinforces the protagonist's psychological state. This wavering between tones suggests his own inability to commit to either darkness or light, creating an ambiguous space where joy and sorrow blend into something undefined, something that blurs the line between what's real and what's imagined. The music becomes an extension of his inner world, embodying the uncertainty and complexity of human emotions, where nothing is ever fully one thing or the other.

As the song progresses, we find the protagonist sitting "in [his] room now, hiding thoughts," where the room itself serves as a metaphor for his isolation. This self-imposed solitude reflects his disconnection from others, a loneliness that stems from feeling misunderstood or perhaps unable to communicate his innermost struggles. When he expresses a desire to "get out," the ambiguity of this statement leaves us wondering: does he want to escape the physical room, his own mind, or a prison of emotional disillusionment? The line is powerful precisely because it is vague—it invites listeners to share in his confinement, to feel the walls closing in as he searches for freedom or clarity that seems always just out of reach.

In a pivotal moment, he hears a voice that calls his name, breaking a trance that has held him in stillness. "I hear a voice call my name, breaking trance so silent, so I can stay the same." This line introduces a subtle shift, a glimmer of self-awareness, as if some external force—perhaps a fragment of his own mind or spirit—whispers to him, reminding him of his potential. Yet this voice, while it breaks his trance, does not push him to change; instead, it leaves him where he is, unresolved. It's almost as if the universe has reached out to touch him, offering a momentary spark of clarity, only to pull back, leaving him stranded in the in-between, teetering on the edge of transformation but unable to move forward.

"Wait now, many things are left unsaid. This life remains the same but I change." This line captures the profound sense of isolation that can accompany inner change. Here, the protagonist acknowledges that he is undergoing a metamorphosis, but one that remains invisible to the world outside. Life moves forward, untouched and unchanged by his internal shifts, as if his transformation is locked within him, unable to manifest in his external reality. There is a bittersweet quality to this realization—a sense that, while he is evolving, he is doing so in silence, without acknowledgment or validation from the world around him. The weight of unspoken truths becomes a burden he alone must carry, deepening his sense of disillusionment and leaving him wondering if his life is indeed nothing more than an illusion, perpetually beyond his grasp.

The refrain, "Just an illusion," echoes throughout the final moments of the song, each repetition sinking deeper into the listener's consciousness. It's a haunting refrain, a mantra that speaks to the protagonist's profound sense of impermanence, the unsettling idea that everything he feels, hopes for, or fears might not be real. Each repetition of the phrase "Just an illusion" reinforces the existential ambiguity that has plagued him from the beginning, leaving him—and the listener—with an aching sense of incompleteness. It's a refrain that resonates long after the music fades, lingering like the ghost of an unresolved question.

At its core, "Illusion" is a meditation on the thin line between reality and perception, on the heartbreaking struggle to find meaning in a world that often feels hollow. The protagonist isn't merely questioning the authenticity of happiness; he's probing the nature of reality itself, wrestling with whether his existence has substance or is merely a

shadow cast by his mind's restless yearning. His journey is one marked
by a profound sense of loneliness and introspection, as he ventures
deep into the self, knowing that clarity may never come. But even
as he faces this uncertainty, the very act of questioning, of seeking
truth, becomes a testament to his resilience, to the indomitable spirit
of human inquiry that persists even when answers remain elusive.

The song speaks to anyone who has ever felt caught in the in-between, living in the gray spaces of life where certainty is rare, and
meaning feels constantly just out of reach. In this way, "Illusion" becomes more than a song; it becomes a mirror for our own struggles
with purpose and identity, a reminder that we are not alone in our
search for something real in a world that often feels illusory.

This resonance is what gives "Illusion" its power. It captures the
universal struggle to define oneself, to find grounding in a world where
everything is in flux. It speaks to the quiet battles waged within us,
battles that often go unseen, yet shape us in profound ways. The
protagonist's journey is our journey, his questions are our questions,
and his search for meaning reflects the timeless human desire to know
that, even in the midst of uncertainty, there is something real and true
worth holding onto.

As listeners, we are invited into this journey, drawn into the protagonist's inner world, where every chord, every pause, every whispered
lyric is imbued with a sense of fragile beauty. We come to understand
that, like the protagonist, we too live in a world of illusions, shaped by
our perceptions and interpretations. But perhaps, in acknowledging
the illusion, we come closer to understanding our own reality, our own
truths, however fleeting or fragile they may be.

In the end, "Illusion" leaves us with a paradox: that the search for
meaning itself may be the closest we come to finding it. In a world
where everything seems to slip away, where nothing is entirely certain,

it is the act of seeking that gives our lives substance. This journey, filled with doubt and questions, is what ultimately defines us, what gives us strength, and what allows us, even if only momentarily, to touch something real. In this way, Creed's "Illusion" becomes a song not only of despair but of quiet hope—a hope that, despite all appearances, there is something true to be found, if only we continue the search.

Application

In *Illusion,* we are presented with a narrative that captures a deeply felt, universal struggle—a quest for purpose, peace, and something real beyond the transient echoes of daily life. The song's lyrics cut through the surface of existence, illuminating the inner tension of someone wrestling with the unspoken questions many of us grapple with: "What am I living for?" "Is happiness just a passing shadow?" "Is there something solid, unchanging that I can hold on to?"

We begin with the protagonist's sense of isolation—a loneliness that's not merely circumstantial but deeply existential. He feels as if he's adrift, stuck between reality and illusion, caught in the endless loop of questioning and searching, yet not finding the anchor his soul longs for. This experience—where uncertainty and longing replace stability and clarity—is painfully relatable, for it reminds us of the restlessness that arises when we attempt to ground ourselves in the unreliable soil of changing circumstances or fleeting emotions. It calls to mind the words of James, who describes a person "like a wave of the sea, blown and tossed by the wind" (James 1:6). This instability stems from the pursuit of truth or purpose within the confines of a world that itself is always shifting. When we try to build our identity or meaning on what we feel or experience in a given moment, it's as if we are trying to find rest on a moving train—constantly readjusting, but never at peace.

One clear theme in *Illusion* is the protagonist's search for stability—a desire to find something unchangeable amidst all that fluctuates around him. He wonders whether happiness is real or simply an illusion, a fleeting experience that vanishes as quickly as it appears. This longing for happiness, however, is complicated by a deeper, unfulfilled need: a foundation of truth that does not waver. True stability, as he's beginning to realize, cannot depend on circumstances that change, relationships that come and go, or emotions that ebb and flow. In Scripture, Jesus speaks of the wise man who builds his house on the rock, a foundation that withstands the inevitable storms of life (Matthew 7:24-27). This rock is the truth of God's word—a truth that is unwavering, absolute, and capable of grounding us when everything else shifts beneath our feet.

The protagonist's journey also reveals a stark lesson about the limitations of self-reliance. Throughout the song, he hides his thoughts, choosing to confine his struggles within his own mind. There's an impression that he fears vulnerability or perhaps feels that no one could understand his inner turmoil. Yet, in isolating himself, he only deepens his sense of loneliness. The Bible speaks profoundly about the importance of community, of bearing one another's burdens (Galatians 6:2). This call to live in connection with others serves as a safeguard against the kind of isolation that magnifies our inner struggles. We are reminded that even in our darkest moments, we are not meant to carry our burdens alone. In genuine, supportive community, there is not only comfort but also the kind of accountability and encouragement that keeps us grounded in truth when our own perceptions or emotions lead us astray.

The protagonist's sense of resignation offers another powerful insight. He seems to view himself as a passive spectator in his own life, almost as if he's stuck on the sidelines, watching events unfold but feeling powerless to shape them. The line "life goes on" hints at a creeping sense of defeat—a notion that life will continue whether or not he actively engages with it. This resignation is dangerous, for it suggests a surrender to the illusion that he has no control over his life's direction. In this way, *Illusion* serves as a caution against passivity. There is value in actively pursuing truth, in taking intentional steps toward growth, even when we cannot see immediate results. The book of Proverbs highlights this truth by reminding us that wisdom, understanding, and purpose are treasures worth seeking—gifts that lead us away from the complacency of passive living (Proverbs 2:1-5). Actively pursuing change or growth under the guidance of divine wisdom provides a sense of purpose that mere resignation cannot offer.

But the song doesn't merely warn us of the dangers of passivity; it also calls us to examine the nature of our pursuits. The protagonist grapples with the question of happiness and whether it is even attainable. Happiness, as it is often understood, is seen as something circumstantial, reliant on the external factors of life. Yet this perspective reduces happiness to a mere feeling, something that fluctuates and cannot be counted on. Instead, the pursuit of joy—rooted in something far more enduring—becomes a deeper, more fulfilling goal. In *Illusion,* we see what happens when one chases temporary gratification or momentary highs. Real contentment, by contrast, is grounded in purpose that transcends our current circumstances.

This longing for something beyond the temporary echoes the teachings found in Ecclesiastes, where the writer laments the emptiness of pursuing worldly pleasures and achievements, calling them "meaningless, a chasing after the wind" (Ecclesiastes 2:11). When we chase after things that cannot satisfy, we end up feeling hollow, disappointed, and even more aware of our need for something greater. The song subtly guides us toward the idea that real contentment, real peace, is found not in chasing fleeting emotions or external validations, but in something—or Someone—who remains constant, even when life does not.

Perhaps one of the most striking aspects of *Illusion* is its portrayal of inner conflict. The protagonist yearns for clarity yet feels enveloped by uncertainty. His struggle reflects the human tendency to wrestle with doubt, to feel caught between what we know to be true and what we feel in moments of weakness. Doubt itself is not inherently sinful or wrong—it can drive us to seek answers, to press deeper into truth. Yet, when left unchecked, doubt can lead to despair, to a place where we no longer feel anchored in anything sure. The prophet Jeremiah expresses a similar sentiment when he cries out, "Why is my pain unending and my wound grievous and incurable?" (Jeremiah 15:18). This question reflects the deep, unresolved pain of a man who knows God's promises yet feels the weight of his present suffering.

As we examine the protagonist's desire to "get out" of his mental confinement, we're reminded of the essential human need for liberation, for a sense of freedom that allows us to live fully. However, true freedom does not mean escaping reality or ignoring hardship; rather, it involves a freedom that is found in surrendering to a higher truth. Jesus spoke of this freedom when He said, "You will know the truth, and the truth will set you free" (John 8:32). This truth, grounded in God's word, offers liberation from the chains of illusion—the illusion that we must constantly strive for meaning on our own, the illusion that our worth is dependent on what we achieve, feel, or experience.

Illusion also reveals the protagonist's need for a deeper connection, a relationship that goes beyond mere surface-level acquaintance. This desire reflects the innate human longing to be known, fully and without reservation. In the Bible, we see that God knows us intimately, understanding our thoughts, our struggles, and our dreams. Psalm

139 beautifully expresses this truth: "You have searched me, Lord, and you know me... You are familiar with all my ways" (Psalm 139:1, 3). This knowledge is not impersonal or detached; it is the loving, attentive knowledge of a Father who cares deeply for His children. In understanding that we are fully known and fully loved by God, we are invited into a relationship that transcends the isolation the protagonist feels. It is a relationship that fulfills our deepest longing for connection.

At its core, *Illusion* challenges us to reconsider where we find our identity, purpose, and hope. It's a reminder that when we ground ourselves in the ever-shifting sands of emotion or circumstance, we are bound to feel lost, confused, and dissatisfied. The only true foundation is one that transcends the limits of human experience—a foundation built on the eternal, unchanging nature of God and His truth. Just as Jesus taught of building on the rock, *Illusion* calls us to question the structures we've built our lives upon and to seek something more enduring, something that can withstand the winds of doubt, fear, and change.

In the protagonist's journey, we see both the struggle and the possibility for transformation. Though he wrestles with isolation, confusion, and an unsettled heart, there is an implicit invitation to step beyond these illusions and to discover a reality that offers both stability and peace. *Illusion* invites us to reflect on our own lives, to search for those places where we may be clinging to illusions instead of seeking truth, and to begin our own journey toward a foundation that is steadfast, grounded, and ultimately, life-giving.

CHAPTER 8

"Unforgiven"

C reed's "Unforgiven" unfolds as a profound, relentless meditation on personal and existential conflicts. From the moment
the first guitar chords rumble like distant thunder, we are swept into
a world where faith and disillusionment collide in unyielding tension.
Through evocative lyricism and masterful instrumentation, the band
draws listeners into the heart of a spiritual battle, one that teeters
between anguish and a desperate hope. The experience is less a song
and more a pilgrimage into the recesses of the soul—a journey toward
self-acceptance or, perhaps, the stark reality of estrangement from it.

The essence of "Unforgiven" lies in its raw honesty, an unfiltered
exploration of a broken spirit that continues to strive, regardless of its
bruises. Creed crafts this journey meticulously, with each line serving
as a revelation, each riff as a blow to the comfortable illusions we might
hold about forgiveness, grace, and redemption. With lines like, "I kept
up with the prophecy you spoke," we sense the narrative's weariness,
the slow realization that their pursuit of something divine has come
at a personal cost. In this, Creed's lyrics become not just words but
confessions, spoken from the depths of a conflicted heart.

The juxtaposition between distorted guitars and strained vocals
gives shape to the narrator's fractured spirit. These sounds are not
random—they pulse with intention, a purposeful rhythm that seems
to symbolize a battle-worn heart struggling against the inevitabilities

it faces. As the guitars surge and retreat, the listener is enveloped in waves of sound, reflecting the internal turmoil of a soul wrestling with its own fallibility. This struggle, one against an intangible yet omnipresent weight, is Creed's gift to the audience: a raw, unapologetic representation of what it feels like to grapple with the most profound questions of existence.

At the heart of "Unforgiven" is an exploration of faith—a faith that has been twisted, reshaped, and almost unrecognizable by the narrator's painful experiences. In the line, "I kept up with the prophecy you spoke," there is a sense of a lost pilgrimage, a journey that began with hope and direction but has since wandered into darker territory. "The prophecy," in this case, feels as though it could represent any guiding principle or belief structure—a tenet once clear and unshakeable, now obscured by doubt and compromise. This isn't a passive disillusionment; it's an active, agonizing realization that what was once sacred has, over time, become a burden.

The music, too, mirrors this transformation. The melody starts with an almost hesitant purity before descending into more distorted, chaotic riffs. These musical shifts are not random but seem to mirror the progression of a soul in turmoil, as the clarity of faith fades into a muddled, twisted sense of purpose. Creed captures the tension between aspiration and loss, purity and corruption, a struggle that feels inescapable. In this, the listener can't help but question: How often do our own beliefs morph in ways we never intended, leaving us with a haunting sense of having lost something essential?

The phrase "Think I'm unforgiven to this world" becomes a kind of mantra, repeated with a haunting resignation that echoes throughout the song. Here, Creed taps into the profound despair of feeling irredeemable, an alienation not just from others but from the very world itself. This isn't a straightforward guilt over a single misdeed; it's an existential fracture, a realization that some wounds may never heal and that some mistakes might forever separate us from who we want to be.

Repeatedly, this refrain drives home a sense of permanence. In music theory, repetition often serves to solidify a central theme, and in "Unforgiven," it's used to force us deeper into the painful realization of estrangement. Each utterance feels like a descent, as if the narrator sinks further into the darkness with every repetition. And as the guitars grind against the drums, the listener feels the pressure of this weight, the unspoken acknowledgment that some things once broken might not be fixable. It's a rare and powerful commentary on the nature of guilt—a reminder that forgiveness, especially forgiveness of oneself, can sometimes be the hardest thing to find.

Creed brings a crushing intensity to the line, "No more raging innocence." This is no casual observation but rather a devastating confession that innocence, once lost, can never be reclaimed. There's a profound tragedy here—a painful acceptance that the purity of faith or purpose the narrator once knew has been permanently tainted. This moment in the song hits like a revelation, and the vocal delivery—strained, almost broken—captures the raw grief of this loss.

Musically, this shift is reflected in an intensifying tone, as if the very structure of the song mourns this loss alongside the narrator. Creed uses dissonant, harsh chords to create a sense of irrevocability, a one-way descent that cannot be undone. In this, the listener is invited to feel the agony of recognizing that the former self, the one filled with idealistic belief, is forever out of reach. It's a harsh truth, a reminder that growth and maturity often come at the cost of innocence, and that, sometimes, what we learn in life only serves to make us mourn what we once believed.

The line, "Step inside the light and see / The fear of God burn inside of me," brings a new intensity, as the narrator seems to invite divine judgment. This is no gentle, forgiving light; it's a purging flame that exposes every flaw, every misdeed. It's an invitation to be laid bare, to be stripped of all pretense, and to stand in unfiltered truth. There's something profoundly courageous—and terrifying—about this moment. Creed isn't just exploring the notion of divine forgiveness but the brutal, almost surgical clarity of self-reckoning.

This moment in the song feels like a climax, the crescendo where all the suppressed fears and hidden guilt come rushing to the surface. It's as if the narrator willingly steps into a furnace, understanding that the only way to know the depth of their own soul is to burn away everything superficial. Musically, the intensity reaches a fever pitch, with each instrument combining to create a wall of sound that crashes over the listener like a tidal wave. In this, Creed captures the emotional and spiritual agony of confronting one's own failures and shortcomings, a moment that is both painful and purifying.

As "Unforgiven" draws to a close, the refrain "Think I'm unforgiven" lingers in the air, refusing to resolve into a comforting conclusion. This open-endedness is perhaps one of the song's most powerful choices. Instead of offering a neat resolution, Creed leaves us suspended in ambiguity, echoing the uncertainty that defines so much of the human experience. The unresolved chords reflect a journey that hasn't yet found its end, a struggle that might never reach peace. In this, Creed speaks to the enduring nature of inner conflict, to the reality that some questions may never have answers.

This choice leaves the listener in a space of contemplation. The journey toward self-understanding, Creed suggests, is not a linear path but a labyrinth filled with dead ends, painful realizations, and moments of clarity that may only be temporary. "Unforgiven" does not aim to comfort; rather, it challenges the listener to sit with discomfort, to acknowledge that some things are irreconcilable. It's a stark, haunting reminder that the search for meaning and forgiveness is ongoing, an endless process of confronting oneself, even when the answers remain out of reach.

Through a lens of hermeneutic intent, "Unforgiven" reveals itself as more than a song; it's a meditation on the nature of faith, the cost of innocence, and the weight of self-forgiveness. Creed's lyrics invite us to examine our beliefs and to question the paths we've taken in pursuit of purpose or truth. It's a song that embodies the journey of faith not as a source of comfort but as a crucible—a place where one's soul is tested, refined, and, at times, shattered.

The words, the music, the progression—all of it is crafted to convey the fragile beauty of striving for meaning in a world that often seems devoid of answers. By choosing to end on a note of ambiguity, Creed honors the complexity of this journey. Forgiveness, they suggest, may not be something easily given or received. It's a journey that requires resilience, courage, and an unyielding desire to understand oneself, even in the face of painful truths.

In "Unforgiven," Creed offers a powerful reflection on the struggle to reconcile faith with human frailty. The song captures the relentless nature of inner conflict, the inevitable losses we face, and the rare, fleeting glimpses of truth that both guide and haunt us. It is a reminder that the journey toward forgiveness—of oneself, of others, and perhaps even from a higher power—is an arduous path, one fraught with revelations that are as likely to wound as they are to heal.

As listeners, we are left to ponder our own journeys, to sit with the uncomfortable reality that some questions may never find answers, and that true redemption might always remain just out of reach. Through its raw lyricism and intense musicality, "Unforgiven" stands as a testament to the beauty and the agony of striving for meaning in a world that often offers none. It's a song that dares to leave us in the tension, inviting us to confront ourselves with the same unflinching honesty. And in this, perhaps, lies the song's deepest truth: that the journey to understanding, forgiveness, and peace is not one of completion but of endless pursuit.

Application

"Unforgiven" speaks with a voice raw and unflinching, peeling back the layers of spiritual struggle and exposing the painful realities of guilt, isolation, and lost innocence. It's a song that doesn't just describe feelings; it drags the listener into the depths of wrestling with personal failings, grappling with alienation from oneself, and searching for a flicker of hope amid darkness. It's an intensely human journey, echoing the voices of countless souls who find themselves questioning their own worthiness, wondering if they've strayed too far from redemption's reach.

This piece invites us to walk alongside those questions and reflections. Here, the soul stands before itself, honest and vulnerable, acknowledging the desperate need for healing. It's about moving beyond the surface of regret and sorrow and into a realm where transformation isn't just a distant hope but an achievable reality. For anyone standing at a similar crossroads, the narrative within "Unforgiven" offers guiding principles—a way forward, step by step, through acknowledgment, reverence, exposure to truth, and ultimately, grounding oneself in a foundation beyond the self.

The first verse in this journey is deeply introspective. The lyrics trace a path from pride to emptiness, revealing a protagonist who has looked around and found nothing satisfying, no lasting joy or purpose. It's as if everything he has touched has withered, and in his heart, he feels hollow. This portrayal reflects a profound truth about the human condition: the longer we deny our brokenness, the more we construct walls of self-deception and pride that lead to inner desolation. It's a theme resonant with Scriptural wisdom—the constant reminders in Proverbs, for example, that pride comes before a fall, and that humility is the path to wisdom.

To own our condition means to look unflinchingly at our own reflection, flaws, scars, and all, recognizing the ways we've contributed to our struggles. This isn't an exercise in self-condemnation, but in honesty. Blame is a powerful temptation, luring us into justifications: we point to the circumstances that set us up to fail, the people who disappointed us, or even the faith that we feel didn't deliver what it promised. Yet here, "Unforgiven" challenges us to stand naked before our choices, to say, "This is where I am, and I see how I arrived." It's a painful truth, but without it, real change remains out of reach.

One line strikes hard: "the fear of God burn[ing] inside." It's a moment of reverence, a jolting reminder that there's a standard beyond our whims and desires—a standard that transcends human failings and calls us to something higher. Today, the concept of "fear" often carries a negative weight, a sense of shame or terror, but biblically, the fear of God is something entirely different. This kind of fear is rooted in awe, an awareness that we stand before a perfect, all-seeing Creator who cannot be deceived or appeased with hollow gestures.

This fear is transformative. It brings us to our knees, not to crush us under shame but to lift our gaze to God's holiness. It's like fire, burning away self-deception and pride, leaving us humbled yet hopeful, because with reverence comes the possibility of grace. When we let the fear of God take root, we stop seeking validation in worldly measures or fleeting pleasures; instead, we become deeply aware of our accountability before a standard that doesn't shift with culture or circumstance. And while this may sound daunting, this reverent fear becomes the beginning of wisdom, the point where we can finally see our lives in the light of God's truth.

The lyrics continue to call us to a crucial step: "step inside the light and see." This isn't an easy invitation—it's a call to face the truth head-on. In this light, every hidden fault, every masked motive, every ounce of pride or bitterness is exposed. Most of us avoid this level of exposure; it's far easier to stay in the shadows, where we can justify, rationalize, or ignore the parts of ourselves we don't want to confront. But stepping into the light is the only way forward. Jesus speaks to this truth in John's Gospel, declaring that those who seek truth come into the light so that their deeds may be shown plainly.

To step into the light is to allow ourselves to be fully seen, flaws and all, not just by God, but by those we trust. This could be through prayer, laying bare our struggles before God, or in conversations with mentors, friends, or counselors who can walk with us through the refining process. Here, there is no hiding. In the light, our inner darkness is purified, our hearts are clarified, and the weight of hidden guilt begins to lift. It's a painful process, but each step taken in honesty is a step toward freedom.

The phrase "Godless to the extent that I died" conveys a haunting reality—a life spent building on a foundation that ultimately collapses. The song's narrator experiences the hollowness of trying to construct meaning without a higher purpose, only to find himself spiritually dead, his heart numb and desolate. This echoes Jesus' warning in Matthew 7:26-27 about building a house on sand; when storms come, the foundation is swept away, leaving ruin in its place. Without God as our anchor, we drift, at the mercy of shifting circumstances and fleeting satisfactions.

A foundation beyond the self isn't just a nice idea; it's essential. Many search for stability in careers, relationships, or personal achievements, but these are all temporary. They can't bear the weight of our deepest needs and longings. When we root ourselves in Christ, however, we ground our lives in something unchanging, something that doesn't fail or crumble. This foundation becomes a source of resilience, peace, and strength, even when life's storms hit. To "seek first the Kingdom of God" is not just a suggestion—it's a call to build our lives on a rock that withstands any trial.

The song's journey is far from over, and so is the journey of anyone wrestling with guilt and alienation. These reflections are steps, not solutions. Moving from a place of despair to one of renewal requires courage—a courage fueled by the hope that change is possible, that grace is real, and that forgiveness can be found. The willingness to own our condition, to humble ourselves in reverent fear, to embrace the light of truth, and to build our lives on God's foundation isn't a path for the faint-hearted. But it is a path that leads to life, a life restored and redeemed.

As we continue down this path, it's vital to remember that this transformation isn't a one-time event. It's a daily surrender, a continual renewal of the mind, as Paul writes in Romans 12:2. The journey to wholeness is one that unfolds over time, each day inviting us to draw nearer to God, to lay down our pride, and to live with a purpose rooted in something beyond ourselves.

"Unforgiven" echoes the cry of many souls, but it also points toward hope—a hope that isn't based on our ability to be good enough, but on God's willingness to redeem us where we are. There's no need to sugarcoat the struggle, no need to pretend the road is easy. The power of grace is found not in the absence of hardship but in the midst of it, in the moments when we think we've gone too far only to find that God's love has been waiting for us all along.

This journey is ongoing. And with each step, we uncover more layers of ourselves, more places where grace can seep in, transforming wounds into wisdom and pain into purpose. The themes in "Unforgiven" remind us that even in our darkest moments, even when the weight of our past feels unbearable, we are not beyond the reach of grace. It's a story of brokenness but also of healing—a journey from isolation to connection, from despair to hope. And as we walk this path, we find ourselves growing, not by our own strength, but by the strength of the One who walks with us, who calls us out of darkness and into His marvelous light.

There is much more to be said, many more depths to explore in this narrative of transformation. The journey is ongoing, and the hope remains that, as we press forward, we draw closer to a truth that does not waver and a grace that does not fail.

CHAPTER 9

"Sister"

C reed's song "Sister" dives deep into the experience of someone hidden in the margins, a person shaped by silent struggle, resilience, and ultimately, self-realization. Through rich, evocative lyrics and powerful musicality, the song paints a portrait of "little sister"—an overlooked, invisible figure who has silently borne the weight of unspoken expectations and familial disappointments. Her story, layered with unresolved tension and muted sorrow, resonates as both an aching lament and a rallying cry for transformation.

In the opening verse, we encounter "little sister" as one "caught up in the middle," where her "birthright" has somehow been "forgotten." These words convey a profound sense of dispossession, as if she has been born into a role defined more by sacrifice than celebration. She is the character in the background, the one whose presence is neither celebrated nor acknowledged. In many ways, she's the backbone of the family, the quiet strength that holds things together, yet she is left unseen, unheard, and unappreciated. Musically, the song's tone is subdued and restrained here, mirroring her muted presence within the family. The introductory guitar line reflects her quiet resilience, a sound that is calm yet carries an undercurrent of tension, as if this quiet strength is waiting for the right moment to be unleashed.

The repetition of "little sister" and "overlooked little girl" becomes almost like a chant throughout the song, a haunting reminder of her invisibility. This echo serves not just as a reinforcement of her position within the family but also as an invitation to the listener to look deeper into her experience. In music theory, Creed's use of minor tonality in these sections conveys a sense of unresolved sorrow, the kind of sadness that lingers and nags at the soul. This progression, paired with the gentle yet steady pulse, symbolizes her yearning for recognition, a quiet but powerful demand to be seen and valued. Each time the refrain returns, it deepens the emotional weight, pulling the listener further into her journey of quiet endurance and growing awareness.

The chorus brings to light a more intense and painful reality. Here, we meet a woman who has spent her life "bottled up and empty," conditioned to hold herself together and absorb the disappointments and neglected affection that were perhaps directed toward others in the family. She's the recipient of "love given to the younger," a line that speaks volumes about the inequities in her family dynamics. It's a portrayal of emotional inheritance, where one child receives the adoration while the other silently bears the absence of it. This kind of experience breeds a unique kind of resilience—a strength built not on validation, but on the ability to hold pain without allowing it to consume her.

As the chorus unfolds, it's clear that she's no longer content to remain confined by this narrative. Her resolve to "get back" emerges as a declaration of intent, a desire to reclaim her own sense of self-worth and identity. Musically, this shift in the song is marked by an intensification of the guitar chords, mirroring her own rising intensity and yearning for freedom. The music builds in power, as if to illustrate the breaking of chains, a release from the confines of her past. Her journey is no longer about survival—it's about actively reshaping her story, about moving from passive endurance to purposeful action.

In the latter half of the song, a significant transformation takes place. The lines "Now realize, little sister" serve as a pivotal moment of self-recognition. Here, she transitions from being a passive observer of her own life to someone who fully understands her position and her power to redefine it. The music crescendos with this realization, building to a point of catharsis that mirrors the intensity of her inner breakthrough. The bridge of the song, laden with heavier and more textured guitar riffs, becomes an anthem of defiance and strength. This part of the song doesn't just imply a desire for change; it's a re-sounding demand for it. She's not merely longing for a new path—she is forging it herself, shaking off the limits placed on her by family and circumstance.

The significance of this transformation cannot be overstated. "Sister" is, in a sense, both a lament and a victory anthem. The song captures the duality of her experience—the sorrow of being overlooked and the fierce strength required to emerge from that shadow. She begins as a peripheral figure, someone who exists in the background, yet by the song's conclusion, she has found her voice, claiming her place with quiet but unyielding strength. She is no longer the "over-looked little girl"; she is her own person, fully aware of her value and unapologetically asserting it.

In many ways, her journey reflects a universal struggle. How often do people find themselves in the margins, cast in roles that minimize their worth? How frequently do we witness individuals quietly ab-sorbing the weight of others' expectations, all while denying them-selves the right to be seen and valued for who they truly are? "Sister" brings this quiet struggle to the forefront, transforming it into a narra-tive of empowerment and self-acceptance. Through the protagonist's journey, we are reminded of the strength that lies within us all—the ability to redefine our own stories, to step out of the shadows, and to claim the recognition we deserve.

The song's composition plays a significant role in conveying these themes. Creed employs a melancholic yet assertive musical progression that reflects her journey from suppression to self-assertion. The restrained beginning mirrors her suppressed voice, while the gradual intensification represents her journey toward self-realization. The rise and fall of the melody echo her inner emotional landscape—a mixture of sorrow, strength, and finally, resolve. By the time the final chorus arrives, the music has taken on a life of its own, matching her demand for acknowledgment with a raw, unfiltered power. Each note, each chord, resonates as an embodiment of her newly claimed voice, as if the music itself is breathing life into her transformation.

What makes "Sister" particularly poignant is the juxtaposition of vulnerability and strength. The protagonist is not without scars; she carries the marks of her past, the remnants of being "bottled up and empty." Yet these very experiences become the foundation of her resilience. Her story is a testament to the transformative power of pain—how sorrow can become strength, and how endurance can lead to empowerment. Her journey is not about erasing the past but embracing it, using it as a catalyst to step into her true identity. Through her resilience, we see a reflection of our own potential to rise above limiting narratives and emerge with a clearer sense of self.

In a broader sense, "Sister" also challenges us to reflect on the roles we assign ourselves and others. How often do we unknowingly confine ourselves or others to the margins, overlooking the silent struggles they endure? The song invites us to look beyond surface-level assumptions and recognize the depth of experience within every individual. It serves as a reminder that no one should be left unseen or unheard and that every voice has the right to be acknowledged. In this way, the song's message transcends the individual, speaking to a collective need for empathy, understanding, and the courage to break free from limiting roles.

In conclusion, "Sister" by Creed is a powerful ode to resilience and self-realization. It tells the story of an overlooked figure who rises above her circumstances to reclaim her identity, moving from the shadows to the center of her own life. The song's melancholic yet fierce composition serves as a fitting backdrop to this journey, capturing both the sorrow of her past and the strength of her transformation. Through this narrative, we are reminded of the strength that lies within each of us to redefine our paths, to embrace our voices, and to claim our place in the world—no longer silent, no longer overlooked. The song is both a reminder and an inspiration, urging us to seek out our own moments of self-realization and to find the courage to step fully into our own stories.

Application

The song *Sister* resonates with an often unspoken pain—an ache rooted in the raw realities of feeling unseen, undervalued, and misunderstood. In this tension, there's a recognition of the human struggle to find identity and worth in a world filled with broken relationships and unmet expectations. The song's lyrics offer a quiet invitation to explore what it means to be shaped not by the failures or neglect of others but by a deeper, transformative understanding of self. For anyone who has walked this path, these words resonate with the yearning to be known, to be seen beyond the labels others have placed upon them.

The initial step in this journey is a brave one: acknowledging the hidden pain that lingers just beneath the surface. Pain that's ignored does not disappear; it festers, shaping our view of ourselves and the world. And so, the first step toward transformation is a willingness to confront these emotions rather than burying them beneath the day-to-day routine or beneath a mask of contentment. This is the very essence of vulnerability—to peel back the layers we use to protect ourselves and to face the places where we've been hurt. In the lyrics of *Sister*, we hear this cry for recognition—a yearning to be seen, to be acknowledged for who one truly is. It's a reminder that healing begins not with solutions or quick fixes but with honesty, with naming what has long remained unspoken.

Sharing these burdens with others—whether a trusted friend, a mentor, or a counselor—can provide a safe space to release this weight. Sometimes, the silence of our own thoughts becomes too heavy, and bringing another voice into the dialogue can create the kind of clarity that helps us take the next steps. Scripture encourages us to "bear one another's burdens" (Galatians 6:2), a call to support each other in the midst of life's hardest places. Bringing our struggles into the open with others who can listen, empathize, and offer guidance is an act of courage and humility, one that God can use to foster healing and restoration.

This journey also involves reclaiming one's identity beyond the roles and expectations placed upon us by others. The lyrics of *Sister* reveal a character who, in her search for acknowledgment, is invited to consider her value beyond the roles she's been given or the disappointments she's experienced. It's a powerful reminder that we are not defined by how others see us or by the labels they place upon us. In the Christian faith, identity is rooted not in the ever-changing views of people but in the steadfast love and purpose given to us by God. Psalm 139 paints a beautiful picture of this truth, describing how God intimately knows each of us—our thoughts, our ways, our very being. Reflecting on this truth, we can begin to see ourselves not through the eyes of others but through the lens of divine love, as uniquely crafted individuals who are seen, known, and valued.

For many, this realization can begin with practices like journaling or meditating on affirmations of worth. Such practices create moments of reflection, helping us uncover aspects of ourselves that may have been dismissed or undervalued over time. They help us move from viewing ourselves through the distorted lenses of rejection or failure to embracing a perspective grounded in truth and purpose. As we journal or reflect on these affirmations, we may find ourselves exploring questions like, *What does God say about me? What gifts or values do I possess that reflect His character?* These reflections allow us to define our identity from within, rather than allowing it to be shaped solely by external circumstances.

Yet, as we seek to build a secure sense of self, we inevitably confront the reality of broken relationships—the wounds left by people we trusted, respected, and, in many cases, loved. The song's mention of a "broken father, broken brother" echoes the pervasive effects of fractured relationships. These wounds often have deep roots and can shape how we view ourselves and others, often causing us to put up walls or withdraw. The weight of unprocessed pain can linger like a shadow, influencing our interactions and shaping our expectations. Here, the invitation is not simply to ignore the hurt but to engage it with intentionality.

While the past cannot be changed, the process of healing allows us to rewrite our relationship with it. Healing might mean forgiving someone who has hurt us, not because they necessarily deserve it but because holding onto bitterness only deepens our wounds. Forgiveness does not mean excusing or forgetting the harm done; it's a conscious choice to release the grip that resentment has over our lives. In some cases, healing may also involve creating boundaries, especially if a relationship continues to be a source of harm. Jesus Himself demonstrated the importance of boundaries throughout His ministry, knowing when to withdraw to quiet places to pray, when to confront, and when to walk away. This balance—of grace and discernment—helps us move toward peace without compromising our own well-being.

As we take these steps toward reclaiming our identity and processing our pain, the refrain of *Sister*—"change, change, change"—calls us to embrace transformation. Change, especially when it involves inner growth, is seldom easy. It requires us to let go of familiar patterns, even those that have kept us feeling safe but stunted. Stepping into change means acknowledging our limitations and recognizing the areas where we desire to grow. This journey often requires us to confront our own choices, to take responsibility for what we can control, and to release what we cannot. Transformation, then, is not an instantaneous shift but a gradual, often uncomfortable process of aligning our lives with the values and truths we hold dear.

Scripture reminds us in Romans 12:2, "Do not conform to the pattern of this world, but be transformed by the renewing of your mind." This renewal is not passive; it calls us to actively engage with our thoughts, our habits, and our choices. Practical steps—such as identifying specific areas in our lives where change is needed or seeking accountability from trusted friends—can guide us along this path. By actively choosing growth, we begin to build lives that reflect our true values and aspirations, moving away from patterns that have held us back and stepping into a more authentic way of being.

Another theme that *Sister* addresses is the trap of comparison—a common struggle for anyone who feels overshadowed or unappreciated. Comparison is a thief of joy; it convinces us that our worth is tied to how we measure up against others. This struggle is amplified in a culture that constantly encourages competition and performance. But true peace comes when we release the need for comparison, embracing instead the unique journey God has set before us. In John 21, after the resurrection, Peter asks Jesus about John's future, only to be told, "What is that to you? You follow me." This response is a call to focus on our own path, to steward our gifts and callings without being distracted by what others may or may not have.

Contentment grows from a place of gratitude, from focusing on what we have rather than on perceived lacks or inequities. As we turn our attention away from the achievements or recognition of others, we begin to see our own lives with fresh eyes, appreciating the unique strengths and opportunities we've been given. This perspective shift frees us from the need to measure up, allowing us to walk our path with confidence and peace. The words of *Sister* remind us that feeling overlooked does not equate to insignificance. In God's eyes, each of us has inherent worth and a purpose that cannot be diminished by the opinions or recognition of others.

Ultimately, this journey—from hidden pain to open acknowledgment, from fractured relationships to healing, from comparison to contentment—requires patience and persistence. It is a lifelong process of learning to see ourselves as God sees us, embracing the identity He has given us, and walking in the freedom that comes from knowing we are deeply loved. In this way, *Sister* invites us to step into a vision of self that is rooted in something eternal, something unshakeable. As we continue to explore and add to this narrative, let this be a reminder that transformation is a continual process, one that leads us closer to a life marked by resilience, peace, and purpose. The journey is far from over, and with each step, we come closer to the person we were created to be, anchored in truth and defined not by the world's shifting standards but by an unchanging, divine love.

CHAPTER 10
"What's This Life For"

I n *What's This Life For,* Creed's words and music unravel like a storm breaking open, one that has been quietly brewing under layers of suppressed questions and existential ache. The song doesn't just tell a story; it beckons us into a deeply reflective, raw, and visceral search for meaning—a journey marked by loss, disillusionment, and a faint but persistent hope. The band masterfully weaves together lyrics and instrumentation, plunging listeners into an experience that resonates on both a spiritual and emotional level. It's as though each note and line is crafted to unearth the listener's own buried questions and struggles, creating a shared space for contemplating the fundamental purpose of existence.

The song opens with a line that strikes at the heart of human fragility: "Hurray for a child that makes it through." Immediately, we're introduced to the notion of survival—an achievement that's not just physical but deeply psychological and emotional. This isn't merely about enduring life's trials; it's about the miracle of arriving at a place of inner knowing, of pushing through despair and uncertainty to glimpse a sense of purpose. In this line, the songwriter conveys an empathetic acknowledgment of life's difficulty. Finding meaning isn't guaranteed; it's a path fraught with barriers, both external and internal. The lyrics allude to countless souls who never made it, lives cut short or dimmed before they could answer the call of purpose, making the "hurray" feel both celebratory and bittersweet.

As the song builds, we're drawn into a repeated question: "What's this life for?" This question, more than a line of curiosity, becomes a mantra of longing—a lament from the depths of spiritual unrest. Creed's minor chords and gritty guitar riffs lend a somber weight to this question, each progression pulling the listener further into the reflective and turbulent waters of existential uncertainty. The minor tonality amplifies the feeling of searching in the dark, as if each note adds another layer to the journey's gravity. The music does more than accompany the lyrics; it underscores the relentlessness of seeking purpose, mirroring the discomfort and yearning that define the human condition.

The song's thematic core emerges in lines that confront the narrator's yearning for connection: "I see your soul, it's kind of gray. You see my heart, you look away." Here, Creed captures the profound loneliness that often accompanies self-reflection and vulnerability. The desire to connect—to have one's inner struggles acknowledged by another—is met with avoidance or misunderstanding. The "gray" soul represents a life dulled by apathy or confusion, lacking the vibrancy that comes from understanding one's purpose. This grayscale imagery is powerful; it paints a picture of lives that fade into numbness when the hunger for meaning goes unsatisfied. The contrast between the narrator's open heart and the other's averted gaze is deeply relatable, reflecting a familiar frustration: the hope for understanding met with the coldness of indifference.

When the lyrics shift to "I know your pain...I know your purpose on your plane," there's a poignant turn toward empathy. This acknowledgment suggests that even amid the chaos and suffering, meaning might still exist. Purpose isn't absent but perhaps buried, masked by life's hardships and struggles. It's a line that offers a glimmer of hope—a hint that, on some plane of existence, there's a reason we endure. This empathetic insight suggests that even when life feels chaotic and disconnected, there's an underlying purpose that binds us together. But it remains just out of reach, obscured by the fog of human frailty and the unpredictability of existence.

As the song moves forward, it introduces a thematic shift—one of unity under "one king." This king is undefined, an enigmatic presence that suggests a universal force or divine authority presiding over life's uncertainties. There's a beauty in this ambiguity; the refrain feels like a revelation and a resignation, an invitation to surrender to something larger than ourselves. Creed doesn't explicitly define this "king," leaving room for listeners to interpret it as they see fit—whether as God, fate, or the natural order. This openness allows each person to connect with the song on a personal level, to project their own beliefs or doubts onto its words.

The line "Don't have to settle no goddamn score" emerges as a pivotal moment, rejecting the notion of vengeance or the need to constantly make sense of every hurt or injustice. Under the reign of this "one king," the need for retribution dissolves. This line is raw and unfiltered, capturing the release that comes when we let go of the need to control or balance every aspect of life. It's a powerful acknowledgment that life, in all its pain and confusion, doesn't require us to endlessly strive for justice or payback. Instead, there's a shared destiny, a sense that each person's struggles and triumphs are interwoven into a larger, unexplainable tapestry. The music crescendos here, creating a sonic landscape that mirrors the acceptance of life's ambiguities, a surrender to the shared experience of existence.

In the final verse, the song circles back to the initial question—"What's this life for?" But now, after the journey through empathy, unity, and surrender, the question feels different. It's no longer just a cry of confusion; it becomes a quiet meditation on life's mysteries. The repeated phrasing, the cyclical guitar riffs, and the throbbing bass create a sensation of returning to the beginning, but with a changed perspective. The journey has brought the narrator—and the listener—to a place where the question doesn't demand an answer. The beauty of life, the song seems to suggest, may lie not in definitive answers but in the courage to ask and to live fully in the tension of the unknown.

Through *What's This Life For,* Creed captures the human experience of grappling with questions that defy easy answers. The song paints a portrait of resilience, of pressing forward even when the road is dark and purpose is hidden. The listener is invited to reflect on their own journey, to wrestle with life's hardest questions, and to find solace in the possibility of a greater unity—a "one king" who might see us all as equal in our struggle. By the end, we're reminded that life's purpose might not be a destination but a journey of perpetual seeking, a dance between fragility and strength, between despair and hope.

In this song, Creed holds space for those who feel lost, who've felt the weight of existence pressing down with unanswered questions. It resonates with those who have grappled with life's meaning, feeling the constant pull between wanting to find answers and surrendering to the mysteries that surround us. The song's final notes don't resolve; instead, they linger, leaving room for each listener to continue their own journey, to ponder, and perhaps to find peace in knowing that some questions might never be fully answered.

Creed's artistry in *What's This Life For* lies in its ability to channel the universal human experience of searching for purpose. The band doesn't shy away from the darker aspects of this journey, acknowledging the pain, disillusionment, and struggles that often accompany our attempts to find meaning. And yet, amid the heaviness, there is an undeniable sense of hope—a feeling that even though life's purpose may be elusive, the search itself is worthwhile. In the end, the song suggests that perhaps the answer isn't as important as the willingness to ask the question, to face life's uncertainties with an open heart, and to hold onto the faint but persistent hope that we are part of something greater than ourselves.

As the final notes fade, we're left with a sense of quiet contemplation, an invitation to look inward and outward, to consider our own lives in light of the song's message. *What's This Life For* isn't just a song; it's a call to confront the depths of our souls, to seek connection with others who share our questions, and to embrace the beauty of a life lived in pursuit of understanding. It reminds us that while the journey may be challenging, filled with moments of doubt and struggle, it is also rich with the possibility of discovery and connection. The song's impact lies in its ability to resonate long after the music ends, leaving a lingering echo of both the question and the hope that drives us forward.

Application

The themes woven into "What's This Life For" take us to the depths of human experience, touching on our raw need to find meaning amid suffering and to understand the purpose of our journey. These aren't just abstract philosophical musings; they're questions that emerge from the very heart of our pain, our longing, our brokenness. Creed's lyrics echo the ancient cry of Ecclesiastes: *What does man gain from all the toil at which he toils under the sun?* This question, like a shadow, lingers over our lives, especially in moments of grief or confusion. Yet the song doesn't leave us in despair—it traces a path forward, calling us to embrace suffering as a gateway to endurance and to find meaning in the midst of our struggles.

The line "Hurray for a child that makes it through" seems simple at first, a fleeting acknowledgment of survival, yet it's laden with a rich and even bittersweet truth. It's not just about the sheer act of surviving, but about the triumph of moving through hardship and coming out transformed. This is more than just optimism; it's a nod to the Scriptures' understanding of endurance. James 1:2-4 invites us to "consider it pure joy...whenever you face trials of many kinds, because you know that the testing of your faith produces perseverance." This perspective radically shifts how we perceive suffering—not as an enemy to be avoided, but as a process that shapes us, revealing strength and cultivating wisdom.

Surviving hardship is never without scars, and it's in those scars that we find our story—our mark on the world. It's tempting to think that life's value lies only in the good, the beautiful, the victories. But enduring life's battles, grappling with the dark valleys, builds in us a resilient faith. It's like the refining fire spoken of in Malachi, which purifies gold. The hardship itself doesn't define us, but our response to it—the way we walk through it—becomes our victory. *The child that makes it through* becomes a testament to courage and resilience, living proof of God's sustaining grace.

Then comes the haunting question, "What's this life for?"—a question that many of us, if not all, have whispered in the quiet of our hearts. The repetition of this question in the song becomes a refrain not of despair but of earnest searching. By asking, we acknowledge that we're not alone in our longing for answers, and perhaps therein lies the comfort. This question has been asked through the ages, by prophets, poets, and every person who has ever looked at life and wondered what it all means. To ask, "What's this life for?" is to connect ourselves with the cloud of witnesses that came before us. It's as if the song beckons us to join that sacred assembly, to recognize that we're not isolated in our questioning but part of a much larger story.

The power of shared suffering is something Scripture recognizes well. Hebrews speaks of us being "surrounded by so great a cloud of witnesses" (Hebrews 12:1), reminding us that our faith journey is not solitary. Our questions and struggles are not unique but woven into the collective human experience. This realization should urge us to seek out communities of faith, to find solace in shared journeys and collective wisdom. It's in these communities, in the trusted arms of others, that we can be vulnerable about our struggles, ask hard questions, and explore together what God might be doing in our lives. Sometimes, peace isn't found in answers but in the comforting presence of others who walk alongside us in faith.

As the song moves toward the idea of living "under the reign of one king," it opens the door to surrender—a concept that is deeply countercultural yet profoundly biblical. The imagery of a king reigning over us suggests an acknowledgment of something greater, something sovereign. To live under this reign is to lay down our striving, our self-sufficiency, and to yield to a higher authority. This kind of surrender doesn't negate our pain; rather, it reorients it within a larger, divine story. The Apostle Paul speaks of this in Romans 8:28, where he assures us that "in all things, God works for the good of those who love him." When we trust that there is a King who is sovereign over every detail of our lives, we can find rest, knowing that we are held even when the road is unclear.

In our modern age, surrender is often misunderstood as weakness or passivity. Yet surrender, as depicted in Scripture, is an act of profound faith. It requires humility and a recognition that we don't control every outcome. When life feels chaotic, when our hearts are burdened with unresolved questions, we are invited to lay down our anxiety and trust in the One who reigns. This act of surrender doesn't remove our burdens, but it allows us to carry them with a lightness, knowing we're not alone. Jesus himself invites us to "come to me, all who labor and are heavy laden, and I will give you rest" (Matthew 11:28). Living under His reign, we find a peace that transcends understanding—a peace that exists not in the absence of struggle, but in the presence of divine companionship.

Then there's the powerful line, "Don't have to settle no goddamn score," a raw and poignant reminder of the freedom that comes with letting go of bitterness and resentment. This phrase speaks to the often-overlooked reality of forgiveness—that it is as much for our own hearts as it is for those we forgive. The need to "settle the score" is a heavy burden to bear, one that leaves us shackled to past wrongs and grievances. But forgiveness, as Christ taught, is a release, a breaking of those chains. He calls us to forgive "seventy times seven," an invitation to let go of the weight of vengeance and choose freedom instead.

Forgiveness doesn't erase the wrongs we've suffered, nor does it invalidate our pain. Rather, it allows us to move forward unburdened by the bitterness that can fester within us. In releasing the need to "settle the score," we align ourselves with the grace of God, who forgave us while we were yet sinners. It's a call to humility and a reminder that, in a broken world, none of us is without fault. We find freedom not in holding onto past grievances but in relinquishing them, trusting that ultimate justice lies with God alone. As Romans 12:19 reminds us, "Beloved, never avenge yourselves, but leave it to the wrath of God, for it is written, 'Vengeance is mine, I will repay, says the Lord.'" In choosing forgiveness, we take on the posture of Christ, who, even in His suffering, prayed, "Father, forgive them."

Each of these themes—endurance through suffering, communal solidarity, surrender to a greater purpose, and the release of bitterness—paints a picture of a journey. It's a journey that doesn't shy away from the hard questions but meets them with faith, hope, and an understanding of God's sovereign hand. While the answers may remain veiled, the call is clear: to live fully, to seek the wisdom that suffering imparts, and to find peace even when clarity eludes us.

"What's This Life For" doesn't offer us a simple resolution. Instead, it serves as an invitation to live in the tension of not knowing, of wrestling with the mysteries of existence while anchored in a trust that goes beyond human understanding. This journey is not about arriving at an easy answer but about growing in trust, becoming people who can bear witness to God's goodness even in the midst of suffering. Each step we take, each battle we endure, adds depth to our story and ultimately draws us closer to the heart of God.

As we reflect on these lyrics, we're reminded of the call to abide. In John 15, Jesus speaks of the vine and the branches, urging us to remain in Him. Abiding in Christ doesn't remove our trials but transforms our perspective. In abiding, we find that life's purpose is less about a final destination and more about the One we walk with. The path may be hard, the questions may be many, but we are held by the One who has already overcome the world. Through every heartache and every question, He remains our constant, our guide, and our peace.

CHAPTER II

"One"

In *One*, Creed pulls us into the throbbing heart of a world divided—a place where unity is more than an ideal; it's a hard-won goal constantly at odds with forces of fragmentation. This song captures the paradox of human connection: the primal desire for oneness clashes against societal structures and internal conflicts that tear us apart. The tension between unity and division feels almost tactile, underscored by Creed's heavy instrumentation and raw, introspective lyrics. We are taken on a journey through societal and personal landscapes marred by conflict, yet illuminated by a flickering hope for unity.

The song's first line, "Affirmative may be justified," introduces a startling paradox, a dissonance that frames the entire piece. "Affirmative" often signifies agreement, a nod to something worthwhile or valuable, yet "justified" hints at something more complicated. What one person perceives as justifiable action may feel like oppression to another. The tone here challenges us to grapple with this contradiction, to examine the intentions behind actions that may strive to unify but unintentionally divide. There's no comforting resolution here, only the unsettling realization that even well-meaning pursuits can perpetuate cycles of separation. In these opening moments, *One* begins as a plea for reflection—not only on society's actions but on our own internal contradictions.

Musically, Creed captures this tension with intensity. The guitar riffs are melodic yet heavy, grounding the song in a sense of resistance and resolve. The throbbing bassline and steady percussion create a firm backbone, mirroring the weight of the song's themes. Each chord progression feels like a step forward, but with an undercurrent of struggle—a sonic reminder that the path to unity is not smooth but filled with obstacles. There's a primal quality to the instrumentation, as if the music itself is reaching back to something elemental, tapping into a universal struggle for cohesion amidst division. The structure speaks as loudly as the lyrics, building a soundscape where each beat feels like a heartbeat—a pulse keeping time with the shared experience of human conflict and reconciliation.

As we move deeper, the lyrics present a plea for a simplistic form of unity, a childlike hope that sharing and connection can bridge the divides. "Take from one, give to another / The goal is to be unified / Take my hand, be my brother." These lines articulate an almost innocent optimism, suggesting that equality can be achieved through redistribution and empathy. But as the song continues, this hope is swiftly complicated. The systems we look to for justice are "sanctified by oppression," revealing that even institutions designed to unite us can be complicit in creating divisions. This line is a stark reminder that unity is not just a matter of good intentions; it's a pursuit constantly undermined by systemic forces that thrive on inequality. The music responds, the distortion growing heavier as if fraying at the edges, reflecting a descent into chaos as the vision of unity "took a back seat, sliding further into regression." Here, Creed illustrates the harsh reality that without vigilance, even the most hopeful pursuits can spiral into a cycle of alienation and retreat.

The refrain—"One, oh one / The only way is one"—emerges as both a mantra and an anchor in the storm. The repeated "one" is not just a symbol of sameness; it's an insistence on recognizing our inter-connectedness, a reminder of our shared fate. This repetition grounds the listener, giving the song a focal point amidst the surrounding chaos. It's as if the refrain is a lifeline, a tether to an underlying truth that remains undeniable even in a fractured world. The music sup-ports this mantra, building with each repetition, layering sound to create a sense of determination. There's an urgency here, as if Creed is urging us not to lose sight of our common ground, despite the forces that push us apart.

Then, the song turns inward, revealing the raw emotions that sur-face when faced with a world that feels irreparably broken. "I feel angry, I feel helpless / Want to change the world, yeah / I feel violent, I feel alone." These lines lay bare the frustration, the helplessness that can consume anyone grappling with injustice. This section of the song is deeply personal, transforming the social commentary into a confession of inner turmoil. The guitar's tone sharpens, matching the intensity of these emotions. This shift in tone, both lyrically and musically, conveys the isolation that often accompanies the desire to change the world—a feeling of standing alone against something vast and unyielding. The music theory behind this choice deepens the impact; the tension builds as if the song itself is straining against the weight of a divided world, amplifying the sense of struggle within.

As the song reaches its crescendo, Creed's lyrics address society's most enduring divisions. "Society blind by color / Why hold down one to raise another?" Here, the song tackles the destructive nature of discrimination. Creed rejects the zero-sum mentality that suggests one group must be diminished for another to rise. This line captures the poison of prejudice—how it seeds resentment and perpetuates cycles of division. The music mirrors this rejection with intense rhythms and heavy, unresolved chords, as if echoing the cyclical violence and harm caused by a world mired in discrimination. The minor chords and shifting progressions emphasize that this tension is far from resolved; it's a conflict that, while voiced, remains painfully present.

The climax of the song confronts us with an unsettling truth: "The world is heading for mutiny / When all we want is unity." In these lines, Creed acknowledges the painful irony of humanity's relentless drive toward division even as we long for harmony. The word "mutiny" suggests a rebellion, a breaking away from a larger whole, even when unity is the ultimate desire. This tension—the pull between mutiny and unity—is at the heart of the human experience, a testament to the fragility of connection in a world marked by competing desires and conflicting values. The music intensifies here, creating a sense of urgency that underscores the precariousness of this quest for unity.

In the final moments, Creed presents an ironic twist of fate with the lines, "We may rise and fall / But in the end, we meet our fate together." It's a powerful reminder that no matter how hard we strive to remain divided, we are ultimately bound together in our shared mortality. This realization doesn't come as a comforting resolution but as a stark acknowledgment of our collective fate. The music reflects this sentiment, fading out in a way that leaves the listener in a state of reflection. It's as if the song itself is asking us to confront the role we each play in sustaining division, urging us to take responsibility for the difficult path toward unity.

One does not provide easy answers or a sense of closure. Instead, it leaves us with a lingering call to examine ourselves and our world. By the end, the refrain of "one" feels almost haunting, echoing in our minds long after the music fades. Creed doesn't pretend that unity is easily achievable or that division can be overcome with simple platitudes. The song's power lies in its honesty—a willingness to stare into the complexity of human relationships, to acknowledge the forces that drive us apart, and to hold space for the dream of unity even when it seems impossible.

Through *One*, Creed crafts a narrative that transcends music, speaking to the core of human experience. This song becomes a mirror, reflecting not just the fractures within society but also the conflicts within ourselves. It reminds us that the path to unity is both a social and personal struggle, one that requires introspection, empathy, and the courage to face uncomfortable truths. The repetition of "one" is a reminder that we are not as separate as we might think; our lives are woven together in ways that can be both beautiful and challenging.

Ultimately, *One* is a call to action, a challenge to break free from the systems and beliefs that keep us divided. Creed invites us to see ourselves in others, to recognize the shared humanity that binds us even amidst differences. This song doesn't end with a solution because it isn't meant to. It's an invitation to begin, to take that first step toward understanding, toward connection, and toward the oneness that lies just beyond the reach of our divided world.

In a world increasingly defined by fragmentation, *One* stands as a testament to the enduring hope for unity. It calls us to examine the systems we uphold, to confront the ways we contribute to division, and to hold onto the belief that oneness is not just a lofty ideal but a possibility worth striving for. As the music fades, we are left with a quiet resolve to face the challenge head-on, to look beyond the lines that divide us, and to see ourselves as part of a larger whole—bound together, for better or worse, in the shared journey of being human.

Application

The song "One" by Creed dives into a tension as old as time, capturing the visceral ache we feel when facing division and discord in our lives. The lyrics resonate with the struggles of feeling isolated, misunderstood, and embattled by forces that seem beyond our control. Yet, woven through these verses is an invitation—a beckoning toward unity, healing, and ultimately, transformation. This path is challenging, no doubt, but it's within these challenges that we often find the deepest avenues for growth, for discovering something of ourselves and of God's nature that we might otherwise miss.

The themes of division and frustration that the song raises are unmistakably relevant today, especially in a culture rife with polarization and tension. People live estranged from each other, families are fractured, and communities often seem defined more by their conflicts than by their common ground. This fragmentation is not just a modern issue but part of the human condition, an outcome of our brokenness and the sin that so often divides us from one another. The Apostle Paul writes about this struggle in Romans, lamenting that even the good he wants to do, he finds himself unable to carry out consistently. This inner conflict mirrors the relational discord we see all around us—a discord that can sometimes feel overpowering.

The first lesson the song offers is to face the pain of oppression and division, not with denial or bitterness but with honesty. This is a tough and countercultural approach in a world that often rewards retribution and bitterness. Division typically festers where there are wounds left untreated, whether between individuals or within our own hearts. Bitterness can entrap us, isolating us from the healing that could come from releasing these burdens to God. Hebrews 12:15 warns about letting "any root of bitterness" take hold, lest it corrupt us and those around us. When we feel wronged, oppressed, or marginalized, there's a strong inclination to hold tight to that hurt. Yet, this song reminds us that freedom begins with examining the anger and resentment we carry. It encourages us to name the hurt and, with God's help, move beyond it.

Ask yourself: what feelings are you holding onto that may be closing off your heart to God's healing work? In Proverbs 4:23, we're told
to guard our hearts above all else because everything we do flows from
it. If we allow bitterness to harden our hearts, it restricts the flow of life,
compassion, and connection that God intended for us. The journey
toward unity and reconciliation often begins when we take an honest
look at what's inside our hearts.

The song then speaks to the brokenness that comes from lack of
unity, a division that isn't just external but lies at the core of human
nature. We often find ourselves competing, judging, and even resent-
ing others without truly understanding why. This is more than just
personality clashes; it's the effect of sin working within us, pushing
us away from the unity we were made for. "Take my hand, be my
brother," the lyrics plead, challenging us to overcome our own judgments and grudges. Ephesians 4:3 reminds us to "make every effort
to keep the unity of the Spirit through the bond of peace." Unity is
not passively maintained; it must be actively pursued through grace,
humility, and a willingness to reach across divides.

Unity, though, doesn't mean the absence of conflict; it's a commitment to work through that conflict in a spirit of love. This small step of
reaching out, of offering forgiveness even when it's hard, can become a
powerful antidote to division. When we forgive, we're not condoning
wrongdoing but rather refusing to let it govern our responses and
attitudes. Forgiveness, in this sense, is an act of liberation, of reclaiming control from the bitterness that might otherwise consume us.
Jesus commands us to forgive "seventy times seven"—not because it's
easy, but because forgiveness frees us from the chains of resentment,
allowing us to grow into people who reflect God's own mercy.

The song's refrain, "The only way is one," speaks to this idea that
true freedom and peace come not from isolation but from a recogni-

tion of our shared journey. Often, when we're hurt or struggling, it's easy to feel isolated, as though no one else understands the depth of our pain. This is a lie that sin whispers, separating us from each other and from God. But when we see ourselves as part of a larger community—of fellow believers, of humanity itself—we begin to realize that we are not alone in our struggles. Galatians 6:2 encourages us to "carry each other's burdens," recognizing that in our shared journey, we find strength and resilience.

There's something liberating in acknowledging that we're not alone, that others are also grappling with similar pains, disappointments, and fears. This recognition can be a profound source of comfort, a reminder that God designed us for fellowship and mutual support. When we come together, sharing both our burdens and our joys, we participate in a form of resistance against the isolation that division tries to impose on us.

It's here that we find the most powerful lesson from the song—a call to choose how we respond to the world's brokenness. There's a reality we all have to confront: we cannot change every circumstance, nor can we force others to act differently. But we do have the ability to control our own responses. When faced with injustice, anger, or isolation, we can choose to respond with grace and humility. Philippians 4:5 reminds us, "Let your gentleness be evident to all. The Lord is near." By choosing to act with kindness and patience, we create a ripple effect that can soften even the hardest hearts, including our own.

While the world around us may continue in its cycles of discord and division, we're called to live differently, to "overcome evil with good" (Romans 12:21). This doesn't mean that we ignore or downplay the reality of injustice but rather that we choose to confront it with a spirit rooted in God's love and truth. It is a call to live with integrity, kindness, and compassion, to extend the same grace we ourselves have received. In doing so, we find that even in the face of seemingly insurmountable divisions, we can be agents of healing and reconciliation.

The song also challenges us to seek change within our own spheres of influence. The temptation to focus on grand gestures or sweeping reform is strong, but often the most impactful changes come from our everyday interactions. Jesus tells us in Matthew 5:16 to "let your light shine before others," so that they may see our good deeds and glorify our Father in heaven. Sometimes, this light shines brightest in the small, faithful steps we take to love and forgive those around us.

Reflecting on the song's call to unity, it's clear that this isn't merely about being "one" in the abstract, but about embodying unity in tangible ways. It's about seeing our relationships, even those that are strained, as opportunities to practice grace. When we love our neighbors, including those who may have hurt us, we bear witness to a love that transcends our own human limitations—a love rooted in the gospel.

Ultimately, as we grapple with the themes of "One," we're reminded that the pursuit of unity is deeply spiritual, requiring us to lean not on our own strength but on God's. Isaiah 40:31 promises that those who wait on the Lord will renew their strength, that they will "soar on wings like eagles." This journey toward unity, healing, and reconciliation is not one we undertake alone; it's empowered by the Holy Spirit, who strengthens us in our weaknesses and guides us when we feel lost.

If you're feeling discouraged by the divisions you see—whether in your own relationships, your community, or the world around you—remember that God is faithful. His grace enables us to forgive, to love, and to bridge divides in ways we could never accomplish on our own. This song reminds us of that higher calling, encouraging us to take the first step toward healing and connection, no matter how small. It's an invitation to participate in the quiet, patient work of building unity, beginning with the choices we make today.

In the end, the journey toward unity is one of continual transformation and self-discovery. Each act of forgiveness, each moment of kindness, each bridge we build is a step closer to becoming the people God created us to be—people who reflect His love and carry His light into a divided world. It's a long, sometimes painful journey, but it's one that brings us ever nearer to the heart of God, teaching us the beauty and strength of living as "one."

As the song captures the cry for unity, may we also remember that this unity is not just a concept but a call to action, a way of life that echoes the prayer of Jesus for His followers to be one, as He and the Father are one (John 17:21). We're not promised that the journey will be easy, but we are assured that it will be worth it, that in the pursuit of unity we find a path of peace, hope, and transformation. And as we walk this path, we draw closer to a truth greater than ourselves, a truth that reminds us we're all bound by the same longing, and ultimately, by the same love – with the condition, that we repent and believe. That is the only way we will ever be truly united to each other and more importantly to God (Ephesians 5:11-20).

PART III
A Field of Human Clay

CHAPTER 12
"Are You Ready"

This isn't a song that lingers on the surface or gently eases the listener in. Instead, it dives headfirst, plunging the listener into a soul-stirring reckoning. It's a call to action—loud, profound, and unyielding. From its opening chords, the song carries a weighty tone and texture, with each lyric crafted to pulse with urgency, challenging the listener to confront their readiness to face the unknown, to embrace life in its entirety. The song resonates as much in its questions as it does in its affirmations, pushing us toward the journey of self-discovery.

The song introduces us to "Mr. Seeker," a figure who encapsulates the human yearning for truth and meaning. In him, we find a restlessness that's familiar, an urge to break from shallow experiences and well-worn paths. He's a character who can't be satisfied with mere surface-level answers or transient wisdom; he craves a deeper understanding of himself and the world. The line, "Hold on to this advice: If you can seek, then you will find," is pivotal here. It feels like a whisper from ancient times, an echo of timeless wisdom found in biblical narratives and spiritual teachings. This line is Creed's nod to a path that requires commitment and resilience. It reminds us that genuine revelation and understanding come not from easy answers but through the willingness to persist and dig deep.

The intensity of this message is mirrored in the music itself. Creed's choice of heavy, deliberate chords, almost like the rumble of distant thunder, intensifies the sense that we're on the brink of something monumental. This isn't just music to listen to—it's music meant to be felt, to resonate within each listener's core. The brooding power chords of the guitar mirror the depth of this journey; they convey a weight and a gravity that amplify the sense of undertaking something daunting, something significant. This is not a casual exploration but a daring venture into the mysteries of life and self.

As the song progresses, the structure intensifies, with a relentless rhythmic build that mirrors the rising tension within the listener's own heart. By the time Creed's frontman Scott Stapp asks repeatedly, "Are you ready? Are you ready?" the listener has been pulled into a state of introspection. The question becomes deeply personal, pressing the listener to reflect on their own readiness to embark on a transformative journey. This moment is devoid of space for hesitation; it's a call to commitment. To listen to this song and remain indifferent feels impossible, as though Creed is demanding that each listener confront their own barriers to growth, their own readiness for change.

The song also brings in the figure of "Mr. Hero," who walks a "thin, fine line / Under the microscope of life." In these lyrics, Creed presents us with a powerful image of vulnerability, of the courage required to live openly and face the inevitable scrutiny and judgment of others. Mr. Hero represents those who dare to stand in the spotlight, to be visible and authentic, even when it means being subjected to the harsh realities of public life. The lyrics remind us that heroes "come and go," a sobering acknowledgment of the transient nature of heroism and the constant challenge of living up to one's ideals. This portrayal of Mr. Hero is a recognition that even those who inspire us, who appear strong and unwavering, have moments of vulnerability and doubt.

The music swells as Creed guides us to a threshold. Here, the sound builds with a fierceness that mirrors the emotional weight of this journey. For those who feel the weight of public scrutiny or the pressure to live authentically, Mr. Hero's plight resonates deeply. The lyrics seem to speak directly to those navigating the tension between being true to themselves and facing the external expectations placed upon them. It's as though Creed is extending a hand of solidarity, a reminder that courage doesn't mean an absence of fear, but the determination to press on despite it.

An iconic element of the song is the countdown sequence—10, 9, 8... This countdown, far from being a mere musical filler, serves as a symbolic pulse, a ticking clock that heightens the sense of urgency. It's as if time itself is narrowing, pushing the listener closer to a moment of decision, a point of no return. The countdown introduces a sense of inevitability; there's an unspoken understanding that something monumental is about to occur. The sequence feels like the edge of a cliff—a last moment to pause before plunging into the unknown. It encapsulates the feeling of standing at the brink of transformation, poised for a rebirth, as if the listener is on the precipice of a significant life shift.

When Creed finally sings, "Life has just begun," the words carry a weight that goes beyond mere optimism. They suggest a profound awakening, a reawakening to the significance of one's existence. This isn't just the beginning of another day; it's a call to a new way of seeing, a renewal of perspective. The music, which had been shadowy and tense, now transforms, embodying the energy of breaking free. There's a palpable sense of liberation in the chords, a soaring affirmation that the listener is, indeed, ready to embrace life's calling with open arms and a fearless heart.

At its core, "Are You Ready?" is both a question and a challenge. The cinematic quality of the song—its deliberate build-up, its heavy yet hopeful melody—creates a space for listeners to pause, to wrestle with their own thoughts. In this moment, we're all asked the same questions: Are we truly prepared to confront the unknown? Are we ready to embrace life in its fullest, rawest form? Creed's song challenges us to shed our hesitations, to let go of the fear of vulnerability, and to step boldly into the possibilities ahead.

For many listeners, "Are You Ready?" is more than a song; it's a roadmap for self-discovery. In an age when it's easy to get lost in the distractions and noise of everyday life, the song invites us to look inward, to reconnect with what truly matters. It asks us to consider the journey we're on and whether we're pursuing it with intention and purpose. Creed's message isn't one of passive acceptance; it's an active, forceful urging to live fully, to engage with life's challenges rather than shy away from them.

"Mr. Seeker" and "Mr. Hero" aren't just characters in a song—they're archetypes that reflect aspects of ourselves. "Mr. Seeker" represents the part of us that yearns for meaning, the part that's willing to question, to look beyond the obvious for answers. His journey is one of exploration, a quest for truth that isn't satisfied with easy conclusions. Meanwhile, "Mr. Hero" embodies the part of us that strives for courage, that's willing to stand out, to be seen, even when it's uncomfortable. He is the side of us that dares to confront the world, to face our fears, and to live in authenticity.

As the countdown continues, we feel the weight of the impending transformation. There's a sense that we're on the cusp of something new, something profound. The song doesn't just ask if we're ready for a new beginning; it dares us to believe that we already are. It's a powerful reminder that change is inevitable, but how we approach it is up to us. Will we face it with courage, or will we shrink back in fear? Will we embrace the unknown, or will we cling to what's familiar?

The song closes with an affirmation that feels like a call to arms: life has begun. This is not just an observation—it's a call to awaken, to engage with life fully, to seize each moment with intention. Creed's message is clear: the time to live is now, and the time to start is immediate. Life waits for no one, and the question "Are you ready?" becomes not just a lyric but a personal challenge to the listener.

In its entirety, "Are You Ready?" is a masterful blend of music, poetry, and philosophy. It calls to those who feel the urge to seek, to find, to understand. It reaches out to the brave souls willing to walk the line of authenticity, to live under the microscope, to endure the challenges of being genuine. Creed's song is an anthem for those who refuse to settle for complacency, for those who dare to dream, to search, to believe that life has meaning and purpose.

Listening to this song is like embarking on a journey of self-reflection and transformation. It leaves the listener with a choice: to stay where they are, rooted in comfort, or to step boldly into the unknown. It challenges each of us to become our own "Mr. Seeker," our own "Mr. Hero," and to live with a sense of purpose that's as relentless as the song itself. Through its haunting lyrics and intense instrumentation, Creed's "Are You Ready?" becomes a soundtrack for personal growth, urging each of us to ask ourselves, "Am I truly ready for this journey called life?"

And as the final notes fade, one can't help but feel a renewed sense of purpose, a desire to face the world with courage and openness. For those who listen closely, "Are You Ready?" isn't just a song—it's a turning point, an invitation to live with intention, to seek out truth, and to embrace life with all its uncertainties and possibilities. Creed has crafted not just a musical experience, but a transformative encounter, one that leaves each listener pondering their own readiness to step into the future with conviction. Are we ready, indeed? Perhaps, by the song's end, we find that the answer is yes.

Application

"Are You Ready?" by Creed doesn't waste time, nor does it allow for passive listening. The song opens like the roll of thunder, deep and rumbling, foreboding yet exhilarating. From the first notes, it shakes us out of complacency, pulling us into something intense, almost primal. It's a call to action—a kind that defies you to sit idly by. There's a defiance in its tone, an unyielding insistence that stirs within the listener, as if awakening something hidden, something long-buried. Creed isn't here to play softly in the background. No, this song demands your full attention, urging you to reckon with your own state of readiness to confront the mysteries of life and the reality of the soul's deeper needs.

This is not just a melody or a beat; it's a challenge wrapped in sound. When the lyrics begin, the words come with a force that feels almost like a spiritual summons. We meet "Mr. Seeker," a character who, on the surface, might just seem like a wanderer or a dreamer. But Mr. Seeker is more than that; he is the personification of humanity's deep-rooted desire for meaning, for something real that transcends the shallows of ordinary experience. In him, we see a familiar restlessness, the unquenchable thirst that refuses to be satisfied by surface-level experiences. Mr. Seeker craves depth and authenticity, and he can't be appeased with superficial wisdom or transient pleasures.

The lyrics' directive, "Hold on to this advice: If you can seek, then you will find," carries an ancient weight, as if echoing from centuries past. It's a nod to the biblical promise that the act of seeking holds the key to discovery. This idea that true revelation comes from perseverance—through digging deeply, rather than accepting easy answers—aligns seamlessly with the scriptural exhortation found in Matthew 7:7: "Seek, and you will find; knock, and the door will be opened to you." Creed's words, whether intentional or not, resonate with this timeless truth, reminding us that the path to understanding demands commitment, resilience, and, often, struggle.

In this journey, we realize that the quest for truth isn't meant to be easy; it's supposed to test our dedication. The song's heavy, deliberate chords reinforce this message, building a kind of sonic foundation that feels immovable, almost eternal. The music feels less like something created and more like something unearthed—a primal sound, reminiscent of distant, rolling thunder. It has the weight and gravity of an ancient, resonant truth. This isn't just a casual listen; it's an invitation to experience something deeply real. The deliberate heaviness of each note, each strum, mirrors the gravity of seeking answers to life's most profound questions. It's a reminder that the journey to self-discovery is no lighthearted affair; it requires strength, commitment, and courage.

As the song unfolds, the rhythm builds, carrying the listener on a journey that feels increasingly intense and introspective. The structure itself becomes a kind of progression, mirroring the unfolding of one's own inner journey toward truth. And then Scott Stapp's voice—raw, impassioned, with a quality that feels almost pleading—asks, "Are you ready?" The question rings out repeatedly, pressing upon the listener, almost daring them to look inward and face their own reflection. Stapp's voice isn't merely singing; it's imploring. It's as if he's asking whether we're prepared to face the unknown within ourselves, to let go of our reservations and take that step into uncharted territory. By the time the chorus swells, the listener is enveloped in a feeling of profound introspection, compelled to answer that question honestly. Are we ready to confront what we find when we strip away the layers and confront our core selves?

And then we meet "Mr. Hero," another figure whose journey is both inspiring and sobering. He "walks a thin, fine line / Under the microscope of life," a line that captures the tension and vulnerability inherent in living authentically. To be under the microscope—to be seen, to be scrutinized—is not for the faint of heart. It requires a level of openness and courage that few are willing to endure. Mr. Hero isn't portrayed as some invincible figure; instead, he's someone who embodies the courage to live in the open, to be transparent about his struggles, knowing full well that this path comes with a cost. He represents the part of us that is willing to endure the discomfort of being seen, judged, and sometimes even rejected, for the sake of authenticity.

In presenting Mr. Hero, Creed acknowledges a fundamental truth about heroism: it is transient and imperfect. Heroes, as the lyrics remind us, "come and go." Heroism is not a static trait but rather a fleeting moment of courage, a series of choices that can waver or falter. Even the most inspiring figures have moments of doubt and vulnerability. It's a reminder that true heroism isn't about perfection; it's about persistence, about standing firm in one's convictions even when faced with adversity and scrutiny. The plight of Mr. Hero resonates deeply, especially in a world that often places impossible expectations on those who dare to live with conviction. It's as if Creed is saying that even the strongest among us need grace, and even the most courageous can feel the weight of their choice.

As the song progresses toward its climactic moment, the countdown sequence—10, 9, 8...—introduces an urgent sense of anticipation. It feels almost like a clock ticking down, each number drawing us closer to a pivotal moment. There's a tension here, a sense of impending change, as if we are standing on the edge of a precipice. The countdown is more than just a musical choice; it's a symbol of the passing of time and the inevitability of decision. We can't remain on the sidelines forever; sooner or later, we must step forward, must answer the call. Each count feels like a heartbeat, a reminder of our mortality, of the fact that our time is limited. It's an unspoken nudge that life will not wait for us to feel ready—it simply moves forward, and we must choose to either follow or be left behind.

When the countdown reaches zero, there's a shift. Creed's lyrics proclaim, "Life has just begun." It's a statement that is both exhilarating and humbling. This is more than just a new day; it's an invitation to a whole new way of living, a renewed perspective on existence. These words suggest a rebirth, a fresh start, as if the slate has been wiped clean. This isn't a mere optimism—it's an awakening to something deeper, a realization that life holds more meaning and purpose than we may have previously understood. The music, which had been dark and intense, transforms in this moment, lifting into something brighter, freer. There's a sense of liberation, as if the song itself has broken free from its own weightiness, allowing us to feel the hope that lies beyond the struggle.

Yet, even in this new beginning, Creed doesn't offer us a neatly packaged resolution. "Are You Ready?" leaves us with questions rather than answers, with challenges rather than reassurances. It's a song that, like life itself, is open-ended. The cinematic quality—the deliberate build-up, the rising intensity, the climactic release—invites us into a story that is still unfolding, that requires our participation to find its resolution. We are left with a sense that this journey is ongoing, that self-discovery and transformation are not destinations but continuous processes.

In its raw honesty, "Are You Ready?" doesn't merely invite reflection; it compels us to engage with it actively. We are asked to consider our own readiness, to evaluate our willingness to confront life with all its uncertainties. The characters of Mr. Seeker and Mr. Hero aren't

just symbolic; they are parts of us that Creed brings to life, urging us
to explore our own depths, to seek our own truths, to stand boldly in
our own authenticity. We are all seekers in our own right, all heroes in
our own small but significant ways.

This song is a journey, one that beckons us not to shy away from
its weight but to carry it with us, to let it shape and refine us. It is a
soundtrack for the soul's search for meaning, for courage, for purpose.
Creed's music here becomes a bridge between the listener and something greater, something that cannot be fully expressed in words. The
listener is left on the brink, with the final chords resonating like an
unanswered question, like a door left slightly ajar.

And so, as the final notes fade, we're left not with closure, but with
a sense of anticipation—a readiness, perhaps, to step into whatever
lies ahead. For Creed has done more than play a song; they've issued
a challenge, asking each of us to live not in half-measures, but with a
fullness of purpose.

CHAPTER 13
"What if?"

I n their song "What If?" Creed crafts a visceral landscape where words become sharper than swords, cutting into the human psyche and confronting us with fundamental questions about pride, betrayal, and the primal drive for justice. More than a vehicle for expressing anger, the song explores deep-seated emotions that linger beneath our wounds—provocative questions that don't settle comfortably, questions that echo long after the last note fades.

The song begins with a striking paradox, as the speaker laments, "I can't find the rhyme in all my reason." This declaration immediately captures our attention, plunging us into a chaotic internal world. It's as if the speaker's mind has become a fractured landscape, where logic, once orderly, now appears jagged and disrupted. This opening line sets the stage for the journey ahead, where the usual patterns of life are dismantled, and an unsettling discord takes hold. The song's tone, reinforced by hard, grating guitar riffs and relentless percussion, mirrors this mental chaos, creating an atmosphere of discord and disorientation that pulls the listener into the speaker's internal struggle.

As we move further into the lyrics, images of instability and powerlessness become more frequent and vivid. Lines like "Lost sense of time and all seasons" and "Feel I've been beaten down / By the words of men who have no grounds" amplify the sense of losing grip on life's stability. Time and seasons are symbols of natural order and change, yet here they feel irrelevant, swept away in the speaker's turmoil. Losing this connection to time suggests that the speaker is trapped in an emotional present, unable to find solace or grounding in the natural rhythms that usually bring comfort and predictability. Musically, the chords mirror this sense of entrapment, with a repetitive and relentless progression that mimics a cycle of thoughts that the speaker cannot escape, creating a sense of being psychologically bound to the pain.

A powerful metaphor emerges: "Can't sleep beneath the trees of wisdom / When your ax has cut the roots that feed them." The image of the ax cutting the roots transforms into a metaphor for destruction at a fundamental level. These "trees of wisdom" symbolize a source of ancient understanding, stability, and perhaps moral guidance. But when those roots are severed, the foundations of clarity and peace are obliterated. The speaker is left restless and unmoored, unable to rest beneath the shelter of wisdom because it has been desecrated by betrayal or by criticism that feels unjustified. The ax isn't just a tool—it's a symbol of betrayal, of actions that sever what should be unbreakable, leaving the speaker grappling with the disorienting aftermath of this destruction.

The line "Forked tongues in bitter mouths" brings up imagery that taps into ancient archetypes of deceit and betrayal. The "forked tongue" is a classic Biblical allusion, often associated with the snake in the Garden of Eden, a creature symbolic of temptation and deception. This imagery paints betrayal as something inherently vile and corrupt, leaving a "bitter" taste that poisons from within. This bitterness isn't merely a feeling; it is something so potent that it physically "bleeds from inside out," as if the betrayal has infiltrated the speaker's very essence. The music intensifies here, matching the heaviness of the lyrics, with guitar and drums mimicking the rawness of the speaker's inescapable pain and anger.

"What if you did? What if you lied? What if I avenge? What if eye for an eye?" These lines form the song's heartbeat, pulsing with tension as the lyrics turn to the question of retribution. The repetition of "What if" transforms these words into a kind of chant, a meditative refrain that forces the listener to confront the darker side of human nature. The speaker's questions linger on the brink between contemplation and action, as if considering the ramifications of taking justice into their own hands. This invocation of "eye for an eye" draws from one of humanity's oldest laws of retribution, found in ancient Mesopotamian and Biblical texts, suggesting a universal conflict between revenge and forgiveness. The musical intensity heightens in these moments, with aggressive guitar riffs and an unrelenting beat that drive home the weight of these questions, leaving the listener no choice but to confront their own inclinations toward vengeance.

This struggle is far from theoretical; it taps into the raw human instinct to demand justice, to make others feel the same pain they inflicted. Yet, woven into this contemplation of revenge is an awareness of its potential consequences. "What if you lied? What if I avenge?" These words suggest a recognition that the pursuit of vengeance is a slippery slope, fraught with the risk of becoming as morally compromised as the person who committed the initial wrong. It's a question that Creed leaves unresolved, leaving us, like the speaker, suspended in a state of inner conflict.

The line "What consumes your thoughts controls your life" serves as a sobering realization amidst this emotional storm. While much of the song navigates themes of betrayal and the desire for revenge, here is a moment of introspective clarity. It's a line that warns of the dangers of letting anger define one's existence. In this moment, the speaker seems to acknowledge that hatred is a double-edged sword, one that imprisons as much as it empowers. Anger may feel like a force, but it is also a cage—a mental state that binds the individual, preventing true freedom and peace. The words convey a universal truth: the thoughts that dominate our minds ultimately shape the way we experience the world. In this way, the song isn't merely a depiction of external conflict but also an exploration of an internal battle, a struggle to avoid being consumed by bitterness.

The final verses revisit the haunting refrain, but the tone has subtly shifted. The questions remain—"What if you did? What if you lied? What if I avenge?"—yet now they feel like echoes, unresolved but less urgent, as if the speaker has come to a point of acceptance, acknowledging the weight of these questions without needing immediate answers. The line "What if your words could be judged like a crime?" encapsulates the song's central message about the potency of language. Words may seem ephemeral, yet they have the power to wound as deeply as physical harm. This line forces us to consider the ethical responsibility we hold when we speak and the potential for words to carry consequences as serious as any other action.

The repetition of "What if, what if, what if..." in the closing moments has a hypnotic effect, almost as if the speaker is caught in an endless loop of reflection. This final repetition leaves the listener in a space of suspended introspection, mirroring the unresolved nature of the questions posed. Creed doesn't provide answers, nor does the song offer closure. Instead, it leaves us with the profound ambiguity that often accompanies moral conflict, the sense that some questions are meant to remain open-ended, echoing in our minds long after the song ends.

Musically, the song's structure and choice of instruments intensify this sense of unease and inner conflict. The heavy distortion on the guitar mirrors the dissonance within the speaker's mind, while the relentless beat drives a sense of inevitability, as if pushing the speaker closer to a breaking point. The use of minor chords throughout creates a dark, brooding atmosphere, evoking the tension between justice and revenge, between anger and forgiveness. The layered instrumentation, with the bass and drums grounding the track, feels almost like a heartbeat, a reminder of the physical reality of the speaker's pain.

In "What If?" Creed doesn't just deliver a rock song; they create an experience that invites the listener to grapple with fundamental moral questions. The song taps into universal themes of betrayal and the desire for retribution, using both lyrics and music to create a cinematic journey through the landscapes of human vulnerability. It reminds us that while anger and betrayal may be inevitable parts of the human experience, they are forces that we must confront with caution. Left unchecked, these emotions can consume us, leading us down paths that may compromise our own values.

By refusing to offer easy answers, Creed compels us to sit with these questions, to feel the weight of unresolved conflicts that exist within all of us. The song's cinematic, transformative style leaves the listener in a state of suspended reflection, asking themselves: What if I had been in the speaker's place? What would I have done? It's a song that doesn't just play through the speakers; it lingers in the mind, inviting the listener to wrestle with the questions long after the music has faded. In this way, "What If?" becomes more than a song—it's a journey into the depths of the human soul, an exploration of the thin line between justice and vengeance that resonates on both an emotional and philosophical level.

Application

The power of Creed's *What If?* lies in its ability to unearth visceral, almost primal emotions buried deep within us. It is not a song that simply laments betrayal or rages against injustice; it probes the complexities of human nature, asking questions that shake us to our core, leaving us with a lingering sense of both unease and self-recognition. With a biblical lens, we find that these themes are age-old, woven into the fabric of humanity's story as we grapple with the same questions of vengeance, pride, and redemption that reverberate through Scripture. Creed has crafted an anthem that invites listeners not merely to sympathize with the speaker's pain, but to confront their own shadow, to look at their own anger, and to ask themselves: what if?

The song's beginning line, *"I can't find the rhyme in all my reason,"* is a paradox that reflects the turmoil within. The speaker is caught between logic and emotion, unable to find coherence in a world suddenly devoid of familiar patterns. This line strikes at the heart of the human experience, particularly in moments of betrayal or loss, when we are plunged into an existential fog where even the most stable parts of our lives feel shattered. This state of disarray reflects what the Bible often describes as a state of brokenness, a loss of shalom—God's intended peace and order. Just as the speaker's mind becomes fragmented, Scripture speaks to the disordered human soul that has been torn from its purpose, as described in the Psalms and the laments of Job.

The imagery grows sharper as we progress, with phrases like *"lost sense of time and all seasons"* conveying a sense of being unmoored, of floating in a dark ocean with no compass or landmarks. Time, seasons—these symbols of order have been replaced by a suffocating, disorienting present. Biblically, time and seasons are ordained by God to bring rhythm and meaning to our lives, with Ecclesiastes 3 reflecting on "a time for every activity under heaven." In losing that rhythm, the speaker is experiencing something akin to spiritual exile, a state of being disconnected not only from God but from the grounding truths that define existence. Here, Creed mirrors the cries of figures like David, who in Psalm 22 laments, *"My God, my God, why have you forsaken me?"*—a state of abandonment that pulls us into the very depths of human sorrow and isolation.

The metaphor of *"trees of wisdom"* further enriches the song's portrayal of betrayal, suggesting that the speaker's connection to understanding and guidance has been severed. The ax that cuts the roots becomes a symbol of willful destruction, an act that strips away what should be stable, sacred, and nourishing. In Proverbs, wisdom is often portrayed as a "tree of life" (Proverbs 3:18), a source of sustenance that connects us to God's understanding and life itself. By cutting these roots, the speaker—or perhaps the betrayer—has committed an act that goes beyond simple harm; it's a spiritual desecration, a severing of the very things that ground us in truth and morality. This destruction resonates with the fall of man, where Adam and Eve, through their actions, severed humanity's direct connection with God, and since then, humanity has been left grappling with the consequences of broken wisdom and lost innocence.

As we move deeper, the imagery of *"forked tongues in bitter mouths"* taps into a well of archetypal symbols. In the Bible, the forked tongue represents deception, most notably seen in the serpent in the Garden of Eden. The serpent's words led to a rupture between God and humanity, introducing bitterness that would plague creation. This metaphor extends beyond the song's context, touching on the corrosive power of deceit in all relationships, whether personal, professional, or spiritual. The bitterness that "bleeds from inside out" captures a truth about how betrayal festers within us, turning something pure and whole into a source of internal torment. The New Testament speaks to this when it warns about "the root of bitterness" (Hebrews 12:15) that can defile and destroy if allowed to take hold. Bitterness, once planted, grows until it chokes out joy and peace, transforming a person's life and even their very soul.

Then comes the question that echoes throughout the song: *"What if you did? What if you lied? What if I avenge? What if eye for an eye?"* Here, Creed taps into the ancient human inclination for retribution. "Eye for an eye," taken from Mosaic Law (Exodus 21:24), represents a strict sense of justice where wrongs are directly answered with equal consequences. But Jesus in the New Testament challenges this concept, urging instead a radical forgiveness: *"You have heard that it was said, 'Eye for eye, and tooth for tooth.' But I tell you, do not resist an evil person. If anyone slaps you on the right cheek, turn to them the other cheek also"* (Matthew 5:38-39). This radical departure from retribution calls listeners—and the speaker—to consider the cost of vengeance. What if, in seeking justice, we only perpetuate the cycle of pain and estrangement?

Creed's refrain *"What if"* becomes a chant that pulls us into this moral struggle. The tension between justice and mercy, between vengeance and forgiveness, is one that runs through the whole of Scripture, reflecting the heart of God's relationship with humanity. There's an allure to vengeance; it feels like power, like taking control back from someone who has wronged us. But the Bible cautions us that vengeance belongs to God alone, as stated in Romans 12:19: *"Do not take revenge, my dear friends, but leave room for God's wrath, for it is written: 'It is mine to avenge; I will repay,' says the Lord."* The unresolved refrain of *"What if"* is a reminder that some questions do not have easy answers and that the pursuit of justice, without the guidance of grace, can lead us down a path as dark as the one that hurt us.

The line *"What consumes your thoughts controls your life"* is a sobering moment of self-awareness. It is a truth that resonates with the biblical admonition to guard our hearts, *"for everything you do flows from it"* (Proverbs 4:23). Here, the speaker realizes that anger, if left unchecked, doesn't just affect others; it begins to shape who we are. This line echoes Paul's instruction in Philippians 4:8 to dwell on whatever is "true, noble, right, pure, lovely, admirable." Creed's lyrics are a reminder of this biblical wisdom—the thoughts we harbor influence our actions, our character, and ultimately, our destiny. To dwell on vengeance is to let bitterness take root, shaping a life that becomes more defined by anger than by love, more by judgment than by grace.

In the song's latter verses, the repeated *"What if"* takes on a quieter, more introspective tone, as if the speaker has come to a moment of reflection rather than immediate action. The line *"What if your words could be judged like a crime?"* crystallizes a fundamental truth about the power of language. Scripture often speaks of the weight words carry: *"The tongue has the power of life and death"* (Proverbs 18:21). Words can heal or they can wound, they can build up or they can destroy. Creed's reflection on the impact of words challenges us to consider how we use our voices, whether in anger or compassion. Just as betrayal has wounded the speaker, so too do our words have the capacity to wound others, to act as agents of grace or instruments of pain.

The unresolved nature of the song, where the speaker remains in a space of suspended reflection, mirrors the ongoing journey of the believer who grapples with questions of forgiveness and justice. In this tension, Creed draws listeners into a place of vulnerability, where they are invited to consider their own responses to betrayal. What if we choose forgiveness, not out of weakness, but out of strength? What if, instead of exacting retribution, we allow God to be the ultimate judge, trusting in His justice rather than our own?

Musically, the song's structure mirrors this journey. The minor chords, the relentless beat, and the dark intensity of the guitar riffs all evoke the weight of inner conflict. The music itself becomes a metaphor, a journey from chaos to contemplation, mirroring the journey the listener is invited to take through the lyrics. The cinematic quality of the music, with its moments of intense buildup and quiet reflection, captures the struggle to move from anger to peace, from vengeance to forgiveness.

What If? is more than a song; it is an exploration of the human soul's darkest corners, an invitation to wrestle with questions that do not come with easy answers. It reminds us that we all carry the capacity for anger and the desire for justice, but we are also capable of grace and mercy. In this, Creed's song is a modern-day psalm of lament and introspection, leaving us with questions that we must carry with us, not for the purpose of easy answers, but to spur deeper reflection, transformation, and ultimately, redemption.

What if, indeed. In this reflection lies the challenge—and the invitation—to find a way forward that does not compromise our humanity, but instead calls us to a higher understanding of justice, one rooted not in vengeance, but in the transformative power of forgiveness and grace.

CHAPTER 14
"Beautiful"

T he song "Beautiful" by Creed speaks to a profound disillusionment, a kind of painful awakening that unfolds as one
grapples with the empty allure of beauty and the illusory promises it
holds. Through careful consideration of each lyric, we see how the
song's protagonist confronts beauty's power to seduce, only to find
that its depths are hollow. There is an emotional trajectory here, from
fascination to revelation, as beauty strips away illusions and leaves one
raw, facing difficult truths.

The song opens with an image: "She wears a coat of color." There's
a visual richness in this phrase, suggesting that beauty comes cloaked
in something eye-catching, captivating, even hypnotic. The colors are
undoubtedly vibrant and bold, each hue designed to allure, to draw
in those who are susceptible to surface appearances. This coat of
color is as much a protective layer as it is a weapon, crafted to both
conceal and attract, creating a paradox. The phrase is intentionally
ambiguous—"color" here suggests vibrancy, but it could also imply
something artificial, like makeup or a mask. It's both a presentation
and a cover, a shield and a lure.

This coat of color marks beauty's dual nature: "Loved by some,
feared by others." Beauty is enchanting and often adored, yet there's
a danger inherent in its influence. The song invites listeners to explore
why beauty might be feared. In many ways, beauty holds a seductive

power that can overtake reason. This is the kind of beauty that stirs primal instincts and desires, affecting people in ways they may not fully understand or control. Its lure can pull people toward actions that defy their better judgment, leading them to regret and even self-destruction.

There's a haunting sense that beauty—personified as "she"—is more than just an appearance; she's an influence, an entity with an almost supernatural grip on the observer. She is "immortalized in young men's eyes." This line evokes the timeless nature of youthful fascination with beauty, a fascination that often disregards depth in favor of allure. Youthful eyes are impressionable, and beauty becomes a kind of idol. Yet, beauty here is a fleeting deity, one that demands loyalty but gives nothing in return. In this fixation, we see the seeds of disillusionment; beauty as an idealized figure becomes an obsession, a distraction from more profound and enduring truths.

Then comes the phrase, "Lust she breeds in the eyes of brothers / Violent sons make bitter mothers." Here, the lyrics explore how beauty, as a symbol of desire, can warp relationships and fuel destructive passions. The "brothers" who are drawn to her are united in their attraction yet divided by competition, jealousy, and rivalry. This attraction transforms into a kind of lustful violence, an uncontainable urge that can spill into aggression. Such a force fractures family bonds, leaving mothers embittered by their sons' actions. This line could also signify how societal values glorify beauty, breeding envy and rivalry, which ultimately harms not only individuals but families, communities, and even generations.

The music accompanying these lyrics reflects the tension within the words. Minor chords and dissonant notes underscore the darker themes, each chord a reminder of the disquiet beneath beauty's surface. There's a progression here that starts with a sense of awe and moves into a haunting, even unsettling tone, hinting that what seems beautiful from afar holds hidden dangers. The melody is strikingly somber, almost mournful, amplifying the sense of loss and regret that permeates the song.

As the chorus emerges, "Beautiful is empty / Beautiful is free / Beautiful loves no one / Beautiful stripped me," we're confronted with the core revelation: beauty, in its superficial form, is hollow. The repetition of "beautiful" reinforces its allure and the harsh realization of its emptiness. Beauty is described as "free," implying that it exists independently of our desires or needs—it has no obligation to reciprocate the feelings it provokes. Beauty takes, but it does not give; it draws others toward it yet offers no lasting fulfillment. It's an indifferent force, caring nothing for those who are captivated by it.

The line "Beautiful loves no one" underscores the neutrality, even cruelty, of beauty. There is no reciprocal relationship here; beauty does not care for those who idolize it. It is as though the protagonist is coming to terms with a one-sided love affair with an ideal that will never love back. This disillusionment is both painful and enlightening—it marks a turning point, a moment of clarity where the protagonist sees through the surface to the reality beneath. Beauty, in this context, has stripped the protagonist of his illusions. Each repetition of "stripped me" brings with it a deeper level of self-awareness, as if each instance is peeling back a layer of naivety, leaving the protagonist exposed and vulnerable.

Musically, the rawness of the stripped-down chords mirrors this vulnerability. The sound grows in intensity, like a descent into self-realization. Each note resonates with a visceral impact, stripping away pretense and digging into the truth of what beauty has done to the speaker—leaving him bare and exposed. There's no attempt to soften this journey; instead, the music amplifies the theme of exposure, like a spotlight illuminating hidden scars.

"In your mind she's your companion / Vile instincts often candid." This line speaks to the deceptive intimacy that beauty offers. Beauty can feel like a companion, a presence that seems close and intimate, especially in the imagination. But this companionship is insidious; it brings out instincts and desires that one might not openly acknowledge. The word "candid" here suggests that these instincts are raw and unfiltered—there's an honesty in lust, envy, or obsession that, while uncomfortable, reveals truth. Beauty's presence forces the protagonist to confront parts of himself he might otherwise deny, unveiling the "vile" instincts lurking beneath the surface.

As the song nears its end, the lyrics repeat, "She told me where I'm going / And it's far away from home." The "she" here still refers to beauty, now almost a siren leading the protagonist away from his roots, his true self. Beauty's allure is powerful enough to pull him far from home, far from comfort and familiarity, leading him into an unknown and perhaps isolating path. Home represents authenticity, warmth, stability—qualities that are absent in the world beauty promises. This departure from "home" is symbolic of the internal distance one creates from one's true values when seduced by superficial ideals.

"I think I'll go there on my own." This line suggests a kind of acceptance, perhaps even resignation, as if the protagonist recognizes the inevitability of this journey. There's a sense of autonomy in these words, a decision to face the consequences of pursuing beauty, knowing full well that the path is a solitary one. In essence, he's choosing to confront the truth alone, embracing the painful, transformative journey that lies ahead. This acceptance is bittersweet—it speaks to the necessity of self-discovery, even when the truths one discovers are difficult to bear.

In the final repetition of the chorus, the lyrics echo with a new-found resignation. The protagonist is now stripped not only of his illusions about beauty but also of his illusions about himself. He has confronted the emptiness of beauty, recognizing that its freedom is a kind of aloofness, an inability to reciprocate or fulfill. This under-standing leaves him changed, no longer an admirer caught in beauty's thrall but someone who has seen its limitations and, in turn, has discovered his own vulnerabilities.

"Beautiful" is more than a song about physical beauty or attraction; it's a powerful meditation on the illusions that beauty creates and the painful yet necessary journey of seeing through those illusions. The song explores themes of seduction, rivalry, disillusionment, and ultimately, self-awareness. Beauty, in its superficial form, is alluring yet empty, captivating yet indifferent. Through this journey, the pro-tagonist comes to understand that true fulfillment cannot be found in chasing illusions. This hard-earned wisdom—achieved through pain and stripping away of pretense—leaves the protagonist bare yet stronger, ready to walk away from the hollow allure of beauty and seek something deeper, something that aligns with his truest self.

The transformation here is stark and revelatory. The song's chords and progression mirror this journey, moving from enchantment to despair to acceptance, each musical element amplifying the emotional weight of the lyrics. Through this interpretation, Creed invites listen-ers to question the ideals they chase and consider the cost of pursuing superficial beauty at the expense of authenticity. In the end, the song is a call to self-discovery, to shed the allure of empty promises, and to walk a path that, while challenging, leads to a more profound and lasting sense of self.

Application

In this song, we find profound reflections on allure, emptiness, and the illusion of beauty—a meditation on the false promises that seduction and superficiality bring. With each line, a deeper truth is unearthed: the idolization of beauty, the allure of the forbidden, and the profound emptiness it leaves in its wake. These themes echo biblical warnings, presenting beauty as both an intoxicating and destructive force, capable of ensnaring the heart and leading it away from genuine life. The Scriptures offer insight into the soul's yearning for something greater than appearances—something real, lasting, and deeply fulfilling. Here, the lyrics speak almost prophetically about beauty's deceptive nature, its hollow core, and its power to rob a person of true self-worth and fulfillment.

The opening lines, "She wears a coat of color, Loved by some, feared by others," suggest the way beauty is often cloaked in appearances that draw admiration and fear alike. Beauty, when idolized, can evoke feelings of both adoration and intimidation; it is both worshipped and feared. Yet, the "coat of color" is just that—a coat. Inwardly, beauty often masks something less permanent, less fulfilling. The Bible reminds us of this in 1 Samuel 16:7, where God tells Samuel, "Man looks at the outward appearance, but the Lord looks at the heart." This verse challenges our inclination to judge worth by external attributes. The allure of physical beauty is powerful, yet God teaches us that true beauty lies deeper than what meets the eye. It resides in the character and heart of a person.

Beauty, as suggested in these lyrics, has a way of ensnaring the eyes of men and evoking lust and envy, creating fractures in relationships. When it says, "Lust she breeds in the eyes of brothers, violent sons make bitter mothers," it recalls the strife that unchecked desire can stir in families and communities. It brings to mind the story of David and

Bathsheba from 2 Samuel 11, where David's lust for Bathsheba led him into a cycle of sin, ultimately resulting in betrayal and violence. David's coveting was not only a private failing but one with ripple effects that hurt his family, his people, and his standing before God.

This obsession with the beautiful, with the temporary, always leads to emptiness, for beauty in and of itself "loves no one" and can "strip" us of our dignity and peace. David's regret was severe, and in Psalm 51, he cries out, "Create in me a pure heart, O God, and renew a steadfast spirit within me." Here, the song resonates with David's remorse, suggesting that beauty can indeed "strip" us of our true selves when it becomes an idol, leaving us with the need to return to God and seek restoration.

The refrain, "Beautiful is empty, beautiful is free, beautiful loves no one, beautiful stripped me," portrays a sense of desolation. The irony is palpable: beauty, though attractive and coveted, is ultimately hollow if it lacks love and truth. It offers freedom but an illusory one, a "freedom" that leads to slavery of the heart. In biblical terms, this emptiness of beauty without substance can be likened to the "chasing after the wind" described in Ecclesiastes 1:14: "I have seen all the things that are done under the sun; all of them are meaningless, a chasing after the wind." The writer of Ecclesiastes understood that earthly pursuits—wealth, pleasure, beauty—are ultimately vain pursuits without God.

The refrain's description of beauty as "empty" and "stripped" points to a deeper truth about misplaced priorities. Many people pursue external beauty, achievements, or pleasures to fill an internal void, only to discover that these pursuits fail to satisfy. Beauty promises but cannot deliver; it offers temporary satisfaction but leaves a deeper hunger unfulfilled. Jesus spoke to this in Matthew 16:26, asking, "What good will it be for someone to gain the whole world, yet forfeit their soul?" Pursuing beauty or external gains at the expense of the soul's well-being leaves one stripped of purpose, integrity, and peace.

The singer's realization that "beautiful loves no one" and "beautiful stripped me" exposes beauty as a poor substitute for true, enduring love. In Scripture, we are taught that "God is love" (1 John 4:8), which highlights the chasm between a beauty that "loves no one" and a love that is rooted in God's eternal nature. This understanding is crucial for the believer. Genuine fulfillment comes not from the transient or the beautiful but from the deep, abiding love of God. Beauty devoid of love is ultimately lifeless and cold.

The line "In your mind, she's your companion" speaks to a common human experience: the creation of mental idols. Often, individuals are captivated by an image or idea, building it up in their minds as something to long for, only to discover that it is a mirage. This is reminiscent of the biblical warning against idolatry. Colossians 3:5 calls on believers to "put to death, therefore, whatever belongs to your earthly nature: sexual immorality, impurity, lust, evil desires and greed, which is idolatry." When we allow an idealized image of beauty to fill our minds, we risk idolizing it, placing it on a pedestal that belongs only to God.

The words "Vile instincts often candid" reveal the raw reality of sinful desires that can seem honest and candid yet are destructive. Here, the song addresses the regret that follows succumbing to these base instincts. The aftermath of giving in to lust or the worship of beauty is always regret. "Your regret is all that's left" points to the heartache of realizing too late that these desires are empty and costly. This echoes the experience of the prodigal son in Luke 15, who squandered his inheritance on reckless living only to find himself in poverty and regret. The prodigal son's story shows us that the path of indulgence leads to a pit of despair, yet it also offers hope, for he finds redemption when he returns to his father's house.

As the song progresses, there is a subtle shift in tone. "She told me where I'm going, and it's far away from home." This line conveys the distance that sin creates between the individual and their true purpose, their true home. When we stray from God's design, we find ourselves far from the place of belonging He has prepared for us. Isaiah 53:6 states, "We all, like sheep, have gone astray, each of us has turned to our own way." The longing for home is a universal cry of the human heart—an ache to return to the presence of God, from which sin and worldly enticements separate us.

Yet, there is also a sense of resignation in the words "I think I'll go there on my own." This mirrors the self-reliance often found in human nature, the desire to fix our lives by our own means. The Bible continually reminds us, however, that we are incapable of saving ourselves. In John 15:5, Jesus tells His disciples, "Apart from me you can do nothing." The realization that "going on my own" leads only to further emptiness and distance should bring us to the understanding that true freedom and homecoming are only found in surrender to God.

This journey home, this longing for rest and redemption, is at the heart of the Christian faith. The soul's true home is with God, and only there will we find the fulfillment that beauty and fleeting pleasures cannot provide.

The repeated refrain, "But beautiful is empty... beautiful stripped me," carries a somber note, but it also subtly invites the listener to seek beauty that does not strip away dignity or peace. The Bible provides a redemptive answer: true beauty is found in Christ and in the lives transformed by His love. Psalm 27:4 expresses this longing for true beauty: "One thing I ask from the Lord... to gaze on the beauty of the

Lord and to seek him in his temple." Unlike the hollow beauty of the world, the beauty of the Lord is rich, fulfilling, and eternal.

Christ redeems what the world has perverted. Where beauty once led us away from God, Jesus offers beauty that draws us closer. In Christ, we discover a beauty that fills rather than empties, that frees rather than enslaves. This redeemed beauty speaks of purity, love, and grace. In 1 Peter 3:3-4, Peter encourages believers to seek "the unfading beauty of a gentle and quiet spirit, which is of great worth in God's sight." This beauty is not external but is rooted in the heart and character transformed by God's Spirit.

The song's powerful and haunting lyrics remind us that without God, beauty and earthly desires will always leave us feeling empty. They call us to recognize the insufficiency of the temporal and to seek the eternal. The refrain's cry—"stripped me, stripped me"—echoes the human soul's experience when it has been deceived by false promises. Yet, there is hope in Christ, who fills what is empty, restores what is broken, and clothes us in a beauty that is unshakable and eternal.

The listener is left with a choice: to continue down the path that leads to emptiness or to turn towards the beauty that is found in a life surrendered to Christ. True freedom, true love, and true fulfillment are found not in fleeting

CHAPTER 15
"Say I"

In *"Say I"* by Creed, we find ourselves plunged into a hauntingly desolate landscape that serves as both metaphor and reality—a world shaped by humankind, yet eerily void of the divine touch that originally breathed life into it. This song's intense urgency and underlying melancholy create a journey of searching, introspection, and a desperate cry for self-definition and salvation in the face of a collective abandonment.

The opening line, "The dust has finally settled on the field of human clay," immediately sets the tone. Here, "dust" and "human clay" evoke a biblical image, recalling the Genesis story in which God forms humanity from the dust of the ground. Yet, now the dust "settles," suggesting a world where creation has paused, and something profound has shifted. This is not a serene rest but an absence, as though the world has been left unfinished, or, worse, neglected by the hand that made it. In this image, Creed confronts humanity's awareness of its incompleteness. There's a raw, haunting acknowledgment here that something vital has departed—a sense of our Creator withdrawing from the very creation made in His image.

The line "Just enough light has shown through to tell the night from the day" is essential to the song's theme. It implies a world suspended in twilight, a liminal space where clarity and obscurity blur. This faint light allows for a minimal discernment, but not enough to illuminate the path forward. It's a world that gives glimpses of truth and insight yet remains shrouded in ambiguity, pushing humanity to strain for meaning while groping in spiritual darkness.

The music, meanwhile, complements these existential reflections through its structure. The composition shifts between haunting still-ness and explosive cries, mirroring the oscillation between despair and the urgent plea for identity that is so central to the song. The soft opening, like a deep intake of breath, is followed by powerful chords that surge forward, simulating the rush of pent-up human desire clashing against a seemingly silent heaven. The distorted guitar riffs and rhythmic pulses evoke a sense of weariness yet determination—a journey that drains but also demands resilience.

As the song continues, we encounter the phrase, "We're incomplete and hollow, for our maker's gone away." Here, Creed taps into the notion of divine absence, a deeply troubling reality where the very essence of humanity—its purpose and vitality—feels drained because the One who breathed life into us is no longer near. This line expresses a collective lament, not just for personal struggles but for a universal condition: humanity feels abandoned by God, grappling with the weight of its "hollowness." This void is not a simple emptiness but one that echoes with all that is unresolved within each soul.

The refrain, "Say I," begins as a subtle invitation but crescendos into a desperate demand. It's not just a call for individual declara-tion but an insistence on self-awareness and acknowledgment. The repetition is relentless, pressing listeners to confront who they are in a world devoid of the divine. "Say I" becomes a plea for identity, an urge to find oneself amidst the noise, confusion, and fragmentation of modern existence. It's a call to each listener, a demand for each person to confront their inner void, to declare who they are, especially when divine guidance feels absent.

In "The stillness is so lifeless with no spirit in your soul," the song touches on a deeply spiritual yet achingly barren reality. This line speaks to an internal deadness, a numbness that has overtaken humanity. The absence of the "spirit" suggests a disconnect from the very source of life, leaving only a mechanical, empty existence. The starkness of this description paints a picture of people moving through life, doing what they are told—"like children with no vision"—as they follow directives without purpose or passion. This visionless state leads humanity into a metaphorical "desert," where strength fades and where the trials are ceaseless and relentless, mirroring the biblical desert where people wander aimlessly in search of a Promised Land that remains out of reach.

The instrumental progression mirrors this sense of wandering, moving from a restrained opening to an intense and climactic midsection. The lead guitar's melancholy tone mirrors a cry in the wilderness, longing for direction, while the percussive elements embody a tribal rhythm that feels both grounding and exhausting. It's as if the music itself is experiencing this desert, reflecting the fatigue and relentless demand for endurance in the face of a seemingly endless struggle.

As the bridge progresses, we hear a refrain: "Frantic, faction, focus...This misconception we call man." Here, Creed points to the inherent chaos in human nature, a fracturing of focus, as if humanity has splintered into countless "factions," all seeking their own truth yet collectively unable to find meaning. The "misconception we call man" suggests a bitter realization that humankind, in its attempt to define itself, has become misguided, losing sight of its original purpose. This fragmented self-awareness is a reflection on human pride and our propensity to reshape our identities outside of divine intention. The line "we speak, they don't own us" is a defiant declaration against conformity and external control—a rejection of false identities imposed upon us.

The bridge concludes with the declaration "but I don't know him," alluding to humanity's disconnect from its true self or perhaps from the Creator. This "he" may be the divine image humanity was meant to reflect but has lost sight of. The dissonance in the music here underscores this confusion, as the guitar distorts and stretches, like an identity being pulled beyond recognition. It's an existential crisis wrapped in sound—a sense of reaching out and finding nothing but static, an attempt to connect to something eternal only to encounter emptiness.

Then comes the haunting line, "Because he lies, they lie." This passage can be interpreted as a rejection of false promises—of a world or culture that has led humanity astray with half-truths, illusions, and distractions. Creed is laying bare the human tendency to accept facades and deceptions, especially when facing the fear of spiritual abandonment. In a world that thrives on these illusions, who can be trusted? The instruments swell here, building tension, mirroring the internal struggle as humanity tries to discern truth from lies. This musical buildup speaks to a universal human condition: the quest for truth amid a world saturated with noise and deceit.

In the closing repetition of "Say I," the song culminates in an intense, almost primal cry. This repetition can be seen as a final push, urging each listener to take a stand and to claim their identity—whatever fragmented, imperfect form it may take. It's as if Creed is calling on each of us to rise above the confusion, to stake a claim in our own existence despite the absence of definitive answers. The music, heavy and pulsing, acts like a heartbeat, a reminder of life and agency even in the midst of existential uncertainty.

Throughout *"Say I,"* the recurring themes of divine absence, spiritual desolation, and the struggle for self-definition resonate deeply. The music reflects these themes with its dynamic shifts, capturing the tension between despair and defiance, between feeling lost and the urge to find oneself. This is a song that doesn't offer easy answers but instead challenges us to sit with the discomfort of unknowing. Creed's message here is ultimately about the courage to confront our own hollow places, to ask the hard questions, and, perhaps most importantly, to choose to exist authentically despite the silence from above.

In this sense, *"Say I"* serves as both an anthem and a lament. It's a reminder that self-discovery is neither clean nor complete—it's an ongoing process filled with dark nights of the soul and moments of fleeting clarity. This song calls each listener to reckon with their own humanity, their own imperfections, and their longing for something transcendent. And while the dust may settle and the rain may fall, *"Say I"* reminds us that even in a world devoid of simple answers, the pursuit of identity and truth is a journey worth undertaking.

Application

In this moment, allow yourself to stand in the quiet of your soul, in the stillness that often eludes us in the noise of daily life. As you read these words, consider what they reveal about the state of our hearts, the condition of our lives, and the ache that lies beneath every fleeting distraction and shallow answer the world offers. Humanity, as the song suggests, walks on a dusty field, often empty and broken, straining to see the light in a world where shadows seem to cling. This image isn't abstract; it mirrors the way so many of us feel: hollow, incomplete, longing for something — Someone — who can fill the empty spaces, who can make the broken pieces whole.

Imagine yourself on this field, where every step is marked by a sense of separation from what is most essential, from the One who gives life and meaning. There is a sense of abandonment, as if our Maker, the One who designed us for communion with Him, has gone away, leaving us to grapple with our own limitations and emptiness. Yet the reality is not that God has left us, but rather that we, as humanity, have often turned away from Him, seeking satisfaction in things that cannot fulfill, and then wondering why we feel desolate. This distance is not His doing; it's ours. And as the rain comes, as trials and sufferings pour down, the hollow, unanchored heart begins to melt away. Without God, we're like clay without a potter's hand to shape it, like seeds without soil, struggling to survive under the weight of our own frailty.

Pause and think about those moments when you've felt this way: when life seemed lifeless, as if each day passed by without meaning or purpose. We've all been there, haven't we? Like children without vision, we do what we're told by the world around us, wandering through deserts that drain our strength and leave us parched. Maybe you've experienced this in seasons of chasing success, relationships, or approval, only to find yourself emptier than before. We think we're seeking life, but we're walking into deserts that strip us bare, consuming every ounce of our inner strength, until we're left dry and directionless.

In these deserts, it's easy to wonder, "Who is to blame?" We question ourselves, the people around us, and often God Himself, looking for answers to the dissatisfaction we can't shake. We think, "Why would a loving God let me wander here? Why does He seem distant, leaving me to face the rain and heat alone?" And yet, even in these dry, hollow places, God's call echoes. The rain that seems to melt us away, that feels like it's breaking us down, can actually become the very tool He uses to mold and reshape us if we let Him. He allows us to see the emptiness of a life without Him so that we might hunger for something real, something eternal.

The truth is, God has not abandoned us. He stands closer than we realize, waiting patiently for us to stop running, to stop seeking life in things that can never give it, and to turn to Him with all of our being. Like a parent who watches a child make mistakes, knowing that sometimes they must fall to understand what's truly safe, God allows us to wander, but He does not leave us. He waits with open arms, ready to fill us with His Spirit, to breathe life into the dry and lifeless places, and to give us the strength that lasts. He wants us to see that without Him, we are indeed clay, but with Him, we can become something beautiful, something purposeful.

As you reflect on these words, consider what it would mean for you to "say I" — to own up to the truth of your own need, to recognize that the strength you've been relying on is finite, and that only through surrender to God can you truly be whole. Saying "I" is an act of humility, an admission that we cannot make it alone, that we are in desperate need of a Savior who can rescue us from the lifelessness we so often feel. It's not about admitting defeat; it's about acknowledging reality — that apart from Him, we're just dust.

The song speaks of a frantic, misguided world, one that chases illusions and misconceptions. We are bombarded with voices that try to define who we are, what we should be, and how we should live. The world's narrative is so loud that it's easy to lose sight of God's voice, of His truth that has stood unshaken from the beginning of time. "They lie," the lyrics say, and yes, the world lies to us, offering us temporary pleasures, false assurances, and empty promises. We're told to look within ourselves for meaning, to shape our own truths, but if we're honest, we know that truth doesn't come from within us

— it comes from God alone. We don't have the power to define what is right, good, and fulfilling. Only He does.

Imagine what it would be like to step away from the voices of the world, to quiet the noise and listen to the One who knows you more deeply than anyone else. This is the One who formed you, who knows every hidden place of your heart, every secret pain, and every longing that you have. He doesn't just see you; He knows you, and His love for you isn't dependent on your accomplishments, your status, or your appearance. It's a love that's anchored in His unchanging character, in His goodness and mercy. And He calls you to Himself, not because you are perfect, but because you are loved.

To apply this truth is to come before God with honesty, to let down the walls and be real about where you are. Are you empty? Are you wandering in a desert? Have you tried to find fulfillment in places that only leave you thirsting for more? Take a moment to lay these things at His feet. Confess the ways you've sought life in other places, the times you've believed the lies, and ask Him to fill you with His Spirit, to revive the parts of you that have felt lifeless and barren. This is not a one-time action; it's a daily turning, a daily reliance on Him, a daily rejection of the world's false promises.

The beauty of God's grace is that it doesn't just cover us; it transforms us. He takes the clay and forms it into something new, something strong, something beautiful. You may feel fragile, but in His hands, you become resilient. The desert places in your life can become gardens when He is with you. The rain that once threatened to melt you away can become the waters that nourish and grow you into the person He has called you to be.

As you continue through life, keep saying "I" in the sense that you're acknowledging your need for Him, your dependence on His strength. Say "I" not to claim independence, but to claim your identity as His beloved, as someone who is known and valued by the Creator of the universe. In every trial, every desert, every moment of emptiness, remember that He is with you, that He never truly left, and that His love for you is constant, unwavering, and powerful enough to carry you through.

So stand on the field of human clay, but stand with confidence, knowing that your Maker has not abandoned you.

CHAPTER 16
"Wrong Way"

"Wrong Way" by Creed is one of those hauntingly reflective pieces that reaches out to each of us and confronts universal questions about purpose, mortality, and the often difficult search for truth. Its lyrics seem deceptively simple, yet they pull the listener into a state of self-examination and wrestle with ideas that are challenging to articulate. Creed's instrumentation, tonal choices, and the underlying tension between melody and lyrics work together to craft a cinematic, introspective journey—one that seeks understanding and reflects on missteps, all while yearning for a way to live rightly.

At the start, the lyrics echo questions that many of us have asked at some point: *"What makes you touch? What makes you feel?"* These questions seem innocuous but reveal a quest for something deeper—what compels us to engage with the world, to feel joy, to notice beauty? This line, like a lens turning to focus on life's simplest, yet most profound experiences, invites the listener to pause and consider the things that move them, that make life worth living. Musically, the chords remain subdued but steady, underscoring this sense of gentle wonderment. It's as if the music, like the lyrics, is inviting us into a state of curiosity and openness, capturing the sensation of an open field where anything might be possible if we only take the time to notice it.

As the song progresses, we sense a shift in tone. The question transforms from one of curiosity to one of introspection and potential guilt: *"What makes you unclean?"* It's a jarring line, especially after the reflective start, which feels almost like a calm before a storm. With these words, Creed pulls the listener into an uncomfortable space, a reminder of the imperfection and inherent brokenness in human nature. The question demands that we consider our flaws, our mistakes, and the regrets that might weigh on us. In this line, the music swells slightly, taking on a darker, more somber undertone. The change in musical atmosphere underscores a sense of unease—an acknowledgment of the things we'd rather ignore but must confront.

What follows is a powerful contemplation of life and death: *"What makes you laugh? What makes you cry? / What makes our youth run from the thought that we might die?"* Here, Creed touches on the bittersweetness of existence. We are drawn to laughter and joy, yet there's always a shadow—the reality of mortality. For many, the thought of death is overwhelming, even frightening. There's a tension here between the urge to fully embrace life and the instinct to flee from anything that hints at our own end. Creed, through the instrumentals, paints this dichotomy with a mixture of fast and slow tempos, as if the music itself is torn between pacing forward and pulling back, echoing the human desire to both confront and evade our fears.

The refrain, *"Somebody told me the wrong way,"* punctuates the song like a painful confession. It's a phrase of both accusation and realization. There is a sense of betrayal, as though the speaker's life has been marked by falsehoods, by misguided advice or teachings. This line reverberates with regret and longing for truth. In these moments, the instruments take on a stronger, almost aggressive tone, amplifying the frustration and confusion of realizing one has been misled. The music's intensity builds, mirroring the growing realization that much of what we follow, much of what we are told, may not lead us where we want to go.

This refrain, repeated throughout the song, is crucial—it points to a sense of collective error, a wrong path taken not just by the individual but possibly by all of us. The "wrong way" could refer to societal values that prioritize material success over spiritual or emotional fulfillment, or it could be a personal struggle with direction and purpose. The speaker feels the weight of having been misdirected, and now grapples with the need to correct their course. In this, there is a profound sense of isolation, as though the realization of this misdirection is a lonely burden to bear. The music complements this, with dissonant notes and heavy bass that underscore the pain of recognizing one's own lostness.

But the song doesn't end in despair; rather, it reaches towards redemption. *"What if I died? What did I give? / I hope it was an answer so you might live."* Here, the lyrics take on a tone of sacrificial love—a willingness to give of oneself for the sake of others. The character singing doesn't just want to find personal redemption; they hope that their journey, with all its wrong turns and mistakes, can still be of value to someone else. This wish to help others live fully, even if it means facing their own mortality, is both humbling and inspiring. The softer notes in the music during this segment serve as a balm, a moment of tenderness in the midst of all the song's angst and tension. There's a glimmer of hope, an almost prayer-like quality to the wish for one's life to be an "answer."

At the core, this song's heart is the desire to be useful, to live a life that matters. The repetition of *"I hope I helped you live"* is like a mantra, a wish to redeem the past by offering something good to the future. The voice behind the lyrics isn't merely lamenting their mistakes; they are yearning to make amends, to transform their life into a source of hope and inspiration for others. There's a universality to this sentiment—many of us reach a point where we look back on our lives and hope that despite the missteps, we've done something meaningful, that we've contributed in some way to someone else's journey.

The ending of the song circles back to the refrain, *"Somebody told me the wrong way,"* but now it carries a different weight. It's less of an accusation and more of an acknowledgment—a realization that we may all be following paths that don't lead to where we want to go, that the search for meaning and truth is not straightforward. There's a humbling awareness that everyone is navigating life with imperfect maps, often relying on flawed guidance. The music fades, leaving the listener with a sense of unfinished business, of questions still unanswered, as if urging us to question and redefine our paths.

In many ways, "Wrong Way" is an exploration of human frailty and the courage it takes to confront the truth of our lives. The use of darker tones, crescendos, and haunting pauses in the music echo the inner turmoil of a soul seeking clarity in a world full of conflicting voices. The repetition of phrases reflects the circular, often frustrating nature of self-discovery, where we find ourselves returning to the same questions, wrestling with the same doubts. The song's structure, in its raw honesty and emotional intensity, mirrors a journey that isn't linear but full of backtracking and revisiting old wounds.

Creed, through both lyrics and music, brings forth a powerful message: that life is full of questions that can be both painful and transformative. The pursuit of purpose, of living a life that matters, is fraught with difficulty. There will be times when we feel lost, when we discover that we've been going the wrong way. But even then, there is hope. The desire to live a meaningful life, to make a difference, is not in vain. There is redemption in the very act of seeking, in the wish to help others, and in the humility that comes from recognizing our own fallibility.

Ultimately, "Wrong Way" isn't just a song about regret; it's about the resilience to keep moving forward even after discovering we've taken the wrong path. It's about the courage to ask difficult questions, to confront uncomfortable truths, and to try, in whatever small way, to leave something behind that helps others. In this, Creed has crafted a piece that resonates deeply with anyone who has ever felt lost, who has questioned the meaning of their life, and who has found strength in the desire to be a light for others.

The song ends not with clear answers but with a sense of resolve. The questions remain, the doubts linger, but there is a newfound sense of purpose: to live in a way that benefits others, that contributes to a larger story of hope and redemption. In this way, "Wrong Way" is both a lament and a call to action, a reminder that our lives, with all their imperfections, have the potential to inspire and uplift. It's an invitation to live intentionally, to face the hard truths, and to find meaning in the journey—however winding it may be.

Application

The words of *"Wrong Way"* by Creed can feel like a poignant call, pulling us into a space where self-reflection meets a longing to make sense of life's deepest questions. It's like looking into a mirror that shows not just our own face but also the burdens, questions, and struggles we carry inside. These words resonate with anyone who has ever wondered if they've been heading down the wrong path, and in many ways, they invite us to consider how we might turn even our detours into steps toward something meaningful.

The song begins by asking, "What makes you touch? What makes you feel?" and this question may seem almost innocent at first, yet it invites us to consider what truly moves us. It's easy in today's world to get caught up in superficial joys, in fleeting distractions that satisfy us momentarily but leave us feeling empty in the long run. But what if we took a moment to examine what really touches our hearts, to notice what stirs us to kindness, to empathy, to genuine connection? This is a call to discover the things that make us feel alive—not just for our own enjoyment but to bring something deeper into the world around us.

When we take the time to reflect on what moves us, we begin to uncover the parts of our lives that hold the greatest meaning. These moments of clarity aren't always obvious, but they might show up in unexpected ways—a conversation with a friend, a quiet walk in nature, or even in times of struggle when we're forced to dig deeper into who we are. Recognizing these moments helps us orient our lives around the things that truly matter, reminding us that life is about more than surface-level success or comfort. It's an opportunity to reconnect with the essence of what it means to live fully.

The song then shifts with the question, "What makes you un-clean?" In this line, Creed invites us to a place of introspection that is both uncomfortable and necessary. Confronting our own brokenness, our failings, and even the things we try to hide from ourselves is never easy. But it's in these moments that we begin to understand the weight of our choices and how they shape us. Each of us has moments we're not proud of, times we've hurt others or failed to live up to our own standards. Rather than turning away from these truths, facing them head-on can lead to transformation.

This doesn't mean dwelling in shame or guilt, but it does mean taking responsibility for the ways we've fallen short. It's a recognition that our mistakes, as painful as they might be, offer a chance for growth. When we acknowledge these moments openly, we begin to see that they don't define us—they are simply part of our journey. With a humble heart, we can look back on these missteps as opportunities to learn, to forgive ourselves, and to approach others with greater compassion. There's strength in vulnerability, in admitting where we've gone wrong, and in choosing to pursue a better path.

In the line, "What makes you laugh? What makes you cry?" Creed reminds us of the beauty and fragility of life. Laughter and tears are two sides of the same coin—expressions of the highs and lows that make us human. There's something deeply powerful about experiencing joy, even in the smallest moments. These moments of laughter can serve as a balm to the soul, reminders that even in the midst of life's challenges, there are glimpses of hope and beauty. Similarly, our tears are often an acknowledgment of things that matter deeply to us—people we love, dreams we've fought for, or losses we've endured.

To reflect on what moves us to laughter or brings us to tears is to connect with the depths of our humanity. These are the things that bring richness to our lives and remind us that we're part of something greater. In a world that often tells us to suppress our emotions, to focus on productivity and achievement, taking the time to feel deeply is an act of courage. When we embrace our laughter and our tears, we open ourselves to a fuller experience of life, one that includes both joy and sorrow in a way that shapes us and helps us grow.

As the refrain echoes, "Somebody told me the wrong way," there's a sense of realization, a painful awakening to the ways we may have been led astray. This line feels like a cry from the heart, acknowledging that sometimes we follow paths that don't lead us to where we truly want to go. Society often gives us mixed messages about what success looks like, encouraging us to chase after wealth, status, or approval. But when we reach these goals, we might find ourselves feeling empty, wondering if we've been climbing the wrong ladder all along.

It's a sobering thought, to consider that we may have been pursuing things that don't truly satisfy. But there's a quiet strength in recognizing this. Rather than feeling defeated, this awareness can be a turning point, a chance to reevaluate our priorities and make choices that align with who we are at our core. It's never too late to change direction, to seek out a path that brings genuine fulfillment. This may mean letting go of certain ambitions or redefining our idea of success, but in doing so, we open the door to a life that is grounded in authenticity and purpose.

As the song moves toward its climax, the lyrics ponder mortality with the lines, "What if I died? What did I give?" These words confront us with a question that each of us must face at some point—what legacy will we leave behind? It's easy to live as though our time here is unlimited, but the reality is that each day is a gift. When we consider the impact we want to have, it shifts our perspective from self-centered goals to a desire to make a positive difference in the lives of others.

Living with this awareness doesn't mean we have to achieve grand gestures or monumental accomplishments. Often, it's in the small acts of kindness, in the quiet moments of support and encouragement, that we leave the most profound impact. Perhaps it's a comforting word to a friend in need, a listening ear to someone who feels unheard, or a simple act of generosity that brightens another person's day. These actions, though seemingly small, are the threads that weave together a life of meaning.

When Creed sings, "I hope it was an answer so you might live," the song takes on a selfless tone—a desire to give something of lasting value. This line reflects the heart of sacrificial love, a willingness to pour out our lives for the benefit of others. It's a call to live in a way that considers not only our own happiness but also the well-being of those around us. This kind of love requires humility and a recognition that our lives are interconnected. When we choose to invest in others, we create a ripple effect that extends far beyond our immediate circle.

Each of us has the power to leave a legacy of love, to live in a way that offers hope and encouragement to others. This might mean mentoring a young person, volunteering in our community, or simply being present with our loved ones. We don't have to have all the answers or be perfect—our willingness to show up, to care, and to offer whatever we can is enough. Through these small but meaningful actions, we become part of something greater, a force for good in a world that desperately needs it.

As the song circles back to "Somebody told me the wrong way," it's no longer a statement of defeat but a gentle acknowledgment that life is a journey of constant learning. We may have taken wrong turns, but those detours don't have to define us. Instead, they become part of the story, lessons that shape who we are and help us grow. By embracing our imperfections, by accepting that we are all learning as we go, we find a sense of peace in the journey.

Life's path is rarely straightforward, and each of us will encounter moments of doubt and uncertainty. But in these times, we can choose to trust that our mistakes are not wasted. They are opportunities to learn, to draw closer to others, and to gain a deeper understanding of ourselves. This perspective allows us to move forward with grace, knowing that our worth isn't defined by our successes or failures but by the love and kindness we bring into the world.

In the end, *"Wrong Way"* serves as both a reminder and an encouragement. It speaks to the universal desire to live a life of purpose, to make a difference, and to find redemption in our journey. The questions remain, the uncertainties linger, but there is a quiet resolve—a commitment to live in a way that brings light and hope to others.

CHAPTER 17
"Faceless Man"

I n "Faceless Man," Creed delves into the profound and often unsettling journey of self-confrontation, the grappling with one's
inner darkness, and the human yearning for redemption. This song
operates on multiple levels, integrating introspective lyrics, atmos-
pheric instrumentation, and layered spiritual motifs, all of which invite the listener into a journey that is as much about the unseen,
internal struggles as it is about the external battles we face. Through
its lyrics, melody, and musical composition, "Faceless Man" paints a
portrait of the soul's wrestle with shadows, the search for truth, and
the hope of finding an unshakeable foundation upon which to stand.

The journey begins by the river, an ancient symbol of cleansing,
renewal, and reflection. The opening line—*"I spent a day by the river"*—is both literal and symbolic, setting the stage for a moment of
solitude in nature. Rivers are timeless, ever-flowing, yet still in some
places, mirroring the dual nature of life as both relentless and yielding.
The protagonist's decision to spend time in quiet, in communion
with nature, reveals a desire to reconnect with what is authentic and
unchanging. In our noisy world, silence is rare and often uncomfortable, yet here, it becomes a sanctuary—a reminder that there is more
to life than the transient demands and pressures of existence.

The river's stillness is matched by *"the wind [that] stood still,"* giving
the scene an almost supernatural calm. It suggests a suspension of

time, a sacred pause in which the protagonist is stripped of distractions, forced to confront himself without the usual comforts or pretenses. The lyric *"It's funny how silence speaks sometimes when you're
alone"* reveals a fundamental truth about human nature: in silence,
we come face-to-face with the thoughts and emotions we often avoid.
This moment of quiet, then, is not an escape but a confrontation. The
world may be still, but within, the internal battle is awakening.

The song's next lines bring in the central figure of "the faceless
man." Here, Creed uses a powerful image: the faceless man as the
embodiment of all that is dark, elusive, and unknown within the
protagonist. This "faceless man" is a specter, an undefined and potentially destructive force that lacks identity, yet holds sway over his mind
and spirit. By standing against this faceless adversary, the protagonist
signals a willingness to confront the parts of himself he fears or fails
to understand. This battle is both existential and deeply personal,
reflecting a struggle common to humanity—the confrontation with
the void within us, the aspects of our character that we can neither
define nor fully comprehend.

As the song progresses, the listener is introduced to a figure on
the water, a "face on the water" who appears *"humble but willing to
fight."* This figure is a direct counter to the faceless man: he has a face,
an identity, and a purpose. The face on the water can be understood
as an embodiment of the divine or, at the very least, a higher moral
force that stands for truth, righteousness, and inner peace. The de-
scriptions—*"his yoke is easy and his burden is light"*—are clear references to biblical language, alluding to Christ's words in the Gospel of
Matthew, where he invites the weary to find rest in Him. This figure is
humble, yet resolute, embodying a paradox of strength and gentleness,
inviting the protagonist into a state of spiritual submission and trust.

The face on the water serves as a mentor, a guide who "looks [the protagonist] right in the eyes, direct and concise, to remind [him] to always do what's right." This moment is transformative; the protagonist is reminded of a path of integrity, one where courage and moral clarity lead him. There's a resonance here that implies the face on the water sees into the depths of the protagonist's soul, understanding his struggles and yet offering a compassionate challenge to rise above them. In looking into this face, the protagonist glimpses a part of himself he longs to realize: strength coupled with humility, purpose rooted in love.

Musically, Creed intensifies this reflection through their instrumentation, which carries a raw, almost primal quality. The guitar riffs are heavy yet introspective, evoking both power and vulnerability. The chord progressions shift between minor and major keys, mirroring the internal tug-of-war between despair and hope. The soundscape is layered, creating a sense of vastness that pulls the listener into a place of reverence and introspection. It's as if the music itself is echoing the protagonist's journey—a powerful yet restrained force guiding him toward self-discovery.

One of the song's most poignant moments comes when the protagonist confronts the darkness within himself, articulated through the line: *"If the face inside can't see the light, I know / I'll have to walk alone."* Here, the "face inside" seems to refer to his own soul, the core of his identity, which, despite his desire for transformation, still harbors shadows. The threat of "walking alone" to the "other side" speaks to a fear of spiritual isolation, the terror of an existence where the light of purpose and connection is out of reach. This realization that he may have to face his battles in solitude is a sobering one, yet it's an essential step in his journey toward authenticity. To stand in the light, he must first confront his own darkness, acknowledging it without letting it consume him.

The closing verses offer a powerful resolution: *"Next time I see this face, I'll say I choose to live for always / So, won't you come inside and never go away?"* These lines capture the essence of a conversion moment, a surrender not to the faceless darkness but to the transformative light of the face on the water. The protagonist's choice "to live for always" represents a decision to embrace an eternal perspective, a life rooted in something greater than himself. He is inviting this presence to take up residence within him, to become a permanent part of his being. This invitation, this surrender, reflects a deep yearning for redemption and lasting peace.

In these lines, Creed brings the journey full circle. The protagonist has moved from confrontation to transformation, from standing alone by the river to inviting the face on the water into his life permanently. This is a moment of union, where the protagonist's desire for truth, strength, and purpose is fulfilled not through his own efforts but by welcoming an external, divine force to reside within him. It's a moment of profound humility, a recognition that true strength lies in dependence, not self-reliance.

Through this lyrical and musical exploration, Creed captures the complexity of the human soul's journey toward wholeness. The faceless man may represent our fears, our failures, and our regrets—those parts of ourselves that threaten to erode our identity. In contrast, the face on the water symbolizes the divine, the embodiment of love, truth, and purpose that we long to embrace. The song's heavy riffs, haunting melodies, and introspective lyrics work in harmony to create a soundscape that is both grounded and ethereal, reflecting the earthly and the spiritual elements of this journey.

At its core, "Faceless Man" is a modern psalm, a cry from the depths of a soul yearning for redemption, meaning, and peace. It speaks to the universal struggle of grappling with one's inner shadows while reaching for the light of truth. This is a song of courage—a reminder that while we may stand alone at times, facing our faceless fears, there is a path to freedom and transformation. Through surrender, humility, and an invitation to the divine, we find the strength to transcend our limitations, to stand against the darkness, and to embrace the light that offers us hope and healing.

In this way, Creed invites us not only to listen but to journey alongside the protagonist, to confront our own faceless shadows, and to find, in the quiet of introspection, the face on the water—a reminder that we are not alone in our struggles and that there is a purpose worth pursuing, a life worth living, and a light worth following. The song is a call to choose life, to stand firm in the face of fear, and to allow the presence of the divine to guide us to a place of enduring peace and unwavering strength.

Application

To apply the words of "Faceless Man" in our lives, start by embracing the practice of reflection and solitude, much like the protagonist standing by the river. Setting aside time to step away from the noise and distractions of everyday life can serve as a powerful gateway to real, honest introspection. In the stillness, we come face-to-face with our inner struggles, the unresolved fears or regrets that we may be carrying. This act of quiet confrontation is transformative; it can reveal areas where we have allowed shame or guilt to take root, creating obstacles to our growth.

Engaging in this self-confrontation can feel unsettling, but it is essential to move forward. Facing these shadows head-on—without distraction or avoidance—allows us to strip away illusions and see ourselves clearly. Often, we may hesitate to confront these parts of ourselves, fearing what we might find. Yet, this moment of vulnerability, if embraced fully, becomes a starting point for growth. It allows us to acknowledge our shortcomings without self-condemnation, leading us toward a path of healing and renewal.

Once we have taken that time for honest introspection, it's crucial to define who or what our "faceless man" is—those fears, anxieties, or unresolved hurts that often linger in our minds without clear identity. Acknowledging them is the first step in disempowering them. The "faceless man" gains strength from our inability to see him clearly, feeding off our doubts and insecurities. But as we begin to recognize these areas, they start to lose their grip on us. Simply by giving voice to these challenges, we reclaim a measure of control. Naming our fears, confessing our regrets, and identifying our weaknesses can free us from their power, allowing us to move beyond them.

At the same time, we need to actively look for the "face on the water"—the presence of wisdom, truth, and guidance that can provide clarity and strength. For many, this may be a connection to the divine or a moral compass that embodies strength coupled with humility, a model of integrity. Holding ourselves accountable to this higher standard, this "face on the water" can remind us to act with courage, honesty, and conviction even when the path forward is unclear.

Aligning ourselves with this "face on the water" means making deliberate choices to embrace humility, recognize our dependence on something greater than ourselves, and accept that real transformation requires surrender. This surrender is not a sign of weakness but a courageous act of entrusting our lives to a purpose beyond our understanding. When faced with moments of decision, seeking the guidance of this "face" can lead us to a path marked by moral clarity and inner peace, despite the uncertainties we may face.

Practically, this can look like adopting specific habits of integrity in our day-to-day lives. Making decisions based on what is right and true—regardless of the personal cost or inconvenience—deepens our character and strengthens our ability to face adversity. Each small, intentional act of kindness, honesty, and resilience builds a foundation that fortifies us against the storms of life. When we commit to these values, we are less likely to be swayed by fleeting fears or shallow temptations. Instead, we anchor ourselves in something lasting, creating a steady base from which to navigate the complexities of life.

The line, "If the face inside can't see the light, I know / I'll have to walk alone," speaks to a profound reality many of us must confront: at times, we will have to stand alone, guided solely by our inner conviction. This might mean making difficult decisions that others do not understand or support. In these moments, we need to draw strength from the principles and values we have internalized, trusting that they will sustain us even when external encouragement is lacking. Choosing to walk in alignment with truth, even in solitude, empowers us to transcend the fears that would otherwise hold us back. The light within becomes our compass, guiding us toward a life that reflects a commitment to something greater than ourselves.

Finally, embracing the closing lines, where the protagonist resolves to "choose to live for always," can be seen as a call to live with an eternal perspective. Making this choice is not about ignoring life's challenges or avoiding struggles; it's about grounding ourselves in the knowledge that our lives have a purpose that reaches beyond the here and now. This perspective encourages us to live with intentionality, recognizing that every thought, every choice, every action shapes our character and impacts those around us.

Inviting the presence of this guiding "face" into our lives—allowing it to "never go away"—is an invitation to constant companionship, wisdom, and strength. In a practical sense, this might look like developing regular practices that remind us of this purpose, such as meditation, prayer, or reading. These practices reinforce the values we aspire to and re-center us when we feel overwhelmed or distracted.

Living with this perspective also means holding fast to the hope of redemption and transformation. No matter how many times we stumble or face setbacks, this path invites us to rise, to continue growing, and to seek a life marked by integrity and love. In our darkest moments, when the "faceless man" seems strongest, this light within can remind us that we are not defined by our failures but by our ability to rise, seek forgiveness, and choose growth over despair.

In our relationships, applying these principles means treating others with the same humility, respect, and compassion we desire for ourselves. By choosing to approach others with empathy, we acknowledge that they too are wrestling with their own "faceless men," and we can offer understanding rather than judgment. This approach fosters a spirit of community, encouraging others to embrace their own journeys toward wholeness.

Creed's song thus becomes more than a melody; it's a call to action. It urges us to take ownership of our lives, to confront the darkness within, to seek the presence of a guiding "face," and to choose a path of integrity and purpose. This journey may be fraught with challenges, yet each step we take brings us closer to a life that reflects not just survival but transformation.

CHAPTER 18
"Never Die"

To understand Creed's "Never Die" is to step into a deeply reflective journey—a confrontation with age, innocence, and the fight to keep a part of ourselves untouched by time. The song, both in lyrics and instrumental tone, is a call to rediscover the purity of youth and to preserve a spirit that defies the wear of years. It's an invitation to look within, to hold onto what's childlike, even as life layers on experiences that might obscure it. This song speaks to something both universal and profoundly personal.

Let's look at the opening lines: "Hands on a window pane / Watching some children laugh and play." This imagery is potent, a kind of portal. A pane of glass separates the observer—presumably an adult—from the world of children. It's as though the speaker is a ghost or an outsider, looking in at something familiar yet inaccessible. Creed's use of a physical barrier here mirrors the psychological one. Age, responsibilities, the losses that come with living—all create a pane, separating the adult self from that childhood world. The image of hands on glass evokes a longing, a desire to reach out and cross that threshold, as if by touching the window, the speaker might breach the distance between who they are now and who they were then.

Musically, Creed underscores this tension with a deep, introspective guitar that resonates alongside Stapp's yearning vocals. There's a mix of melancholy and a subtle ferocity, a tension that captures the essence of desire meeting resistance. Creed has always been known for blending rock with reflective intensity, and here, the instrumental undertones evoke a struggle—softened edges that border on sorrow, yet are hardened by a refusal to surrender.

The line "Inspired to question / What makes us grown-ups anyway?" cuts to the core of the song's theme. This question isn't just rhetorical; it's a challenge. What are the markers of adulthood? Is it the weight of responsibility, the struggle, the scars we bear from the trials of life? Or is it the quiet resignation to leave behind wonder, imagination, and play? The song presses us to consider that adulthood might be defined not so much by chronological years, but by the ways we surrender to cynicism, practicality, and even hopelessness.

In the words, "Let's search for the moment / When youth betrayed itself to age," the betrayal here is subtle but profound. Creed suggests that aging isn't just a physical process; it's something that happens within, in the moments when the heart stops allowing space for the child within. This line asks the listener to search backward, to find where they let go of their wonder and play. Was it a moment of hurt, when innocence felt inadequate to handle the pain? Or perhaps a moment of disappointment when dreams felt naive and practicality crept in as a necessary shield? This internal search becomes a journey of self-discovery—a quest to trace the cracks and try to find the point where the foundation shifted.

The chorus, repeating the words "So let the children play / Inside your heart always," shifts the tone slightly. There is a tenderness here, a plea. The idea of letting the children play is simple but layered. It is an invitation to allow playfulness, wonder, and curiosity to continue living within. This line speaks to a universal truth: within each person resides the echoes of every stage of life. The children here are both literal and metaphorical—the past selves we carry with us and the youthful spirit that longs for release. It's as if the song is saying that to truly live, we must remain open to the presence of all these selves.

"Death you will defy / 'Cause your youth will never die." This line embodies the song's central message: defiance against not just physical death, but spiritual erosion. In the song's framework, "death" isn't just about mortality; it's also the quiet dying that happens each time we surrender our childlike awe. Each decision to abandon dreams or let go of simple pleasures marks a kind of death. Creed draws on the idea that youth is an undying force, capable of defying age and mortality if only we allow it to play freely within us.

As the song progresses, it turns its attention to the process of "searching for substance." Here, Creed brings attention to the fact that many spend their lives searching for something meaningful, often losing sight of that meaning in the haze of struggle. The "clouded by struggle's haze" line reflects the burdens we accumulate over time—the responsibilities, expectations, and losses that obscure clarity and simplicity. In adulthood, many are so entrenched in responsibilities that they lose sight of the joy in simplicity, the purity of laughter, and the meaning found in moments of pure experience.

The line "Remember the meaning / Of playing out in the rain" carries a sense of nostalgia but also holds a symbolic significance. Rain often signifies renewal, a washing away of the old, allowing for new growth. Playing in the rain, therefore, isn't just an act of youthful indulgence; it's a surrender to the forces of life, a willingness to be vulnerable and open to the unknown. It's a return to the days when getting wet wasn't an inconvenience but an adventure. This line suggests that to revive youth within, one must remember and reconnect with the willingness to be free, to embrace life in its unfiltered form.

In "We swim in the fountain / Of youth's timeless maze," the song ties itself to a longstanding mythos—the fountain of youth. But

Creed's perspective here is nuanced. This fountain isn't a literal place; it's a maze, suggesting that the pursuit of timeless youth isn't straight-forward. It's winding and complex, filled with dead ends and challenges. This maze reflects the inner journey, the search within oneself for a place where wonder and resilience intersect. The invitation to drink from this fountain implies that youth, vitality, and spirit are choices, available to those willing to embark on this maze-like journey of rediscovery.

The refrain "Never die" echoes repeatedly, both as a declaration and a mantra. Musically, the intensity crescendos here, with the instruments layering a defiant energy. The repetitive nature of the refrain hammers in the message: this youthful spirit is immortal, unyielding. It's a powerful assertion against not only aging but also the surrender of the soul. The use of a rock anthem sound here is essential—it gives weight and volume to the idea that this inner youth is something to fight for, something worthy of being proclaimed from the depths.

As the song continues, it intensifies with the line, "I won't let go of that youthful soul / Despite body and mind, my youth will never die." This is a personal vow, a refusal to give in. Here, Creed takes a stand, suggesting that youth isn't something you passively retain; it's something you fiercely defend. This line speaks to the battles one fights against time, cynicism, and despair. It's a reminder that one's spirit can remain untarnished, even if the body and mind undergo wear. This refusal to let go is not just an act of rebellion but a profound declaration of self-preservation. It implies that within each person lies a core that can resist the harshest realities of life.

The song's final repetition of the chorus takes on a new layer of meaning. It's as if the song itself is guiding the listener through a rite of passage, inviting them to make the same vow—to let the children play, to defy death by nurturing the child within. The tone is both triumphant and contemplative, as though each repetition of "Never die" is a heartbeat, keeping the spirit of youth alive.

In many ways, "Never Die" is a meditation on self-preservation. Creed is asking, almost begging, that we hold onto the aspects of ourselves that first made life beautiful. This song isn't merely nostalgic; it's a directive. It asks the listener to adopt an active stance against time, a refusal to surrender to the grayness that can so easily creep into life. The song reminds us that age need not diminish the soul, and that by nurturing the inner child, we preserve not only our youth but also our essence.

In sum, "Never Die" challenges us to break through the glass of self-imposed barriers, to confront the ways we've let struggle and age define us, and to drink deeply from the fountain of timeless youth. Creed uses powerful rock instrumentation, vivid lyrics, and a thematic depth that encourages us to consider how we can live fully, with hearts unburdened by age's weight. This song becomes not just a statement but a way of being—a call to resist, to remember, and to embrace life with the same fervor we did as children.

Application

To apply the words of *Never Die* to your life is to embark on a journey inward, peeling back the layers of age and experience to find the core of who you are—the part that has always been there, waiting for you to look back and recognize it. In Creed's words, there is an invitation to look beyond the years, responsibilities, and struggles that may have clouded that pure part of yourself. It's an invitation to reconnect with a resilient spirit that defies the gradual erosion of innocence and joy.

Imagine standing before that windowpane, with children laughing and playing on the other side. As you observe, let yourself feel the separation, the invisible barrier that has slowly, perhaps imperceptibly, come between you and that childlike part of yourself. Start by acknowledging that barrier—the busyness, the "shoulds" and "have-tos" that life imposes, the moments where you traded wonder for worry or dreams for duty. Recognize that this separation doesn't mean you've lost the child within; rather, it's a veil of experiences that have merely obscured it. Take a moment here to simply let your heart rest, to hold your hands on that pane and acknowledge the longing to cross back over.

The words of the song, "Inspired to question / What makes us grown-ups anyway?" challenge you to rethink the life you've built. It's a moment to reevaluate what markers have come to define your adulthood. How much of your present life was built on values you once held as sacred? And how much is a reflection of things you took on simply because they were expected? As you wrestle with this, ask yourself, where did your youthful dreams and innocent spirit get crowded out? Which moments marked the "growing up" that left parts of your heart behind? This process of tracing back is a powerful tool for introspection. It's an invitation to face those moments, and to see them as opportunities to reclaim, rather than merely mourn, parts of yourself that you thought were lost.

Consider letting "the children play / Inside your heart always." This line calls for intentionality—making room within yourself for spontaneity, curiosity, and play. Find moments where you can allow your heart to be light. Perhaps it's as simple as laughing freely with a friend or taking a walk where you aren't focused on productivity but on just being. Let this line shape small choices in your day: pause in moments of beauty, let your mind wander to creative dreams, or sit with the questions that once filled you with wonder. It's about creating space in your heart, even amid responsibilities, for that playful spirit to thrive. Allowing "the children" to play within isn't about abandoning maturity; it's about weaving wonder into the fabric of your daily life.

When the song declares, "Death you will defy / 'Cause your youth will never die," there is a powerful invitation here. Take this line to heart. It isn't about clinging to physical youth but about cultivating a spirit that isn't diminished by the hardships of life. Think of areas where you may have let go of joy or curiosity. Notice where doubt or cynicism has crept in, and recognize that this isn't a loss you're required to accept. Decide here and now to defy the subtle "death" of wonder that comes with settling for a life devoid of joy. This isn't a call to deny reality but to find the resilience that says, "I can still hope, still dream, still believe in the beauty of this world." This inner vow is one you can renew each day—an affirmation to live from a place of openness and awe.

The line "clouded by struggle's haze" is a call to acknowledge the burdens that obscure joy. Each of us faces struggles that can feel overwhelming. But in this line, there's an invitation to look through the haze, to find glimpses of light even in dark times. Consider the struggles you carry, and challenge yourself to search for moments of meaning within them. When life feels heavy, find ways to honor the strength it takes to keep moving. Remember that you're not required to be consumed by your struggles; you're allowed to seek moments of reprieve, to nurture your spirit with small acts of kindness, joy, and creativity. This doesn't erase the haze but gives you the strength to navigate through it.

"Remember the meaning / Of playing out in the rain." This is a call to rediscover joy, even in the midst of the unknown or uncomfortable. To "play in the rain" is to accept life in its raw, unpolished form. Embrace moments that feel imperfect—let yourself laugh at life's small absurdities, find joy in the midst of hardship, and give yourself permission to find beauty even when things aren't as you'd like them to be. Reflect on ways you can incorporate this spirit into your daily routine. It might look like trying something new without fear of failure, or simply finding humor in the middle of a challenging day. In doing so, you practice a kind of resilience that not only endures life's rain but dances in it.

The idea of "swimming in the fountain / Of youth's timeless maze" acknowledges that the journey to reclaiming youthful joy and wonder isn't straightforward. You may feel lost, may come up against obstacles within yourself that make it hard to connect with this inner youth. Accept that this process is a maze—a journey that requires patience, perseverance, and a willingness to try again even when you hit a dead end. Each time you encounter a memory or an aspect of yourself that feels difficult, see it as part of the maze. You don't need to rush or force your way through. Instead, trust that with each step, you're moving closer to that timeless place within yourself where youth and joy reside. Remember, this is not a race but a journey of rediscovery. Allow yourself the grace to get lost sometimes, knowing that in the search, you are continually drawing closer to the heart of who you are.

Finally, let the refrain "Never die" echo within you as a mantra, a vow to keep alive the parts of yourself that make life rich and meaningful. Take this as a commitment to nurture what's best in you—your dreams, your compassion, your curiosity. It's a decision to live fully, without reservation, to let your spirit radiate in a way that resists the erosion of time and hardship. As you carry these words with you, let them become a guide, reminding you to hold fast to the essence of who you are, no matter the years that pass.

In this way, Creed's "Never Die" becomes not only a song but a way of approaching life with openness, resilience, and a deep-seated joy. The song invites you to make a conscious choice each day: to keep alive the spirit within that defies age, to embrace life's wonder, and to live from a place of wholeness, with a heart unburdened by time's passage. As you go forward, hold onto this vow to live fully, to nurture the child within, and to carry the light of youth in every step you take.

CHAPTER 19
"With Arms Wide Open"

The song *With Arms Wide Open* by Creed, penned by Scott Stapp, unfolds as a deeply personal, transformative experience—a man's journey into fatherhood, wrapped in vulnerability, awe, and hope. Here, we see Stapp, both as an artist and a soon-to-be father, grappling with the enormity of this new chapter. The layers of the song are both spiritual and grounded, and each element—lyric, tone, and musical structure—reveals the depth of transformation and self-discovery that fatherhood brings.

From the very first line, *"Well, I just heard the news today"*, Stapp sets a scene of realization. The phrasing is simple, almost conversational, as if the narrator is still absorbing the gravity of the moment. The words don't rush; they hang in the air with weight, reflective of a man on the edge of a life-changing discovery. He's received the news that will alter his path forever: he is going to be a father. There's an element of shock mingled with reverence—a kind of sacred pause that invites introspection.

The line, *"I closed my eyes, begin to pray / Then tears of joy stream down my face"*, reveals a raw, almost primal response to this revelation. In these words, Stapp captures the duality of this experience—the initial urge to seek guidance or strength through prayer, and then the emotional release as he is overcome by the beauty and enormity of the situation. The simplicity of his language mirrors the universality of the moment. Prayer, here, is a posture of humility, surrender, and gratitude—a recognition that something far greater than himself has entered his life.

The next verse introduces a note of trepidation: *"Well, I don't know if I'm ready / To be the man I have to be."* There's a profound vulnerability here. He questions his own worthiness, his readiness to guide and nurture another life. This line resonates with an almost existential doubt, a fear that he may not live up to the image of a father he hopes to embody. Stapp acknowledges his own imperfections, his own struggles, even perhaps his own past mistakes. This admission is essential; it shows that fatherhood is not a badge of honor easily earned. It's a mantle that demands self-reflection, humility, and a willingness to confront one's own limitations.

There's something poetic, almost cinematic, in this humble acceptance. He doesn't sugarcoat the fears, nor does he shield himself from them. Instead, he faces them with honesty, breathing deeply, grounding himself in the presence of his partner, *"I'll take a breath, I'll take her by my side."* The imagery of "taking her by his side" suggests unity, partnership—a reminder that he's not alone in this journey. It's a shared transformation, one that binds them in a sacred experience of bringing life into the world.

Musically, *With Arms Wide Open* reflects the emotional progression of the lyrics. The intro is quiet and contemplative, with soft guitar strums that mimic the reflective tone of a man who is sitting with his thoughts, digesting life-altering news. The initial, gentle acoustic guitar creates a sense of intimacy, almost like a heartbeat, steady and grounding.

As the song progresses, the music swells, becoming more powerful, mirroring the rising emotions within the narrator. This progression from a quiet contemplation to a grander, fuller sound signifies the journey from shock and awe to a sense of resolved purpose. The power chords and resonant drumbeats that build in the chorus give the song a sense of reverence, almost like a hymn or anthem—fitting for a moment as sacred as becoming a father.

In musical terms, the structure follows a crescendo of discovery and acceptance. Each verse brings a layer of revelation, matched by the intensifying music. It's as if each chord, each strum, and each beat are all part of a larger conversation, mirroring the lyrics in a kind of sonic symbiosis. The crescendo in the chorus, *"With arms wide open under the sunlight / Welcome to this place, I'll show you everything"*, is an invitation. There's an overwhelming sense of openness, of laying down barriers and welcoming this new life wholeheartedly.

The chorus, *"With arms wide open under the sunlight"*, captures the essence of the song. "Under the sunlight" suggests a divine or universal presence, as if he's standing under a watchful eye, ready to embrace this role with sincerity. Sunlight often symbolizes clarity, warmth, and truth. Here, it's as though Stapp is standing before life itself, stripped of any pretense, basking in the raw beauty of what's to come. The phrase *"With arms wide open"* embodies an attitude of acceptance, vulnerability, and eagerness. There's an almost Christ-like imagery here, as if Stapp is echoing a posture of self-giving love.

As he repeats the line *"With arms wide open"*, it becomes more than just words. It's a mantra, a promise, a commitment to his unborn child. This repetition is powerful—it symbolizes the resolve growing within him, each repetition fortifying his commitment to fatherhood. He's declaring to his child that he's here, ready to love and nurture, despite his fears.

Toward the end, the tone shifts slightly as he sings, *"If I had just one wish, only one demand / I hope he's not like me, I hope he understands."* This line is haunting in its honesty. Stapp wishes for his son to be free from his own flaws and mistakes—a poignant hope for any parent. It suggests a desire for redemption, not just for himself, but for his lineage. There's a subtle sense of repentance, as if he's acknowledging the battles he's fought within himself and wishing to spare his son from similar struggles.

"I hope he understands that he can take this life and hold it by the hand." Here, Stapp conveys a beautiful piece of fatherly wisdom. He wishes for his son to approach life with purpose, intention, and strength—to greet the world with curiosity and courage. "Hold it by the hand" evokes tenderness, an image of leading and guiding, yet also empowering his child to take ownership of his life. It's a reminder that life, with all its uncertainties, is still a gift, something to be embraced and cherished.

With Arms Wide Open is more than a song about fatherhood; it's a narrative of transformation, a journey that invites the listener to witness a man's encounter with humility, fear, and ultimately, love. Through the lyrics, Stapp bares his soul, exposing his doubts and his hope for a better future for his son. Musically, the song complements this journey, building from quiet contemplation to a resonant declaration, mirroring the emotional highs and lows of the moment.

The song's beauty lies in its honesty. It doesn't present fatherhood as an easy path but as a transformative one, requiring courage and a willingness to confront one's inner struggles. Stapp invites us to consider what it means to love unconditionally, to stand vulnerable before life, and to greet the unknown with open arms. Through this journey, he discovers the strength that lies in openness—the kind of strength that has nothing to prove, but everything to give.

In *With Arms Wide Open*, we see a man willing to set aside his fears, to let go of past mistakes, and to embrace the present with hope. In this vulnerable posture, he finds transformation—not only for himself but for the legacy he wishes to impart. He stands, open-hearted, a father waiting to guide his son with love, understanding, and a vision for a life lived fully. In this openness, he finds peace, redemption, and the courage to become the father he hopes to be.

Application

Life holds moments when we're called to something greater than ourselves, inviting us to open our hearts in profound surrender, to see beyond our own limitations, and to step forward with courage. With Arms Wide Open by Creed, through the lens of the Bible, can illuminate the call to glorify God in our daily lives, embracing this purpose with vulnerability and trust.

In fatherhood, as in all facets of life, we're reminded of our primary purpose: to glorify God and to enjoy Him forever. This journey of faith and growth often begins when we humble ourselves before Him, recognizing our need for His wisdom and strength. Just as Scott Stapp's song describes a man on the edge of a profound transformation, we too stand at the edge of life's transitions, realizing that our purpose and identity are found in Christ alone.

Scripture guides us, grounding us in the truth that we were made to reflect God's glory. As Paul says in 1 Corinthians 10:31, "So, whether you eat or drink, or whatever you do, do all to the glory of God." This verse speaks to all moments, both monumental and mundane. In fatherhood, or any new role, this call remains: we are to honor God in every act, reflecting His character in our words, our actions, and our attitudes. It means leaning on Him for the courage to guide our families, to teach them His ways, and to love them with the grace we've first received from Him.

The vulnerability expressed in With Arms Wide Open, where the father-to-be confesses his uncertainty—"Well, I don't know if I'm ready / To be the man I have to be"—echoes the same sentiment expressed in countless stories of God's people. Moses, when called to lead the Israelites, admitted his doubts, asking, "Who am I that I should go to Pharaoh and bring the Israelites out of Egypt?" (Exodus 3:11). Yet, God reassures him, saying, "I will be with you" (Exodus 3:12). In our own lives, the reminder is the same: God is with us, equipping us with His Spirit to fulfill His calling, whether as parents, spouses, friends, or disciples.

In moments of self-doubt, our focus must shift to God's faithfulness. Ephesians 2:10 reminds us, "For we are his workmanship, created in Christ Jesus for good works, which God prepared beforehand, that we should walk in them." Our purpose in each new chapter of life, even one as humbling as parenthood, is part of God's larger plan for us to walk in His ways, to reflect His love and righteousness. The assurance is that He's prepared us for these moments, shaping our hearts and molding us through His Word.

The song also speaks to a posture of humility and openness—"With arms wide open under the sunlight." In this posture, there's an invitation to embrace God's grace, to stand open before Him, ready to receive His guidance. As Stapp expresses a desire to be there fully for his child, it reminds us of Jesus' call to follow Him with a heart wide open, free from self-sufficiency, and ready to walk in His light. Jesus says in Matthew 11:28-30, "Come to me, all who labor and are heavy laden, and I will give you rest." In trusting Christ, we find rest, a rest that strengthens us to carry our responsibilities with humility, knowing that He bears our burdens alongside us.

The lyrics "If I had just one wish... I hope he's not like me" reveal a father's desire for his child to live a better life, free from his own mistakes. This desire for redemption is echoed in our relationship with God. He, too, wishes for us to live righteously, turning away from sin, and embracing His truth. In Psalm 51:10, David prays, "Create in me a clean heart, O God, and renew a right spirit within me." As parents or as spiritual mentors, our hope is to see the next generation grow with a heart set on God, not repeating the errors of the past but striving for His righteousness. This yearning aligns with God's promise to renew and transform us when we seek Him.

Each verse in the song mirrors the gradual deepening of realization and acceptance, which parallels our spiritual journey. Just as the song crescendos, our relationship with God is meant to grow, transforming us day by day. Philippians 1:6 reassures us of this transformation: "And I am sure of this, that he who began a good work in you will bring it to completion at the day of Jesus Christ." God works within us to mold our character, strengthening our faith, and enabling us to walk in His light, even through the challenges and uncertainties we face.

Finally, the act of welcoming a child into the world with open arms serves as a reminder of God's own embrace. Just as the father in the song vows to guide his child, God assures us of His presence and guidance. In Isaiah 41:10, He promises, "Fear not, for I am with you; be not dismayed, for I am your God; I will strengthen you, I will help you, I will uphold you with my righteous right hand." Our lives should reflect this same trust and surrender, knowing that God holds us close, teaching us, leading us, and equipping us for every good work.

When we hold our arms wide open, it's not just an expression of love or acceptance; it's a surrender to God's will. To live fully, with the purpose of glorifying God, we must remain open to His leading, trusting Him with our fears, doubts, and uncertainties. Life's journey requires this openness—an openness to His grace, an openness to grow and be transformed, and an openness to give all of ourselves in the service of His Kingdom.

CHAPTER 20
"Higher"

The opening lyrics of Creed's *Higher* introduce us to an intimate, almost vulnerable realm—the world of dreams, where the protagonist, engulfed in tranquility, feels a pull toward an ethereal escape. The setting evokes a calm, a place where the burdens of the waking world dissolve, replaced by the "comfort of this place." Each return to this dream world is not only a reprieve but a necessary refuge, hinting at a life filled with unresolved longings. And while "Higher" opens in an almost somber, introspective tone, this dream world isn't a static escape. Instead, it becomes a bridge between worlds, a place where glimpses of something greater—something otherworldly—begin to take form.

The music itself plays a pivotal role in framing this journey. The melody, climbing gradually yet persistently, mirrors the protagonist's longing to transcend, to escape. Guitar riffs rise and fall in waves, resembling the ebb and flow of our most sacred aspirations. This layering effect—softened, and at times intensified, by Stapp's powerful voice—emulates the rhythm of a soul wrestling with what it means to experience life "higher," beyond mere physical existence. The harmony suggests a yearning for transformation, a breaking free from earthly constraints. It's as though each chord progression pushes the listener up, lifting the protagonist toward the "place where blind men see."

Theologically, "higher" evokes notions of spiritual ascent, of glimpsing eternity. The protagonist's dream—a place of escape and solace—draws from this theme and reflects a universal human desire to move beyond the mundane, to taste freedom from personal and societal limitations. It recalls the age-old tension between the ephemeral and the eternal. The protagonist does not simply want to evade reality; he seeks an encounter with the transcendent. The chorus, echoing with urgency, is almost a plea, as though he is addressing something greater, perhaps divine, asking, "Can you take me higher?" Here, the words become a petition, almost a prayer, to reach a place that will provide clarity—where "blind men see." This metaphor, "a place where blind men see," might signify spiritual enlightenment, an unshackling from ignorance, or the gift of seeing truth and meaning that isn't accessible in the waking world.

The call to be "taken higher" has echoes of ancient Psalms, which speak of ascending to the hills, of searching for something loftier than what life on the ground can provide. The music crescendos at the chorus, reinforcing the idea of longing not only to witness but to exist in this place of sight and insight, to step into a world with "golden streets." Such a place evokes images of paradise, perhaps even heaven itself—a vision of what is ultimately real, pure, and unsullied by human failings. Golden streets are symbols of spiritual richness, of a realm beyond scarcity, envy, and suffering. They signify fulfillment, a reward for those who seek earnestly.

In the verse that follows, we see a shift from yearning to reflection. The protagonist acknowledges the necessity of dreams, admitting that they help him "appreciate those nights and those dreams." He values them not just as temporary escapes, but as glimpses of something authentic, fragments of a life that could be. Yet, he doesn't desire to dwell only in these dreams. Rather, there's an eagerness to unify the dream world with his waking reality: "I'd sacrifice all those nights if I could make the earth and my dreams the same." Here, the journey becomes one of integration, a merging of vision and reality. This is not an abandonment of earthly life but a commitment to transforming it. He realizes that true escape is not merely evasion but a call to something greater—to bridge the gap between what is and what could be.

The dreamer's desire to bring heaven to earth, to live in a world where "love replaces all our hate," is perhaps the most striking transformation in the song. This plea for love over hate—an age-old longing found across spiritual traditions—suggests a profound shift within him. He's no longer content to dream of golden streets or celestial realms; he now desires a world here, in this life, where compassion reigns, where love is the governing force. Such a sentiment is deeply resonant with the human spirit's cry for a world where brokenness gives way to unity, where anger yields to understanding. This transformation, from personal escape to collective hope, marks a journey from self-centered longing to altruistic vision.

Instrumentally, the song's intensity begins to mirror this evolution. The music swells, the vocals become more impassioned, driving home the weight of this transformation. Up "higher," the protagonist senses strength, a realization that he is "alive for the very first time." This is a revelation moment, an awakening. The metaphorical ascent to heights brings clarity and renewal, offering not only refuge but a profound shift in self-perception. He declares, "I'm strong enough to take these dreams and make them mine." This marks a movement from passive dreaming to active pursuit, from a mere longing for something better to a conviction that he possesses the power to realize it.

There's an undercurrent of hope that shines through the lyrics and music alike—a hope that transformation is within reach, that love can indeed replace hate, that what was once elusive in dreams can be seized and lived. The protagonist's final words are not those of a man asking for escape but of someone who has glimpsed his true potential and is resolved to make his dreams reality. The chords reverberate with this newfound resolve, a crescendo that speaks of strength and determination.

In the end, "Higher" isn't simply about leaving behind the sorrows of earth; it's a song about bringing the beauty glimpsed in dreams into the fabric of everyday life. It's about transcending personal limits and realizing that the power to transform our world lies within us. As the music fades, we're left with a sense of empowerment, a reminder that we, too, can take our dreams and make them ours—replacing hate with love, blindness with sight, fear with faith. Through its journey, "Higher" invites each listener not only to yearn for more but to participate in the transformation of their own lives and the world around them.

Application

In a world dominated by the temporal and material, it is natural to feel the urge to escape, to seek solace in moments that lift us beyond the mundane. The opening of "Higher" resonates with this deep human inclination. When we read the protagonist's desire to ascend to a place of "comfort" and peace, we see a yearning not just for a release from earthly burdens, but for a sanctuary where life's cares are momentarily suspended. Yet, as much as it draws him in, this place is not merely a shelter from reality. Instead, it becomes a point of connection—a bridge to something transcendent.

Each of us, too, can find this kind of space within our lives. While the dream world here is presented in musical and lyrical form, it reflects a universal longing for spiritual sanctuary, a quiet place where we can reflect and seek restoration. In practical terms, this might look like setting aside time in our day for personal reflection, prayer, or meditation—moments where we pause to recalibrate, to distance ourselves from life's demands, and to engage in spiritual renewal. Just as the protagonist finds reprieve and direction in his dreams, we are called to find intentional stillness, to listen, and to reconnect with a higher purpose.

However, we are not meant to stay in this space of retreat. Just as the song's protagonist does not dwell only in his dream world but brings back with him a desire for transformation, we, too, are called to return to our daily lives with a renewed perspective. Time set apart for introspection or prayer should lead to a reintegration with life, not an evasion from it. Dreams and visions serve as reminders of the possibilities that lie within us and the changes we can effect in the world. For the believer, these moments become occasions of communion with the divine, glimpses of eternity that help us face temporal concerns with a new resolve.

As the melody rises and builds, echoing the protagonist's desire to reach "a place where blind men see," it captures a deep yearning for enlightenment, for a life of sight and understanding. We, too, are often blind—not in the physical sense, but spiritually. Our eyes are closed to what truly matters, to the ultimate truths that lie beyond materialism and self-interest. In the pursuit of higher truths, we can cultivate discernment, a "sight" that perceives beyond the surface. Scripture often speaks of spiritual blindness as a barrier to knowing God, urging us to pray for wisdom and insight. This spiritual ascent, then, is not just about knowledge, but about seeing the world, and our place within it, with clarity and purpose.

This call for sight also challenges us to confront our own misconceptions, biases, and shortcomings. As we ask to be taken "higher," we must be willing to leave behind the baggage that blinds us: pride, anger, prejudice, and all forms of selfish ambition. True vision requires humility, an openness to be corrected, and a willingness to learn from the One who sees all things. The words, "a place where blind men see," signify the humility required to acknowledge our limitations and the courage to pursue a more excellent way of living. This is not merely about escaping but transforming, refining ourselves in the light of higher truths.

In his reflections, the protagonist also reveals an important desire to bring what he has seen in his dreams into his waking reality. He wants to "make the earth and [his] dreams the same." This is a profound realization, urging us to live with an undivided heart, to ensure that our deepest values are not confined to isolated moments but are evident in every aspect of our lives. Rather than seeing spiritual experiences or ideals as separate from our day-to-day interactions, we are challenged to bring those principles into everything we do. We must not separate our sacred convictions from the life we live in the marketplace, in our families, or in our communities.

This means allowing the love, joy, peace, and patience we experience in moments of reflection or worship to permeate our dealings with others. We strive not only to be transformed personally but to be instruments of transformation, agents of change who embody the principles we cherish. This pursuit of an integrated life is a calling to all who seek a higher way of living. It is not enough to visit "golden streets" in our minds or dreams; we must bring the essence of that paradise into our relationships, our work, and our attitudes toward the world.

The song's evolution from personal longing to a broader vision of love replacing hate is particularly instructive. As the protagonist moves from seeking his own peace to desiring a world where compassion triumphs over division, we witness a journey from self-centeredness to selflessness. This shift is a powerful reminder that any pursuit of higher living must include a concern for others. We are called not only to personal transformation but to act as vessels of love and reconciliation, to be peacemakers in a world marred by conflict and animosity.

Applying this to our lives means making a conscious effort to replace hatred, envy, and anger with love, forgiveness, and understanding. In our workplaces, neighborhoods, and families, we have opportunities to embody this shift. It requires daily intentionality, choosing to respond with grace rather than retaliation, with kindness rather than judgment. Such choices may seem small in isolation, but collectively, they contribute to the greater transformation of the world. To seek to live "higher" is to choose to be an agent of God's love, a conduit of His peace.

As the song builds toward the protagonist's declaration that he feels "alive for the very first time," we recognize the profound truth that transformation brings new life. There is a vibrancy, a spiritual awakening, that occurs when we pursue a higher way. The joy and strength found in living according to our highest values are unparalleled. However, this vitality is not a result of our strength alone. Just as the protagonist declares his new strength to "take these dreams and make them mine," we, too, realize that true strength comes from a power greater than ourselves. We lean not on our own understanding but on divine wisdom and guidance.

This new life is not without challenges, but it is marked by resilience and purpose. The journey upward is steep and often requires sacrifices. Yet, as we yield to the process of transformation, we become stronger, more compassionate, more attuned to the needs of those around us. This ascent is not about reaching an unattainable height on our own, but about allowing ourselves to be lifted, to be shaped by a divine purpose that far surpasses our limited understanding.

The song closes with a sense of empowerment, a resolve to live according to a vision glimpsed in dreams. This, too, is our calling: to live with a firm conviction, to pursue what is noble, true, and loving, and to bring light into dark places. When we commit to this path, we join a lineage of those who have sought to make their lives a reflection of the divine, who have endeavored to bring hope, healing, and love to a world in need.

In the end, the pursuit of "higher" living is not a solitary journey. It is a shared calling, one that unites us in a common purpose, to build a world where love triumphs over hate, where understanding replaces prejudice, and where every individual lives with a sense of worth and dignity. Each step we take toward this vision brings us closer to the ultimate reality we long for—a world redeemed, a life fully aligned with truth, and a soul at peace with God and others. Through the grace extended to us, we are invited to not only dream of this life but to live it, here and now, with courage, faith, and unwavering hope.

CHAPTER 21
"Wash Away Those Years"

The haunting depth of "Wash Away Those Years" emerges from its tone, words, and layers of sonic intensity, tracing a path of transformation through pain—a theme Creed frequently immerses itself in, both lyrically and instrumentally. "Wash Away Those Years" carries a cinematic quality, as if the song itself is a screenplay of grief and redemption, marked by an intimacy that invites listeners to explore their own shadows while keeping their gaze fixed on the light of hope. It is a journey of hardship and the persistent, aching hope for cleansing, for renewal.

The song opens as if someone has stepped into a private, vulnerable moment. "She came calling one early morning," the song begins, setting a time of day often associated with the dawning of clarity, a moment suspended between night and day, dreams and waking. This unnamed woman, draped in symbols of suffering—a "crown of thorns"—brings to mind an image of quiet endurance, a figure bearing a burden with a dignity that speaks of her strength. She enters the scene quietly, but her story reverberates with the weight of sorrow and resilience.

Her "crown of thorns" symbolizes not just her pain, but a particular kind of suffering: the burden of innocence lost, of trust shattered. This thorny crown may draw the listener's mind to images of martyrdom and sacrifice, yet here it takes on a personal, almost sacramental meaning, representing the wounds inflicted on her spirit. The woman whispers her story, suggesting both the difficulty of speaking such pain and the softness needed to share it. "About how she had been wronged," she confides, a phrase that distills complex trauma into a simple expression. Here, the woman's pain is both deeply personal and universal, resonating with anyone who has suffered.

As the song continues, it grows darker and heavier. The words "as she lay lifeless, he stole her innocence" convey not just an event but a devastating stillness—the emotional death that follows profound betrayal. She carries on in the shadow of this violation, enduring a kind of emotional paralysis. The music here swells to reflect this weight, deep, resonant chords underscoring the gravity of her experience. Creed's instrumentation intentionally mirrors her inner state, oscillating between moments of quiet reflection and intense, crashing waves, mimicking the journey of someone wrestling with hidden wounds. The guitars swell in layered progression, almost as if symbolizing the rise of anger and sorrow within, then pulling back, reflecting the tension between outward calm and inner turmoil.

The song brings the listener into the woman's interior world as she attempts to "close her eyes and imagine everything's alright." In this moment, there's a sense of longing for escape, a desire to pretend, even if only briefly, that the wounds of the past are not etched so deeply. Yet the lyrics underscore that such a strategy is ultimately futile. Her tears betray her. No matter how much she tries to "hide" them, they surface, seeking release. The tears are "sent to wash away those years," suggesting that grief—raw and exposed—is a necessary part of healing. The song implies that her tears are not a weakness but a mechanism through which her spirit can finally begin to process and release the hurt she has buried.

Creed introduces a shift in the perspective with the line, "My anger's violent, but still I'm silent when tragedy strikes at home." Here, a second voice steps in—a narrator observing from a distance, yet personally affected. This narrator's anger is "violent," but it remains "silent," encapsulating a common reaction to trauma. There's a recognition here of the internalized rage many feel but do not express, the silent struggle with pain that feels too volatile to unleash.

Yet the song quickly transitions to a message of solidarity: "I know this decadence is shared by millions." It's as if Creed is reaching out to everyone who has felt broken by life, extending a hand to remind them that they're not alone. This line captures a crucial element of the song: it acknowledges the collective weight of human suffering, which so often feels isolating but is, paradoxically, shared. The phrase "decadence shared by millions" speaks to a universal human experience of grappling with pain in a world marked by betrayal, sorrow, and decay. The song becomes an anthem for the wounded, a place where listeners can gather and confront their hidden burdens without shame.

In the repeated refrain, "do not hide your tears, 'cause they were sent to wash away those years," there's a return to the imagery of tears as cleansing agents. This refrain emphasizes that suffering and grief have a purpose, not merely to be endured but to be expressed. There's an almost redemptive quality here, as if the tears—far from being a sign of weakness—are divinely appointed to heal the wounds of the past. They're a release, a pathway through which the soul can find peace and move forward.

From a musical perspective, the song's structure reinforces this theme of release and renewal. The chords swell and recede, building tension before letting it fall, a dynamic pattern that evokes the process of confronting pain, allowing it to wash over, and then finding relief. The use of minor chords underscores the heaviness of the subject matter, while shifts to major chords hint at moments of hope, suggesting that though the journey is dark, there is light at the end.

The bridge of the song offers a reflective pause, almost as if the narrator has taken a step back to consider the journey so far. "We have crossed many oceans," the lyrics say, suggesting the vastness of the trials the characters have endured. The image of crossing oceans implies both struggle and distance, as if their pain has been a journey unto itself, with waves of suffering and temporary islands of respite.

The next line, "we labor in between," captures the ongoing nature of their struggle—healing isn't immediate; it requires persistent effort. Life, with its many "quotients," is an equation they're still trying to solve. They hope to find "the mean," a balance or sense of peace amidst the chaos. The word "mean" here might also refer to meaning—a hope that, in time, they will understand the purpose behind their suffering. Musically, the bridge is quieter, more contemplative, giving the listener space to reflect on the journey.

The final repetition of the refrain intensifies in both sound and emotion, like a wave that has been building and now crests. The repeated line "close your eyes and just imagine everything's alright" sounds less like an invitation to escape and more like a meditation—a reminder that while pain is real, there's also a place for hope. In those last words, "maybe we can wash away those years," the song closes on a note of cautious optimism. The pain may not be gone, but perhaps it can be cleansed, piece by piece, moment by moment.

"Wash Away Those Years" is ultimately a song about the courage to face one's wounds, to confront the past without hiding from it. The tears that the woman sheds aren't merely expressions of pain—they're active agents of change. She's not erasing the past but finding a way to live with it, to allow her scars to become part of her strength.

The musical progression throughout mirrors this transformation. Each crescendo is followed by a moment of quiet, suggesting that healing isn't a single triumphant moment but a process with its own rhythm, its own peaks and valleys. The guitars, at times biting and harsh, give voice to the anger and sorrow that words alone can't express. The drums carry a steady beat, a reminder that life moves forward, even when the soul is burdened.

The song's theological undertones hint at a kind of baptismal cleansing, as if the tears themselves are a sacrament—a visible sign of an invisible grace. They "wash away those years," not by making them disappear but by transforming their meaning, by allowing the person to emerge on the other side of suffering with a deeper sense of self and a renewed capacity for life.

Creed's song does not offer an easy resolution; rather, it presents a path, a journey that each person must walk in their own way. It acknowledges the reality of pain but also the hope that lies within it. For the woman, and for everyone who finds resonance in her story, the journey toward healing is long and winding, marked by moments of despair and hope. But in facing her tears, in allowing herself to feel deeply, she finds a kind of redemption—a washing away of bitterness and shame, leaving behind a spirit that, though wounded, is stronger and more compassionate.

The song, with its rich layers of meaning and musical complexity, offers a space for listeners to confront their own pain and perhaps, like the woman, find a way to carry on, not by erasing the past but by allowing it to become part of their strength.

Application

The song "Wash Away Those Years" is not merely a melody or a set of poetic lyrics but a profound exploration of human suffering, resilience, and the grace found in brokenness. Through its emotional layers, it paints a vivid picture of pain transformed, sorrow met with hope, and the slow, persistent journey of healing that each person must confront. We can find in this song a blueprint for our own lives, especially when we face wounds that seem too deep to ever heal and burdens that seem too heavy to ever lift. There is a way to approach such suffering that can lead us to renewal rather than despair.

The song's imagery begins by inviting us into a private, vulnerable moment, as if we're stepping into a scene already heavy with significance. Early morning, the time of day chosen in the lyrics, is symbolically rich; it's when darkness begins to give way to light, the hour when clarity begins to break through confusion. Just as morning light dispels shadows, so too does an honest confrontation with our pain bring understanding and ultimately peace. The woman who appears in this scene is described as bearing a "crown of thorns," and it's an image that resonates deeply for anyone familiar with suffering. Such a symbol is powerfully evocative, representing not only her individual sorrow but a universal experience of injustice and anguish. The crown is not just a mark of pain but a reminder of dignity in suffering, the idea that even in our most painful moments, there can be meaning, even beauty, in enduring with faith.

Her "crown of thorns" also speaks to a suffering that is undeserved, inflicted upon her rather than sought. It calls to mind moments in our own lives when we've suffered through no fault of our own. This might be a betrayal by someone we trusted, an experience of loss that shattered our world, or the consequences of others' mistakes that deeply wounded us. In this woman's endurance, there's a powerful reflection of the redemptive potential of suffering. While it is tempting to let such experiences harden us or lead us to despair, her quiet endurance suggests another response: to accept the suffering not as something meaningless but as something we can offer up, something we can live through with dignity, knowing that our pain is seen and that, ultimately, it can be used for good.

As the song progresses, her story becomes one of unspeakable violation and profound trauma. The lyrics, "as she lay lifeless, he stole her innocence," are stark and brutal, depicting a moment that robbed her of a precious part of herself. This moment represents the kind of experiences many of us have faced in different ways—a breaking point where something sacred within us was lost or taken away. When faced with such pain, the natural reaction is often to withdraw, to bury it deep and try to carry on as if it never happened. And yet, the lyrics reveal that this approach only prolongs the hurt, keeping it festering beneath the surface.

Her response is one we can all relate to: she tries to "close her eyes and imagine everything's alright." It's a defense mechanism we often use, an attempt to cover our wounds rather than truly heal them. In our culture, we're often encouraged to "move on" quickly from our pain, to gloss over it with platitudes or distractions. But here, the song warns against that. Her tears, described as "sent to wash away those years," serve a different purpose. They're not something to hide but to embrace. Just as water purifies, her tears are a form of cleansing, a way of confronting and releasing her sorrow rather than allowing it to remain buried.

When we face our own wounds, it's essential to allow ourselves this same freedom to grieve. Grieving is often seen as weakness, especially in a culture that idolizes strength and resilience. But true strength lies in the willingness to face our brokenness openly, to allow our sorrow to flow freely rather than repress it. In acknowledging our pain, we find a path toward healing; our tears become a form of release, a necessary step in moving forward.

There's a moment of striking empathy in the lyrics when another voice enters, expressing anger at the injustice faced by others but acknowledging the temptation to remain silent. This silent anger is something many of us can relate to—anger over wrongs we see in the world, whether they affect us personally or those we care about, but a hesitancy to speak out or confront that injustice head-on. There's a lesson here about the importance of voicing our experiences and supporting others in their pain. Remaining silent can sometimes make us complicit, allowing injustices to persist unchallenged. But speaking up, especially about our pain, not only validates our experience but can bring comfort to others facing similar struggles. It is a reminder that our story is part of a larger human story, that our struggles are shared and understood by countless others who walk similar paths.

The line "this decadence is shared by millions" beautifully captures the communal aspect of suffering. We are not alone in our pain, though it often feels that way. There is solidarity in understanding that others, too, carry heavy burdens. When we acknowledge our shared struggles, we can begin to support one another, lifting each other up instead of allowing pain to isolate and divide us. This community of shared experience allows us to confront our burdens with a renewed sense of strength, knowing that we are never alone in our darkest moments.

The repeated refrain, "do not hide your tears, 'cause they were sent to wash away those years," reinforces the idea that grief is not an obstacle to be overcome but a process to be embraced. The phrase suggests an almost divine purpose in tears, as if they were given to us as a way to heal, to restore, to cleanse. This is a radical view in a world that often pressures us to hide our sorrow, to maintain a facade of happiness or composure even when we are breaking inside. The song encourages us to let go of that mask, to be honest with ourselves and with those around us, to recognize that our tears are part of the healing process. There is no shame in grief; rather, there is a deep, enduring beauty in allowing ourselves to be vulnerable, to express the pain we feel so that we can eventually let it go.

Musically, the song mirrors this journey, with moments of intense, crashing sound followed by quieter, reflective interludes. This musical ebb and flow represents the natural rhythm of healing. Just as the music swells and recedes, so too does our own journey of processing pain. There are moments of overwhelming emotion, times when the hurt seems too much to bear, followed by moments of calm where we can breathe and reflect, gradually coming to terms with what we've endured. This dynamic reminds us that healing is not a linear process but one filled with ups and downs, periods of progress, and setbacks. Yet, through it all, there is a steady forward movement, an assurance that even the darkest night eventually gives way to dawn.

The bridge of the song, with its image of "crossing oceans" and "laboring in between," speaks to the long, often arduous nature of healing. It's a process that requires patience and perseverance. There's no shortcut to restoration, no quick fix that will instantly make every-thing right. Instead, healing is something we must work for, a labor of love and faith. The word "labor" is telling; it implies effort, struggle, but also purpose. We don't labor in vain; rather, we labor toward something greater, a peace that only comes through wrestling with our pain.

In our own lives, we can draw strength from this example. When we face challenges that seem insurmountable, it's tempting to give up, to think that the pain will never end. But just as the song's characters continue moving forward despite their hardships, we too can persist. Each step, each tear, each prayer brings us closer to wholeness, even when progress seems slow. And as we labor, we find meaning in our struggles, a sense of purpose that transforms our suffering into something redemptive.

The final repetition of the refrain holds a subtle shift in tone, a note of hope and possibility. When the lyrics say, "close your eyes and just imagine everything's alright," it's not a denial of pain but an encouragement to envision healing, to allow hope to take root in our hearts. It's an invitation to see beyond our current suffering to the restoration that lies ahead. This hope is not blind optimism but a faith that, despite the scars we carry, we can be made whole.

CHAPTER 22
"Inside Us All"

When we step into the world Creed builds in "Inside Us All," there's an immediate sense of solitude and quiet reflection. The first lines set a stage of isolation, where the protagonist finds themselves alone, waiting by a silent phone. There's a restless heaviness in these initial words—a universal ache that feels familiar to anyone who's wrestled with their own shadows. This image of waiting, of looking for validation or connection, feels like a moment of vulnerability. The phone, something typically lifeless, becomes a symbol of connection, reminding the protagonist that they are still here, that their existence is real, despite the oppressive silence around them.

The song's atmosphere—drawn from haunting guitar arpeggios and the open, resonant chords—sets a tone that is introspective and heavy, yet filled with an underlying hope. The pacing of the music, neither rushed nor stagnant, mirrors the tempo of self-reflection. This tempo, paired with the minor key, crafts an air of searching, as if each chord progression is another step into the protagonist's internal landscape.

There's a duality in the lyrics that reflects a struggle between inner peace and inner turmoil, a wrestling with both personal disconnection and the longing for something more profound. When the lyrics shift to "When shadows paint the scenes / Where spotlights used to fall," we are given a glimpse into a life that once held brightness—a life where moments and memories were once in the light, but now feel like shadowed reflections of their former selves. This imagery serves as a metaphor for the loss of meaning or joy that many experience, especially in times of hardship, when the things that once illuminated our path are no longer within reach.

The chorus, with its simple but powerful refrain, "There's a peace inside us all / Let it be your friend," invites us to look inward. It's a reminder that the journey toward peace is not one of adding something external but of uncovering something internal. This line isn't a demand but an invitation, almost whispered, as if this peace were a quiet, gentle presence that's always been there, waiting to be recognized.

In a sense, the song embodies a journey of self-discovery through the layers of suffering and solitude. The chord progressions, steeped in melancholic minor tones, create an emotional weight, but there's a shift as the melody unfolds. When the lyrics encourage, "Let it be your friend," the music subtly lightens, mirroring the notion that embracing this inner peace can lift even the heaviest burdens. The tone feels like the rising of dawn—a gradual illumination from within that doesn't erase the night but gives it purpose.

The phrase "Life can hold you down / When you're not lookin' up" conveys a simple yet profound truth. There's a quiet warning here: if we remain focused only on our struggles, our grief, or our loneliness, life itself can become a weight that feels inescapable. But the invitation to "look up" suggests a shift in perspective—a reminder that sometimes the relief we seek is just beyond the narrow focus of our pain. The instrumentation reinforces this concept; it carries an upward arc, lifting in a way that feels like breaking free, as if the music itself were leading the listener to a higher place.

This song doesn't ignore the scars we carry; instead, it encourages us to "tear down the walls / And show the scars we're covering." Here lies a profound call to authenticity. The walls represent the barriers we build to protect ourselves from further pain, but these same walls also isolate us from others. The invitation to show our scars isn't just about vulnerability—it's about acknowledging our shared humanity. The lyrics subtly remind us that while our experiences might differ, our underlying struggles are often the same. This is a plea for unity in a world that's increasingly divided by appearances and the masks we wear.

The repetition of "There's a peace inside us all" is not simply a refrain but a grounding truth that echoes throughout the song. It's as if the song is beckoning the listener back to this central truth whenever the verses drift into darkness or doubt. This repetition serves as a steady pulse, a reminder that no matter how far we drift from ourselves, that peace remains within, waiting. It becomes a constant, a heartbeat, something we can return to even when we feel most lost.

The song's structure—verse, chorus, verse, and chorus, ending with an extended outro—mirrors the cyclical nature of our own journeys with peace. We often rediscover and lose our inner tranquility in waves, sometimes momentarily forgetting that it's within us, only to be reminded again. The closing lines, with their gentle insistence on "let it be," act as a benediction. It's not a forced peace but an invitation to allow it to dwell within us, to surrender to it as a friend who has always been there.

From a music theory perspective, Creed uses a blend of minor chords and subtle harmonic shifts to evoke a feeling of yearning and release. The key changes in the chorus, where the music reaches its emotional peak, enhance the listener's connection to the lyrics, making each repetition of the word "peace" resonate more deeply. The melody's movement in these moments of tonal shift reflects an ascent, as though peace itself were rising within, becoming a tangible presence.

The interplay between lyrics and music in "Inside Us All" speaks to an inner transformation—an awakening. The protagonist begins in isolation, grappling with shadows and questions about the value of it all, yet the chorus gently reveals a pathway to peace. By turning inward and making peace a friend, the protagonist finds a way to carry on, not through avoidance but through acceptance. This peace is not about the absence of struggle or the resolution of every question. Instead, it's a quiet assurance, a steadfast anchor that helps us to endure.

Through "Inside Us All," Creed taps into the universal search for inner tranquility in a turbulent world. The song is both a mirror and a guide for anyone who has felt weighed down by life's burdens. It encourages a shift from external validation and superficial peace to something much deeper—a peace that exists beyond circumstance, untouched by the changes in the world around us.

Ultimately, the song suggests that peace is not something that can be manufactured or obtained from outside. It is a constant presence within, a quiet strength we can draw upon when we choose to let down our walls and embrace the scars that make us human. Creed's lyrics and music converge to create a message that is both personal and universal, pointing to a path of self-discovery, transformation, and enduring peace that resides, waiting to be uncovered, inside us all.

Application

In times of hardship, when familiar sources of comfort and assurance feel distant, we are often forced into a place of deeper searching. This search compels us to examine ourselves, to peel back the layers we may have long avoided. We look within, seeking something lasting, an anchor that holds when the world around us trembles. Here, the song's refrain, "Let it be your friend," encourages us to uncover peace not by avoiding or escaping our reality but by embracing what lies within.

Scripture often reminds us of this deep, enduring peace. Jesus, in His words to His disciples, gave them an invaluable promise: "Peace I leave with you; my peace I give to you. I do not give to you as the world gives. Do not let your hearts be troubled and do not be afraid" (John 14:27). This peace is unlike any worldly comfort or pleasure, which are fleeting by nature. Christ's peace is grounded in His very character and in His abiding presence. His peace transcends circumstances, whether we are in times of joy or trial. In Him, we find peace that does not waver with the winds of life but endures through them.

The song suggests that peace comes through an openness to what lies within, including our vulnerability. Vulnerability is a difficult reality to embrace, for it requires us to set aside our defenses and confront the parts of ourselves that we often hide from others—and even ourselves. When we confront our fears, our insecurities, and our longings, we take the first step toward genuine transformation. The Psalmist echoes this kind of searching: "Search me, O God, and know my heart; test me and know my anxious thoughts. See if there is any offensive way in me, and lead me in the way everlasting" (Psalm 139:23-24). This prayer is a call for God to reveal even the deepest parts of the heart, for only by confronting these inner realities can we find the healing and peace that come from Him alone.

The song's lyric, "Life can hold you down when you're not lookin' up," points us to the need for a greater perspective in times of adversity. When we focus solely on our challenges, they can indeed weigh us down, leaving us feeling overwhelmed. Yet, when we "look up," we remember the greater truth of God's sovereignty. The writer of Hebrews urges us, "Let us fix our eyes on Jesus, the author and perfecter of our faith" (Hebrews 12:2). Here, we see that fixing our gaze upward, toward God's promises and His purposes, provides the strength to endure, even in the most trying seasons. Looking beyond our immediate struggles reveals that we are part of a larger story, one in which even our sufferings have purpose.

The Bible frequently calls us to lift our eyes from earthly troubles and fix them on heavenly realities. Colossians 3:2 exhorts, "Set your minds on things above, not on earthly things." This shift in perspective reminds us that life's present trials, while painful, are temporary and cannot compare to the eternal glory that awaits us. Our struggles are not meaningless; they are often the means by which God refines us and draws us closer to Him. When we look up, we are reminded of His promises, His faithfulness, and His purposes. This upward gaze transforms our perception of hardship, allowing us to see it not as an end in itself but as a means by which God molds us.

When the song encourages us to "tear down the walls and show the scars we're covering," it calls for a life of authenticity. Many of us are tempted to hide our scars—those experiences of pain, loss, and failure. We fear judgment or rejection, so we build walls to protect ourselves. Yet, these very scars are often the greatest testimonies of God's grace and healing. The Apostle Paul, writing to the Corinthians, did not boast in his strengths but in his weaknesses, saying, "Therefore I will boast all the more gladly about my weaknesses, so that Christ's power may rest on me" (2 Corinthians 12:9). Paul understood that vulnerability, rather than diminishing him, allowed God's strength to shine through him.

Our scars, when shared openly, can become sources of encouragement and connection for others. We are not alone in our struggles, and when we reveal our vulnerabilities, we invite others into genuine community. James 5:16 encourages us to "confess your sins to each other and pray for each other so that you may be healed." There is a healing that takes place in this openness—a freedom that comes from stepping into the light and allowing others to see the journey we have walked. Rather than isolating us, our shared experiences draw us closer, allowing God to work in us and through us as we bear one another's burdens.

The peace the song speaks of is not something we create or manufacture; it is a gift that exists within, often hidden beneath our worries, distractions, and ambitions. Scripture calls this peace the "peace of God, which transcends all understanding," and assures us that it "will guard your hearts and your minds in Christ Jesus" (Philippians 4:7). This peace is not conditional; it does not depend on our circumstances or achievements. Rather, it is rooted in our relationship with Christ, in the trust that He is sovereign and good.

In our fast-paced, noise-filled world, this peace may seem elusive. We are often too distracted to notice it, too focused on the next task or the next goal. Yet Jesus Himself modeled a life of quiet and peace, regularly retreating to solitary places to pray and commune with the Father. He understood the importance of seeking stillness, of quieting the soul to hear God's voice. Psalm 46:10 calls us to "Be still, and know that I am God." In the stillness, we recognize that God is present, and His peace is available to us, even in the midst of life's storms.

Our journey with peace, much like the structure of the song, is often cyclical. There are moments when peace feels tangible, when the presence of God is so near that our troubles seem to fade. Yet, there are also times when peace feels distant, when the weight of life presses heavily upon us. In those moments, we may feel as though peace is slipping away, but Scripture assures us that God's peace is constant. Isaiah 26:3 promises, "You will keep in perfect peace those whose minds are steadfast, because they trust in you." Peace is not absent; it is waiting, constant, like a river that flows quietly beneath the surface.

The simple call to "let it be" in the song's conclusion speaks to a posture of surrender. True peace is found not in our ability to control every aspect of life but in releasing our burdens to God. Jesus invites us, saying, "Come to me, all you who are weary and burdened, and I will give you rest" (Matthew 11:28). This rest, this peace, is a gift we receive when we let go of our striving and place our trust in Him. Just as dawn brings light to the night, God's peace illuminates our hearts, giving us the strength to face each day with courage and hope.

In essence, "Inside Us All" offers a pathway to a peace that exists not apart from life's challenges but within them. It is a peace that sustains, comforts, and empowers us to live with purpose. Paul, writing to the Romans, speaks of this peace as a gift that accompanies our faith: "Therefore, since we have been justified through faith, we have peace with God through our Lord Jesus Christ" (Romans 5:1). This peace is not merely an emotional state; it is a reconciliation with God, a restored relationship that anchors us.

As we walk this journey, we may find that peace is indeed a friend who walks with us through every season of life. The prophet Isaiah foretold of a Savior who would be called the "Prince of Peace" (Isaiah 9:6), and in Christ, this prophecy is fulfilled. He is our peace, our guide, and our strength. Though life may bring shadows, the light of His peace remains constant, unwavering, and present.

PART IV
Rusted And Weathered

CHAPTER 23

"Bullets"

"Bullets" by Creed captures a primal, gut-wrenching exploration of internal and external conflict, with a depth that only emerges fully when you hold the lyrics and music in tension, alongside each instrument's cry and Scott Stapp's impassioned, almost tortured vocal performance. In "Bullets," the listener is pulled into a battle—both spiritual and existential—where the protagonist is simultaneously victim and warrior, pierced by a society that often seeks to wound rather than understand.

The journey begins with the sound of footsteps, each step weighted with questions and doubts, as if the earth itself is crying out. In the opening line, "Walking around I hear the sounds of the earth seeking relief," there's a profound awareness that the world itself is groaning. There's almost a biblical undercurrent here, echoing Paul's words in Romans about creation groaning for redemption. The earth isn't silent—it is active, restless, as if aligned with the protagonist's own search for meaning and release from unseen burdens. The production captures this movement through a relentless, almost haunting beat from Scott Phillips, whose drums don't just set the tempo but echo the protagonist's every step through a chaotic world.

Stapp's lyrics reveal a desperate search for life's purpose amidst "mindless clutter" and the "thorns" piercing his side. These are not thorns of a minor nuisance but rather those that drive deep into the flesh, like Paul's thorn that kept him humble. In this image, there is a personal agony, and we are shown the juxtaposition of wanting to live fully while being hampered by pain inflicted by unseen forces. Stapp repeats, "Oh, these thorns in my side," bringing the listener into a rhythmic awareness of the pain's persistence. This ache is not occasional; it is constant. There is also a subtle defiance, an unspoken will to press forward despite the suffering.

As the song intensifies, Tremonti's guitar plays a crucial role in setting the tone. His riffs are abrasive, almost angry, mirroring the lyrics' cry for release. Tremonti doesn't play to soothe but to break through, each note piercing like the very bullets the protagonist describes. His guitar work is gritty, rough-edged, and deliberate, as if he, too, is questioning and fighting alongside Stapp. There is a power here that refuses to be silenced or ignored, underscoring the protagonist's resilience. Each note feels crafted to reflect the inner chaos—a dissonance that refuses to resolve, mirroring life's own unresolved tension.

The chorus brings a stark realization: "I think they shoot 'cause they want it." In these words, Stapp reflects on society's tendency to attack what it cannot understand or possess. To "shoot" becomes a metaphor for attempts to destroy or diminish others out of jealousy, hatred, or fear. There's a sense that these forces aren't random—they're intentional, driven by desire. In this line, he alludes to the human tendency to attack what represents freedom or life because it reminds others of their own perceived lack. It's a sobering statement on humanity's darker inclinations, suggesting that the "bullets" aimed at us are born out of others' unresolved internal battles. They are not just attempts to harm but are often fueled by envy, as if by "shooting," they might somehow capture or extinguish what they envy.

The plea, "At least look at me when you shoot," is a call for acknowledgment, a demand to be seen even by those who seek to wound. There's something profoundly human in this line—a need to be recognized, even by one's enemies. It echoes the painful irony that even in moments of hostility, there is a cry for connection. Stapp is not asking for pity; he's asking for respect, for the dignity of recognition. This plea transcends the personal; it speaks to a universal longing to be seen, to be understood, even when standing in opposition.

The music swells here, a storm of sound that amplifies the emotional crescendo. Scott Phillips' drums resonate like the sound of distant artillery, driving forward with a relentless force. The arrangement itself feels almost cinematic, pushing the listener to the edge of what they can bear. The music theory behind "Bullets" leans heavily on minor chords and dissonant intervals, which invoke a feeling of unrest. These choices are intentional; they serve to unsettle, to keep the listener on edge, mirroring the protagonist's own psychological turmoil.

As the song progresses, the protagonist grapples with feelings of "disgrace, jealousy, and lies," laughing aloud at the irony of his life being absorbed into someone else's mind. This laughter is not joy—it's the laughter of resignation, the kind that erupts when one recognizes the absurdity of life's struggles. Here, Stapp might be touching on the modern phenomenon of projection, where others' insecurities and issues are often thrust upon those who challenge or expose them. He laughs because he understands that this external hatred has less to do with him and more to do with the insecurities of those around him. He laughs because he sees the tragic humor in how people project their fears onto others, like shadows cast on a wall.

The protagonist's cry for "something real, something I can touch and feel" resonates with a deep-seated human longing for authenticity. There's an urgency in this desire—an impatience with the superficial, a craving for truth. His words resonate with anyone who has felt disconnected, as if they're floating through life without anchoring to anything substantial. It's not a cry for escape but for grounding, a need to hold onto something that will not shift or shatter. Tremonti's guitar work underscores this yearning, shifting between aggression and moments of melodic clarity, as if he, too, is searching for a moment of peace amid the chaos.

In the verse "Why do we live this life with all this hate inside?" the song touches on the destructive power of bitterness. Hate, in this sense, is depicted as an illness, something that festers and spreads within, poisoning not just the person but their interactions and relationships. Stapp's voice, heavy with weariness, conveys the toll that such hatred takes on the soul. He doesn't just want to rid himself of it; he wants to "give it away," to unburden himself. This relinquishing is crucial—it's a surrender, a choice to release what was never meant to be carried.

The protagonist's plea for "a place somewhere far away" speaks to a desire for sanctuary, a retreat from the constant barrage of hostility. This is not a retreat born of cowardice but of self-preservation, a longing for a space where he can exist without the constant assault. He doesn't demand paradise; he simply asks for peace. This request feels universal, echoing a collective desire for a reprieve from the world's chaos. It's the longing for a place untouched by the cynicism and cruelty that have tainted his current reality.

In the closing repetitions of "Look at me, look at me," the protagonist demands visibility, a raw, almost primal need to be acknowledged, to be validated. He stands exposed, unshielded from the metaphorical bullets, yet he insists on facing them head-on. There is defiance here, a refusal to be erased or forgotten. The repetition reinforces his resilience, his unwillingness to fade quietly. Stapp's voice rises, almost pleading, as if he knows this is his final chance to be truly seen.

This refrain is both an invitation and a challenge—an insistence that, regardless of others' intent, he will remain standing.

The song's climax is not in resolution but in the protagonist's choice to confront his attackers, to look them in the eye and demand acknowledgment. There is no peace, no resolution, no easy answers. The music fades with a sense of unresolved tension, a final chord that leaves the listener suspended, much like life itself—caught between struggle and hope, between suffering and the faintest glimmer of redemption.

"Bullets" leaves us with a lingering question: what will we do with our own bullets, both those we fire and those we endure? Stapp's closing words echo like a challenge, a reminder that to live fully, one must confront both the darkness within and the forces outside that seek to consume. In the end, "Bullets" is more than a song—it is an anthem of survival, a testament to the strength found in vulnerability, and a call to be fully seen, even amidst life's fiercest battles.

Application

To apply the insights from Creed's "Bullets" to your own life in a way that aligns with Christian teaching, we must first acknowledge the song's raw depiction of suffering, longing, and internal struggle. This deeply resonates with biblical themes, especially the experience of trials and the desire for authenticity, connection, and purpose. These are essential parts of the human condition that Scripture addresses time and again, offering not only a framework for understanding them but also a path toward peace, fulfillment, and transformation through Christ.

In listening to "Bullets," you're witnessing a vivid portrayal of internal and external battles—spiritual warfare, existential pain, and a longing to break free from a hostile, often superficial society. The lyrics present a cry for meaning and a search for something true and tangible amid life's chaos. This echoes the Apostle Paul's description in Romans 8:22 of creation "groaning" for redemption, alongside humanity's yearning for liberation from pain and decay. In Christian terms, this reflects the inherent human need to find refuge, purpose, and ultimately salvation that can only be fulfilled in a relationship with God through Jesus Christ.

First, as Christians, we must remember that suffering is part of our earthly journey, but it is not without purpose or hope. In 2 Corinthians 4:8-9, Paul writes, "We are hard pressed on every side, but not crushed; perplexed, but not in despair; persecuted, but not abandoned; struck down, but not destroyed." This passage speaks to the resilience we can have in Christ, not by avoiding suffering but by finding strength and redemption through it. The protagonist in "Bullets" feels the weight of society's hostility—represented metaphorically as "bullets"—which often stems from misunderstanding or envy. As Christians, we encounter similar opposition, as Christ himself warned that we would face trials and even hatred because of our allegiance to Him (John 15:18-20). The challenge, then, is to respond not with resentment or despair but with a heart transformed by God's grace.

The protagonist in the song calls for recognition, pleading, "At least look at me when you shoot." This speaks to a deeply human desire to be seen and validated, even in times of hardship. But as believers, we understand that true validation and identity are found in our relationship with God, who knows us intimately and values us beyond measure. Psalm 139 beautifully illustrates this truth, describing how God perceives every thought, every movement, and every part of our being. When we seek our worth in God's unchanging love and acceptance, we're liberated from the need for external validation, finding freedom and confidence in His approval alone.

In dealing with life's "bullets," whether they come in the form of personal attacks, societal pressures, or spiritual battles, Scripture encourages us to put on the "full armor of God" (Ephesians 6:10-18). This armor isn't meant to isolate us from the world or make us callous; rather, it equips us with truth, righteousness, faith, and the Word of God so that we can stand firm in faith. This standing firm doesn't mean an absence of pain or vulnerability; it means trusting that God is our protector and guide through every trial.

The cry for "something real, something I can touch and feel" reflects the human longing for authenticity and stability, a search for an anchor in a world filled with distractions and superficiality. Jesus speaks directly to this need, inviting us to build our lives on a firm foundation, the "rock" of His teachings, rather than the shifting sands of worldly values (Matthew 7:24-27). Through a personal relationship with Christ, you gain access to a truth that transcends human fallibility—a truth that remains steadfast regardless of life's storms. In times of uncertainty or discouragement, consider drawing near to God in prayer and through His Word, asking Him to reveal Himself to you in a way that meets your need for real, unshakeable purpose.

The song also addresses the corrosive effects of bitterness and hatred, posing the question, "Why do we live this life with all this hate inside?" This line touches on a crucial aspect of Christian life: forgiveness and releasing resentment. Jesus teaches us that hatred corrodes the soul and distances us from God. In Matthew 5:44, He instructs us to love our enemies and pray for those who persecute us. This radical approach frees us from the spiritual poison of bitterness, allowing us to experience God's peace and to reflect His love even in challenging relationships. Forgiveness is not about denying the pain inflicted on us; it's about releasing that pain to God, trusting that He is both just and merciful. When we do this, we can experience healing and let go of the "thorns" that would otherwise hinder our spiritual growth.

At the heart of "Bullets" is a cry for peace, a "place somewhere far away" from the hostility and burdens of this world. This mirrors the promise Jesus offers in Matthew 11:28-30: "Come to me, all you who are weary and burdened, and I will give you rest." Jesus doesn't offer escape from life's hardships, but He does provide rest for our souls and strength for the journey. The peace He promises isn't the absence of trouble but the presence of His Spirit within us, empowering us to face challenges with hope and endurance. As you seek peace, remember that it's found not in isolation or withdrawal but in abiding in Christ, who walks with you through every storm.

Lastly, the closing refrain, "Look at me, look at me," underscores the song's theme of resilience and the protagonist's determination to be seen even amid life's battles. In a world that often seeks to reduce people to labels or statistics, the Christian message is one of profound worth and individuality. God sees you fully—every struggle, every triumph, every pain, and every joy. He invites you to come as you are, without fear of rejection. In Christ, you are a new creation (2 Corinthians 5:17), loved beyond measure and called to live a life that glorifies God and blesses others.

In applying the message of "Bullets" to your own life, I encourage you to reflect on these key biblical principles: finding identity and worth in God's unchanging love, standing firm in faith amid adversity, pursuing authenticity through a relationship with Christ, releasing bitterness by embracing forgiveness, seeking peace in God's presence, and living resiliently as a testament to His grace. When you anchor yourself in these truths, the "bullets" of life lose their power to harm or define you. Instead, they become opportunities to demonstrate the strength, love, and redemption found in a life surrendered to Christ.

Let the song's intensity drive you deeper into Scripture, where you'll find both the challenges and the hope that come with a life in Christ. Embrace the struggles as refining fires that shape you more into His image, and trust that every trial, every "thorn," and every "bullet" can be used by God for a greater purpose. In Him, you have the assurance of a peace that transcends understanding and a hope that does not disappoint, for He is with you always, even to the end of the age (Matthew 28:20).

CHAPTER 24
"Freedom Fighter"

C reed's *Freedom Fighter* unfolds like a rallying cry—raw, defiant, and relentless. Each line carries the weight of conviction and a sense of purpose sharpened by the pain of opposition and betrayal. This isn't just a song; it's an anthem for those who find themselves standing against forces determined to silence, diminish, or control. Stapp's lyrics and Tremonti's guitar work draw us into a battlefield of the soul, where personal integrity clashes with the envy and deceit that surround it. Together, they shape a sonic landscape that feels both timeless and immediate, urging the listener to confront hard truths.

The opening lines—"The mouths of envious always find another door"—capture the essence of persistent opposition. The word "envious" highlights the source of much human malice: a bitterness born from a sense of lack or inferiority. These envious mouths aren't silent; they're insidious, searching constantly for ways to undermine, manipulate, or dismiss. "Another door" suggests that even when one way is blocked, these forces persistently seek another path, another angle, another attack. There's an inevitability in it, a relentless nature that parallels the experience of anyone who's ever stood out or defied the expectations of others. Stapp's voice, rough and resolute, doesn't waver as he paints this picture, grounding the song in the reality of continuous resistance.

At the gates of paradise, they "beat us down some more." The juxtaposition of paradise—a place of peace and fulfillment—and the act of being beaten down speaks volumes. It's as though every step closer to purpose or fulfillment is met with greater resistance. Paradise is near, within sight, yet just as they approach it, they are confronted again. The imagery suggests that paradise isn't simply a destination but a state that must be fiercely defended, with each step requiring perseverance. This isn't a passive vision of paradise; it's a struggle, a relentless push forward, and an acknowledgment that progress, even spiritual progress, will face fierce opposition.

"Our mission's set in stone, 'cause the writing's on the wall." There's a feeling of destiny here—a purpose that transcends the individual, a calling that is immovable, as unyielding as stone. The phrase "writing's on the wall" carries prophetic weight, often associated with an inevitable reckoning. In this context, it suggests that the path forward is both unavoidable and divinely sanctioned. The phrase calls to mind the biblical story of Belshazzar, where the writing on the wall foretold the king's fall. Here, it's almost a warning to those who would stand in the way, a reminder that pride comes before a fall, that no amount of envy or resistance can ultimately alter the course that has been set.

Stapp's voice rises as he declares, "I'll scream it from the mountain tops." This isn't merely a statement; it's a commitment to truth that refuses to be silenced. There's an Old Testament prophetic tone here—a voice in the wilderness proclaiming a message that must be heard, a message that cannot be contained. Mountain tops have long symbolized places of revelation, places where the divine meets the earthly. By choosing this imagery, Stapp aligns himself with those who have spoken hard truths, even at great personal cost. There's a raw urgency in his delivery, a promise that no matter the opposition, the truth will not be hidden.

The refrain, "Pride comes before a fall," is a warning wrapped in wisdom. It's a timeless reminder of the dangers of arrogance and the inevitability of justice. For those who have wielded power with a sense of invincibility, it is a reminder that no one is above consequence. Here, it's directed at those who would use deceit or force to control or suppress, as if to say that their actions will ultimately lead to their own undoing. This line serves as both a caution and a prophecy, a reminder that no one who builds on lies will stand forever.

Tremonti's guitar work intensifies as Stapp continues with, "So many thoughts to share, all this energy to give." Tremonti's riffs are relentless, almost overpowering, matching the surge of emotion and purpose in these words. His guitar isn't simply accompanying the lyrics; it's amplifying the protagonist's inner fire. There's a sense of urgency, a need to give, to share, to release. This isn't a passive energy—it's almost volcanic, as though the words have been held back for too long and can no longer be contained.

Stapp's commitment to truth shines through in the line, "Unlike those who hide the truth, I tell it like it is." In a world filled with illusions, half-truths, and distortions, this line speaks to the value of authenticity. To "tell it like it is" requires courage, especially when the truth is uncomfortable or inconvenient. Stapp's delivery here is unapologetic; he doesn't soften the blow, nor does he ask for approval. There's an almost prophetic quality in his stance, a willingness to risk rejection or retaliation in favor of speaking what he knows to be true. In this context, truth is not just a concept—it's a calling, a responsibility that transcends personal gain.

The next line—"If the truth will set you free, I feel sorry for your soul"—is as haunting as it is powerful. Here, Stapp acknowledges that freedom is not something everyone desires. For some, the chains of deception, envy, or hatred are preferred because freedom would require facing hard truths. There's a pity in his tone, almost a sadness, as though he recognizes the tragedy of those who will never break free because they refuse to face reality. The reference to the "bell tolling" evokes a sense of finality, a reminder of mortality, and the inevitability of judgment.

As the chorus begins, Stapp declares himself "a freedom fighter, no remorse, raging on in holy war." This is not a call to violence but a declaration of purpose. His battle is spiritual, a struggle against forces that would seek to corrupt or control. The phrase "holy war" here speaks to the intensity of conviction, a commitment so deep that he's willing to sacrifice comfort, safety, even acceptance, to stand for what he believes is right. The term "freedom fighter" elevates his stance from mere opposition to a mission—a mission to liberate, to protect, to defend. This is a fight for the soul, a refusal to yield in the face of overwhelming opposition.

The repeated line, "Face to face with me," brings a sense of impending confrontation. There is an inevitability in it, a sense that the time for deception or avoidance is over. This isn't a fight that can be waged from a distance; it's personal, direct, unflinching. Stapp's voice here is both a challenge and a promise. He's not hiding, nor is he backing down. There's a quiet strength in his delivery, a readiness to stand, face to face, no matter the cost. It's an invitation and a warning to those who would oppose him, as if to say that their reckoning is near, that they can no longer hide behind shadows or lies.

"Can't you hear us coming? People marching all around," he sings, bringing to life an image of solidarity, a movement of individuals united by purpose and truth. This is not a solitary fight; it's communal, a collective stand against forces of deceit and oppression. The drums and guitar amplify this unity, creating a sense of power in numbers. This isn't just Stapp's fight; it's the fight of all who have been silenced or dismissed. The line "Close your eyes, it's over now" has a dual meaning, speaking to both the end of deception and the inevitability of facing truth.

As the song crescendos, the repetition of "Can't you see we're coming?" becomes almost like a chant, a mantra that refuses to be ignored. Tremonti's guitar and Phillips' drums create a relentless momentum, a feeling of unstoppable force. The music theory here leans on driving rhythms and relentless chords that build without release, creating a tension that reflects the protagonist's intensity. It's a sound that doesn't ask permission; it demands recognition.

In the closing refrain, Stapp repeats, "I'm just a freedom fighter, no remorse." The emphasis on "no remorse" underscores his commitment. This isn't a fight waged with regret or hesitation; it's wholehearted, a conviction so deep that it doesn't waver. As he declares "soon there'll come a day when you're face to face with me," there's both a promise and a challenge. This day is inevitable, a moment of truth where all illusions will be stripped away. Stapp's voice holds a quiet confidence, a certainty that no matter the resistance, the truth will prevail.

Freedom Fighter leaves the listener with a powerful message: truth is worth fighting for, even when the odds seem insurmountable. The song is a call to arms for those who refuse to compromise their integrity, a reminder that the fight for authenticity is ongoing, relentless, and often lonely. It speaks to the courage required to stand in the face of opposition, to confront forces that would seek to diminish or silence. Through Stapp's passionate vocals, Tremonti's fierce guitar work, and Phillips' driving rhythm, *Freedom Fighter* becomes not just a song, but an anthem for all who choose to live boldly, authentically, and unafraid of confrontation.

In the end, the song reminds us that truth, once found, must be defended. It is a call to remember that in a world filled with envy, deception, and fear, there will always be those willing to stand for what is right. The battle may be fierce, the cost may be high, but the fight is worthy.

Application

In considering the message of Creed's "Freedom Fighter," we see a powerful illustration of standing firm for truth and righteousness amidst fierce opposition. The song captures the intensity of a battle for integrity, a rallying cry against forces of deceit and envy. This is profoundly relevant to the Christian life, where followers of Christ are called to stand for truth, even when the world around them may push them toward compromise. In applying this song's themes to your walk with Christ, let's explore how the biblical truths of courage, resilience, and dedication to truth can shape and strengthen your life.

The opening line, "The mouths of envious always find another door," reflects a reality many believers face: opposition and criticism, often from those driven by envy or misunderstanding. This aligns with Jesus' own teachings about persecution, where He reminds us that as His followers, we will encounter resistance just as He did. In John 15:18-20, Jesus says, "If the world hates you, keep in mind that it hated me first... If they persecuted me, they will persecute you also." This isn't a call to embrace suffering for suffering's sake but to understand that truth will often provoke hostility. Envy, as described in the song, is a natural response to righteousness because it reveals others' insecurities and confronts their conscience. Therefore, when you face opposition, recognize that it can be a mark of standing for what is right, and ask God to help you respond with grace and perseverance.

The song speaks of "beating down" the protagonist as he nears "the gates of paradise," a vivid image of how progress in one's faith and life can often meet with increasing obstacles. Scripture repeatedly speaks of this spiritual reality, particularly in James 1:2-4, which encourages believers to "consider it pure joy... whenever you face trials of many kinds, because you know that the testing of your faith produces perseverance." Trials, though painful, refine and strengthen us. Every step closer to your "paradise" in Christ—the fullness of joy, peace, and purpose—will likely be met with resistance. Yet, God calls us to persevere, trusting that He is with us every step of the way, fortifying our character and deepening our faith.

The lyrics refer to a mission "set in stone," rooted in the "writing on the wall." This phrase, in a biblical sense, refers to Daniel 5, where God sends a message to the Babylonian king Belshazzar, foretelling his kingdom's downfall due to pride and idolatry. In the context of "Freedom Fighter," the line conveys a sense of divine purpose and destiny—a calling that is unchangeable and divinely appointed. As Christians, we too are called to a purpose set in stone, to live as witnesses of the Gospel and to embody the love and truth of Christ in every aspect of our lives. In 1 Peter 2:9, we are called "a chosen people, a royal priesthood, a holy nation, God's special possession, that [we] may declare the praises of him who called [us] out of darkness into his wonderful light." When you feel the weight of this calling, remember that it is God who works in you to accomplish His purposes. Your mission is not fueled by your strength alone; rather, the Lord equips you to fulfill His calling.

The anthem-like declaration "I'll scream it from the mountain tops" echoes the prophetic boldness seen throughout Scripture. This stance is reminiscent of John the Baptist, who boldly declared God's truth, regardless of the opposition he faced. In the same way, Chris-

tians are called to speak truth without fear or compromise, proclaiming the message of salvation with courage and conviction. Matthew
5:14-16 reminds us, "You are the light of the world. A town built on a
hill cannot be hidden." To "scream it from the mountain tops" is not
only an act of courage but also of faithfulness to God's command to
make His truth known. Let this call to boldness inspire you to share
your faith openly and live out the Gospel fearlessly.

One of the central themes of the song is the reality that "pride
comes before a fall," a clear biblical principle from Proverbs 16:18:
"Pride goes before destruction, a haughty spirit before a fall." This
serves as both a warning and a reminder that no one is immune to
accountability. Those who attempt to manipulate, control, or diminish others often do so out of pride, which ultimately leads to their
downfall. For the Christian, humility is the antidote to pride, and it's
a virtue God values deeply. Jesus himself modeled humility, showing
that greatness in the Kingdom of God is defined not by domination
or self-exaltation, but by service, compassion, and sacrifice. As you
navigate your own life and relationships, let humility guide you. Resist
the temptation to respond to others' pride with pride of your own,
and instead trust that God will bring justice and vindicate those who
walk in humility and truth.

Stapp's line, "Unlike those who hide the truth, I tell it like it
is," underscores the Christian call to authenticity and integrity. In a
world that often values convenience over honesty, Scripture teaches
that truth is foundational to the Christian life. Ephesians 4:15 urges
us to "speak the truth in love," balancing honesty with compassion.
Authenticity is not about bluntly expressing every thought but about
living in alignment with God's truth and being willing to stand for
what is right, even when it's unpopular. Jesus declared in John 8:32
that "the truth will set you free." When we live honestly, without

hiding or distorting truth, we experience freedom and enable others to see God's light shining through us.

Stapp's statement, "If the truth will set you free, I feel sorry for your soul," is a poignant reminder that many resist truth because of what it demands. True freedom in Christ often requires sacrifice and the willingness to confront uncomfortable realities about ourselves and the world. Many reject this freedom because it means relinquishing control or letting go of deeply held deceptions. But for the Christian, embracing truth leads to liberation, peace, and transformation. In your journey of faith, seek to open yourself to God's truth, even when it challenges you or requires you to change. Pray for the courage to surrender to His will, trusting that true freedom is found in obedience to His Word.

As Stapp declares himself a "freedom fighter, no remorse, raging on in holy war," it's important to recognize that the battle we face as Christians is spiritual, not physical. Ephesians 6:12 reminds us that "our struggle is not against flesh and blood, but against the rulers, against the authorities, against the powers of this dark world and against the spiritual forces of evil." We are called to be "freedom fighters" for God's kingdom, standing firm in faith and resisting the forces of darkness. This battle requires the armor of God—truth, righteousness, faith, salvation, and the Word of God (Ephesians 6:13-17). Engage in this "holy war" by strengthening your relationship with Christ, praying diligently, and living in a way that reflects His love and grace.

The imagery of people "marching all around" brings to mind the power of unity within the Body of Christ. As believers, we're not alone in this battle; we're part of a larger community, the Church, which Christ established as His instrument of hope and redemption in the world. Hebrews 10:24-25 encourages us to "consider how we may spur one another on toward love and good deeds, not giving up meeting together, as some are in the habit of doing, but encouraging one another." Stand alongside your fellow believers in faith, encouraging one another, and drawing strength from God's promises and from the support of His people.

As the song closes with the repeated refrain, "I'm just a freedom fighter, no remorse," we are reminded of the unwavering commitment required to follow Christ. The call to discipleship is not for the faint of heart; it requires a willingness to surrender all to Christ and to stand firm in the face of opposition. Jesus Himself said in Luke 9:23, "Whoever wants to be my disciple must deny themselves and take up their cross daily and follow me." This is the cost of following Jesus, but it is a cost that brings ultimate reward. Commit yourself fully to God's purpose, without regret or hesitation, trusting that He will be with you every step of the way.

Creed's "Freedom Fighter" ultimately challenges us to live with integrity, courage, and faithfulness. As you apply these truths to your life, remember that the true "freedom fighter" is one who fights for the freedom and redemption found in Christ. Let this song's message inspire you to stand for truth, to resist the pressures of the world, and to live boldly as a follower of Christ, knowing that your reward is not found in human recognition but in the eternal, unshakable Kingdom of God.Top of Form

Bottom of Form

CHAPTER 25
"Who's Got My Back?"

"Who's Got My Back?" by Creed is a soul-stirring lament, an anguished search for meaning in a fractured world. This song speaks to the heart of disconnection—disconnection from truth, from unity, from something sacred that once bound us together. In Stapp's words and Tremonti's haunting guitar, we hear the echo of a covenant that has been broken, leaving humanity adrift, longing for something stable and true. The song doesn't offer easy answers; instead, it wrestles with an existential crisis, asking questions that don't yield simple solutions. The listener is drawn into an emotional pilgrimage, a search for something, or someone, to trust in a world that feels deceptive and hollow.

The opening line, "Run, hide all that was sacred to us," feels like a warning, as if the protagonist is urging us to shield what little remains of our ideals, our values, our sense of purpose. "Sacred to us" suggests something deeply personal, something once held in reverence. But the sacred is no longer safe—it's something we must hide to protect. The use of "run, hide" conveys a sense of urgency and danger, setting the tone for a journey into a world where what was once holy is now under threat. It speaks to a loss of innocence, a world in which trust has been eroded, leaving us vulnerable and exposed.

The line "See the signs" serves as an awakening, a call to confront the reality of our situation. In this phrase, there's an implication that the signs have been there all along, visible to those who would look, but ignored or overlooked in the rush of modern life. Here, the protagonist draws our attention to a broken covenant—a relational or moral agreement that humanity has failed to uphold. There's almost a biblical weight to this concept, as if this "covenant" is foundational, something woven into the fabric of existence. By breaking it, humanity has created a breach, a rift that leaves us stranded, "with no shoulder to rest our head on." The repetition of this line—"to rest our head on"—reinforces the need for comfort, for something or someone that can bear the weight of our sorrow.

The refrain, "Who's got my back now?" is both a question and a plea. In a world that feels unreliable and filled with deception, the protagonist is searching for an anchor, a point of stability. It's a question that speaks to the loneliness of the modern experience, where individualism and division have often left us feeling isolated. This line is not just about protection; it's about loyalty, about someone who will stand by us when everything else has fallen away. Stapp's delivery is filled with vulnerability, a raw openness that exposes the depth of his longing. He's not merely asking who will protect him physically; he's asking who will stand with him, who will provide the emotional and spiritual support that he so desperately needs.

The phrase "When all we have left is deceptive" captures the hollow feeling of living in a world where truth seems elusive. There's a profound sense of betrayal here, as if the very foundation on which life was built has crumbled. The word "deceptive" speaks to a pervasive feeling of disillusionment, a sense that what we once relied upon is no longer trustworthy. It's a subtle nod to the fragmentation of truth in an age filled with misinformation, spin, and hidden agendas. The protagonist feels cut off, "so disconnected," and in this disconnection, he is left searching for something real.

"What is the truth now?" becomes the song's central question, one that reverberates with desperation. This line isn't rhetorical; it's an earnest, almost primal cry. In a world where even the idea of truth feels fractured, this question is an attempt to find a grounding force. Stapp's voice takes on a pleading tone, as if he's appealing not just to the listener but to some higher authority, something beyond himself. He wants clarity, honesty, something untainted by deception or half-truths. The repetition of this question throughout the song reinforces its urgency, its importance. He's not merely asking for intellectual knowledge—he's seeking something that will resonate with his soul, something he can build his life upon.

The line "There's still time, all that has been devastated can be recreated" offers a glimmer of hope. It's a reminder that while much has been lost, not all is beyond redemption. There's a quiet resilience here, a belief that healing and restoration are possible, even in a world that feels irreparably broken. But this recreation is not something that happens passively; it requires action, commitment. The protagonist calls on us to "pick up the broken pieces of our lives," suggesting that healing is a communal effort, a collective act of rebuilding. This line is filled with both hope and responsibility, a recognition that while there's a chance for restoration, it will require courage and intentionality.

"Giving ourselves to each other, ourselves to each other" is perhaps the song's most powerful line. In these words, we hear a call to unity, to a sense of shared purpose that transcends individualism. This is not a passive act; it's a self-sacrificial choice to bear each other's burdens, to be the "shoulder" that the song has been searching for. This line speaks to the deepest human need for connection, for intimacy, for a bond that is built on trust and mutual support. In a world that has left the protagonist feeling betrayed and isolated, this act of giving becomes a form of resistance, a choice to create something sacred even amidst the brokenness.

As the refrain repeats, "Who's got my back now?" the question becomes more than just a search for support—it becomes an accusation, a challenge to those who have abandoned or deceived. Stapp's voice takes on a confrontational edge, as if he's daring the world to step up, to prove itself. The drums and guitar swell here, creating a sense of urgency, a feeling that this question cannot be ignored any longer. There's a restless energy in the music, an intensity that mirrors the protagonist's frustration and determination.

The repeated plea for "the truth" intensifies as the song builds, each repetition carrying more weight. It's as though the protagonist is stripping away layers of deception, searching for something pure, something real. This search is not gentle; it's a relentless pursuit, a demand for authenticity in a world that has often offered only illusions. Tremonti's guitar riffs here are raw and unpolished, mirroring the grit of this search. There's a feeling that the protagonist is willing to dig through the muck, to confront uncomfortable realities, if it means finding something true.

In the song's final moments, the refrain "Tell us the truth now" becomes almost like a chant, a collective cry. It's no longer just the protagonist's question; it's the voice of all who feel betrayed, disillusioned, and lost. Stapp's voice rises, filled with both desperation and defiance, as if he's rallying a movement, calling others to join him in this search. The repetition is hypnotic, almost trance-like, pulling the listener into the intensity of the plea. There's a rawness here, an emotional honesty that cuts through the noise and strikes at the heart of human longing.

"Who's Got My Back?" ends with the feeling of unresolved tension, a question left hanging in the air. The protagonist hasn't found all the answers, but he has refused to be silenced. In this way, the song becomes a testament to the power of questions, to the importance of seeking truth even when it seems elusive. It's a reminder that in a world filled with deception and disconnection, the search for authenticity is an act of courage, a refusal to settle for anything less than what is real.

Creed leaves us with a challenge: to ask ourselves who, or what, has our back in a world that often feels unreliable. The song reminds us that while we may feel isolated, we are not alone in our search. In our shared longing for truth and connection, we find solidarity, a bond that goes deeper than words. "Who's Got My Back?" is more than just a song—it's a call to resilience, a reminder that even in the darkest moments, there is a part of us that will not give up, that will continue to seek, to question, to hope.

Application

o apply the message of Creed's "Who's Got My Back?" to your life as a Christian, let's begin with the song's profound exploration of longing for truth, connection, and stability. These are deeply rooted human desires, and they resonate strongly with biblical principles. This song presents a journey of lament, an acknowledgment of brokenness, and a relentless search for truth in a world that often feels fractured and unreliable. As you seek to live out these themes, consider how Christ provides the ultimate fulfillment of these needs, offering a firm foundation in a world that constantly shifts.

The song opens with a powerful line, "Run, hide all that was sacred to us," capturing the sense of disconnection and loss. As believers, we know that the things sacred to us—our faith, values, and relationship with God—are under constant threat in a fallen world. Jesus warns in John 16:33 that "in this world, you will have trouble," a reminder that we are not immune to suffering or opposition. But He doesn't leave us in despair; He follows this with, "But take heart! I have overcome the world." Christ's victory over sin and death gives us the strength to persevere, even when the sacred seems vulnerable. Rather than running or hiding, Scripture encourages us to hold fast to God's truth, trusting that He is our ultimate protector.

The line "See the signs" serves as a wake-up call, a reminder to recognize the brokenness around us. The "signs" point to a world marred by sin, where humanity has broken its covenant with God. This echoes the story of Israel in the Old Testament, where time and again, God's people abandoned their covenant, resulting in disconnection and exile. Yet, through prophets like Isaiah, God repeatedly called them back to Himself, urging them to return and rebuild the relationship they had forsaken. As Christians, we're reminded that our own covenant with God, established through Christ's sacrifice, must be guarded with vigilance. When you feel the weight of brokenness, allow it to draw you closer to God, seeking His wisdom and presence to restore what has been lost.

The refrain, "Who's got my back now?" resonates with a universal longing for protection, loyalty, and a sense of belonging. In a world that often feels unreliable, this question speaks to our need for a steadfast source of support. In Psalm 91, God promises His unwavering protection: "Whoever dwells in the shelter of the Most High will rest in the shadow of the Almighty." This psalm is a powerful reminder that God is always with us, providing refuge and strength. As a Christian, you can find assurance in knowing that God "has your back" in every situation. His presence is constant and unchanging, offering you a stability that transcends any earthly relationship or source of support.

The song's line "When all we have left is deceptive" captures the pervasive sense of disillusionment in a world where truth often seems fragmented. Jesus addresses this in John 8:31-32, where He says, "If you hold to my teaching, you are really my disciples. Then you will know the truth, and the truth will set you free." In Christ, truth is not an abstract concept; it is embodied in Him. By anchoring yourself in His Word and His teachings, you gain a foundation that withstands the confusion and deception that may surround you. When you feel disconnected or lost, seek God's truth as revealed in Scripture, allowing it to ground you in what is real and unchanging.

"What is the truth now?" becomes the song's central question, reflecting a deep yearning for something solid and reliable. This question speaks to the human soul's need for an anchor, especially in times of confusion. In John 14:6, Jesus boldly declares, "I am the way, the truth, and the life." This statement reveals that truth is not merely factual knowledge but a person—Christ Himself. When you are searching for truth, seek to know Jesus more deeply. By drawing near to Him, you'll find that He is not only the answer to your questions but the One who can sustain you in times of uncertainty.

The line "There's still time, all that has been devastated can be recreated" offers a glimpse of hope amidst the lament. The Bible speaks often of God's redemptive power, His ability to restore what has been broken. In Joel 2:25, God promises to "repay you for the years the locusts have eaten," a powerful assurance that He can redeem even the most painful losses. When life feels shattered, remember that God specializes in restoration. Trust that He can recreate and renew what has been devastated, bringing beauty from ashes and hope from despair. Allow this promise to encourage you, knowing that God is continually working to heal and transform both your heart and the world around you.

"Giving ourselves to each other, ourselves to each other" reflects a call to unity and mutual support that resonates deeply with the teachings of Christ. In Galatians 6:2, Paul instructs believers to "carry each other's burdens, and in this way, you will fulfill the law of Christ."

The Christian life is not a solitary journey; it is one that thrives in community. By investing in relationships with fellow believers, you become both a recipient and a giver of support and encouragement. In a world that often feels disconnected, this bond of unity in Christ becomes a powerful testament to God's love. Embrace the opportunity to serve and support others, building relationships that reflect the unity and compassion of God's Kingdom.

The repeated refrain, "Who's got my back now?" takes on an almost confrontational tone as the song progresses, challenging the world's systems and values. This echoes the Christian's call to be "in the world but not of the world" (John 17:14-16). In Christ, you are called to stand apart from worldly values, pursuing righteousness even when it sets you at odds with popular culture. This separation doesn't mean isolation; rather, it calls you to live as a witness of God's love and truth. When you feel at odds with the world, remember that Christ has overcome it. He calls you to stand firm, knowing that your identity and purpose are secure in Him.

The final plea for "the truth" becomes almost a chant, a collective cry for something real and unbreakable. In Matthew 7:24-27, Jesus speaks of building one's life on a solid foundation, comparing His teachings to a rock that withstands the storms. When life feels uncertain or disorienting, return to this foundation. The pursuit of truth in Christ is not always easy, but it is a journey that leads to life and fulfillment. Allow the cry for truth to deepen your commitment to Christ, seeking Him not only as Savior but as the guiding force for every part of your life.

As "Who's Got My Back?" ends with unresolved tension, we're reminded that in this world, we will always feel a measure of longing and incompletion. Yet this tension invites us to fix our hope on eternity, where every question will be answered and every longing fulfilled.

Revelation 21:4 offers the promise of a day when God "will wipe every tear from their eyes. There will be no more death or mourning or crying or pain, for the old order of things has passed away." Until that day, we are called to live in faith, trusting that God holds every answer and fulfills every need.

In response to the questions raised by "Who's Got My Back?" embrace your faith in God as the ultimate answer to these longings. Seek His truth, find your stability in His promises, and allow His presence to be the "shoulder" you can rest on. Though life may bring seasons of disconnection, remember that God is always near, offering a love that is constant, a truth that is unchanging, and a hope that is eternal. Let this song's message of searching and longing draw you deeper into relationship with Him, where every question finds its answer and every need finds its fulfillment in the steadfast love of Christ.

Bottom of Form

CHAPTER 26

"Signs"

I n Creed's *Signs,* the listener is drawn into a reflective, almost urgent search for clarity in a world obscured by superficial divisions. Each line feels like an unraveling, a peeling back of layers that we often use to shield ourselves from uncomfortable truths. Through Stapp's impassioned voice and Tremonti's evocative guitar, the song invites us to question and transcend the boundaries of age, belief, race, and desire—to see beyond the surface and grasp the deeper signs that surround us. It's a journey not just into self-awareness, but into a shared human consciousness, where we are challenged to look past distractions and see what truly matters.

"This is not about age," the song begins, immediately rejecting one of the most superficial markers we use to define ourselves and others. Age is typically a shorthand for experience or wisdom, yet Stapp dismantles that notion, reminding us that "time served on the earth doesn't mean you grow in mind." It's a critique of the assumption that mere years translate to maturity or insight. Instead, Stapp points us toward a more profound understanding of growth—one that requires intentionality and depth. His voice carries both frustration and hope, as if he's urging the listener to go beyond these simplistic markers and consider what real wisdom looks like. Tremonti's guitar plays with a haunting, almost subdued resonance here, underscoring the contemplative tone of this revelation.

"This is not about God," he continues, addressing the complicated relationship society has with spirituality. The line "Spiritual insinuations seem to shock our nation" points to the discomfort many feel with matters of faith in a public or personal setting. There's a deep irony here: while spirituality can be a source of unity, it often becomes a point of division. Stapp isn't dismissing spirituality but challenging us to look beyond the divisions it can create when misunderstood or wielded as a weapon. His tone is one of sadness mixed with defiance, as if he's tired of seeing something as sacred as faith twisted into a tool for separation. Tremonti's chords grow heavier, reflecting the weight of this critique and the societal tension around spirituality.

"Come with me, I'm fading underneath the lights," Stapp invites, almost like a call into an intimate, hidden space away from the harshness of public scrutiny. This fading, this movement away from the lights, speaks to the need to step out of society's relentless spotlight. The "lights" are not just physical but symbolic—representing the glare of judgment, expectation, and societal pressures. Here, Stapp's voice softens, becoming almost a whisper, as if he's leading us into a place of vulnerability, a place where we can examine ourselves away from the world's gaze. Tremonti's guitar mirrors this invitation with a subtle, almost beckoning melody, one that feels both intimate and slightly haunting.

"This is not about race," he declares, addressing another profound divider in society. The phrase "It's a decision to stop the division in your life" challenges the listener to take responsibility for the biases and separations they carry. Race, often a focal point of prejudice and division, is presented here not as an insurmountable obstacle but as a choice—something we can choose to see differently. Stapp's tone is resolute, filled with a quiet strength as he speaks these words. He's not dismissing the reality of racial difference, but rather calling for an end to the divisions that arise when we fixate on these differences. Tremonti's guitar shifts, becoming more assertive, as if emphasizing the power of unity over division.

"This is not about sex" points to the pervasive power of desire, especially in a society where "sex sells and the whole world is buying." The statement isn't prudish; it's a critique of a world that often reduces relationships and value to physical desire. Stapp's tone here feels almost weary, as if he's saddened by how the sacredness of intimacy has been commodified, transformed into a product rather than a genuine connection. "We're buying, yeah," he observes, casting a spotlight on our complicity. It's not an accusation, but a somber acknowledgment of how we've let desire shape our values and relationships. Tremonti's chords take on a mournful tone, underscoring the sense of loss that accompanies this realization.

As the chorus rings out—"Can't you see the signs? See the signs now"—the repetition intensifies, becoming almost hypnotic, as if Stapp is urging us to break free from these distractions and see the underlying truths. There's an urgency in his voice, a desperation that builds with each repetition. It's not just a question; it's a demand, a plea to wake up. The signs, he suggests, are all around us, but we're often too distracted by superficial concerns to notice them. The repetition becomes a mantra, urging the listener to focus, to look beyond the obvious and see the deeper reality. The music swells, amplifying this urgency, creating a sense of movement, as if we're being pushed to the edge of something profound.

"Come with me, I'm fading underneath the lights," Stapp repeats, reinforcing his invitation to step away from the noise and chaos of the world. There's a vulnerability in this repeated line, as if he's offering himself as a guide but also acknowledging his own weariness. It's a moment of shared humanity, a reminder that the journey toward truth is one we take together, not alone. Tremonti's guitar becomes more subdued, almost like a heartbeat, grounding this moment in a raw, unfiltered emotion.

In the final verses, the refrain of "Can't you see the signs?" becomes almost like a chant, a relentless call that refuses to be silenced. By now, the signs are no longer abstract—they're all around us, visible if we only choose to look. Stapp's voice is insistent, filled with both hope and frustration. He's not asking us to believe blindly; he's asking us to open our eyes, to acknowledge the truths that lie beneath the surface. Tremonti's guitar intensifies, creating a sense of urgency that mirrors the climax of the song, as if to say that the time for ignorance or avoidance is over.

As the song reaches its close, the refrain of "Come with me" becomes almost like a prayer, a call for unity and purpose. Stapp's voice, filled with conviction, urges us to let go of the divisions and distractions that have held us back. He's not promising easy answers, nor is he offering a simple solution. Instead, he's inviting us to take the first step, to join him in a journey toward clarity and understanding. The repetition of "see the signs" in the final moments leaves the listener with a lingering question: will we continue to look away, or will we finally open our eyes to the deeper truths that surround us?

Signs is more than a song—it's a call to awareness, a plea to see beyond the surface and grasp the realities we often ignore. Through Stapp's impassioned vocals and Tremonti's evocative guitar work, Creed challenges us to confront the distractions, divisions, and desires that keep us from connecting with ourselves and each other. In a world filled with noise and confusion, *Signs* serves as a reminder that the path to truth begins when we stop looking outward and start searching within.

Application

Creed's "Signs" presents a powerful call to look beyond the surface distractions of age, race, desire, and belief, challenging us to confront our assumptions and pursue a deeper, unified understanding of truth. The song resonates with a biblical perspective on transcending worldly divisions and embracing the unity that Christ offers. As you seek to apply these themes as a Christian, let's explore how this pursuit of clarity aligns with God's call to look beyond the temporal and see His eternal truths.

The song begins with "This is not about age," challenging the listener to discard the superficial marker of age as a measure of wisdom or understanding. Scripture, too, teaches that true wisdom does not come with age alone. In James 1:5, we're reminded that wisdom is a gift from God: "If any of you lacks wisdom, you should ask God, who gives generously to all without finding fault." In Proverbs, we also see that wisdom is "the beginning of the fear of the Lord" (Proverbs 9:10). True growth and maturity are found not in the number of our years, but in our relationship with God and our openness to His guidance. Just as the song urges us to seek a depth that transcends years, the Bible calls us to grow in spiritual maturity, rooted in a dependence on God and a desire to live according to His Word.

"This is not about God" seems initially contradictory, but in context, it challenges the ways society often misconstrues or divides over spirituality. Many people feel uncomfortable discussing faith in public because they fear judgment or misunderstanding. Jesus Himself encountered this tension, and in John 4, we see a profound example of it in His interaction with the Samaritan woman. When Jesus speaks to her about "living water" and worship "in spirit and in truth" (John 4:24), He transcends societal boundaries of race, gender, and cultural expectations. His message is clear: true spirituality isn't about external markers or cultural labels but about an authentic relationship with

God. Similarly, Creed's lyrics invite us to examine our own beliefs and biases, to recognize where we might have allowed religion to divide rather than unite. As Christians, we're called to move beyond shallow judgments and seek a faith that unites us in truth, fostering love and understanding rather than division.

"Come with me, I'm fading underneath the lights" is a poignant invitation to step away from the pressures of society, symbolized by "the lights," which represent the harshness of public opinion and the expectations that often cloud our understanding. Jesus often withdrew from the crowds to pray and seek clarity in solitude, reminding us of the value of stepping away from worldly distractions to find truth in God's presence. In Matthew 6:6, Jesus teaches, "When you pray, go into your room, close the door, and pray to your Father, who is unseen." Taking time in quiet reflection allows us to tune out the noise of the world and focus on what God is speaking into our lives. In your own walk, consider taking moments away from the demands and distractions of life to seek God's presence, allowing Him to provide the clarity and peace that the world cannot offer.

"This is not about race" challenges us to examine the divisions that arise from focusing on physical differences. The Bible affirms that all people are created in the image of God (Genesis 1:27), and Galatians 3:28 teaches that "there is neither Jew nor Gentile...for you are all one in Christ Jesus." In the Kingdom of God, unity transcends race, culture, and background. Creed's message here aligns with the biblical call to view each person as a unique and valuable creation, deserving of respect and love. As Christians, we are called to be peacemakers, bridging the divides that society may impose. When we focus on unity in Christ, we can overcome biases, foster understanding, and build relationships that reflect God's love.

The line "This is not about sex" critiques a culture that often reduces relationships to physical desire, missing the sacredness of genuine intimacy. In Scripture, intimacy within the bounds of marriage is presented as a gift from God, reflecting a deeper spiritual unity and commitment (Ephesians 5:31-32). However, when society distorts this gift, it can lead to emptiness and brokenness. Creed's words remind us of the need to look beyond fleeting desires and seek relationships built on love, respect, and genuine connection. In 1 Corinthians 6:18-20, Paul reminds believers that their bodies are temples of the Holy Spirit, calling them to honor God in how they live. This perspective encourages us to approach relationships with intentionality and purity, recognizing that true fulfillment is found not in superficial attraction but in a deeper connection with God and others.

As the song's chorus urges, "Can't you see the signs? See the signs now," we're reminded of Jesus' words in Matthew 16:3, where He rebukes the people for being able to interpret the sky but failing to understand the "signs of the times." In today's world, distractions, biases, and worldly values can cloud our ability to see God's hand at work around us. The call to "see the signs" is a call to discernment, to seek a God-centered perspective on life. Hebrews 12:2 encourages us to "fix our eyes on Jesus, the pioneer and perfecter of faith." By focusing on Christ, we can begin to see beyond worldly distractions and understand the deeper truths that God reveals through His Word and creation.

"Come with me, I'm fading underneath the lights" is repeated throughout the song, emphasizing the importance of vulnerability and shared humanity. In a culture that often prizes independence and self-reliance, this line is a reminder that we are called to journey together. Galatians 6:2 urges believers to "carry each other's burdens," a call to unity and mutual support. Just as Jesus shared in our suffering and bore our burdens, we, too, are called to support one another. In your faith journey, look for ways to connect with others, sharing both joys and challenges, and allowing God's love to flow through these relationships.

The repeated line "Can't you see the signs?" becomes almost a chant, a persistent reminder to open our eyes to the deeper truths around us. Jesus frequently called His disciples to look beyond the physical, challenging them to understand spiritual truths through His parables and teachings. In Matthew 13:16-17, He tells them, "Blessed are your eyes because they see, and your ears because they hear." As Christians, we're called to a higher awareness, recognizing God's presence and purpose in all aspects of life. Allow this call to "see the signs" to inspire a deeper attentiveness to God's voice, actively seeking His will and discerning His direction in each situation.

As the song ends with the refrain "Come with me," Stapp's voice seems to carry a note of both urgency and invitation. This echoes Jesus' invitation to His disciples to "come, follow Me" (Matthew 4:19), a call to leave behind worldly distractions and embark on a transformative journey. When we respond to Christ's call, we step into a life that is not free of challenges, but one filled with purpose, love, and hope. This journey requires us to let go of divisions, biases, and fleeting desires, choosing instead to pursue a life centered on God's eternal truth.

"Signs" challenges us to confront the divisions, desires, and distractions that hinder our relationship with God and with one another. By focusing on the deeper "signs" of God's presence and purpose, we can move beyond the surface-level concerns that often preoccupy us. As you apply this message, remember that God's truth is eternal and unchanging, calling you to a life of unity, authenticity, and love. Seek to cultivate a heart that discerns His signs, embracing the journey of faith with a spirit of openness and humility. In a world filled with confusion, let your life be a testament to the clarity, hope, and peace that only Christ can provide.

CHAPTER 27
"One Last Breath"

C reed's *One Last Breath* is a haunting meditation on despair, regret, and the fragile thread of hope that keeps us holding on when it feels like we're on the verge of falling apart. The song pulls us into the mind of someone standing on the edge—literally and figuratively—caught between the desire to escape pain and a lingering belief that there's still something worth living for. Scott Stapp's voice, Tremonti's evocative guitar, and the steady drumbeat work together to paint a picture of a soul in crisis, grappling with the weight of past mistakes and the fear of letting go. The song becomes a deeply introspective journey, an invitation to explore the raw moments when life feels unbearably heavy yet somehow worth fighting for.

"Please come now, I think I'm falling," Stapp begins, setting the stage with a sense of vulnerability. This opening line is a plea, an admission of fragility that feels almost childlike in its honesty. The phrase "I think I'm falling" speaks to the uncertainty that often surrounds moments of despair. It's not a definite statement—it's tentative, as though the protagonist is not fully convinced of his own reality, questioning whether he is really at his breaking point or if there's still something left to cling to. Stapp's voice trembles with a kind of restrained anguish, hinting at an internal struggle that he hasn't yet surrendered to. The guitar's gentle but mournful tones mirror this tentative reach for help, creating a sense of quiet desperation that underscores the vulnerability of this opening.

"I'm holding on to all I think is safe," he continues, drawing us into the mindset of someone grasping at whatever remnants of stability he can find. The line suggests that the safety he clings to is tenuous, possibly even illusory. There's a hint of self-awareness here—a recognition that what he considers "safe" may not truly offer the security he seeks. It's a line that speaks to the human tendency to cling to the familiar, even when it doesn't serve us, out of fear of the unknown. Tremonti's guitar shifts slightly, becoming more tense, as if to underscore the fragility of this "safety" the protagonist is holding onto.

The phrase "It seems I found the road to nowhere, and I'm trying to escape" captures the heart of the song's existential crisis. There's a sense of frustration here, a realization that the path he's been following has led him to a dead end. The imagery of a "road to nowhere" conveys a profound sense of emptiness, as if all his efforts have been in vain. This line speaks to the universal fear of meaninglessness, the terror of looking back on one's life and feeling as though it's amounted to nothing. Stapp's voice carries a weight of resignation, but there's also a note of defiance—a desire to escape this empty path and find something more. The guitar here grows more forceful, as though pushing against the inertia of despair, adding a layer of urgency to his quest for purpose.

"I yelled back when I heard thunder, but I'm down to one last breath," he confesses, acknowledging his past attempts to fight back against the forces that have worn him down. Thunder, often a symbol of divine or external power, here represents the challenges or perhaps the warnings he's faced. His response—yelling back—suggests a defiance, a refusal to be passive in the face of adversity. But now, as he's left with "one last breath," there's a sense of weariness, a recognition that his strength is nearly gone. This line marks a turning point in the song, as he realizes just how close he is to the edge, literally "six feet" from the brink. Tremonti's guitar intensifies, capturing the weight of this realization and amplifying the tension as he faces his final moments.

"Hold me now, I'm six feet from the edge, and I'm thinking maybe six feet ain't so far down," Stapp sings, his voice tinged with both despair and contemplation. This line is filled with haunting ambiguity. "Six feet" evokes the traditional depth of a grave, suggesting that he is inches from death. Yet there's also a strange comfort in the thought—"maybe six feet ain't so far down." It's as if he's trying to convince himself that the descent wouldn't be as frightening or final as he fears. Stapp's voice here is vulnerable, almost tender, revealing a moment of deep introspection as he contemplates his mortality. The music softens, creating a sense of intimacy, as though he's sharing his innermost thoughts with the listener.

"I'm looking down, now that it's over, reflecting on all of my mistakes," he continues, moving into a moment of reflection and regret. There's a solemnity in this line, a quiet acceptance of responsibility for the path that led him to this point. It's not a simple wallowing in self-pity; rather, it's a sober acknowledgment of the choices and actions that have shaped his life. This introspection carries a sense of humility, a willingness to face his past without flinching. Tremonti's guitar shifts to a softer, more reflective tone, mirroring the introspective mood and allowing space for the protagonist's thoughts to unfold.

"I thought I found the road to somewhere, somewhere in His grace," he confesses, adding a spiritual dimension to his journey. This line speaks to a search for redemption, for something greater than himself that might offer forgiveness and purpose. The mention of "His grace" introduces the possibility of divine intervention, a hope that perhaps he hasn't been entirely abandoned. Yet there's a sense of loss in this line, as though he once believed in this grace but now feels distant from it. Stapp's voice is filled with yearning, a quiet hope mingled with doubt. The guitar becomes almost ethereal, suggesting the possibility of transcendence, of reaching beyond the darkness.

"I cried out, 'Heaven, save me,' but I'm down to one last breath." This is a moment of raw desperation, a final plea for help from a higher power. The juxtaposition of a cry to heaven with the acknowledgment of his last breath creates a poignant tension. It's as if he's holding onto the slimmest thread of hope, even as he feels himself slipping away. This cry is both a surrender and a defiant refusal to give up entirely. Tremonti's guitar swells, building a sense of urgency that mirrors the protagonist's desperation, as though echoing his plea into the void.

"Sad eyes follow me, but I still believe there's something left for me," he reflects, introducing a glimmer of hope amid the darkness. The "sad eyes" suggest the presence of those who care, those who perhaps see his pain and long for him to find healing. Their sorrow adds weight to his struggle, but it also reminds him that he's not entirely alone. Despite everything, he clings to the belief that there's still something left for him, a purpose or a connection that makes life worth living. This line is a turning point, a shift from resignation to the faintest hope of redemption. The guitar here becomes softer, almost gentle, as though offering comfort.

"So, please come stay with me, 'cause I still believe there's something left for you and me," he pleads, reaching out for connection, for companionship. This isn't just about his own survival; it's about the shared journey, the hope that by staying together, they might find healing and purpose. This line speaks to the power of human connection, the idea that even in our darkest moments, we are not meant to face life alone. Stapp's voice softens, filled with a tenderness that suggests vulnerability and a desire for companionship. Tremonti's guitar becomes almost melodic, underscoring the hope and intimacy of this moment.

As the chorus returns—"Hold me now, I'm six feet from the edge, and I'm thinking maybe six feet ain't so far down"—there's a shift in tone. What once felt like resignation now carries a hint of strength, a decision to hold on despite the pain. Stapp's voice rises, filled with determination, as if he's choosing to live, to face whatever lies ahead rather than succumb to the darkness. The repetition of this line becomes almost a mantra, a reminder to himself that he can survive, that the edge is not the end.

In its final moments, *One Last Breath* leaves us with a sense of bittersweet hope. The protagonist hasn't found all the answers, but he has chosen to keep going, to believe that there is still something worth fighting for. Through Stapp's heartfelt lyrics and Tremonti's evocative guitar, Creed captures the universal experience of facing despair, of standing on the edge and choosing, however tentatively, to hold on. The song reminds us that even when life feels overwhelming, even when we're down to "one last breath," there's still a chance for redemption, for connection, for something meaningful to emerge from the darkness.

One Last Breath is more than a song; it's a testament to the resilience of the human spirit. It speaks to the power of vulnerability, of reaching out for help, and of finding strength in the smallest glimmers of hope. In a world that often feels isolating and unforgiving, this song serves as a reminder that even at our lowest, there is always the possibility of grace, of connection, of something more.

Application

Creed's "One Last Breath" brings to life the weight of despair and regret, yet it also holds the smallest glimmer of hope—a hope that resonates deeply with the Christian faith. The song captures the journey of someone standing on the edge, wrestling with the desire to escape pain and the instinct to hold on. The emotions expressed here mirror the struggles that many face in times of hardship and loneliness, and they invite us to look to God as the ultimate source of strength, redemption, and hope. Let's explore how this song's message aligns with biblical truths and how you can apply it to your own life in faith.

In the opening line, "Please come now, I think I'm falling," the protagonist expresses a vulnerability that feels raw and deeply human. This plea for help echoes a familiar cry throughout Scripture, where individuals reach out to God in moments of despair. Psalm 34:17-18 tells us, "The righteous cry out, and the Lord hears them; he delivers them from all their troubles. The Lord is close to the brokenhearted and saves those who are crushed in spirit." In acknowledging his need for help, the protagonist reflects the humility required to draw near to God. Admitting our need for God is often the first step toward healing, as it allows Him to enter into our struggle and lift us up. When you feel overwhelmed, remember that God is always near, ready to catch you when you fall.

"I'm holding on to all I think is safe" reflects a common human tendency to cling to anything that seems stable, even if it's only a temporary illusion of security. Many people place their trust in things that ultimately can't sustain them—money, relationships, status, or personal achievements. But Jesus calls us to build our lives on a foundation that endures. In Matthew 7:24-27, He describes the wise builder who "built his house on the rock," a metaphor for living according to God's Word. When life's storms come, it is this foundation that will hold. Rather than relying on temporary comforts, seek to anchor yourself in the love and promises of God, who is your true source of safety and stability.

The line "It seems I found the road to nowhere, and I'm trying to escape" captures the sense of futility that often accompanies feelings of despair. The protagonist's realization that he's been on a "road to nowhere" reflects a life that lacks purpose or direction. Ecclesiastes 1:14 speaks to this existential struggle, as Solomon writes, "I have seen all the things that are done under the sun; all of them are meaningless, a chasing after the wind." This search for meaning is a universal human experience, and in the Christian faith, it finds its answer in Christ. Jesus says in John 14:6, "I am the way and the truth and the life." Only in Him do we find true purpose, a path that leads not to emptiness but to eternal life and fulfillment.

"I yelled back when I heard thunder, but I'm down to one last breath" speaks to the weariness that comes from fighting against life's challenges. Thunder here symbolizes the trials and storms we face, and yelling back signifies a resistance, a desire to confront or overcome these struggles. Yet the admission of being "down to one last breath" shows that his strength is nearly gone. In 2 Corinthians 12:9-10, Paul shares that God's grace is sufficient, saying, "for my power is made perfect in weakness." When we reach the end of our strength, God's power is revealed, allowing us to rely on Him rather than ourselves. In your own journey, remember that even when you're down to "one last breath," God's strength is available to sustain you.

"Hold me now, I'm six feet from the edge, and I'm thinking maybe six feet ain't so far down" conveys the tension between despair and the faint hope that there's still something worth holding onto. The "edge" here symbolizes the brink of giving up, yet the line also suggests a curiosity—a questioning of whether it's truly the end. Psalm 40:1-2 captures this hope in times of despair: "I waited patiently for the Lord; he turned to me and heard my cry. He lifted me out of the slimy pit, out of the mud and mire." When you feel close to giving up, remember that God can lift you from the depths, giving you a reason to hold on. Even when you feel close to the "edge," know that God is present, reaching out to draw you back to safety.

"I'm looking down, now that it's over, reflecting on all of my mistakes" brings a moment of introspection, where the protagonist faces the reality of his choices. This kind of reflection aligns with the biblical practice of repentance. In 1 John 1:9, we're told, "If we confess our sins, he is faithful and just and will forgive us our sins and purify us from all unrighteousness." Honest reflection is essential for growth, but as believers, we're also invited to receive God's forgiveness and to let go of regret. When you look back on past mistakes, do so with a heart open to God's grace, allowing His mercy to guide you forward rather than letting guilt hold you back.

The line "I thought I found the road to somewhere, somewhere in His grace" introduces a spiritual dimension to the protagonist's journey, hinting at a past hope in divine grace. This search for grace reflects a yearning for redemption and connection with God. In Ephesians 2:8, Paul reminds us, "For it is by grace you have been saved, through faith—and this is not from yourselves, it is the gift of God." God's grace is a gift that brings purpose and meaning, even in the darkest moments. When you feel distant from God, remember that His grace is always available, inviting you back into relationship with Him.

"I cried out, 'Heaven, save me,' but I'm down to one last breath" is a raw expression of desperation, a final plea for rescue. In times of deep struggle, calling out to God can be an act of surrender, an acknowledgment that we need His help to make it through. Psalm 18:6 reflects this cry: "In my distress I called to the Lord; I cried to my God for help. From his temple he heard my voice." God hears every plea, and His love reaches into even the darkest places to offer comfort and healing. When you reach the end of your own strength, don't be afraid to cry out to God, trusting that He is near and ready to answer.

"Sad eyes follow me, but I still believe there's something left for me" introduces a glimmer of hope, a belief that there's still something worth living for. The presence of "sad eyes" suggests that others care for him, and their empathy serves as a reminder that he's not alone. Ecclesiastes 4:9-10 emphasizes the importance of companionship: "Two are better than one... if either of them falls down, one can help the other up." In times of hardship, remember that God has placed people in your life to offer support and encouragement. Lean on your community, allowing others to be a source of strength and hope.

"So, please come stay with me, 'cause I still believe there's something left for you and me" is a call for connection, an acknowledgment of the healing power found in relationships. This plea echoes the biblical call to bear one another's burdens, as we see in Galatians 6:2: "Carry each other's burdens, and in this way you will fulfill the law of Christ." As Christians, we're invited to be a source of comfort and support for others, reminding one another of God's love and purpose. When you're struggling, seek companionship and connection, remembering that you're not meant to face life's challenges alone.

As the song's chorus repeats, "Hold me now, I'm six feet from the edge, and I'm thinking maybe six feet ain't so far down," it becomes a statement of resilience, a choice to hold on despite the darkness. Philippians 4:13 declares, "I can do all this through him who gives me strength." When you feel close to giving up, rely on the strength that comes from God, trusting that He will provide the endurance you need. Through faith, you can find the courage to face each new day, knowing that God walks with you.

Ultimately, "One Last Breath" serves as a reminder of the resilience and hope found in the human spirit, especially when anchored in faith. In moments of despair, when you feel close to the edge, turn to God, trusting in His promises and embracing the strength He offers. He will carry you through, offering a love that is steadfast and a hope that endures, even when life feels overwhelmingly difficult. Let the message of this song inspire you to reach out for God's grace, to lean on those around you, and to believe that there is always something worth fighting for—something that God has planned for you, no matter how close you may feel to the edge.

CHAPTER 28
"My Sacrifice"

*M*y Sacrifice by Creed is an evocative reflection on friendship, redemption, and the healing power of connection. The song's lyrics carry a sense of nostalgia, warmth, and depth, like a reunion of souls who have weathered storms and found solace in each other's presence. Through Stapp's passionate delivery and Tremonti's tender yet powerful guitar, we are drawn into a reunion not just between friends but between fragments of the self—a return to a place of inner peace, reconciliation, and freedom. *My Sacrifice* isn't just about reconnecting with another person; it's a journey into the heart, where memories of love and shared struggles bring clarity and healing.

"Hello my friend, we meet again," the song opens, with a greeting that feels intimate, almost sacred. The word "friend" here resonates on multiple levels, encompassing not only an external relationship but an internal one as well, as if the protagonist is reconnecting with an aspect of himself he had lost touch with. The line "It's been a while, where should we begin?" suggests a long absence, a separation that has left both parties changed. There's an acknowledgment here that while time has passed, the connection remains intact. Stapp's voice is warm and inviting, filled with a mixture of relief and yearning, as if he's finally returning home after a long journey. Tremonti's gentle guitar echoes this sentiment, creating an atmosphere of reunion and peace.

"Within my heart are memories of perfect love that you gave to me," he continues, delving into the emotional reservoir of past experiences that have shaped him. These "memories of perfect love" suggest a profound, unconditional connection that has left an indelible mark on his heart. This love isn't merely romantic; it's transformative, an experience of being seen and accepted without reservation. Stapp's voice softens here, filled with reverence, as he reflects on the gift of this love. It's not something he can hold onto physically, but it lives on within him, shaping his understanding of himself and the world. The guitar swells gently, as if underscoring the depth and purity of this love, a love that transcends time and distance.

"When you are with me, I'm free; I'm careless, I believe." These lines capture the essence of liberation that true connection brings. The freedom he describes isn't merely physical; it's emotional and spiritual—a release from the burdens of self-doubt, fear, and insecurity. To be "careless" here is not recklessness; it's a lightness, a feeling of being unencumbered by life's pressures and judgments. There's a trust, an implicit faith that allows him to let go and believe in the beauty of the present moment. Stapp's voice here is filled with a sense of surrender, a willingness to open himself completely. Tremonti's guitar takes on a soaring quality, mirroring the sense of flight and elevation that comes with this freedom. Together, they create a moment of transcendence, a reminder of the purity that connection can bring.

"Above all the others, we'll fly," he sings, suggesting that this bond lifts them beyond the ordinary, beyond the struggles and limitations of everyday life. There's a sense of ascension here, a belief that together, they can rise above whatever obstacles they face. This line is not about superiority but about transcendence—a reminder that true connection elevates us, bringing us closer to something divine. Stapp's voice carries a quiet awe, as though he's marveling at the beauty of this shared experience. Tremonti's guitar adds a layer of intensity, capturing the exhilaration and wonder of this flight, a moment where everything else fades away, leaving only the purity of connection.

"This brings tears to my eyes," he confesses, allowing the depth of his emotion to surface. These are not tears of sorrow but of gratitude, a recognition of the beauty and fragility of the moment. The simplicity of this line underscores its authenticity; he's not trying to mask his emotions or make them palatable. Instead, he lets the listener feel the raw impact of this reunion, this rediscovery of something sacred. Stapp's voice trembles slightly, revealing a vulnerability that adds depth to his expression. Tremonti's guitar takes on a softer, almost weeping quality, as if echoing the protagonist's tears and amplifying the emotion.

"We've seen our share of ups and downs; oh, how quickly life can turn around in an instant." This line shifts the song from the present moment of reunion to a broader reflection on life's unpredictability. The protagonist acknowledges the highs and lows they've faced, the moments of joy and sorrow that have shaped their journey. There's a bittersweet quality here, a recognition that life's beauty is inseparable from its challenges. Stapp's voice is filled with both nostalgia and acceptance, as though he's learned to embrace the fullness of life's experiences. Tremonti's guitar becomes more introspective, capturing the complexity of this reflection, the way that joy and sorrow are woven together in the tapestry of life.

"It feels so good to reunite, within yourself and within your mind. Let's find peace there." These lines bring the song into a deeply introspective space, as the protagonist recognizes that true peace comes from within. This reunion isn't only with a friend but with his own sense of inner calm, a return to a place where he feels whole and grounded. There's a gentle encouragement here, a reminder to seek peace not in external circumstances but within one's own heart and mind. Stapp's voice is soft, almost meditative, as he invites the listener to join him in this inward journey. Tremonti's guitar takes on a soothing tone, creating an atmosphere of serenity that feels almost like a balm, a moment of respite from life's chaos.

The chorus repeats, "When you are with me, I'm free; I'm careless, I believe. Above all the others, we'll fly." This refrain becomes a mantra, a reminder of the freedom and elevation that come from connection. Each repetition deepens the feeling, allowing the listener to sink into the experience of liberation and joy. Stapp's voice grows more intense with each iteration, as if he's reaffirming this truth to himself, anchoring it in his soul. Tremonti's guitar soars alongside him, capturing the exhilaration of release, the way that love and connection can lift us beyond ourselves.

"I just want to say hello again," he sings, returning to the simple joy of reconnecting. This line is filled with warmth, a desire to renew a bond that has brought him so much peace and strength. The word "hello" here is loaded with meaning; it's not just a greeting but a recognition, a way of saying, "I see you, and I am grateful for you." Stapp's voice is filled with tenderness, a softness that suggests he's fully present, fully appreciative of this moment. The music slows slightly, creating space for the intimacy of this moment to settle.

In the final repetitions of the chorus, "When you are with me, I'm free; I'm careless, I believe," the song reaches a crescendo of emotion. This isn't just a reunion with a friend or a loved one; it's a reunion with himself, a reconnection with the parts of his soul that he may have lost along the way. The phrase "My sacrifice" takes on a new depth here, suggesting that whatever he's given up, whatever he's endured, has led him to this place of peace and connection. Stapp's voice is filled with a mixture of gratitude and reverence, as though he's finally found something worth holding onto. Tremonti's guitar swells, capturing the magnitude of this moment, a celebration of love, resilience, and faith.

My Sacrifice is more than a song about friendship or love; it's a meditation on the beauty of reconnection, the way that relationships can ground us and lift us up simultaneously. Through Stapp's heartfelt lyrics and Tremonti's soulful guitar, Creed invites us to reflect on the people and memories that bring us back to ourselves, the moments of connection that remind us of our capacity for love and freedom. It's a reminder that even when life's struggles feel overwhelming, there is always the possibility of reunion, of rediscovery, of finding peace within ourselves and each other.

In the end, *My Sacrifice* leaves us with a sense of gratitude—a recognition of the gifts we receive through connection, through shared experiences, through love that transcends time and hardship. It's a song that encourages us to look beyond the surface, to seek the deeper meaning in our relationships, and to hold onto the memories and moments that remind us of our capacity for joy, resilience, and peace.

Application

Creed's *My Sacrifice* is a powerful reflection on friendship, redemption, and the healing found in reconnecting both with others and within oneself. The song takes us through a journey of reunion, where past struggles and shared memories serve as anchors that bring peace and healing. In many ways, this mirrors the Christian experience of reconciliation—first with God and then with others—and the profound sense of freedom, gratitude, and peace that emerges from restored relationships. Through its lyrics and music, *My Sacrifice* points us toward the beauty of reunion, not only with loved ones but with the parts of ourselves we may have lost in life's journey. Here's how these themes align with biblical truths and how you can apply them to your life as a Christian.

"Hello my friend, we meet again" opens the song with an intimate greeting that feels sacred. This reunion is not only with a friend but perhaps also with a part of himself that has been estranged or lost. In the same way, our relationship with God often begins as a reunion—a "meeting again" with our Creator. James 4:8 encourages us, "Draw near to God, and He will draw near to you." When we turn back to God, it's like returning home, reconnecting with the One who has always known us fully. If you've experienced seasons of distance or disconnection from God, remember that He welcomes you back with open arms. Just as the song captures the warmth of reunion, so too does God rejoice when we turn back to Him.

"Within my heart are memories of perfect love that you gave to me" speaks of an enduring love that has left a lasting imprint. This love is reminiscent of the love God shows us, a love that is unconditional, perfect, and transformative. Romans 8:38-39 reminds us that nothing "will be able to separate us from the love of God that is in Christ Jesus our Lord." This divine love leaves an indelible mark on our hearts, shaping our understanding of ourselves and the world. Just as the protagonist in the song cherishes these memories, we too can hold on to the knowledge of God's love as an anchor in our lives. When you reflect on your relationship with God, remember the moments when you have felt His presence, and let those memories bring you comfort and encouragement.

"When you are with me, I'm free; I'm careless, I believe" describes a liberation that comes from being in the presence of someone who offers love and acceptance. In a similar way, the Bible speaks of the freedom we have in Christ. Galatians 5:1 tells us, "It is for freedom that Christ has set us free." This freedom is not reckless or without purpose; it is a release from the burdens of sin, fear, and insecurity. In Christ, we find a safe space to be fully ourselves, unencumbered by shame or judgment. Allow this truth to transform the way you see yourself and live your life. Embrace the freedom that comes from knowing you are loved and accepted by God.

"Above all the others, we'll fly" expresses the idea of transcendence—rising above life's struggles and finding joy in connection. This line recalls Isaiah 40:31, which promises that "those who hope in the Lord will renew their strength. They will soar on wings like eagles." When we trust in God, we can experience moments of transcendence, where His presence lifts us above the trials and limitations of this world. This isn't about escaping reality but about gaining a perspective that gives us strength to endure. When life feels heavy, lean into your relationship with God, allowing Him to lift you up and give you a sense of peace and purpose.

"This brings tears to my eyes" captures the gratitude and vulnerability that come from reconnecting with someone dear. In the Bible, we see examples of people moved to tears in moments of profound spiritual revelation or reunion with God. Psalm 126:5 reminds us that "those who sow with tears will reap with songs of joy." Tears are often a part of the healing process, a release that brings renewal. When you experience deep emotions in your walk with God, don't be afraid to let those feelings surface. Whether they're tears of gratitude, sorrow, or relief, God sees your heart and is present in those moments.

"We've seen our share of ups and downs; oh, how quickly life can turn around in an instant" reflects on life's unpredictability, acknowledging the challenges and changes that shape our journey. This aligns with Ecclesiastes 3:1, which says, "There is a time for everything, and a season for every activity under the heavens." Life is filled with highs and lows, yet each season has its purpose. Recognizing this helps us to approach both joy and sorrow with acceptance, trusting that God is with us through it all. As you reflect on your life's journey, find comfort in knowing that every experience, whether joyful or challenging, is part of a greater purpose in God's plan.

"It feels so good to reunite, within yourself and within your mind. Let's find peace there" points to the idea that true peace begins within. Jesus speaks of this inner peace in John 14:27, saying, "Peace I leave with you; my peace I give you. I do not give to you as the world gives." The peace of Christ is not dependent on external circumstances; it is a deep, abiding peace that comes from knowing and trusting Him. By seeking God's presence, you can find a sense of calm and assurance that transcends the chaos of the world. When life feels turbulent, remember to turn inward and seek the peace that God offers—a peace that can sustain you no matter what challenges you face.

"When you are with me, I'm free; I'm careless, I believe" repeats as a refrain, becoming a mantra that reinforces the freedom and trust found in connection. In the Christian life, this freedom is found in communion with God, where we are reminded of our true identity as His children. 2 Corinthians 3:17 says, "Where the Spirit of the Lord is, there is freedom." Living in the presence of God liberates us from fear, doubt, and shame, empowering us to live fully and joyfully. Let this refrain remind you of the freedom you have in Christ, a freedom that gives you confidence to embrace life with hope and trust.

"I just want to say hello again" returns to the simple joy of reconnecting. This greeting is filled with warmth and gratitude, a reminder of the power of presence. In the story of the prodigal son (Luke 15:11-32), we see a beautiful example of reunion, where the father welcomes his lost son back with open arms. This story reflects God's eagerness to reconnect with us, no matter how far we may have wandered. Just as the protagonist in the song rejoices in reconnecting with his friend, we too can find joy in the knowledge that God is always ready to welcome us back. When you feel distant from God, know that you can always return and say "hello" again.

The final repetitions of "When you are with me, I'm free; I'm careless, I believe" reach a crescendo, symbolizing the completeness of reunion. This is not only a reconnection with another person but a reconnection with oneself—a sense of wholeness found in restored relationships. Romans 5:10 tells us that "while we were God's enemies, we were reconciled to Him through the death of His Son." Through Christ, we are reconciled to God, made whole, and brought into peace with Him. This sacrificial love provides a foundation upon which we can build other meaningful connections in our lives, finding unity, healing, and joy in relationships.

"My sacrifice" ultimately reflects the idea that love often involves giving of oneself, enduring trials, and letting go of pride or past hurts. Jesus exemplified this perfectly in His sacrifice for us, laying down His life out of love. John 15:13 tells us, "Greater love has no one than this: to lay down one's life for one's friends." Our relationships, too, may require sacrifices—patience, forgiveness, humility—but through these acts, we find deeper connection and purpose. When you consider the relationships in your life, ask God to show you how you can reflect His sacrificial love, building bonds that strengthen and uplift.

In *My Sacrifice*, Creed captures the beauty and depth of connection, reminding us of the transformative power of love, reunion, and redemption. In times of struggle, loneliness, or joy, allow the message of this song to remind you of the eternal reunion and peace offered in Christ. Through God's love, we find freedom, strength, and the joy of belonging, a gift that brings us closer to Him and to each other. Embrace this truth, knowing that even in life's ups and downs, there is always the hope of reconciliation, healing, and peace that endures.

CHAPTER 29
"Stand Here With Me"

S tand Here With Me by Creed is a heartfelt tribute to a person whose impact has been transformative, a guide who has shown the way through life's complexities. The song is a meditation on gratitude, admiration, and the enduring influence of a presence that has shaped the protagonist's outlook. It's an anthem of remembrance and appreciation, capturing the essence of someone who has provided strength, clarity, and purpose. Through Scott Stapp's evocative vocals and Mark Tremonti's uplifting guitar work, the listener is drawn into a celebration of influence—a recognition of the profound gift of having someone who stands by you, even in spirit.

"You always reached out to me and helped me believe," Stapp begins, establishing the depth of this relationship with simple yet powerful words. This isn't a superficial connection but a lifeline, someone who reached out not just to comfort but to inspire faith and belief. The phrase "helped me believe" speaks to the profound impact of this person, suggesting that their influence brought light into moments of doubt. Stapp's voice carries a tone of reverence here, as though he is recalling a time when his own strength faltered, but this person's support lifted him up. Tremonti's guitar follows with a subtle, reverent melody that amplifies the sincerity of this gratitude.

"All those memories we share, I will cherish every one of them," he continues, with a nostalgic warmth that captures the beauty of shared experiences. The memories aren't just moments in time; they're treasures, each one carrying weight and meaning that he holds close. This line reveals the protagonist's deep appreciation for these experiences, for the moments that have shaped who he has become. There's a timeless quality to this sentiment, a recognition that the person's impact is eternal, held within the heart. Tremonti's chords rise gently, underscoring the intimacy of these memories, as if the music itself is carrying each cherished moment forward.

"For the truth of it is there's a right way to live, and you showed me." This line stands as a testament to the moral and ethical guidance this person has provided. It's not just about actions but a philosophy of life, a code of conduct that the protagonist has come to understand through example. This truth, this "right way to live," speaks to integrity, kindness, and the importance of selflessness. Stapp's voice takes on a tone of quiet strength here, as if he is finally realizing the depth of the lessons he has received. The guitar takes on a richer, fuller sound, mirroring the weight of this realization, grounding the song in a sense of purpose and meaning.

"So now you live on in the words of a song; you're a melody." In this line, the protagonist transforms his appreciation into something immortal. By likening this person's presence to a melody, he suggests that their influence is woven into the very fabric of his being, always present, always resonant. This is not merely a metaphor; it's an acknowledgment that their spirit lives on in a form that is both intangible and eternal, like a song that never fades. Tremonti's guitar echoes this sentiment with a melody that feels timeless, almost as if it could go on forever, embodying the continuous, unbroken presence of this person's legacy.

"'Cause you stand here with me now, yeah," Stapp sings, repeating this line with a reverence that deepens with each iteration. This is the core of the song—the sense that even in their absence, this person's influence remains, standing alongside him as a source of strength. It's an image of spiritual companionship, a reminder that the impact of those we love doesn't disappear but becomes a part of us. Stapp's voice is filled with conviction, as if he truly believes that this presence is tangible, something he can feel in the most challenging and uplifting moments. Tremonti's guitar lifts here, creating a sense of elevation, as though this presence is lifting him beyond his fears and doubts.

"Just when the fear blinded me, you taught me to dream." This line captures the dual role of this person as both a protector and a visionary guide. The protagonist acknowledges his own vulnerability—moments when fear obscured his vision and made him feel lost. But this person didn't just shield him from fear; they inspired him to look beyond it, to dream despite it. There's a transformative quality in this guidance, as though they not only helped him through difficult times but also encouraged him to reach for something greater. Stapp's voice is filled with a mix of humility and gratitude, as he recognizes the profound nature of this gift. Tremonti's guitar becomes more assertive, capturing the strength that comes from having someone who believes in you, even when you doubt yourself.

"I'll give you everything I am and still fall short of what you've done for me." This line conveys a sense of awe at the selflessness and generosity of this person's love. The protagonist is keenly aware of the depth of what he has received, feeling that no matter how much he gives, it will never fully repay the gift of support and guidance he has been shown. There's humility in this line, a recognition that the love he has received is boundless, something that can't be measured or re-paid. Stapp's voice is filled with reverence, as if he's offering a heartfelt tribute to this person's impact. Tremonti's guitar takes on a softer, more reflective tone, underscoring the depth of gratitude and the sense of unworthiness that often accompanies receiving unconditional love.

"In this life that I live, I hope I can give love unselfishly," he sings, expressing his desire to pass on the legacy of love he has received. This is not just admiration; it's a commitment to embody the same values, to live with the same selflessness that he has witnessed. There's a sense of growth in this line, as if the protagonist has internalized the lessons and is now ready to carry them forward. Stapp's voice is filled with resolve, a quiet determination to honor this person's legacy by living in a way that reflects their influence. The guitar builds, becoming more resolute, as if echoing this newfound purpose.

"I've learned the world is bigger than me; you're my daily dose of reality." This line brings a moment of groundedness, a recognition that this person has taught him to look beyond his own needs and see the bigger picture. This "daily dose of reality" is a reminder to stay humble, to remain aware of his place in the world, and to approach life with a sense of perspective. It's a gentle reminder to focus on what truly matters, to let go of ego and embrace humility. Stapp's voice is filled with gratitude for this grounding influence, and Tremonti's guitar takes on a steady, grounding rhythm, reinforcing the sense of stability and clarity this person provides.

In the repeated refrain, "On and on we sing this song," the song becomes a communal act of remembrance and celebration. This refrain is a testament to the endurance of love and memory, a song that will continue beyond the present moment, echoing through time. Each repetition feels like a prayer, a dedication to the person who has made such a lasting impact. Stapp's voice grows stronger with each repetition, as if he is drawing strength from the act of singing, from the acknowledgment that this presence remains with him, always. Tremonti's guitar soars, filling the space with a sense of elevation, as though the song itself is lifting both the protagonist and the listener into a place of reverence and gratitude.

Stand Here With Me is more than just a song of gratitude; it's an ode to the people who guide us, shape us, and leave an indelible mark on our souls. Through Stapp's heartfelt lyrics and Tremonti's powerful, uplifting guitar, Creed captures the essence of spiritual companionship—a connection that transcends time, distance, and even death. It's a reminder that those who impact us deeply never truly leave us; they become a part of us, a melody that lives on, guiding us through life's ups and downs.

This song encourages us to remember the people who have stood by us, to honor their legacy by living with integrity, humility, and love. It reminds us that even when they're not physically present, their influence remains, offering strength, clarity, and purpose. In a world that often feels isolating, *Stand Here With Me* is a reminder of the power of connection, of the enduring bonds that keep us grounded and lift us up. It's a song that celebrates the beauty of being guided by love and the comfort of knowing that those who shaped us are always with us, standing by our side.

Application

Creed's *Stand Here With Me* is a song of gratitude and tribute, honoring the profound influence of a person whose presence has brought guidance, clarity, and strength. The lyrics convey a sense of admiration for someone who has been a steadfast support, shaping the protagonist's life and helping him see beyond himself. This kind of mentorship and companionship resonates with the biblical idea of discipleship and the transformative power of love and guidance in one's life. Let's explore how the message of this song aligns with biblical principles and how you can apply it in your faith journey.

"You always reached out to me and helped me believe" opens the song with words that reflect the lifeline that this person has provided. Their influence extends beyond comfort, inspiring faith and a renewed sense of purpose. In Proverbs 27:17, we read, "As iron sharpens iron, so one person sharpens another." Relationships that bring us closer to faith are gifts that strengthen our resolve and encourage us to pursue a meaningful life. Just as the protagonist expresses gratitude for someone who "reached out" and offered support, we are called to both appreciate those who inspire us and be that source of strength for others, helping them find their faith in times of doubt.

"All those memories we share, I will cherish every one of them" emphasizes the beauty of shared experiences and the lasting impact of meaningful relationships. The memories are not just fleeting moments; they are treasured experiences that continue to shape him. In Philippians 1:3, Paul writes to the church, "I thank my God every time I remember you." Cherished memories with those who have walked alongside us are blessings to hold close. When you reflect on those who have left a positive impact on your life, let that gratitude lead you to thank God for the ways He has used people to bring you closer to Him, and to remember that every moment shared in love is a gift.

"For the truth of it is there's a right way to live, and you showed me" highlights the moral and ethical guidance provided by this person. It speaks to the biblical principle of living with integrity, kindness, and humility, as seen in Micah 6:8, which says, "He has shown you, O mortal, what is good. And what does the Lord require of you? To act justly and to love mercy and to walk humbly with your God." The "right way to live" is found in following God's principles, and when we are blessed with mentors or friends who embody these values, their example can guide us toward a life that honors God. If you have someone in your life who models Christlike behavior, let their influence inspire you to pursue integrity and selflessness.

"So now you live on in the words of a song; you're a melody" expresses the idea that the person's influence is both eternal and ever-present. Like a melody that stays with us, their impact remains woven into his life. This is reminiscent of the legacy that godly people leave behind, as described in Proverbs 10:7, "The memory of the righteous is a blessing." A life lived in alignment with God's will creates a lasting influence that inspires others even after they are gone. When you think of those who have left an imprint on your heart, consider how you can carry their legacy forward by living out the values they instilled in you.

"'Cause you stand here with me now" underscores the core of the song, the sense that this person's presence endures, standing by him even when physically absent. Hebrews 12:1 speaks of the "great cloud of witnesses" that surrounds us, reminding us that those who have gone before us are part of our spiritual journey, cheering us on. While these witnesses include people of faith from Scripture, it also applies to loved ones who have guided us in faith. Their impact remains with us as a source of encouragement and strength. Take comfort in the presence of those who have shaped you, knowing that their influence stays with you, strengthening you in both challenging and joyful moments.

"Just when the fear blinded me, you taught me to dream" conveys the powerful encouragement this person provided, helping him see beyond his fears and believe in something greater. This resonates with the encouragement found in 2 Timothy 1:7, which says, "For the Spirit God gave us does not make us timid, but gives us power, love, and self-discipline." Having someone who encourages you to overcome fear and pursue your dreams is a gift, and in our Christian walk, God often uses others to remind us of His promises and to embolden us to step forward in faith. When you face doubt or fear, remember the encouragement of those who believe in you and trust that God is with you, guiding you to dream beyond your limitations.

"I'll give you everything I am and still fall short of what you've done for me" expresses a humble acknowledgment of the selfless love and support he has received. It mirrors our response to God's grace, which is a gift we can never fully repay. Ephesians 2:8-9 tells us, "For it is by grace you have been saved, through faith—and this is not from yourselves, it is the gift of God—not by works, so that no one can boast." Just as the protagonist feels indebted to this person, we recognize that God's love and grace are boundless and cannot be repaid. Let this humility inspire you to live with a grateful heart, appreciating both God's love and the selflessness of those who have shown you kindness.

"In this life that I live, I hope I can give love unselfishly" reveals his desire to carry forward the legacy of love he has received. This aligns with Jesus' teaching in John 13:34-35, where He says, "A new command I give you: Love one another. As I have loved you, so you must love one another." The love we receive is not meant to be held onto but to be shared generously with others. As you live your life, seek to reflect the love that others have shown you, embodying the selflessness and generosity that have inspired you. By loving others unselfishly, you honor the legacy of those who have loved you well.

"I've learned the world is bigger than me; you're my daily dose of reality" speaks to the grounding influence this person has provided, teaching him humility and perspective. Philippians 2:3-4 reminds us, "Do nothing out of selfish ambition or vain conceit. Rather, in humility value others above yourselves, not looking to your own interests but each of you to the interests of the others." Realizing that the world is bigger than ourselves calls us to live with humility and compassion, considering others' needs and perspectives. When you reflect on the influence of those who have grounded you, let their example encour-age you to live with humility, valuing others and serving with a heart that reflects God's love.

The repeated refrain, "On and on we sing this song," transforms the song into a shared act of remembrance and gratitude. This refrain echoes the biblical call to remember and celebrate the blessings in our lives. Psalm 77:11 says, "I will remember the deeds of the Lord; yes, I will remember your miracles of long ago." In both faith and relation-ships, remembering the good that has been done for us strengthens our spirit and reminds us of God's faithfulness. When you sing this "song" of gratitude for those who have impacted you, let it become a prayer of thanks, recognizing the ways they have drawn you closer to God.

Stand Here With Me is more than a song of thanks; it's an anthem celebrating the legacy of love, guidance, and support from those who have shaped us. Just as this person's presence continues to inspire the protagonist, the love we receive becomes a part of who we are, shaping our journey and helping us grow in faith. This song serves as a reminder that those who walk with us, guide us, and love us are gifts from God, and their influence can uplift and ground us, bringing us closer to Him.

In the Christian life, *Stand Here With Me* encourages us to remember and honor those who have helped us see God's truth, strengthened us in times of weakness, and taught us to live with pur-pose. As you reflect on the people who have impacted you, let their influence inspire you to walk in faith, gratitude, and love, carrying forward the legacy they've left in your life. Through God's grace, may you be a source of strength and encouragement for others, embodying the love, humility, and guidance that have been gifted to you.

CHAPTER 30
"Weathered"

The song *Weathered* by Creed captures a deep, almost visceral struggle between fragility and resilience. Beneath the jagged edge of Scott Stapp's voice and Mark Tremonti's raw, grinding guitar chords lies an aching portrait of endurance and human vulnerability, channeled through a haunting melody that feels both timeless and distinctly personal. In a way, the music and lyrics invite us to travel down a desolate road, each phrase and chord peeling back layers of inner conflict and weariness, exposing a soul that feels worn yet somehow refuses to yield entirely.

The opening lines immediately plunge us into a place of unrest. Stapp's vocal delivery—almost haunted—draws us into the dark interior world of a mind battling with its own existence. "I lie awake on a long, dark night / I can't seem to tame my mind," he sings. There's a loneliness here, a familiar one, echoing the moments when we too have lain awake, unable to quiet the voices within. In the music, there's a restrained tension in the first chords, a slow and steady build that matches this restlessness. Tremonti's guitar, heavily textured and layered with distortion, adds weight to each line, as if to amplify the inescapable pull of these inner shadows. The resonance of these notes feels almost like a heartbeat, muted but insistent—a reminder of the ceaseless demands of life, pulsing beneath the surface of exhaustion.

This song is a journey of self-confrontation, and its progression mirrors the fluctuations of that journey. The protagonist grapples with self-acceptance, singing, "Maybe I can't accept the life that's mine." In this line, Stapp captures the universal struggle of wrestling with one's place in the world. There's a sense of resistance here—a resistance to the cards life has dealt, a refusal to settle into what feels like an ill-fitting role. And yet, there's resignation too. The complexity of these conflicting emotions creates a tone that is at once raw and subdued, as if he's aware of his limitations but is still fighting against them.

As the song continues, the lyrics move into themes of self-isolation and numbness: "Simple living is my desperate cry / Been trading love with indifference." These lines suggest a retreat from the vulnerability of connection. The phrase "trading love with indifference" is especially telling—it captures the way we sometimes shield ourselves from hurt by withdrawing emotionally, allowing a protective numbness to settle in. The musical choices here reflect this inward retreat, with Tremonti's guitar creating a fuller, almost suffocating atmosphere that mirrors the weight of indifference. This is not a light withdrawal; it's a burden that dulls the senses, leading to a "calloused" existence.

The phrase "I try to hold on but I'm calloused to the bone" speaks to a hardness born of survival. Calluses, in their essence, are formed by repeated friction, a protective response to pain. In this case, the calluses are metaphorical, marking a life that has been worn down by constant hardship. There's an almost tragic acceptance in Stapp's voice here; he's aware of his own isolation, of the toll it's taken, and yet he feels powerless to break free. "Maybe that's why I feel alone," he admits, acknowledging that his self-protection has also become a prison. It's a poignant moment, exposing the irony of seeking safety in isolation, only to find oneself trapped within it.

The refrain, "I'm rusted and weathered / Barely holding together," is central to the song's theme of decay and endurance. The imagery of rust evokes the slow, inevitable process of corrosion, suggesting that life's struggles have gradually worn away at the protagonist's strength. "Weathered" suggests exposure to the harsh elements—like wood or metal left to the mercy of wind, rain, and sun, slowly breaking down over time. There's a sense of exhaustion here, of a soul that has been battered by life's relentless storms. Yet, there's also resilience in the very act of acknowledging this state; he's still "holding together," however fragile that hold might be.

Musically, this refrain is powerful. The guitar's texture becomes almost abrasive, like metal grinding against stone. It's as if Tremonti is mirroring the rawness of human endurance, each chord and note layered with distortion to evoke the experience of barely keeping oneself intact. The rhythm and pace add to the sense of weariness, capturing the slow, heavy steps of someone carrying an invisible weight.

As the song progresses, there's a shift, a slight turn toward light: "The sun shines and I can't avoid the light." This line holds a subtle tension between surrender and defiance. The "light" here could represent truth, awareness, or even hope. Yet, the protagonist's response is not one of embrace but rather of reluctant acceptance—he "can't avoid" it, suggesting that facing this light is painful. The awareness of truth, of life's demands and disappointments, is not easily borne; it's something he would rather avoid but cannot. The music here shifts subtly, opening up just a bit, as if allowing a sliver of hope to enter the otherwise dark atmosphere.

When he sings, "Ashes to ashes and dust to dust / Sometimes I feel like giving up," there's a solemn recognition of mortality, an awareness that everything ultimately fades. The biblical allusion in "ashes to ashes" evokes the inevitability of death, the inescapable end that awaits us all. Yet, despite this, he doesn't surrender. The phrase "I feel like giving up" is tinged with weariness, but it's also a statement of resistance—he feels like giving up, but he hasn't done so. This acknowledgment of mortality adds depth to his struggle; he's wrestling not just with his own limitations but with the finite nature of life itself.

One of the song's most powerful sections comes toward the end: "Take all this pride and leave it behind / 'Cause one day it ends, one day we die." Here, Stapp seems to reach a moment of clarity. Pride, which often binds us to our own suffering, is revealed as an obstacle to inner peace. By letting go of pride, there's a hint that he might find some form of release. The realization that "one day we die" is sobering, yet it also holds a kind of freedom—the freedom to let go of things that no longer serve us, to focus instead on what truly matters.

The final lines, "Believe what you will, that is your right / But I choose to win, I choose to fight," represent a choice. In the face of decay, isolation, and weariness, he makes a conscious decision not to surrender to despair. This decision to "fight" isn't about external battles; it's an inner resolve to hold onto hope, however fragile, and to resist the corrosion that threatens to consume him. It's a powerful moment of self-affirmation, one that speaks to the human spirit's resilience in the face of suffering.

Throughout *Weathered*, there's a subtle interplay between surrender and resistance, between acknowledging pain and choosing not to be defined by it. The song captures the paradox of human experience—the way we can feel both broken and unbreakable, fragile and resilient, all at once. The music, with its heavy, layered textures and haunting melodies, underscores this paradox, creating a soundscape that feels both intimate and epic, as if inviting us to witness the quiet heroism of endurance.

Ultimately, *Weathered* is a song about transformation—not a dramatic, sudden change, but the slow, difficult work of survival. It's about facing the darkness within and choosing, day by day, to hold on. In the end, there's no easy resolution, no triumph or victory. The protagonist remains "barely holding together," but he's still here, still fighting. In this way, the song becomes a testament to the power of perseverance, to the quiet strength that comes from simply refusing to give up.

Application

Weathered by Creed is a hauntingly beautiful song that explores themes of resilience, weariness, and the inner battle between surrender and survival. The lyrics delve into the struggles of enduring life's challenges, grappling with vulnerability, and confronting one's own limitations. In many ways, this song reflects the Christian journey of faith—one that encounters hardship yet clings to hope, one that recognizes human frailty while relying on God's strength to press on. Let's explore how the song's themes align with biblical principles and how you can draw inspiration from them in your walk with God.

"I lie awake on a long, dark night / I can't seem to tame my mind" opens the song with a raw admission of restlessness, a feeling many of us experience in times of anxiety or despair. These dark, sleepless nights are when fears and worries often feel magnified. In Psalm 63:6-7, David writes, "On my bed I remember you; I think of you through the watches of the night. Because you are my help, I sing in the shadow of your wings." When we lie awake at night, troubled by life's challenges, God invites us to turn our thoughts toward Him, allowing His presence to bring comfort and peace. When you find yourself restless or anxious, take those moments to seek God in prayer, trusting that He is near, even in the darkness.

"Maybe I can't accept the life that's mine" reflects a struggle with self-acceptance, a tension between who we are and who we wish we could be. This resonates with the Apostle Paul's words in Romans 7:15, where he describes his own inner conflict: "I do not understand what I do. For what I want to do I do not do, but what I hate I do." The Christian journey often involves wrestling with our own weaknesses and failures. Yet God calls us to find our identity in Christ, who loves us despite our imperfections. When you struggle to accept yourself, remember that God's love is not based on who you wish you could be but on who He has created you to be, with all your strengths and weaknesses.

"Simple living is my desperate cry / Been trading love with indifference" speaks to the isolation that can arise when we numb ourselves to the world's pain. The Bible reminds us, however, that love is central to the Christian life. In 1 John 4:7-8, we are urged to "love one another, for love comes from God." When we retreat into indifference, we lose touch with this divine call to love others. Numbness might feel like protection, but true strength lies in staying open to love and connection, even when it feels vulnerable. When you're tempted to withdraw emotionally, consider praying for God's grace to keep your heart open, knowing that His love is a source of strength.

"I try to hold on but I'm calloused to the bone" captures the toll that life's hardships can take, building a metaphorical "callous" to shield us from pain. Callouses form through repeated friction, just as emotional callouses form through repeated disappointments and struggles. Yet God offers healing for even the most hardened hearts. Ezekiel 36:26 promises, "I will give you a new heart and put a new spirit in you; I will remove from you your heart of stone and give you a heart of flesh." In Christ, there is hope for renewal. When life's burdens feel overwhelming, ask God to soften your heart, restoring your ability to love, feel, and trust.

"I'm rusted and weathered / Barely holding together" symbolizes a soul worn down by life's storms, yet still holding on. This imagery of "weathered" resilience resonates with 2 Corinthians 4:8-9, where Paul says, "We are hard pressed on every side, but not crushed; perplexed, but not in despair; persecuted, but not abandoned; struck down, but not destroyed." The Christian life acknowledges suffering, but it also holds to the promise that God sustains us, even in our weakest moments. If you feel worn down, remember that God is holding you together, providing strength even when it feels like you're barely holding on.

"The sun shines and I can't avoid the light" introduces a glimmer of hope, representing truth, awareness, or the reality of God's presence. Light in the Bible often symbolizes God's truth and His guiding presence. In John 1:5, we're reminded, "The light shines in the darkness, and the darkness has not overcome it." The protagonist's reluctant acceptance of this light reflects the journey of coming to terms with God's truth, even when it's painful. If you feel reluctant to face certain truths in your life, ask God for courage, trusting that His light brings healing and guidance, even when it exposes uncomfortable realities.

"Ashes to ashes and dust to dust / Sometimes I feel like giving up" reflects a deep awareness of mortality and the finite nature of life. This phrase echoes Ecclesiastes 3:20, which reminds us that "all go to the same place; all come from dust, and to dust all return." Yet, even in moments when giving up seems tempting, God calls us to persevere. Galatians 6:9 encourages, "Let us not become weary in doing good, for at the proper time we will reap a harvest if we do not give up." Though life's struggles may feel heavy, God promises that endurance has purpose, and He is faithful to sustain us as we keep pressing forward.

"Take all this pride and leave it behind / 'Cause one day it ends, one day we die" speaks to the importance of humility and letting go of pride, especially in light of life's brevity. Pride can often lead us to isolate ourselves or to hold onto things that ultimately don't matter. James 4:10 instructs, "Humble yourselves before the Lord, and he will lift you up." Letting go of pride allows us to live with a clearer sense of purpose, focused on what truly matters—our relationship with God and with others. When you face struggles that seem overwhelming, ask God to help you release pride and live with humility, finding strength in His promises.

"Believe what you will, that is your right / But I choose to win, I choose to fight" is a powerful statement of resilience, a decision not to surrender to despair. In 1 Timothy 6:12, Paul encourages Timothy to "fight the good fight of the faith." The choice to "fight" in this song is an inner resolve to endure, to keep hope alive even when life feels heavy. As Christians, our fight is not against flesh and blood but against spiritual forces, as described in Ephesians 6:12. When you feel close to giving up, remember that God equips you with His armor to stand firm in faith, to choose resilience, and to continue fighting for hope.

Throughout *Weathered*, there's an interplay between surrender and resistance, between acknowledging brokenness and refusing to be defined by it. This paradox reflects the Christian experience, where we are called to face hardships with honesty but also with the hope that God provides. Romans 5:3-4 reminds us that "suffering produces perseverance; perseverance, character; and character, hope." The song's protagonist is both fragile and resilient, much like we are in our journey with God. Though we may feel weathered and worn, our faith gives us the strength to endure, knowing that our hope is secure in Christ.

In the end, *Weathered* is a testament to the power of perseverance—the strength that comes from choosing to press on, even when life feels overwhelming. This song encourages us to confront the darkness within, not with a promise of easy resolution but with the assurance that endurance itself is a form of victory. When you feel the weight of life's struggles, remember that God sees your resilience, and He walks with you on the journey. Trust that, in Christ, your hope is unbreakable, and that even when you're "barely holding together," God's love and strength will carry you through.

CHAPTER 31
"Hide"

A s the song *Hide* unfolds, it reveals a tension that aches within every chord, lyric, and rhythm. In each carefully crafted line, Scott Stapp seems to unmask a soul wrestling with its inner shadows. Here is a narrative where redemption feels just beyond reach, hidden behind layers of regret, entangled with the desire for freedom. The music – marked by Mark Tremonti's resounding guitar riffs and Scott Phillips' pulsing beats – provides not merely a backdrop but a powerful, almost cinematic soundscape that breathes life into the words.

From the very start, the words "To what do I owe this gift, my friend? / My life, my love, my soul" frame the scene, almost like a monologue directed at an unseen confidante. There's a vulnerability in addressing this "friend" – a figure who might be a literal companion or a symbolic representation of a spiritual presence. The phrase "gift" suggests a conscious awareness of life as something bestowed, a gracious bestowal that demands reverence. Yet within this line lies a sorrowful undertone: the gift seems both precious and burdensome, as if the weight of life, love, and soul has borne down on him. The music captures this tension beautifully; Tremonti's guitar comes in not with brightness but with a contemplative melancholy, setting a tone that prepares listeners to confront the singer's internal conflict.

In the following lines, "I've been dancing with the devil way too long / And it's making me grow old," the confession grows darker.

Stapp's voice deepens, a slight gravel signaling both the years lost and the wisdom painfully gained. The "dance with the devil" paints a vivid image, as though he's been entangled in a destructive, cyclical movement, one he couldn't – or perhaps wouldn't – break from. The phrase suggests a life of repeated missteps, patterns of rebellion or regret, and the exhausting toll they've taken. This dance is not the youthful kind, bursting with energy; it's heavy, trudging, a reminder that these choices age the spirit, sapping it of vitality. The guitars and drums amplify this weariness, shifting between haunting riffs and heavier sections that feel almost like stumbling under the weight of one's own choices. There's an aching honesty here, a self-reflection that, in itself, reveals a yearning for something more.

When Stapp sings, "Let's leave, oh, let's get away / Get lost in time / Where there's no reason left to hide," a glimmer of hope breaks through. The invitation to "get away" signifies the first hint of transformation, a desire to escape the confines of this cycle, to reach a place of peace, freedom, and transparency. It's as if he's dreaming of a field where masks can finally be shed, where one's soul can breathe without restraint. The music mirrors this yearning; Tremonti's guitar opens up here, finding a lighter, almost ethereal quality as though embodying the possibility of transcendence. There's a nostalgic tone that suggests that this place is not new but rather a return to something forgotten – a purity lost along the way.

The line "What are you going to do with your gift, dear child?" shifts the tone subtly, a question that resonates with profound gravity. Addressing "dear child" creates an emotional distance from the earlier confession, as though the speaker is now an elder or a wiser self, looking back with compassion at a younger, more innocent version. It's a piercing question, one that every listener might ask themselves: *What will I do with the life I've been given?* In this line, the focus pivots from regret to responsibility, from dwelling on the past to contemplating the future. "Give life? Give love? Give soul?" These words echo the earlier description of the gift, but here, they take on a tone of purpose, a call to offer what has been entrusted rather than to waste it. There's a duality in the music at this point; the instrumentation grows more intense, almost demanding, as if urging the listener to confront this challenge.

The next line, "Divided is the one who dances / For the soul is so exposed," returns to the earlier image of dancing, but now the tone shifts. The dance is no longer just with the devil; it's a reflection of the inner division between the self that yearns for redemption and the self that hides from it. There's a vulnerability in the word "exposed" – it implies a risk, a revelation of the soul that is unguarded, unarmored. It suggests that to truly "dance" with authenticity, one must be willing to be seen, to let go of the façades. The line rings with a kind of tragic beauty, as though acknowledging that to live fully, to embrace the gift, requires a stripping away of the very things that have provided protection. The guitars wail here, echoing this tension, as if wrestling with whether to play softly or unleash fully. The music does not provide easy answers; instead, it underscores the vulnerability in self-revelation.

As the chorus returns – "Let's leave, oh, let's get away / Get lost in time" – the desire for freedom becomes almost palpable, like a desperate plea to find this place of peace. It's repeated multiple times, as though Stapp is urging the listener, or perhaps himself, to truly embrace this moment of escape. The call to "run in fields of time" evokes a sense of timelessness, a place where past mistakes no longer define us, where time's endless ticking fades, leaving only the present moment – free, untethered, safe. The repetition of "no reason to hide" becomes a mantra, an insistence that to fully live, one must release the burdens and step into the light, unguarded. The music rises with this repetition, allowing the emotions to surge, encouraging listeners to feel not just the words but the profound yearning behind them. Phillips' drumming, Tremonti's riffs – they all coalesce into a crescendo that almost demands a response, a step toward this field of freedom.

Yet, there's a subtle sadness in the repetition, a hint that this freedom, though so deeply desired, remains elusive. Each iteration of "no reason to hide" feels like a reminder as much as a declaration, almost as if Stapp is trying to convince himself of this truth. The listener is left wondering: is he really ready to let go of the shame, the regret, the fear? Or does he still feel trapped in that dance with the devil, unable to break free entirely?

The song's structure, with its cycles and returns to familiar lines, mirrors the human experience of transformation. True change rarely happens in a single moment; it's a process, a repeated return to hope, a constant wrestling with doubt. The cyclical nature of the music reflects this, grounding us in the reality that letting go is not a one-time act but a continual journey. Each chorus, each echo of "no reason to hide," reinforces the struggle to step out of the shadows, to be seen without shame, and to live with purpose.

The instrumental breakdown in the middle of the song allows a pause, a breath between the verses. Here, Tremonti's guitar takes center stage, creating a haunting, almost ethereal soundscape that feels like an invitation to reflect. The notes linger, reverberate, as if embodying the very struggle between hiding and stepping into the light. The bridge feels like a moment of surrender, a time to let the music speak where words cannot fully express the weight of this transformation. In these moments, the listener is left alone with the music, given space to absorb the weight of Stapp's journey.

In the final choruses, the music reaches its full intensity, as if building toward a breakthrough. But unlike some songs that conclude with
a resolution, *Hide* leaves us in a place of ambiguity. The song's ending
echoes "no reason to hide" again and again, as though it's both a statement of hope and a reminder of the ongoing battle within. There's no
definitive answer, no clean conclusion. It leaves us with an open-ended
invitation – will we accept this call to live exposed, to share our gifts
of life, love, and soul? Or will we continue the dance, keeping our true
selves hidden, even from ourselves?

Hide is not simply a song but a deeply introspective journey that
invites listeners to wrestle with the questions it raises. In its cyclical
structure, raw confessions, and cinematic soundscape, it resonates as
both a plea and a challenge. It dares us to look within, to confront
our own dance with the devil, and to decide whether we will continue
hiding or step into a field of time where, as Stapp so poignantly sings,
there is "no reason left to hide."

Application

Creed's *Hide* is a powerful exploration of vulnerability, self-reflection, and the tension between living openly and hiding behind
layers of shame and regret. The song invites listeners to confront the
struggle between darkness and light, wrestling with inner shadows
and yearning for a release from past mistakes. In many ways, this
mirrors the Christian journey, where we are called to bring our hidden
struggles to God, to seek healing and transformation, and to live a
life that is unguarded and authentic in His light. Let's explore how
the song's themes align with biblical truths and how you can draw
spiritual inspiration from them.

"To what do I owe this gift, my friend? / My life, my love, my
soul" opens the song with a sense of gratitude and reflection. The
protagonist acknowledges life as a "gift" that has been entrusted to

him, echoing a biblical understanding of life as a precious and intentional creation. In James 1:17, we read, "Every good and perfect gift is from above, coming down from the Father of the heavenly lights." Recognizing our lives, talents, and relationships as gifts from God calls us to live in a way that honors Him. When you reflect on your life, take time to thank God for the gift He has given you, even when it feels burdened by trials or struggles. Recognizing life as a gift can reframe even difficult seasons as opportunities to grow and rely on God's grace.

"I've been dancing with the devil way too long / And it's making me grow old" confesses the toll of sin and poor choices, reflecting a cycle of behavior that has aged the spirit. The Bible speaks to the weariness that sin brings, warning that it leads to separation from God and a feeling of emptiness. In Romans 6:23, we learn, "For the wages of sin is death, but the gift of God is eternal life in Christ Jesus our Lord." Sin can make us feel weighed down and disconnected from the vitality of life. Yet, even when we feel "aged" by our mistakes, God's mercy offers a way back. When you recognize patterns of sin in your life, remember that Christ's forgiveness is available to restore you, releasing you from the heaviness of past mistakes.

"Let's leave, oh, let's get away / Get lost in time / Where there's no reason left to hide" introduces a longing for freedom from shame and regret. This desire to step out of hiding reflects the biblical call to come before God with honesty. In John 8:12, Jesus declares, "I am the light of the world. Whoever follows me will never walk in darkness, but will have the light of life." When we bring our struggles to God's light, we no longer have to hide. He invites us to let go of shame, knowing that He sees us fully and loves us still. When you feel burdened by regret, remember that God's light brings healing and freedom, allowing you to live openly in His grace.

"What are you going to do with your gift, dear child?" introduces a moment of self-reflection, challenging the listener to consider how they are using their life. This question resonates with the parable of the talents in Matthew 25:14-30, where servants are entrusted with resources to steward wisely. God calls us to use our lives, not to waste them in hiding or fear, but to serve and love others. When you consider how to use the gift of your life, ask God for wisdom, seeking to live in a way that reflects His love, generosity, and purpose.

"Divided is the one who dances / For the soul is so exposed" expresses the tension between authenticity and self-protection. The Bible encourages us to live with integrity, reminding us that God values a heart that is genuine. In Psalm 139:23-24, David prays, "Search me, God, and know my heart... See if there is any offensive way in me, and lead me in the way everlasting." When we try to hide parts of ourselves from God or others, we end up feeling divided, torn between authenticity and the masks we wear. Yet God invites us to live transparently, knowing that His love holds us securely, even when we feel exposed. When you feel afraid of vulnerability, trust that God's love is a safe place to let go of pretense and to be truly known.

"Let's leave, oh, let's get away / Get lost in time" repeats as a chorus, a call to break free from hiding and step into a place of peace. This longing to "run in fields of time" suggests a desire for timelessness, a place where one can live freely and unburdened. In Revelation 21:4, we are given a glimpse of eternity, where "there will be no more death or mourning or crying or pain." This place of peace reflects the ultimate freedom we have in Christ—a freedom where shame, guilt, and regret no longer bind us. When you feel the desire to "get away" from the weight of life, remember that God's promise of eternal peace is secure, and even now, His presence offers rest for your soul.

"What will you do with your life, your love, your soul?" is a question of purpose, challenging the listener to consider how they are stewarding what God has entrusted to them. In Micah 6:8, we find guidance on how to live with purpose: "To act justly and to love mercy and to walk humbly with your God." God calls us to live a life marked by love, humility, and justice, using our gifts to serve others. Reflect on this call in your own life, seeking ways to live with intention, using your time, talents, and love to make an impact for God's Kingdom.

"Take all this pride and leave it behind" speaks to the necessity of surrender, letting go of pride and self-sufficiency. Proverbs 11:2 teaches, "When pride comes, then comes disgrace, but with humility comes wisdom." Pride can create barriers, keeping us from God and others, but humility opens the door to transformation. Letting go of pride is a step toward freedom, allowing us to live with authenticity and openness. When you feel tempted to cling to pride, pray for God's help to embrace humility, trusting that He will provide wisdom and guidance.

"Believe what you will, that is your right / But I choose to win, I choose to fight" reflects a decision to pursue hope and resilience, a choice not to succumb to darkness. In 2 Timothy 4:7, Paul writes, "I have fought the good fight, I have finished the race, I have kept the faith." The choice to fight in this song is a commitment to persevere, to hold onto hope despite challenges. For Christians, this "fight" is the journey of faith—a journey that requires resilience, trust, and the courage to walk in God's light, even when darkness threatens to pull us down. When you feel close to giving up, remember that God equips you to stand firm, and that by His strength, you can overcome.

Throughout *Hide*, there is an interplay between the desire to escape shame and the yearning to live openly and authentically. This struggle mirrors the Christian experience of seeking transformation while confronting fears and regrets. Romans 12:2 encourages us, "Do not conform to the pattern of this world, but be transformed by the renewing of your mind." Transformation is often a gradual process, one that requires us to revisit God's promises again and again. The song's cyclical structure, returning to the refrain of "no reason to hide," emphasizes the journey of letting go of self-protection, learning to embrace the light of truth, and finding peace in God's love.

In the end, *Hide* is a deeply introspective journey that calls us to examine our own lives and to consider whether we will continue hiding behind masks or step into the freedom that God offers. It's an invitation to embrace vulnerability, to let go of shame, and to live in the light of God's grace. When you feel tempted to hide, remember that God's love holds no condemnation, and in Him, there truly is "no reason left to hide."

CHAPTER 32
"Don't Stop Dancing"

*D*on't Stop Dancing by Creed dives into the heart of human vulnerability and resilience, as Scott Stapp's lyrics paint a haunting, deeply introspective portrait of struggle and hope. Each line pulses with an ache, an inner wrestling that resonates with those who have encountered life's darkness and sought light amid it. Mark Tremonti's guitar and Scott Phillips' drums lend not just accompaniment but emotional heft to each phrase, making the song a kind of collective anthem for anyone grappling with unseen battles.

The song opens with a stark admission: "At times, life is wicked, and I just can't see the light." Stapp's voice, raw and almost pleading, captures a universal sense of despair – a darkness so pervasive that it seems to obscure even the faintest glimmers of hope. The phrase "wicked" isn't chosen lightly; it evokes something more than just difficulty or challenge. It hints at a profound struggle against forces that feel overwhelming, as if they operate beyond mere human comprehension. The chord progression mirrors this sentiment, moving between minor keys that reflect a sense of weight, grounding the listener in the reality of life's unfairness. Tremonti's guitar builds layers of tension, each note resonating with the sense that sometimes, even when we look hard, we can't find the silver lining we so desperately need.

When Stapp sings, "Whatever life brings, I've been through everything / And now I'm on my knees again," he offers a glimpse into his own weariness, an exhaustion born from a life filled with hardship and spiritual searching. The imagery of being "on my knees" is deeply evocative, suggesting both surrender and a plea for help. It's a position of humility, vulnerability, and desperation. And yet, there's a resilience in his words; the acknowledgment of being on his knees is paired with a resolve to rise again. This blend of brokenness and determination feels almost like a prayer – a reaching out to something greater, a silent hope that there's a purpose to the pain. Phillips' drumming here is soft but steady, as though underscoring the beating heart that persists despite the exhaustion.

In the lines "But I know I must go on / Although I hurt, I must be strong," the song shifts from despair to a kind of weary acceptance. There's a recognition here that life's battles are unavoidable, that pain is an inescapable part of the journey. This sentiment is both sobering and empowering; it acknowledges the hurt without letting it dictate the next steps. Stapp's voice takes on a slightly firmer tone, almost as if he's reminding himself of this truth, digging deep to find the strength to keep moving forward. The music follows suit, building in intensity, signaling the internal resolve needed to continue. There's a raw beauty in this moment, as if the song itself is reminding listeners of the strength that comes from embracing both one's vulnerability and resilience.

The refrain "Children, don't stop dancing / Believe you can fly / Away, away" is one of the song's most poignant moments. Here, Stapp shifts his focus outward, speaking directly to those who might be younger or more innocent, the "children" who haven't yet been as deeply scarred by life's trials. It's as if he's trying to protect this purity, urging them not to lose hope, not to let life's darkness quench their spirit. The metaphor of "dancing" evokes a sense of freedom, of living without fear, without restraint. Dancing, in its purest form, is a full-bodied expression of joy, spontaneity, and presence. It's an image of wholeness, a contrast to the pain and shadows Stapp has described. The gentle plea to "believe you can fly" is almost angelic, a reminder that despite life's heaviness, there is still a reason to dream, to reach for heights beyond our current circumstances.

The next verse, "Hey God, I know I'm just a dot in this world / Have You forgot about me?" reaches a new level of vulnerability. Here, Stapp's voice takes on a tremble, as though he's barely holding back a sense of abandonment. Addressing God directly is a powerful act, exposing the raw human need for connection, for reassurance that there's someone out there who cares, who sees. The line "just a dot in this world" encapsulates the smallness we often feel in the face of the universe's vastness. It's a humbling realization that we're part of something much larger than ourselves, yet this vastness can also feel isolating, as though we could be overlooked or forgotten. Tremonti's guitar becomes almost reverent here, with notes that seem to reach out, seeking a response from the silence.

The repeated lines "Am I hiding in the shadows? / Forget the pain and forget the sorrows" reveal a longing for escape, a desire to push the hurt and sorrow into obscurity. Yet the question "Am I hiding in the shadows?" suggests a deeper conflict – an awareness that burying the pain isn't truly facing it. It's as if Stapp is caught in a paradox, torn between the urge to run from his suffering and the understanding that real freedom requires confronting it. The music's tone here becomes introspective, almost haunting, as if echoing this struggle to reconcile pain with the hope of release. The drums pull back slightly, allowing the guitar to take the lead, creating a sense of introspection that pulls the listener deeper into Stapp's emotional landscape.

As the song reaches its final chorus, the repetition of "Children, don't stop dancing / Believe you can fly" grows in intensity, as if Stapp is willing these words to resonate, to reach those who need them most. The refrain has evolved from a gentle suggestion to an impassioned command, a plea for resilience, not just for himself but for anyone feeling crushed under the weight of life's hardships. Each repetition seems to drive the message home: *Keep moving, keep believing, don't let the darkness steal your spirit.* The instrumentation builds alongside this plea, the guitar growing more powerful, the drums more insistent, culminating in a swell of sound that feels like an invocation, a call to push beyond despair.

The closing lines, "Am I hiding in the shadows? / Are we hiding in the shadows?" reveal a subtle but profound shift. The question moves from a personal introspection to a collective query. By using "we," Stapp draws the listener into his journey, transforming the song from a solitary struggle to a shared experience. It's as if he's acknowledging that this battle against pain, against hiding, is not his alone; it's one that many of us face, each in our own way. The music fades, leaving a lingering echo, as if to suggest that while the battle may not be over, there is a shared strength in knowing we're not alone in it.

In *Don't Stop Dancing,* Creed has crafted more than just a song; it's a lifeline for those who find themselves in darkness. Stapp's words, along with Tremonti's evocative guitar work and Phillips' grounding beats, create a soundscape that captures the full breadth of human experience – despair, struggle, resilience, and hope. The song doesn't offer easy answers or quick solutions; instead, it invites us to sit with the tension, to acknowledge both the pain and the possibility of something greater. In doing so, it becomes a reminder that even when we feel like we're just "a dot in this world," there is purpose in our persistence, beauty in our resilience, and freedom in choosing to keep dancing through life's shadows.

Application

Creed's *Don't Stop Dancing* is a powerful anthem that explores themes of vulnerability, resilience, and the deep need for hope amid life's struggles. Through raw, introspective lyrics and evocative instrumentation, the song encourages listeners to hold onto their dreams, even when life feels overwhelming. In many ways, *Don't Stop Dancing* aligns with the Christian journey of persevering in faith, seeking God's light in darkness, and embracing hope when we feel small in the vastness of life's challenges. Let's delve into the song's themes and how they connect to biblical truths and can inspire you in your faith journey.

"At times, life is wicked, and I just can't see the light" opens the song with an admission of despair, a feeling many of us experience in moments of profound struggle. The Bible acknowledges that life's trials can feel heavy and confusing. In John 16:33, Jesus offers comfort, saying, "In this world you will have trouble. But take heart! I have overcome the world." This reminder is a beacon of hope, assuring us that even in life's wickedness, Christ's victory provides a light that transcends our darkest moments. When you feel overwhelmed by life's challenges, remember that God's light is present, even if you can't always see it. He is with you, offering strength and guidance through every storm.

"Whatever life brings, I've been through everything / And now I'm on my knees again" reveals a sense of exhaustion and humility, as the protagonist finds himself seeking help once more. The act of being "on my knees" is a powerful image of surrender and prayer, echoing Psalm 34:17-18, which promises, "The righteous cry out, and the Lord hears them; he delivers them from all their troubles. The Lord is close to the brokenhearted and saves those who are crushed in spirit." When you feel worn down by life, turning to God in humility opens the door to

His comfort and support. In moments of exhaustion, let your prayers be a source of strength, knowing that God hears you and is near.

"But I know I must go on / Although I hurt, I must be strong" reflects a determination to persevere, even when the road is difficult. This echoes the biblical call to press on in faith, trusting that God will sustain us. In Philippians 4:13, Paul writes, "I can do all this through him who gives me strength." The resolve to "go on" despite pain is a testament to the resilience God provides in our times of need. When you face trials that seem unending, remember that God's strength is available to you, empowering you to keep moving forward and reminding you that pain doesn't define your path.

"Children, don't stop dancing / Believe you can fly / Away, away" is a poignant refrain, urging innocence, joy, and resilience. The Bible often highlights the importance of childlike faith, as seen in Matthew 18:3, where Jesus says, "Truly I tell you, unless you change and become like little children, you will never enter the kingdom of heaven." To "keep dancing" and to "believe you can fly" speaks to a sense of trust and openness, a willingness to hope even when life is hard. God calls us to hold onto this faith, trusting that He is guiding us through life's complexities. Embrace the simplicity of faith, allowing it to carry you forward with joy and resilience, just as a child dances without fear or worry.

"Hey God, I know I'm just a dot in this world / Have You forgot about me?" captures a sense of smallness and vulnerability, expressing the fear of being overlooked. In Psalm 8:4, David marvels, "What is mankind that you are mindful of them, human beings that you care for them?" This verse reflects the wonder that, despite the vastness of creation, God sees and loves each of us intimately. When you feel small or insignificant, remember that you are never forgotten by God. He knows you completely, and His love reaches even the smallest "dots" in His universe, offering purpose and care to every life.

"Am I hiding in the shadows? / Forget the pain and forget the sorrows" expresses a desire to escape from pain and sorrow, while also questioning if hiding is the answer. The Bible invites us to bring our struggles to God, rather than hide them in the shadows. In Psalm 139:12, we read, "Even the darkness will not be dark to you; the night will shine like the day, for darkness is as light to you." God's light penetrates even our deepest shadows, offering healing and release. When you feel tempted to hide your pain, remember that God invites you to bring it into His light, where He can transform and heal it. Embrace His love as a safe place to confront and work through your struggles.

As the song reaches its final chorus, "Children, don't stop dancing / Believe you can fly" grows in intensity, becoming a powerful command to persevere. The call to "believe" and to keep "dancing" resonates with the biblical theme of enduring in faith. Hebrews 10:23 encourages, "Let us hold unswervingly to the hope we profess, for he who promised is faithful." The determination in these words reflects the encouragement to not give up, to hold onto hope even when life feels heavy. Let this refrain remind you to keep moving forward in faith, trusting that God is faithful to carry you, no matter the weight you bear.

"Am I hiding in the shadows? / Are we hiding in the shadows?" transitions from personal introspection to a collective question, acknowledging that we all face hidden battles. This shift to "we" reflects the shared nature of human struggle. Galatians 6:2 calls us to "carry each other's burdens, and in this way you will fulfill the law of Christ." God created us for community, to support each other and to bring our struggles into the light, where we can find strength together. When you face your own shadows, know that you're not alone; others share similar struggles, and God's design is for us to encourage and uplift one another on the journey.

In *Don't Stop Dancing*, Creed offers a deeply introspective and hopeful message. Stapp's lyrics and Tremonti's soulful guitar create a soundscape that holds both the weight of human pain and the beauty of resilience. The song doesn't promise easy answers or immediate relief, but it offers a reminder to hold onto hope, to trust in something greater, and to keep dancing even when life's shadows press in. In the Christian walk, this song resonates as a call to faith – a reminder that even when we feel small and weighed down, God's love gives us a reason to keep moving forward.

Through *Don't Stop Dancing*, you're invited to reflect on your own journey, to embrace both the struggles and the joy that come with walking in faith. Allow God's promises to be the melody that keeps you dancing through life's challenges, knowing that in Him, there is always a reason to hope, to dream, and to believe that He is with you, guiding you through every shadow and into His marvelous light.

CHAPTER 33
"Lullaby"

The song *Lullaby* invites us into an intimate and quiet space, a world built on the simplest and yet most profound of human expressions: love and peace. Unlike the heavier, often conflicted themes that mark much of Creed's work, *Lullaby* is like a whisper in the dark, a tender moment between two souls where words serve as a gentle balm rather than as a means of revelation or introspection. The composition, with its understated instrumentation and soothing rhythm, creates an atmosphere of calm, allowing each word to fall softly, like a lullaby spoken in the stillness of night.

"Hush my love now, don't you cry / Everything will be alright." The song begins with this timeless promise, one that echoes through countless lullabies across cultures and eras. It is a quiet reassurance that everything, despite the chaos of life, can be calmed, if only for a moment. Here, Scott Stapp's voice is different – softened, more tender. It's as though he is wrapping his words around someone precious, providing comfort with the certainty of a loving parent. The melody, gentle and undulating, mirrors the rhythmic rocking one might imagine, a kind of musical embrace that encourages rest and peace.

"Close your eyes and drift in dream / Rest in peaceful sleep." In these lines, Stapp paints a picture of complete surrender to tranquility. Sleep, in this context, becomes a space of solace, a safe haven where all troubles are suspended. The choice to use phrases like "drift in dream" and "peaceful sleep" reflects the tender simplicity of a moment where defenses fall, where vulnerability is protected by love. It's a scene that needs no embellishment; there's beauty in the quietness, a kind of unspoken reverence for the purity of resting in love's arms. The music follows suit, with delicate guitar tones and a subtle rhythm that carry the listener along, mimicking the sensation of drifting into a dreamscape.

"If there's one thing I hope I showed you / Just give love to all." This refrain is both the heart of the song and the wisdom it seeks to impart. In the same way a parent might impart a single core value to their child, this line carries a message that feels both personal and universal. It's not a complex philosophy or a list of dos and don'ts; it's an invitation to live a life centered on love. Stapp's delivery of these words is almost pleading, as if this single truth – to "just give love" – is the only thing worth passing on. The words are repeated, like a mantra, an affirmation, or perhaps even a prayer. Through each repetition, they sink deeper, not only into the listener's mind but also into the soul, embodying the song's mission to nurture and heal.

As the song continues, "Oh, my love in my arms tight / Every day you give me life," there's a shift from the singer as a giver to a receiver. Stapp acknowledges the reciprocal nature of love, revealing that the act of comforting and nurturing another also brings life and meaning to the one offering it. The line "every day you give me life" is a revelation; it expresses the profound impact of this love, that it breathes life into him daily, even as he holds the other close. The instrumentation here is subtle, with minimalistic accompaniment that doesn't intrude but instead supports the intimacy of the words. This musical restraint amplifies the sincerity of the sentiment, allowing each line to be felt deeply.

In "As I drift off to your world / Rest in peaceful sleep," we see a continuation of the reciprocal relationship. Now, Stapp himself drifts, suggesting that the roles of protector and comforted have blurred. There's an understanding that love, in its truest form, creates a shared space where both souls can find rest and peace. It's as if the "world" he drifts into is one where both the singer and the one he sings to are united, where boundaries dissolve, and where they can share in a tranquil, almost sacred silence.

"I know there's one thing that you showed me / That you showed me / Just give love to all." With these words, the song shifts slightly, revealing that the lesson of giving love wasn't only taught by the singer but also learned from the one he holds. This realization brings a sense of humility to the song, as if acknowledging that even in his role as a protector or guide, he has been equally shaped and changed by the other. The repetition of "that you showed me" underlines this discovery, as if he's marveling at it, internalizing that love is not merely something he offers but something he has learned to embody through this relationship. The music swells here, subtly reinforcing the significance of this revelation without overwhelming it.

As the song approaches its conclusion, "Let's give love to all" becomes the guiding refrain, growing from a personal sentiment into a universal call. The shift from "just give love" to "let's give love" transforms the song from an individual plea to a communal invitation, a reminder that love, though deeply personal, has the power to transcend individual relationships and reach others. Stapp's voice, still soft but now imbued with conviction, communicates this as a choice, a commitment to live a life marked by love. The refrain, repeated over and over, feels almost like a benediction, a blessing bestowed on the listener.

Throughout the song, the music remains gentle, never overpowering the lyrics but serving as a quiet anchor that supports each word.
Tremonti's guitar, tender and melodic, underscores the emotional
weight of the song, adding subtle layers of harmony that create a
feeling of warmth and safety. The restraint shown in the music allows
the song to become almost like a whispered prayer, a lullaby in the
truest sense – not merely a song to induce sleep but a song to soothe
the soul, to impart wisdom, to fill the listener with peace.

Lullaby offers a moment of respite, an oasis of calm in a world
that often feels too loud and too fast. In this space, Scott Stapp and
the listener connect over a shared need for peace, love, and rest. It's a
simple song, yet in its simplicity, it touches on something profoundly
human. The invitation to "just give love to all" is not new, but here,
in the context of this quiet, reflective lullaby, it becomes a gentle yet
powerful reminder of life's most essential truth: love, freely given and
freely received, is what ultimately sustains and heals us.

Application

Creed's *Lullaby* is a gentle, tender song that draws us into a space
of calm, peace, and love. Unlike the band's other, more intense pieces,
Lullaby feels like a whispered message, reminding us of the importance
of love, simplicity, and human connection. The song's themes mirror
many Christian principles: the reassurance that God's love offers us
peace, the mutual nature of love, and the idea that love is the highest
calling and deepest source of life. Let's reflect on how the song's message aligns with biblical truths and how it can inspire you in your walk
with God.

"Hush my love now, don't you cry / Everything will be alright."
These opening words evoke a sense of calm and reassurance, much like
God's comforting presence in our lives. The Bible often speaks of God
as a source of comfort and peace in times of distress. In Isaiah 66:13,

God says, "As a mother comforts her child, so will I comfort you." Just as a parent's gentle words can soothe a child's fears, God's promises reassure us that even amid life's challenges, we are not alone. When you face moments of worry or sorrow, allow these words to remind you of God's tender care, trusting that He is with you, calming your fears and holding you in His embrace.

"Close your eyes and drift in dream / Rest in peaceful sleep" continues this theme, inviting a sense of surrender to peace. The Bible emphasizes that true rest is found in God's presence, where we can let go of burdens and find renewal. In Psalm 4:8, David writes, "In peace I will lie down and sleep, for you alone, Lord, make me dwell in safety." God calls us to trust in His protection, allowing our souls to find rest in Him. When life feels chaotic, remember that God offers you rest, a space where you can lay down your worries and simply be held in His peace.

"If there's one thing I hope I showed you / Just give love to all" captures the essence of the song's message – a simple but powerful call to love. This mirrors Jesus' teaching in Matthew 22:37-39, where He says, "Love the Lord your God with all your heart and with all your soul and with all your mind... and love your neighbor as yourself." This is the core of the Christian life, a commandment that transcends all others. The call to "just give love to all" reminds us of our highest purpose: to reflect God's love in our relationships and interactions. Let this refrain inspire you to seek opportunities to share love freely, knowing that it is the greatest gift you can offer others.

"Oh, my love in my arms tight / Every day you give me life" acknowledges that love is not only given but also received, creating a relationship that sustains both people. This sentiment echoes the mutual love between God and His children, as seen in 1 John 4:19: "We love because he first loved us." Our love for others springs from the love God pours into our lives each day, a love that breathes life into our spirits and inspires us to give in return. When you think about the people who bring you joy and meaning, thank God for these relationships, recognizing that His love flows through them, renewing and encouraging you daily.

"As I drift off to your world / Rest in peaceful sleep" shifts the song's perspective, suggesting a reciprocal relationship where love creates a shared space of peace. This idea of resting in each other's presence reflects the communal nature of love, as described in Ecclesiastes 4:9-10: "Two are better than one... if either of them falls down, one can help the other up." God designed us for relationships that uplift and support us, where we can find mutual rest and encouragement. When you feel weary, remember that God provides community and companionship, a reminder that we are not meant to walk through life alone.

"I know there's one thing that you showed me / Just give love to all" reflects a humble realization that love is not only something we give but also something we learn from others. This mirrors the Bible's teaching on mutual edification in relationships. Proverbs 27:17 states, "As iron sharpens iron, so one person sharpens another." The people we love and care for often teach us how to be more compassionate, patient, and kind. Embrace these moments of learning, allowing them to shape you into a person who loves more fully, reflecting the love you receive from others and, ultimately, from God.

"Let's give love to all" transforms the song's message into a collective call, reminding us that love is meant to reach beyond personal relationships. Jesus taught His disciples to be "the light of the world" (Matthew 5:14-16), a light that reflects God's love to everyone. This shift from "just give love" to "let's give love" invites all of us to join in a shared commitment to love. Let these words encourage you to be a part of something greater, choosing to share God's love not only with those closest to you but with everyone you encounter.

Throughout *Lullaby*, the music remains gentle, creating a peaceful atmosphere that echoes the quiet strength of love. The soft instrumentation mirrors the gentleness of God's love, which is not forceful but comforting, wrapping around us like a warm embrace. This subtlety reflects the way God works in our lives, often in quiet, unassuming ways that bring peace and reassurance. When you feel burdened by the noise and stress of life, seek God's presence as a refuge, where His still, small voice can soothe your soul.

Lullaby is a simple yet profoundly moving song that reminds us of life's most essential truth: love is what sustains and heals us. In its quietness, *Lullaby* captures the heart of God's message to His children – that we are loved deeply, called to love others in return, and invited to find peace in the simplicity of giving and receiving love. Let this song inspire you to live a life marked by love, knowing that God's love is the source of all comfort, joy, and purpose.

As you reflect on *Lullaby*, allow its message to lead you into a deeper understanding of God's love, a love that is both tender and powerful, quiet yet all-encompassing. Embrace the call to "just give love to all," recognizing that love is not only a gift we offer others but a reflection of the love God has given us. In a world that often feels too busy and complex, remember that the most profound truths are often the simplest – love freely, love deeply, and find peace in the knowledge that God's love holds you securely, now and always.

PART V
Coming Full Circle

CHAPTER 34

"Overcome"

O *vercome* by Creed opens with a stark confrontation. Stapp's voice, gritty and resolute, does not merely sing but almost snarls through the words: "Don't cry victim to me." The line has an immediate, visceral impact, thrusting the listener into a space of bitterness and defiance. The tone is set from this very first line; this is not a song of quiet reflection but a battle cry, a fierce declaration of reclamation. As the instruments kick in, Tremonti's guitar grinds with a raw, unpolished edge, mirroring the bruised intensity of Stapp's lyrics. Here, the music itself becomes an embodiment of emotional resistance, adding layers to a narrative of survival and rebirth.

The words "Everything we are and used to be is buried and gone" echo with a finality that feels almost ruthless. There is no wistfulness, no trace of nostalgia—just a clean, brutal severing of the past. This is a song about purging, about ridding oneself of toxicity and refusing to be chained to what once was. Stapp's tone suggests a character who has reached the end of his patience, ready to discard any lingering connections to a painful history. This line speaks to the profound power in declaring something "gone," releasing oneself from its shadow. In the music, there is a forceful cadence, as the instruments drive forward, heavy and unyielding, refusing to linger or look back. It's as though each beat and chord pounds the past further into the ground.

When Stapp sings, "Now it's my turn to speak / It's my turn to expose and release what's been killing me," there's a sense of righteous vindication. The repetition of "my turn" suggests he has long been silenced, perhaps by a person or by circumstances, and now, finally, he claims his voice. The idea of "exposing and releasing" implies that he has been carrying hidden pain or buried truths, and it's in the act of unveiling them that he begins to find freedom. Tremonti's guitar echoes this revelation, growing more intense, as if unleashing everything that has been pent up. There's a catharsis in the music, a sense that each note is a release from something previously held back.

"I'll be damned fighting you / It's impossible, impossible," he continues, his voice sharpened with resignation. The line does not convey a tone of weakness or surrender, however; instead, it seems to be an acknowledgment of futility. He's not giving up—he's choosing to let go of the struggle that has consumed him. In this line, "impossible" resonates as both a personal and universal truth. There are some battles that, no matter how fiercely we fight, are unwinnable, and wisdom lies in recognizing when to let go. The repetition here gives weight to that realization, emphasizing the futility of clinging to a struggle that only drains him. The music complements this sentiment with a steady, relentless beat, as if echoing the exhaustion of a battle long fought.

In the chorus, "I'm entitled to overcome," the word "entitled" holds a sense of reclaimed power. This isn't entitlement in a self-serving sense; rather, it feels like a hard-earned right. Stapp's voice, both raw and defiant, reinforces that he has earned his place of resilience, that he has withstood enough, suffered enough, and now, he deserves to overcome. "Completely stunned and numb" portrays the toll this journey has taken, hinting at the emotional cost of survival. Yet, even in numbness, there is strength, a kind of steely resilience. The numbness becomes a shield, allowing him to keep going, to withstand whatever comes his way. The heavy, driving rhythm in this section amplifies this sense of resilience, creating a powerful atmosphere of endurance.

The line "Knock me down, throw me to the floor / There's no pain; I can't feel no more" reinforces this numbness as a form of invulnerability. He's reached a point where pain cannot touch him; he has absorbed so much that his emotional armor is nearly impenetrable. This is not numbness out of weakness but out of necessity – a survival mechanism forged from repeated blows. In the relentless beat and grinding riffs, the music embodies this defiance. It's almost as if Stapp is daring life to try again, to throw him to the floor, because he knows he will rise. There is a gritty resilience here, a refusal to be broken, even in the face of overwhelming hardship.

"Finally see what's beneath / Everything I am and hope to be cannot be lost" marks a shift in the narrative, a glimmer of introspection beneath the defiance. It's as though he's peering through the pain and bitterness to find something enduring, a self that has survived despite everything. In these words lies a sense of self-discovery, an acknowledgment that his core, his essence, cannot be stripped away. He may have been battered and bruised, but there is something indomitable within him, a truth he can finally see and hold onto. The music, though still heavy, takes on a slightly more hopeful tone here, suggesting that through all the pain, there remains a foundation that endures.

In the bridge, the line "You'll never know what I was thinking before you came 'round" suggests a lost innocence or a former self that existed before the influence of another. There's a sadness here, as though something pure or unbroken was altered by external forces. Yet, rather than mourn this change, he acknowledges it as part of his journey, an unavoidable part of becoming who he is now. The music grows more subdued in this section, allowing the words to stand on their own, inviting the listener to reflect on what might have been lost or sacrificed along the way.

"Take a step, take a breath, put your guard down" feels almost like a whispered invitation, both to himself and to others. In the midst of all this defiance, there is a moment of softness, a brief pause that invites vulnerability. Yet, this openness is fleeting; it's followed by a renewed resolve. "I cannot worry anymore of what you think of me" marks a pivotal moment, a declaration of independence from the opinions and judgments of others. It's a statement of liberation, a shedding of external expectations. In this line, there's a powerful rejection of societal or personal pressures that might have once dictated his actions or self-perception. It's a freeing moment, both lyrically and musically, as though he's casting off the last chains that have held him.

The repetition of "I may be crazy but I'm buried in your memory" reveals a final layer of defiance and acceptance. He acknowledges that, despite everything, he will remain a part of the other's memory, indelibly marked by the relationship that once was. There's a sense of triumph here, as though he has transcended the need for reconciliation or forgiveness. He is content to remain in memory, both as a mark of his resilience and as a testament to the past. The music swells, matching this triumphant tone, signaling that he has truly overcome, not by erasing the past but by rising above it.

In the song's climax, when he repeats, "I'm entitled to overcome," there's a sense of closure, a final assertion of victory. The phrase "I'll fight till I die" punctuates this resolve, highlighting his determination to continue facing whatever comes his way. This is not a declaration of peace but of readiness, a willingness to keep fighting, to remain resilient no matter the cost. The music, with its relentless beat and fierce guitar riffs, reaches its peak here, providing a powerful ending to a journey marked by struggle, survival, and ultimately, self-empowerment.

Overcome is a song that speaks to the universal human experience of facing adversity and emerging stronger. It does not shy away from the darkness but instead confronts it head-on, challenging the listener to consider their own battles, their own journeys of resilience. Stapp's lyrics, combined with the unyielding power of Tremonti's guitar and Phillips' drums, create a soundscape that is both brutal and beautiful, a raw testament to the strength found in overcoming life's trials. Through pain, defiance, and ultimate self-discovery, the song leaves us with a powerful reminder that we all have the right, and perhaps the duty, to overcome.

Application

Creed's *Overcome* is a powerful anthem of resilience, defiance, and reclaiming strength after enduring hardship. From its opening lines to its intense instrumentation, the song explores themes of empowerment, letting go of painful battles, and ultimately rising above the shadows of the past. The themes in *Overcome* resonate deeply with the Christian message of facing adversity with courage, seeking God's strength in our struggles, and finding freedom in letting go of what no longer serves us. Let's examine how the song's message aligns with biblical truths and how it can inspire you to face your own battles with faith and perseverance.

"Don't cry victim to me" opens the song with a sharp refusal to dwell in a place of defeat or self-pity. This bold stance echoes the biblical encouragement to confront hardship with strength and to rise above a victim mentality. In Romans 8:37, Paul writes, "No, in all these things we are more than conquerors through him who loved us." In Christ, we are empowered to face challenges with courage, knowing that God's love makes us victorious, even over life's darkest moments.

When you find yourself tempted to give in to despair, remember that God calls you to be "more than a conqueror," capable of standing strong with His help.

"Everything we are and used to be is buried and gone" reflects the desire to release the past and let go of what once weighed us down. The Bible often speaks of leaving behind the old self and embracing new life in Christ. In 2 Corinthians 5:17, Paul writes, "Therefore, if anyone is in Christ, the new creation has come: The old has gone, the new is here!" This message invites us to let go of past hurts, mistakes, and struggles, knowing that God offers us a fresh start and the strength to move forward. Let this line inspire you to release any old burdens you may be carrying, embracing the new identity and freedom God gives you.

"Now it's my turn to speak / It's my turn to expose and release what's been killing me" captures the need to release hidden pain and reclaim one's voice. This act of confession and release is echoed in James 5:16, which encourages, "Therefore confess your sins to each other and pray for each other so that you may be healed." By bringing our pain into the light, whether through prayer or honest conversations, we invite healing and freedom into our lives. When you feel burdened by unresolved struggles, remember that God calls you to bring them to Him, to release them from the shadows, and to allow His healing power to work in your heart.

"I'll be damned fighting you / It's impossible, impossible" reflects the wisdom of recognizing battles that are futile or toxic. Sometimes, true strength lies in knowing when to let go. Psalm 46:10 reminds us, "Be still, and know that I am God." This verse invites us to let go of control and trust God with the things we cannot change. When you face situations that feel "impossible," trust that God is with you, even in letting go, and that surrendering what you cannot control is not a sign of weakness but of faith.

"I'm entitled to overcome" expresses a hard-won sense of empowerment. This entitlement isn't about pride; it's about claiming the victory that God grants us over life's challenges. In Revelation 12:11, we read, "They triumphed over him by the blood of the Lamb and by the word of their testimony." Through Christ's sacrifice and the testimonies of our faith journeys, we have the strength to overcome. Let this line remind you that God equips you with the tools to rise above adversity, and in Him, you have every right to claim victory over struggles.

"Knock me down, throw me to the floor / There's no pain; I can't feel no more" suggests a resilience that comes from facing repeated hardship. The Bible speaks to the idea that trials, though painful, can build our endurance and strengthen our character. Romans 5:3-4 encourages us, "We also glory in our sufferings, because we know that suffering produces perseverance; perseverance, character; and character, hope." This verse reminds us that God can use even our deepest pain to shape us, preparing us to face life's challenges with strength and hope. When you feel like life has knocked you down, remember that God is refining you, using these moments to deepen your resilience and faith.

"Finally see what's beneath / Everything I am and hope to be cannot be lost" reflects a moment of self-discovery and confidence in one's worth. The Bible assures us of our identity in Christ, emphasizing that our value is secure in God's love. In Psalm 139:14, David proclaims, "I praise you because I am fearfully and wonderfully made; your works are wonderful, I know that full well." No matter what challenges we face, our identity in Christ remains unshaken. Let this line remind you of your inherent worth and the truth that God's love defines who you are, beyond any external circumstances or past hurts.

"You'll never know what I was thinking before you came 'round" suggests a lost innocence or a change brought on by life's trials. This sentiment reflects the reality that hardship often alters our perspective, sometimes revealing depths of strength and resilience we didn't know we had. In 1 Peter 5:10, we're reminded, "And the God of all grace... will himself restore you and make you strong, firm and steadfast." Through trials, God strengthens us, preparing us for what lies ahead. When you reflect on how life's challenges have shaped you, remember that God is always at work, using these experiences to deepen your faith and prepare you for a future grounded in His grace.

"Take a step, take a breath, put your guard down" offers a rare moment of softness, inviting vulnerability amid the defiance. This invitation reflects the biblical call to find peace and trust in God. In Matthew 11:28, Jesus says, "Come to me, all you who are weary and burdened, and I will give you rest." God invites us to lay down our defenses, trusting in His love and protection. When life feels overwhelming, take a moment to "put your guard down" and rest in God's care, allowing Him to carry your burdens and renew your strength.

"I cannot worry anymore of what you think of me" is a powerful declaration of freedom from others' judgments. The Bible encourages us to seek approval from God rather than from people. Galatians 1:10 asks, "Am I now trying to win the approval of human beings, or of God?" When we shift our focus to pleasing God, we find freedom from the expectations and judgments of others. Let this line inspire you to seek God's approval, knowing that His love for you is unchanging and that His opinion is the only one that ultimately matters.

In the climax of *Overcome*, the repetition of "I'm entitled to overcome" serves as a triumphant declaration, a reminder of our strength and right to rise above adversity. Through God's grace, we have not only the ability but the right to overcome life's hardships. 1 John 5:4 assures us, "For everyone born of God overcomes the world." This victory is not a result of our strength alone but a gift of God's love and power in our lives. When you feel overwhelmed by life's challenges, remember that in Christ, you are an overcomer, equipped with the strength to face and rise above any trial.

Overcome is more than a song of defiance; it's an anthem of resilience and a reminder that, no matter how hard life may press us, we have the strength to rise. With God's help, we can let go of what no longer serves us, release past hurts, and claim the victory that He has already won for us. As you reflect on this song, let it remind you of your identity as an overcomer in Christ, drawing on His strength to face life's challenges with courage, hope, and an unbreakable spirit.

CHAPTER 35
"Bread of Shame"

The song "Bread of Shame" by Creed unfolds as a raw introspective journey, one that dives into the internal battle of a man who feels trapped in a world that judges and misunderstands him. The lyrics echo with an ache that runs deeper than surface-level discontent, hinting at an experience where fame, acceptance, and fulfillment come at a high price—an empty, soulless "bread of shame" that barely sustains him. The song doesn't just communicate frustration; it explores the cost of living a life where identity and authenticity are traded for superficial validation.

The opening lines, "If you say I'm alive, I guess I'm living," establish the tone of resignation and detachment. This isn't merely someone questioning their existence, but someone trapped in a life shaped by the expectations and perceptions of others. The phrase "I guess I'm living" doesn't imply true vitality or joy; it sounds more like survival without purpose. It's the existence of someone who has accepted an externally imposed reality, reluctantly yielding to the roles and labels others have placed on him. The ambiguity in "guess your size, a choice I've been given" further reflects this tension: it could refer to society's predefined measures of success or worth, which he's forced to fit into despite their limitations and disconnect from his true self.

Musically, the driving guitar riff is forceful, almost a persistent reminder of the relentless nature of these expectations. The energy of the music builds, wrapping itself around the lyrics, amplifying the pressure he feels to conform. The combination of chords, often leaning on minor progressions, mirrors the mood of the lyrics—a somber and introspective soundscape where the minor tones evoke a sense of melancholy, underscoring the speaker's dissatisfaction. The music feels urgent and oppressive, echoing the claustrophobia of living a life according to others' terms.

When he sings, "Tell me everything's fine and peace is coming; I won't listen to the heartache I'm numbing," we see a man who has trained himself to shut down his emotions. There's a resignation to denial—a conscious numbing that speaks to his coping mechanism for navigating an unfulfilling existence. Peace is something he desperately wants but doesn't truly believe is on the horizon. Here, he willingly blocks out his heartache, hinting at the pain of losing oneself and one's authenticity in exchange for fleeting acceptance. The minor tonal shifts in the song during this section emphasize the sense of disillusionment, underscoring how peace and true contentment feel perpetually out of reach.

As the song progresses, the lyrics turn toward an almost pleading acceptance of his circumstances, marked by the lines, "When the world casts me down and says I've changed; I'll survive on all the promises you made to me." This evokes a sense of dependency on external validation. He's been cast down—an image that brings to mind exile or rejection. He survives on promises, but they're unfulfilled and ultimately hollow. The reference to change suggests that others have perceived him differently over time, perhaps labeling him as an outsider or a "sellout." There's a bitter irony here, as he's accused of changing, yet it's the world's demands and expectations that have shaped him into someone he barely recognizes.

The recurring refrain, "Bread of Shame," is haunting in its simplicity, symbolizing sustenance that doesn't nourish. In many religious
and philosophical traditions, bread is a symbol of life, of something
that gives strength and sustains. But "bread of shame" corrupts this
image, representing sustenance that fills the belly while emptying the
soul. It's the sustenance of someone who's accepted a life devoid of
personal truth, someone who's starved for authenticity yet subsists
on shallow rewards. Shame here acts almost as a currency, something
he's forced to consume repeatedly in the absence of anything real.
The repetition of "bread of shame" throughout the song creates a
litany, driving home the cyclical nature of this existence, where one
continually consumes shame as a substitute for real fulfillment.

The tone shifts subtly as he sings, "As long as you say I'm free; then
keep these chains off me." There's a flicker of irony in this statement.
He wants to feel free, yet it's clear that he's bound by chains, restrained
by others' definitions of who he should be. It's as if he's clinging to the
illusion of freedom, even as he's aware of the restrictions it imposes.
The mention of chains speaks to the internal and external forces holding him back—the chains of societal expectations, the chains of fame,
and the chains of self-doubt that weigh on him. It's a tragic paradox,
this notion of "freedom" granted conditionally, leaving him bound by
the very words intended to liberate him.

The line, "Tell me down is up; I'll let you fill this broken cup,"
illustrates his willingness to accept even the most distorted truths. He's
in such a state of dependency that he's willing to swallow falsehoods
if they promise him even the slightest reprieve. The cup here could
symbolize his spirit or soul—broken, fractured, and in need of healing.
Instead of the pure water that might heal, it's filled with the shallow
promises and empty platitudes of those around him. The music in this
section builds with a rawness that feels both desperate and resigned,

almost as if he's crying out yet simultaneously accepting the futility of his plea.

As the song crescendos, the repeated refrain "Just promise me fame; I'll survive on the bread of shame" reflects the tragic hunger for recognition, even if it means compromising his true self. Fame becomes a hollow objective—something he knows will not satisfy but clings to because it's what's offered. Fame here is almost a cruel irony, a false light that distracts him from a deeper, more meaningful pursuit. He's aware of its emptiness, yet he's drawn to it as if it's his only remaining option. The instrumentation here grows intense, reflecting his inner turmoil, a build-up of frustration that finds no resolution.

The verse "Tell me where I sign my name; inside I find no peace of mind to hide behind; only bread of shame" marks a pivotal moment in the song, where he confronts the loss of inner peace. Signing his name could symbolize an agreement, perhaps a deal with the world or with himself, to continue down this path of compromise and superficial validation. Yet with each signature, he signs away pieces of himself, trading his peace of mind for external approval. The image of signing one's name is powerful—an act that is both personal and binding, a symbol of commitment to something that's ultimately draining his spirit.

"Inside I find no peace of mind" echoes the emptiness that pervades his inner life. He has everything that society says should make him happy, yet he's bereft of peace, a reminder that true contentment doesn't come from fame, acceptance, or external validation. The "bread of shame" has left him hollow, unfulfilled, and lost, and it's as if he's finally acknowledging the full extent of his emptiness.

In the closing moments of the song, as he reiterates, "When the world says I've changed; bread of shame," there's a sense of finality. The repetition doesn't signal acceptance but rather a resigned acknowledgment of his predicament. It's as though he's locked into this cycle, and though he recognizes its futility, he doesn't yet see a way out. The intense, lingering chords at the end leave us with a sense of unresolved tension, mirroring his own inability to break free from the chains of shame and shallow sustenance.

Creed's "Bread of Shame" is a haunting reflection on the human condition, especially in a society that promises fulfillment through fame, validation, and conformity. The song's exploration of shame as sustenance—a twisted form of nourishment—serves as a powerful reminder of what happens when we allow external validation to define us. The music and lyrics work together to paint a stark portrait of a man grappling with his own identity, trapped in a world that offers him everything he thought he wanted, only to leave him starving for something real. The story he tells is deeply personal yet universal, an unsettling reminder of the hollowness that awaits those who abandon their true selves for the empty promises of a superficial world.

Application

Creed's *Bread of Shame* captures a deep, introspective struggle between self-worth and the hollow promises of fame and validation. The song confronts the internal emptiness that can arise when we prioritize external approval over authenticity, a theme that resonates powerfully with the biblical teaching about the dangers of conforming to the world's values rather than finding our identity in God. As we unpack the lyrics of *Bread of Shame*, let's explore how its themes align with spiritual truths and how this song can serve as a reminder to seek fulfillment in God rather than in fleeting, worldly achievements.

"If you say I'm alive, I guess I'm living" opens the song with a resignation to others' expectations. This line mirrors the struggle to find genuine purpose amid society's definitions of success. In Galatians 1:10, Paul writes, "Am I now trying to win the approval of human beings, or of God? Or am I trying to please people?" As followers of Christ, we are reminded that our identity and purpose are not found in others' approval but in God's love and calling. When we feel pressured to conform, remember that true life and joy come from living according to God's purpose, not the world's standards.

"Tell me everything's fine and peace is coming; I won't listen to the heartache I'm numbing" speaks to the temptation to ignore inner struggles and mask pain with superficial reassurances. In John 14:27, Jesus promises us peace, saying, "Peace I leave with you; my peace I give you. I do not give to you as the world gives." The world's peace is often temporary, built on avoidance rather than true healing. When you feel tempted to numb pain or silence your inner struggles, remember that Jesus offers a lasting peace that heals rather than merely covering up wounds.

"When the world casts me down and says I've changed; I'll survive on all the promises you made to me" reflects a dependency on others' validation. This line suggests a reliance on hollow promises, a pursuit of fame or acceptance that leaves one feeling depleted. Jesus warns against storing up "treasures on earth" (Matthew 6:19), which fade and disappoint, instead urging us to store up "treasures in heaven." God's promises are the only ones that sustain us fully, unchanging and faithful. When the world's validation falls short, let this be a reminder that God's love and promises are steadfast and will never leave you empty.

"Bread of Shame" is repeated as a symbol of sustenance that doesn't nourish, representing a life built on shallow achievements. The Bible often uses bread as a symbol of spiritual nourishment, with Jesus declaring in John 6:35, "I am the bread of life. Whoever comes to me will never go hungry." Here, *Bread of Shame* offers a stark contrast to this promise, illustrating the emptiness of seeking validation apart from God. Remember that only Christ can provide true fulfillment, the kind that satisfies our souls rather than leaving us feeling hollow.

"As long as you say I'm free; then keep these chains off me" reflects a tragic paradox: the desire to feel free while being bound by the need for approval. The Bible reminds us that true freedom comes from knowing the truth of God's love and grace. In John 8:36, Jesus says, "So if the Son sets you free, you will be free indeed." When you feel trapped by the pressures and expectations of the world, let this line remind you that freedom in Christ is unbounded, unshackled by the world's demands or judgments.

"Tell me down is up; I'll let you fill this broken cup" reflects a willingness to accept even distorted truths if they promise momentary comfort. This echoes the story of the Samaritan woman at the well in John 4, who sought satisfaction from "broken cisterns" – relationships that ultimately left her unfulfilled. Jesus offers her "living water" that will never leave her thirsty again. When you feel tempted to accept shallow promises or fleeting comforts, remember that God offers living water, a source of true and lasting fulfillment that heals rather than drains.

The repeated phrase "Just promise me fame; I'll survive on the bread of shame" captures the emptiness of fame pursued for its own sake. Fame, here, becomes a hollow idol, something that momentarily distracts but ultimately leaves the soul unfulfilled. In Matthew 16:26, Jesus poses the question, "What good will it be for someone to gain the whole world, yet forfeit their soul?" Fame and approval can never replace the deep satisfaction of knowing and serving God. When you feel drawn to the allure of recognition, let Jesus' words remind you of the eternal value of your soul and the incomparable worth of living a life aligned with God's will.

"Inside I find no peace of mind to hide behind; only bread of shame" acknowledges the profound emptiness that follows a life built on shallow pursuits. This line speaks to the universal human need for inner peace, a peace that only God can provide. Philippians 4:7 promises us "the peace of God, which transcends all understanding" when we turn to Him in faith. Worldly accomplishments, fame, or approval cannot fill this need for peace – it is only found in the presence of God. When you feel unrest, let this line remind you to seek God's peace, a peace that fills the void and brings wholeness.

"When the world says I've changed; bread of shame" speaks to the weight of judgment and the constant feeling of being misjudged or misunderstood. Jesus faced similar rejection, misunderstood even by those closest to Him. In John 15:18, He reminds us, "If the world hates you, keep in mind that it hated me first." When you feel judged or misunderstood, remember that Jesus understands this feeling deeply and invites you to find strength in knowing that God knows your true heart and intentions.

The music in *Bread of Shame* creates a heavy, oppressive soundscape, underscoring the song's themes of inner turmoil and frustration. Yet, even in the song's darkness, there is a reminder of the peace and fulfillment we find in God's presence. Psalm 34:8 invites us to "taste and see that the Lord is good." Unlike the "bread of shame" that leaves the soul starved, God's love fills and sustains us. When life feels heavy or unsatisfying, let the weight of the music remind you of the need to seek God's goodness, a goodness that never fades or disappoints.

In *Bread of Shame*, Creed explores the painful cost of pursuing the world's promises at the expense of one's soul. The song's message serves as a reminder to turn away from shallow pursuits, finding true fulfillment in God's love, peace, and purpose. When you feel the temptation to chase worldly validation or hollow goals, remember that God's love is a source of sustenance that truly satisfies. Seek His presence, His peace, and His purpose, knowing that in Him, you will find rest for your soul and an identity that does not fade or depend on others' approval.

CHAPTER 36
"A Thousand Faces"

In "A Thousand Faces," Creed delves into the complex struggle of facing both oneself and others, exploring themes of identity, betrayal, and self-reflection with a raw intensity. The lyrics paint a picture of a person standing amidst crumbling walls—walls that once confined them but now serve as a reminder of the imprisoning effects of deception and fractured identity. This song is a plea for honesty, both with oneself and with others, set against a backdrop of unresolved pain and a longing for clarity amidst the chaos.

The song begins with a haunting image: "I stand surrounded by the walls that once confined me, knowing I'll be underneath them when they crumble, when they fall." These walls, once seemingly solid, represent a kind of psychological prison, built from misunderstandings, facades, and betrayals. The notion of being "underneath them" when they fall suggests a sense of inevitability, a recognition that the past—the betrayals, the wounds, the lies—will eventually collapse, burying him unless he breaks free. There's a subtle hint of resilience here, though. Even as he acknowledges his confinement, he's willing to confront the moment when it all comes crashing down.

Musically, the song carries a somber, heavy tone, with minor chords and dissonant sounds that intensify the feeling of entrapment and conflict. The instruments mirror the emotional turbulence of the lyrics, building tension that ebbs and flows, much like the process of self-discovery and confrontation with one's own pain. The harshness of the guitar riffs and the driving rhythm add layers of frustration and anger, reinforcing the deep-seated wounds the speaker is struggling to overcome.

As he reflects on his scars, he notes, "Ash still simmers just under my skin. Indifference smiles again." These words suggest that the pain hasn't fully healed; it lingers beneath the surface, a smoldering reminder of past wounds. The "ash" speaks to remnants of something once burning brightly—perhaps a sense of trust, purpose, or belief in others. Now, it's reduced to embers beneath his skin, unresolved, ready to ignite again if provoked. And "indifference" becomes a mask he wears to conceal this simmering pain, a facade to protect himself, or perhaps a shield against the betrayal he's endured. This line sets up the central struggle of the song: the battle between authentic emotion and the masks people wear to protect or deceive.

The chorus, "You wear a thousand faces," echoes this theme of deception and hidden identities. The "thousand faces" signify the many personas people adopt, whether to please others, to protect themselves, or to manipulate. There's a poignant frustration in the plea, "Tell me, tell me which is you." It's a desperate appeal for honesty, for the stripping away of masks to reveal the true self. But the repeated "even though it's there" suggests a painful paradox—he knows the truth is there, somewhere behind the myriad faces, yet it remains obscured, just out of reach. This resonates with the struggle of trying to see through someone's facade, knowing they're hiding something but unable to break through the layers.

As the song moves forward, the lines "So broken mirrors paint the floor; why can't you see the truth?" create a visceral image of shattered self-reflection. Broken mirrors signify a fragmented sense of identity, an inability to view oneself—or others—clearly. The mirrors could represent both his own shattered perception and the distorted reflections he sees in those around him. When trust is broken, it's not only our view of others that fractures, but also our view of ourselves. The floor littered with shards of these broken mirrors suggests a painful landscape he must navigate, a constant reminder of betrayal and fractured truth.

The line, "Eerily, time made no change," is one of the most haunting in the song, speaking to a sense of stagnation. Despite the passage of time, the pain, betrayal, and deception remain. It's as if the events of the past have been preserved in amber, untouched and unhealed. This line is a powerful commentary on how unresolved trauma can keep someone emotionally frozen, locked in a cycle of pain and mistrust. Musically, this section has a more subdued intensity, a quiet rage that underscores the despair of realizing that time alone doesn't heal; it takes active confrontation to move forward.

"Pointing fingers, laying blame; lying over and over," he continues, highlighting the destructive cycle of blame and deception that perpetuates his inner conflict. There's a palpable exhaustion here, the weary frustration of someone who's been betrayed and blamed, scapegoated even, yet still stands. The repetition of "over and over" emphasizes this endless cycle, as if the accusations and lies have taken on a life of their own, refusing to dissipate. The song's rhythm here is relentless, mirroring the persistence of this emotional weight and the difficulty of escaping it.

"Trashed my name, yet here I stand" is a declaration of resilience. Despite the character assassination he's endured, despite the attempts to tarnish his reputation, he remains. This line is a quiet triumph, a refusal to be erased by others' judgments or lies. It suggests an inner strength that's developed in response to hardship. In contrast to the earlier sense of entrapment, there's a glimmer of defiance here—a refusal to let his identity be completely overtaken by others' perceptions.

Yet, the refrain "So much I hide" returns, reminding us that this strength comes at a cost. The hiding isn't just from others; it's from himself as well. There's a certain sorrow in admitting that survival has required him to bury parts of himself, to conceal his pain and vulnerability. The music becomes almost cathartic at this point, with heavier guitar riffs and a rising intensity, expressing the pent-up emotions he's held back for so long.

The plea, "How is stepping back a move forward?" captures the confusion and frustration of self-reflection. Forced to confront his past, he wonders how revisiting these painful memories can possibly help him move forward. This line underscores the paradox of healing—sometimes, to progress, we have to look back, to face what's been left unresolved. He's being asked to confront the "you" he addresses, a person who's worn "a thousand faces." But as he's forced to look behind, he must also examine his own role, his own hidden truths.

The verse "I bleed inside, just let it out" is a cry for release, for the ability to finally express the pain that's been festering within. The repetition of "just let it out" feels both urgent and cathartic, as if he's willing himself to finally face the emotions he's buried. It's a blunt, unfiltered moment of anger and frustration. It's an admission that the walls, the facades, the pretenses have been nothing but distractions from the real, painful truth. The music during this part reaches a fever pitch, embodying the chaotic release of suppressed emotion, as if he's on the edge of breaking free from the lies that have held him back.

In the closing lines, "Tell me which is you," repeated almost like a mantra, we sense a longing for authenticity—not only from the person he's addressing but from himself as well. The repetition is both desperate and insistent, reflecting the futility he feels in his search for truth. The layered vocal delivery here creates a haunting effect, as if he's pleading with multiple versions of the same person, each one wearing a different face. This relentless demand for the truth is not just an accusation—it's a challenge to break the cycle of deception, to face reality with honesty and courage.

Creed's "A Thousand Faces" is a haunting meditation on identity, betrayal, and the struggle to reconcile with one's past. Through layered metaphors, powerful imagery, and intense musicality, the song captures the emotional weight of facing fractured relationships and the masks we all wear. It's a powerful reminder that true healing requires confronting not only the betrayals of others but also the parts of ourselves we hide. As the music fades, we're left with a sense of unresolved tension—a recognition that, while the speaker may have begun the journey toward truth, he has yet to find the clarity he seeks.

The song doesn't offer easy answers. It leaves us with a question: In a world of broken mirrors and thousand-faced masks, can we ever truly know ourselves or others? "A Thousand Faces" invites us to wrestle with this uncertainty, urging us to shed our own masks and confront the painful truths that lie beneath. It's a journey of self-discovery that requires facing our deepest wounds and releasing the pain we carry, even when the cost is steep and the path is unclear.

Application

In Creed's *A Thousand Faces*, we encounter a haunting reflection on identity, betrayal, and the arduous journey of self-discovery—a theme that powerfully resonates with the Christian call to integrity, transparency, and the pursuit of truth. In a world that often encourages us to wear masks, to present different faces in different contexts, this song underscores the consequences of such deception and the yearning for genuine self-understanding and relational honesty. Through deeply personal lyrics, Scott Stapp wrestles with the pain of broken trust and the lingering wounds of betrayal, inviting us to consider what it means to live truthfully before God and others.

The opening line, "I stand surrounded by the walls that once confined me, knowing I'll be underneath them when they crumble, when they fall," paints a vivid image of someone imprisoned by the facades and broken relationships that have shaped them. In many ways, these walls represent the false identities we adopt or the barriers we build to protect ourselves. Yet, as Scripture reminds us, God calls us to "worship in Spirit and in truth" (John 4:24), to break down the walls of pretense and face the reality of who we are before Him. When we construct walls based on deception or self-protection, they eventually collapse, leaving us vulnerable beneath the rubble of our own making. *A Thousand Faces* challenges us to dismantle these walls by seeking God's truth and embracing a life of genuine transparency.

The imagery of "ash still simmering just under my skin" suggests the lingering effects of unresolved pain and broken trust, echoing the biblical call to confront rather than conceal our wounds. Proverbs 28:13 advises, "Whoever conceals their sins does not prosper, but the one who confesses and renounces them finds mercy." The "ash" represents past hurts that may have once burned brightly with anger or betrayal but have now settled into a steady ache, smoldering just beneath the surface. While indifference might seem like a shield, it can harden us, numbing our capacity to heal and to forgive. True peace comes not from hiding our scars but from facing them with courage, asking God to transform the "ash" of bitterness into healing.

The chorus, "You wear a thousand faces," is a powerful reminder of the dangers of living a life fragmented by duplicity. As Christians, we are called to a single-minded devotion to truth and authenticity. James 1:8 warns of the instability that comes from being "double-minded," and here, the thousand faces symbolize the fractured identity of someone who hides their true self. When we adopt different personas to fit into different situations, we risk losing sight of our God-given identity, becoming strangers even to ourselves. This line, "Tell me, tell me which is you," is a plea for truth, echoing the psalmist's cry, "Search me, God, and know my heart" (Psalm 139:23). It is an invitation to strip away the masks and allow ourselves to be known fully.

"So broken mirrors paint the floor" creates a stark image of shattered self-perception, reflecting the internal consequences of deceit. The mirrors symbolize our self-image and the fractured way we see ourselves and others when trust has been broken. In 1 Corinthians 13:12, Paul describes how we now "see only a reflection as in a mirror," suggesting that our understanding of ourselves and others is incomplete. These broken mirrors represent a distorted self-view, reminding us that, without truth, our relationships and self-image remain fragmented. The act of navigating this "floor of broken mirrors" reflects the painful process of walking through the consequences of deception and betrayal, a journey that requires humility and a willingness to seek healing.

When Stapp sings, "Eerily, time made no change," he speaks to the power of unresolved pain to hold us captive, even as time moves on. This line echoes the biblical theme of sin and its lingering effects. Like the Israelites wandering the desert, sometimes we remain in cycles of pain and deception, despite the passage of time, because we haven't confronted the underlying issues. Ephesians 4:22-24 calls us to "put off" our old selves and "be made new in the attitude of our minds." Healing requires not just time but active transformation, a willingness to surrender our pain and ask God to renew us.

"Pointing fingers, laying blame" reflects the human tendency to evade accountability. It's a reminder of the story in Genesis 3, where Adam and Eve, after their disobedience, began to blame each other rather than taking responsibility. This destructive cycle perpetuates the pain rather than healing it. *A Thousand Faces* challenges us to break free from this cycle by taking ownership of our actions, just as Scripture calls us to "confess your sins to each other and pray for each other so that you may be healed" (James 5:16). By acknowledging our role in our brokenness, we open the door for God's grace and healing.

"Trashed my name, yet here I stand" is a line of quiet defiance, a refusal to be defined by others' judgments or betrayals. As believers, we are reminded that our true identity is rooted in Christ, not in others' opinions or accusations. In Isaiah 54:17, God declares, "No weapon forged against you will prevail, and you will refute every tongue that accuses you." This line encourages us to stand firm in the face of slander or rejection, knowing that our worth is found in God's unchanging love for us. Despite the world's attempts to tarnish us, we remain steadfast, not because of our own strength but because of the truth of who we are in Christ.

"How is stepping back a move forward?" encapsulates the confusion we often feel when facing past pain. In our journey of faith, sometimes moving forward requires stepping back and revisiting wounds we'd rather leave untouched. The Bible frequently reminds us of the importance of reflection and repentance, recognizing that true growth often involves confronting the past. Hosea 14:1 calls Israel to "return" to the Lord, to revisit the point of separation in order to find healing. In the same way, *A Thousand Faces* challenges us to examine the places of hurt in our own lives, not to dwell in them but to understand and learn from them, allowing God to transform our past into a stepping stone toward wholeness.

"I bleed inside, just let it out" is a cry for release, an acknowledgment that pain kept hidden will only fester. The psalmists often pour out their anguish before God, modeling a healthy approach to processing pain: "Pour out your hearts to him, for God is our refuge" (Psalm 62:8). In this line, there is a plea for freedom from the weight of unspoken suffering, a reminder that healing begins with honesty. As Christians, we can bring our wounds before God, knowing that He sees and understands our pain. By "letting it out," we begin the process of surrender, giving our pain to the One who heals.

The closing line, "Tell me which is you," repeated almost as a mantra, is a call for authenticity and clarity. In a world filled with "thousand faces," the song resonates with the Christian call to shed all pretenses and live transparently. Jesus warned against hypocrisy, urging us to "let your 'yes' be 'yes,' and your 'no,' 'no'" (Matthew 5:37). In this final plea, there's a longing to strip away the masks and live in truth, both in our relationships with others and with God.

Creed's *A Thousand Faces* captures the pain of betrayal, the cost of living a divided life, and the yearning for self-knowledge and truth. The song serves as a poignant reminder to seek integrity, to break free from the "thousand faces" we might wear, and to confront the wounds that keep us imprisoned. Through its powerful imagery and introspective lyrics, *A Thousand Faces* encourages us to pursue honesty, healing, and wholeness, knowing that true freedom lies in living transparently before God and others. When we are willing to confront the broken mirrors of our past, we open the door to healing and transformation, allowing God's truth to illuminate the darkest corners of our hearts.

CHAPTER 37
"Suddenly"

I n "Suddenly," Creed delves into the powerful themes of identity, guilt, and the vulnerability of self-destruction. The lyrics and music together create a visceral experience of being confronted with one's weaknesses and losses—a moment when the walls of denial collapse, leaving the soul exposed and defenseless.

The opening lines introduce a struggle as ancient as human nature itself: "A nature to nurture, an instinct to sin." This line suggests a duality within each person, an innate tension between the desire to care, love, and nurture and an equally strong instinct toward actions that lead us astray. Here, the concept of sin isn't portrayed as an external force but something embedded within—almost as though it is an inevitable aspect of human existence. There's a sense of frustration in the question, "What's underneath the skin you live in?" as if the speaker himself is struggling to reconcile these conflicting impulses within.

As the song unfolds, "Betrayed, you're an image, oh, precious creation," these lines paint a tragic picture of self-betrayal. "Betrayed" suggests that the speaker feels as though he's turned against himself or that something precious has been lost within him. He is both the creation and the betrayer, and this internal conflict is leading him to a place of submission: "You will submit, you will give in." The language here hints at a powerful inevitability, as if this downfall is unavoidable, like waves crashing on a shore that cannot hold them back. There's a sadness in these lines, as if the speaker knows that giving in to his baser instincts and self-destructive tendencies will destroy him, but he feels powerless to resist.

The music at this point shifts, the rhythm and chords heightening in tension as we're taken to the song's chorus, where the repeated word "Suddenly" strikes like a bolt out of the blue. "Suddenly I have no strength at all, so suddenly hit with all I've lost." This sudden shift marks a turning point, where realization and consequence collide. The repetition of "suddenly" is not accidental; it captures the overwhelming, disorienting experience of facing a truth long buried or ignored. This moment feels cinematic—a freeze-frame where the full weight of his choices crashes down on him all at once, leaving him reeling. The vocals swell with urgency, and the guitar intensifies, pulling the listener into the rawness of his pain and confusion.

With each "suddenly," there's a heightened sense of fragility, like a life built on shaky ground finally crumbling. "Suddenly my world is falling apart, so suddenly." There's a timeless quality to this line, a recognition that sometimes everything can change in an instant, and when it does, it feels like the ground has been ripped out from under him. There's an emotional paralysis here—a sense of feeling overwhelmed, where even finding the strength to process the loss seems impossible.

The lyrics then turn to a darker introspection: "You say you're a victim, but that's just a symptom, it's so very clear you volunteered." This line is a jarring confrontation, an unmasking of the self-deceptions that have likely sustained him. By pointing out that he's "volunteered" for this suffering, there's an implication that he's been complicit in his own downfall. This line stings with the bitter truth that he has, at least in part, chosen this path, perhaps by turning a blind eye to his darker instincts or by allowing himself to be consumed by them. It's not a comforting thought, and the music supports this realization with an edgy, almost accusatory tone.

The next question, "Why are you fighting? Just stop your denying, own up to the sin you bury within," strips away any lingering excuses. The speaker is being forced to confront himself with brutal honesty, to look inwards and own the choices he's made, however painful. This moment is intensely personal; it's as though he's looking into a mirror, unable to escape the harsh truth of his complicity. The tone here becomes almost judgmental, as if he's tired of his own excuses, tired of pretending to be a victim of circumstance. The repetitive questioning forces him to face the guilt and shame he's buried, laying bare his vulnerabilities.

As the song cycles back to the chorus, there's a deepened weariness in the repetition of "Suddenly I have no strength at all." Each repetition feels heavier, more resigned. By now, it's clear that the speaker is overwhelmed by the weight of his own accountability, as if the very act of acknowledgment has drained him of all vitality. It's not simply about a single moment of weakness or regret; it's an admission of a lifetime of small, compounding choices that have led to this breaking point. The instrumentation at this point grows mournful, with the guitar and vocals descending into a solemn resonance, reflecting the depth of his sorrow and exhaustion.

"Suddenly my world falls apart, my world falls apart, my world." The triple repetition of "my world" is almost a chant, each echo seeming to break him down further. His world—everything he's known, everything he's built, however flawed—is now shattered. There's an underlying acceptance here, a kind of submission to the wreckage. The music, too, feels like it's fading, as if each note struggles under the weight of despair. The repetition of the word "suddenly" captures the shock, the abruptness of his reckoning, and also the inevitability of it—a slow-building storm that has finally broken upon him.

In these final lines, we see a man stripped of defenses, humbled by the recognition of his own failings and the consequences they've wrought. The song ends without resolution, leaving the listener suspended in that moment of realization and loss. There's no redemption here, no quick fix, only the stark, uncomfortable truth that he must face. The music fades but lingers in the mind, echoing with the haunting sense of a life irrevocably changed.

Creed's "Suddenly" speaks to the fragility of identity and the hidden, often denied, parts of ourselves that can bring us to ruin. The song's progression from denial to acknowledgment of guilt is painfully human, a reminder of the heavy toll that comes with avoiding responsibility for our own choices. It's a deeply reflective and almost cinematic portrayal of a man's inner collapse, as he's forced to confront the wreckage of his decisions. The song leaves us with a sense of weightiness, a stark reminder that true transformation often requires facing the darkness within ourselves.Top of Form

Bottom of Form

Application

In *Suddenly*, Creed offers a soul-baring exploration of the human struggle with sin, self-deception, and the crushing impact of unaddressed guilt. Through the song's powerful imagery and intense music, Scott Stapp invites listeners to confront their own inner battles—the choices we make, the responsibilities we evade, and the fragile foundations upon which we often build our lives. The song serves as both a caution and a call to self-examination, showing the stark consequences of living in denial and the toll it takes on one's soul.

The opening line, "A nature to nurture, an instinct to sin," speaks to the duality within every person. Scripture acknowledges this conflict, describing the battle between the Spirit and the flesh in Galatians 5:17: "For the flesh desires what is contrary to the Spirit, and the Spirit what is contrary to the flesh." This line encapsulates the tension between our desire to nurture, protect, and love, and our inclination toward sin and self-destruction. It paints a portrait of a human soul caught in the struggle to choose a higher path while continually pulled toward the lesser instincts of the flesh. The question, "What's underneath the skin you live in?" hints at the discomfort of self-examination, calling to mind Psalm 139:23-24, where the psalmist asks God to "search me and know my heart." The lyrics set the tone for a journey of painful introspection, leading the listener to ask: Who am I beneath my actions and desires?

As the song continues with, "Betrayed, you're an image, oh, precious creation," Stapp evokes the feeling of self-betrayal, a poignant reminder of the disconnect between who we were created to be and the ways we often fall short. The idea of being both "precious" and "betrayed" resonates with the Christian understanding of humanity as God's creation, made in His image yet marred by sin. In this line, we're reminded of the fall of humanity in Genesis, where Adam and Eve's betrayal of God's command resulted in separation from Him. This "betrayal" is not just against oneself but also against the Creator, a forfeiting of the true identity for something lesser.

The song's chorus—"Suddenly I have no strength at all, so suddenly hit with all I've lost"—is a powerful moment of realization. Like the story of the prodigal son, who "came to his senses" (Luke 15:17) in the midst of ruin, this "sudden" awareness brings the weight of all he has forfeited crashing down. The repetition of "suddenly" captures the shock and immediacy of self-recognition, a painful yet necessary jolt that forces him to face the reality he has long ignored. The swelling intensity of the music mirrors this revelation, drawing the listener into the character's emotional turmoil as he grapples with the consequences of his choices. In moments like these, we're reminded that true transformation often begins with a raw confrontation with the truth of our own failings.

The line "You say you're a victim, but that's just a symptom, it's so very clear you volunteered" strikes at the heart of human tendencies toward self-justification. In Proverbs 28:13, we're reminded, "Whoever conceals their sins does not prosper, but the one who confesses and renounces them finds mercy." This lyric exposes the ways we often cast ourselves as victims to avoid taking responsibility, masking our choices behind excuses and blame. Yet, the statement that he "volunteered" brings him face-to-face with the painful reality that he willingly chose his path, adding a layer of accountability that is difficult to evade. Here, the song challenges us to see our actions for what they are, to recognize the times when we, too, have "volunteered" for behaviors or mindsets that lead us astray.

"Why are you fighting? Just stop your denying, own up to the sin you bury within" becomes a call for repentance, an invitation to face the hidden sins that weigh him down. Like David's plea in Psalm 51:10—"Create in me a pure heart, O God, and renew a steadfast spirit within me"—this line underscores the importance of facing one's guilt and confessing it, a necessary step for healing. It's a moment of painful clarity, where the speaker is urged to stop hiding and own his choices fully. The harshness of the tone reveals a frustration with self-deception, a desire to break free from the cycle of denial and self-destruction. The music intensifies here, underscoring the urgency of facing this inner darkness before it consumes him completely.

The song's refrain, "Suddenly I have no strength at all," becomes heavier with each repetition, conveying the exhaustion that comes from a lifetime of hidden guilt and unacknowledged responsibility. The weight of his choices has left him drained, mirroring Paul's lament in Romans 7:24, "What a wretched man I am! Who will rescue me from this body that is subject to death?" This moment captures the depth of his weariness, a brokenness that can only find healing through surrender. The music's mournful undertones reflect his resignation, highlighting the struggle to accept accountability without losing hope entirely.

As the final lines echo—"my world falls apart, my world"—the speaker acknowledges the shattering of everything he once held onto. Each repetition feels like a further descent into surrender, a recognition that his self-made world was built on unstable ground. Matthew 7:26-27 warns of the dangers of building one's life on shifting sands, illustrating that only a foundation in truth can withstand life's storms. In this moment, the speaker's world is falling apart because it was constructed on denial, self-deception, and unresolved guilt. The music fades, leaving the listener in a place of unresolved tension, mirroring the speaker's own sense of displacement.

"Suddenly" doesn't provide easy answers or neat resolutions; it presents the painful but necessary confrontation with one's own failings. As the character faces the wreckage of his choices, he is left in a space of vulnerability and uncertainty, an uncomfortable place but a pivotal one. This moment of reckoning calls to mind the Christian call to repentance, the first step in a journey toward transformation. Like the prodigal son who returns to the Father, each of us must first acknowledge our need for grace, recognizing that we cannot bear the weight of our sin alone.

In its raw intensity, *Suddenly* invites listeners to reflect on their own lives, to consider the ways we, too, have buried guilt or denied responsibility. The song is a powerful reminder that true peace comes not from avoiding the truth but from facing it head-on, confessing our failings, and allowing ourselves to be broken open before God. The weight of this confrontation is not without purpose—it is the threshold to a more authentic self, a necessary purging that makes room for healing, restoration, and the strength to rise anew.

Creed's *Suddenly* echoes the biblical call to authenticity and self-awareness, urging us to recognize the darkness within and bring it to light. In this way, the song becomes a modern-day psalm of lament, a testament to the painful but redemptive power of self-reckoning. It leaves us with a sense of gravity, a reminder that though facing our sin is daunting, it is also the first step toward true freedom and renewal.

CHAPTER 38

"Rain"

This song paints the picture of a person who feels trapped, uncertain, and weary from a cycle they can't break. The lyrics carry a kind of resigned exhaustion, mixed with a glimmer of hope, longing for relief and renewal. The sense of being "stuck again" is not unfamiliar to the speaker—it's a place they've found themselves in before. There's an underlying helplessness, like being caught in a relentless storm, longing for a breakthrough but unable to find a way out.

The opening plea, "Can you help me out, can you lend me a hand?" feels vulnerable, like a reaching out in the darkness. This isn't just a casual request; it's a call for real support, a lifeline in a moment of despair. The line, "It's safe to say that I'm stuck again," conveys a frustrating acceptance. The word "safe" is particularly telling—it implies a kind of fatalism, as if he's used to this place of being caught between conflicting realities. He's trapped, "between this life and the light," suggesting a struggle between where he is and where he hopes to be. This phrase is poignant, almost ethereal, hinting that he sees a brighter path but feels unable to reach it.

The music surrounding these lines is subdued yet steady, like the quiet before a storm. The melody seems to mirror his internal state, carrying a sense of stagnation and a haunting repetition that underscores his entrapment. The steady pulse of the chords and the slightly melancholic tone resonate with his exhaustion and weariness.

The refrain, "I feel it's gonna rain like this for days," captures the sense of an unending, inescapable gloom. Rain becomes a powerful metaphor, representing both cleansing and sorrow. It's as if the rain is both his sadness and his hope for something to wash away the past. There's a tension in this refrain; on the one hand, the rain is heavy, unrelenting, something to endure. On the other, it's also a source of renewal. The rain becomes almost a ritual of purification, something that might strip away his confusion and bring clarity.

As he sings, "Let it rain down and wash everything away," there's a surrender to the forces around him. He's allowing the rain to take control, perhaps even welcoming it. It's a release, a way of letting go of the burdens that have weighed him down. This isn't necessarily a resolution, but it's a step toward acceptance, a willingness to confront whatever lies beneath his confusion and sorrow. The instrumentation here grows more intense, reflecting this emotional surrender, as if the music itself is crashing down, embodying the rain he's imagining.

The repetition of "I hope that tomorrow the sun will shine" is his fragile hope, a desire for renewal and a clean slate. There's a kind of longing for light, not just to illuminate his path, but to bring warmth and life back to his weary soul. Yet, even as he hopes, he doesn't quite believe it. The rain is all-consuming, making the possibility of sunshine feel distant and almost unattainable. This line also speaks to the cyclical nature of his struggle—he's been here before, hoping for a better tomorrow, yet he's still caught in the rain. The contrast between the rain and the hope for sun captures the push and pull within him, the desire to move forward clashing with the weight of his current reality.

The second verse digs deeper into his sense of confusion: "I tried to figure out, I can't understand what it means to be whole again." This line is profoundly introspective, reflecting the speaker's deep need for healing. "Whole again" suggests a previous wholeness, a time before he was fractured or lost, and it implies that he's searching for a part of himself that's been missing. His struggle here isn't merely situational but existential—he's searching for a completeness that feels perpetually out of reach. This line also adds another layer of melancholy, hinting that he may not even fully remember what it feels like to be whole.

"Trapped between the truth and the consequence, nothing's real, nothing's making sense," brings out a crisis of reality. This entrapment between truth and consequence suggests that he's grappling with the weight of his own choices or perhaps even an unwanted truth. There's a loss of grounding here, as though he can no longer trust his own perceptions. This line captures the disorientation of someone who's been drifting, perhaps avoiding certain realities, only to find himself lost in the fog of his own decisions and their repercussions. The music here adds to this disorientation, with its rhythm almost feeling like it's suspended, echoing his confusion and sense of disconnection.

The refrain returns, heavier with each repetition. "I feel it's gonna rain like this for days" carries an added weight now. Each time he says it, the listener can sense his desperation deepening. The rain is both his torment and his refuge, something he wishes to escape but also feels he must endure. There's an acceptance here, a kind of resignation that he may be in this place for a while longer. Yet, his hope for sunshine remains, flickering but never fully extinguished.

As the song builds to the bridge, he pleads, "Fall down, wash away my yesterdays." Here, the rain becomes explicitly symbolic of forgiveness and release. "Yesterdays" encompass his past mistakes, regrets, and all the accumulated weight he carries. This line is a cry for liberation, a request for the rain to cleanse him of everything that holds him back. It's an invitation for renewal, a desire to strip away his burdens so that he might emerge lighter, freer. The instrumentation here swells, matching the intensity of this plea, and as he repeats it, the sound crescendos, amplifying the rawness of his need for a fresh start.

The line "So let the rain fall down on me" is a final surrender. The rain isn't just something he feels happening around him; it's something he welcomes upon himself, a force that he hopes will wash over and through him, leaving nothing but what's essential. This line feels almost like a baptism, a transformative moment where he's embracing whatever is necessary to let go of his past and find a way forward. He's no longer merely enduring the rain; he's actively seeking its transformative power.

In the song's closing, the refrain repeats once more, as if cycling through his acceptance of the rain, his hope for renewal, and his uncertainty about what lies ahead. Each repetition of "I feel it's gonna rain like this" leaves a deeper imprint, emphasizing that his journey isn't over. The rain is ongoing, a continuous cleansing that he's willing to endure, no matter how long it takes. The repetition gives a sense of finality yet also leaves an open question, as if he's still waiting for the clouds to break.

Creed's song captures the ache of feeling caught between past regrets and future hope. The rain serves as a poignant metaphor for both sorrow and cleansing, the inescapable weight of his struggles and the potential for transformation. The music and lyrics together create a landscape of emotional endurance, a journey through which he comes to accept that perhaps the rain itself is what will lead him to healing. His hope remains tentative but unwavering, a faint light that guides him forward through the storm. The song's conclusion doesn't promise an end to his struggles, but it leaves him open to whatever lies beyond the rain, symbolizing a fragile but enduring resilience in the face of life's storms.

Application

In *"Rain"*, Creed explores the theme of emotional entrapment and the longing for renewal in a deeply introspective way. The song captures the tension between despair and hope, creating a landscape where rain symbolizes both the weight of life's struggles and the possibility of transformation. Through haunting lyrics and a steady, melancholic melody, Scott Stapp invites us to sit with the heaviness of unresolved sorrow and the quiet yearning for a fresh start.

The opening plea, *"Can you help me out, can you lend me a hand?"*, is laden with vulnerability, evoking the psalmist's cry for deliverance. Psalm 40:13 comes to mind: "Be pleased to save me, Lord; come quickly, Lord, to help me." This is not a superficial request; it's a desperate reach for assistance, a cry for connection amidst isolation. Stapp's use of "safe" in *"It's safe to say that I'm stuck again"* suggests a familiar, almost comfortable resignation—a pattern he's fallen into repeatedly, like the Israelites who longed to break free from the cycle of sin yet struggled to escape its pull. The words *"between this life and the light"* imply a yearning for spiritual release, a place where he can move beyond his current limitations and find peace. This mirrors Romans 7:24's lament, "What a wretched man I am! Who will rescue me from this body of death?"

Musically, the subdued melody reflects this state of stagnation. The chords carry a feeling of suspension, creating an atmosphere that is neither fully despairing nor hopeful. The music's steady pulse reflects the persistence of life's storms, while the slight melancholic undertone underscores the weight he feels, waiting for release.

The refrain, *"I feel it's gonna rain like this for days,"* draws us into a space of unrelenting gloom, echoing the feeling of being overwhelmed by life's circumstances. Rain in Scripture often symbolizes cleansing or the presence of God in times of desolation, as in Joel 2:23: "He has given you the autumn rains because He is faithful." In this line, rain becomes a metaphor for sorrow but also carries an undercurrent of hope, as though he sees the rain as something that might finally wash away his burdens. It's a paradox, the tension between the heaviness of the storm and the promise of renewal it brings.

"Let it rain down and wash everything away" carries an undertone of surrender, much like David's prayer in Psalm 51:2, "Wash away all my iniquity and cleanse me from my sin." This line is a release, a moment where he acknowledges his need for cleansing and lets go of control, inviting the rain to strip away his confusion and despair. Musically, the intensity builds here, mirroring the catharsis in his surrender, as if the music itself is embodying the storm he's enduring. This surrender isn't an end but a step toward acceptance, allowing the forces around him to work on him in the hope of healing.

The repeated line, *"I hope that tomorrow the sun will shine,"* introduces a fragile hope, a belief in the possibility of redemption and renewal. Yet, the hope feels tentative, almost out of reach, much like Lamentations 3:21-23, where amid great sorrow, the writer remembers, "Yet this I call to mind and therefore I have hope: Because of the Lord's great love we are not consumed, for His compassions never fail. They are new every morning." The sun here symbolizes not only physical light but also spiritual warmth and clarity, a sense of life that he yearns to feel again. His repeated hope for a new beginning underscores his internal conflict—a desire for change wrestling against a resigned expectation of continued rain.

The second verse, *"I tried to figure out, I can't understand what it means to be whole again,"* delves deeper into his sense of brokenness, akin to the Israelites' longing to return to their former wholeness. The words *"whole again"* echo a desire for reconciliation with a self he barely remembers, suggesting a time before life's hardships fractured him. His search for wholeness brings to mind John 5:6, where Jesus asks the man at the pool of Bethesda, "Do you want to get well?" This line, though quiet, reveals the depths of his weariness and the search for something he feels he may never attain again.

"Trapped between the truth and the consequence, nothing's real, nothing's making sense" captures a crisis of identity, a state of being torn between reality and the weight of his choices, like the Israelites wandering in the desert, caught between Egypt and the Promised Land. This line suggests a disconnect from his own sense of purpose, much like King David when he wrote, "For I am in trouble; my eye wastes away with grief" (Psalm 31:9). The music here grows more disorienting, echoing his confusion as he confronts a reality that feels fragmented and elusive.

As the refrain returns, *"I feel it's gonna rain like this for days"* takes on a heavier tone, as though each repetition brings a deeper acceptance. The rain is his trial and his hope for purification, something he wishes to escape yet feels bound to endure. It's an acceptance that he may remain in this place longer, that perhaps the rain has a purpose he has yet to understand. But his hope for sunshine flickers, a reminder that his faith remains, however faintly. The push and pull between the rain and the sun is an embodiment of his internal struggle, the tension between resignation and hope.

The bridge, *"Fall down, wash away my yesterdays,"* echoes a longing for forgiveness and a clean slate, much like David's plea, "Purge me with hyssop, and I shall be clean; wash me, and I shall be whiter than snow" (Psalm 51:7). The rain becomes a symbol of divine grace, an invitation for the past's burdens to be washed away. This line is a cry for liberation, for the freedom to let go of everything that has weighed him down. Musically, the song crescendos, mirroring his intense desire for redemption, an eruption of emotion as he begs for release from his past.

"So let the rain fall down on me" marks a final surrender, a baptism of sorts, where he invites the rain to wash over him fully. This is not simply enduring the rain but embracing it, hoping it will cleanse him from the inside out. It recalls the symbolism of baptism in Romans 6:4: "We were therefore buried with him through baptism into death in order that, just as Christ was raised from the dead, we too may live a new life." The rain here becomes not only a force of nature but a purifying agent, one that he hopes will bring him to a new understanding and sense of wholeness.

As the song concludes with the refrain, "I feel it's gonna rain like this for days," the sense of ongoing struggle lingers, yet there's a hint of acceptance. The repetition leaves the listener in a space of unresolved tension, suggesting that his journey isn't over. The rain continues, but it's no longer something he fears; it has become a part of his path to healing. This conclusion reflects a fragile resilience, an acknowledgment that while he may remain in the storm, he's willing to endure it as he waits for the light.

"Rain" captures the tension of feeling lost between despair and hope, symbolized by the relentless storm and his quiet anticipation of sunshine. The song, with its somber melody and introspective lyrics, becomes a meditation on emotional endurance, on the patience required to sit in sorrow while hoping for renewal. The rain serves as both a metaphor for sorrow and a promise of transformation, a

reminder that sometimes the storm itself is the journey, and enduring it with faith can lead to the cleansing and healing we seek.

CHAPTER 39
"Away In Silence"

"Away In Silence" by Creed is a haunting plea for reconciliation, transformation, and redemption. The lyrics and music convey a sense of raw desperation, as the speaker grapples with the profound loss of a relationship and the deep-seated desire to repair what has been broken. The song paints a vivid, almost cinematic portrait of a man standing on the edge, seeking forgiveness while confronting the pain he has caused.

The song opens with a scene of quiet departure: "You walked away in silence; you walked away to breathe." This line captures a profound moment—when words are absent, and the weight of unspoken feelings lingers in the air. "To breathe" suggests that the other person is suffocated by the relationship or perhaps by the mistakes and failures that have accumulated over time. This departure in silence isn't marked by anger or shouting but by a quiet, heartbreaking realization that something has broken between them. There's a sense of abandonment, but also of understanding, as if both parties recognize the necessity of space to find clarity.

The line "Stopped and turned around to say goodbye to me" amplifies this emotional tension. The silence is broken momentarily, only to confirm the finality of the moment. In turning to say goodbye, there's both an acknowledgment of what they shared and a clear intention to leave it behind. This silent farewell leaves the speaker in a state of longing and helplessness, knowing that he's at risk of losing something irreplaceable.

As the music builds, the speaker's pleas intensify: "I'm pleading as you're leaving, I'm begging you to stay." This line reveals the speaker's desperation to mend what's been shattered. The repeated phrase, "I'm not the man I used to be, I've changed," speaks to a deep desire for transformation. He's grappling with the mistakes of his past, wanting to convince the person he loves that he is no longer the person who caused the pain. His words echo with sincerity, yet there's an underlying tension—has he truly changed, or is this plea motivated by the fear of being alone?

The music in this section is both soft and intense, mirroring the speaker's vulnerability and the weight of his realization. The instrumental layers seem to rise and fall, like the ebb and flow of his emotions. The soft intensity of the guitar and the steady, almost hesitant drumbeat reflect his internal conflict, the push and pull between hope and despair.

"Don't give up on us, don't give up on love" becomes the anthem of his plea, a mantra that he clings to in the hope that love is strong enough to withstand the mistakes he's made. This refrain is repeated with increasing intensity, as if each repetition carries a deeper, more urgent appeal. There's a humility here, an acceptance that the relationship may not survive, but he's willing to give everything to fight for it. This refrain captures the core of his struggle—the desperate hope that love can transcend past wrongs and that forgiveness is still within reach.

The line "If my life is the price, then my life it will cost" is profound in its sense of sacrifice. He's willing to pay the ultimate price, to give everything he has to repair what's broken. This isn't a casual statement; it speaks to a man who is willing to put his very existence on the line for the sake of love. The music here grows more intense, amplifying the gravity of his words. The phrase resonates with a kind of solemn commitment, a vow that shows the depth of his remorse and his willingness to do whatever it takes to make amends.

The lyrics then shift to a reflective tone, "Now that I'm picking up the pieces, see the pain that I have caused." This line reveals a moment of clarity, where he's able to look at the situation with honesty and acknowledge his role in the heartbreak. He's no longer in denial; he sees the consequences of his actions, the hurt he's inflicted on someone he loves. The image of picking up the pieces speaks to both the broken relationship and his own brokenness. This process of reassembly is painful but necessary—a step toward healing, even though he knows it may be too late to salvage what they had.

"It's hard to believe in someone you thought was lost" is a painful acknowledgment of the damage he's caused. This line suggests that the other person may have lost faith in him, no longer able to trust him as they once did. There's a sense of guilt here, a realization that he may have pushed her too far, to the point where she can no longer believe in the possibility of his change. It's a difficult truth for him to face, but it adds depth to his plea, showing that he's fully aware of the challenge he's asking her to overcome.

The image of "face down screaming 'God help me please'" is powerful and raw. It captures a moment of absolute vulnerability, a breaking point where the pain and guilt become too overwhelming to bear alone. There's a sense of surrender in this cry for help, a recognition that he needs something beyond his own strength to find redemption. This line speaks to the depth of his despair, his recognition that he cannot rebuild without divine intervention or a profound change within himself. The music here grows somber, almost echoing his cry for help, underscoring the depth of his need for transformation.

The line "Please come back to me, don't you walk away in silence" reflects a final, heartfelt appeal. Silence has become his enemy—a barrier between him and the person he loves. Her silence is more painful than words could ever be, a reminder of the distance that has grown between them. His request for her to break this silence is a request for connection, for dialogue, for the chance to bridge the gap that has formed. This plea is underscored by the music, which builds in intensity, mirroring the urgency of his words.

As the song moves toward its conclusion, he speaks of hope for rebuilding: "We can rebuild and forever, we can go on, go on, and go on." This line holds a fragile optimism, a belief that despite everything, they can start anew. There's a sense of endurance here, a hope that love can persist and grow stronger in the wake of hardship. The repetition of "we can go on" becomes almost like a vow—a promise to persevere, no matter the obstacles. The music here swells with a sense of possibility, a tentative lifting that suggests a sliver of hope amidst the sorrow.

The final lines, "Look at horizons and let the light bring you home," bring a sense of closure and direction. Horizons symbolize new beginnings, a reminder that there is a future beyond the pain of the present moment. He's asking her to look beyond the hurt, to see the light of possibility, and to find her way back. The word "home" resonates with warmth, safety, and the comfort of reconciliation. It's where they can both find peace, if only they are willing to move forward together.

The song closes with a repeated refrain, "Don't give up on us, don't give up on love." These words linger, echoing the core of his plea. He's aware that the choice is ultimately out of his hands; he's done all he can to express his remorse, his hope, and his commitment to change. The repetition serves as a final prayer, a desperate hope that love will triumph over past mistakes. The music fades with a sense of unfinished business, as if the story isn't fully resolved, leaving the listener with the question of whether love will indeed be enough to heal the rift.

In "Away In Silence," Creed captures the journey of a man who has come face-to-face with his own failings and is desperately seeking a second chance. The lyrics and music together tell a story of remorse, transformation, and the fragile hope that love can endure even the deepest wounds. This song is a testament to the resilience of love and the human spirit, a reminder that while forgiveness and redemption are hard-won, they are worth fighting for. The ending leaves us with a sense of both resolution and ambiguity, an acknowledgment that while love may have the power to heal, it's ultimately a path that must be walked together.

Application

In *"Away In Silence,"* Creed explores the profound themes of reconciliation, transformation, and redemption through a haunting portrayal of remorse and longing. The lyrics and music together evoke an emotional landscape of quiet despair, capturing a moment where a man faces the reality of losing someone he loves and grapples with the need to make amends. It is a raw, cinematic portrayal of the depths of human vulnerability, a plea for forgiveness and a recognition of one's own failings.

The song opens with a powerful image: *"You walked away in silence; you walked away to breathe."* The absence of words, the silence, is laden with meaning, suggesting the suffocating nature of the relationship or the pain inflicted over time. There's a sense that the other person needs space—not out of anger, but as a necessary step to find clarity. In these lines, the speaker is left in the stillness of his own mistakes, echoing the biblical lament in Psalm 38:9-10: "All my longings lie open before you, Lord; my sighing is not hidden from you. My heart pounds, my strength fails me; even the light has gone from my eyes." This silence is not merely an absence of sound but a void filled with sorrow, regret, and the weight of unspoken words.

The line, *"Stopped and turned around to say goodbye to me,"* adds a layer of finality to the departure. It is a moment of quiet acknowledgment—a last look back, recognizing both the connection they shared and the necessity of moving on. This brief farewell in silence leaves the speaker stranded in his own helplessness, aware of the permanence of the moment. Musically, the song here remains subdued yet poignant, setting a stage for the plea that follows, as if mirroring the stillness of the moment before the storm of emotion breaks.

As the lyrics progress, the speaker's desperation comes to the forefront: *"I'm pleading as you're leaving, I'm begging you to stay."* Here, his vulnerability is on full display. The repetition of *"I'm not the man I used to be, I've changed,"* is a powerful declaration, showing his determination to repair what he's broken. It echoes the biblical theme of repentance, much like King David's confession in Psalm 51:10: "Create in me a pure heart, O God, and renew a steadfast spirit within me." His words suggest genuine remorse, yet there's an underlying question of whether he's truly changed or is merely grasping at hope to avoid being alone. The music swells in intensity here, echoing the tumult within him, while the guitar and drum beats mirror his inner struggle between hope and despair.

"Don't give up on us, don't give up on love," becomes the core refrain, a mantra repeated with growing fervor. This line is an earnest appeal for the other person to hold onto love despite his past mistakes. There is a humility in his words—a recognition of his own failings and an acknowledgment of the fragility of their love. This refrain captures the essence of his struggle, his hope that love might transcend the pain he's caused. The music intensifies alongside this plea, as though he's

pouring every ounce of himself into these words, hoping that love is strong enough to withstand the damage.

The line, *"If my life is the price, then my life it will cost,"* introduces the theme of sacrifice. It's a bold statement, reflecting his willingness to give everything he has to restore what's broken. This echoes the idea of atonement, where he is willing to pay any price to make things right, similar to the theme in John 15:13: "Greater love has no one than this: to lay down one's life for one's friends." The music here grows more solemn, enhancing the gravity of his words, showing that he's fully committed to redemption, no matter the cost.

As the song continues, he reflects with painful clarity, *"Now that I'm picking up the pieces, see the pain that I have caused."* Here, the speaker reaches a moment of self-awareness, acknowledging the hurt he's inflicted. The image of "picking up the pieces" suggests both the broken relationship and his own fragmented self. This process is painful, yet it's also necessary—a step toward healing, even if it may not restore the relationship. His honesty mirrors the sentiment of James 5:16, "Therefore confess your sins to each other and pray for each other so that you may be healed." This is the beginning of self-reckoning, where he confronts the full scope of his responsibility.

"It's hard to believe in someone you thought was lost," reflects the challenge he faces in regaining the other person's trust. He understands the depth of his betrayal and knows that his actions may have permanently eroded her faith in him. There's a deep guilt in this acknowledgment, a recognition that he may have pushed her too far. It's a humbling realization that adds depth to his plea, showing he's not only aware of his shortcomings but also understands the difficulty of the forgiveness he seeks.

The powerful line, *"Face down screaming 'God help me please',"* captures his moment of ultimate vulnerability. It's a breaking point where the weight of his guilt and regret overwhelms him, leading to a raw cry for divine intervention. This plea for help mirrors David's cry in Psalm 6:6, "I am worn out from my groaning. All night long I flood my bed with weeping." Here, he acknowledges that he cannot find redemption on his own; he needs something beyond his own strength. Musically, this moment is underscored by a haunting intensity, as though the music itself echoes his plea for help.

"Please come back to me, don't you walk away in silence," reflects his ultimate appeal. Silence now symbolizes the distance between them, a void that words can't bridge. Her silence is a painful reminder of the separation, more agonizing than any argument could be. His request for her to break the silence is a request for a chance to rebuild, to reconnect, to bridge the chasm that has formed. The music rises here, matching the urgency of his words and amplifying the emotional weight of his plea.

As the song nears its conclusion, he expresses hope for a second chance: *"We can rebuild and forever, we can go on, go on, and go on."* This line is imbued with fragile optimism, a belief that love can survive and even grow through hardship. The repetition of *"we can go on"* becomes almost like a vow, a promise to endure together, no matter the difficulties. This is reminiscent of the perseverance called for in 1 Corinthians 13:7: "Love bears all things, believes all things, hopes all things, endures all things." The music swells with this sense of possibility, creating a feeling of uplift that suggests a sliver of hope amidst the sorrow.

The final words, *"Look at horizons and let the light bring you home,"* bring a sense of closure and peace. Horizons symbolize new beginnings and a hopeful future, a reminder that there is a path forward. He's asking her to look beyond the immediate hurt, to see the possibility of healing and reconciliation. The mention of "home" evokes warmth, comfort, and the peace of returning to a place of belonging. It's a gentle reminder that true love, if nurtured, can survive even the deepest wounds. The music fades, leaving a sense of both resolution and ambiguity, as if the path to healing remains open but uncertain.

In *"Away In Silence,"* Creed has crafted a deeply introspective journey of a man who has come to terms with his failings and seeks redemption. The song is a poignant testament to love's resilience, a reminder that while forgiveness and reconciliation require humility and sacrifice, they are worth pursuing. The lyrics and music together offer a story of transformation, of a love that, despite the weight of past mistakes, can still find a path toward healing. The ending leaves us with a powerful sense of hope—hope that true love, even after enduring the silence of separation, can emerge stronger and more enduring than before.

CHAPTER 40

"Fear"

I n Creed's "Fear," the lyrics offer a rallying cry for transformation, urging the listener to break free from ingrained beliefs and embrace a new way of thinking. The song centers on the power of change, both on a personal and societal level, and challenges us to confront the fears and barriers that keep us tied to outdated ideas. Through a blend of impassioned lyrics and driving instrumentals, the song builds a sense of urgency, calling for a permanent shift in perspective and mindset.

The opening lines, "The cradle of civilization sparks my fascination," immediately set a broad, historical stage. This reference to the origins of society hints that the forces shaping human thought and behavior are ancient, deeply rooted in the collective psyche. By starting with such a sweeping image, the lyrics suggest that the challenges we face today aren't new—they're legacies we've inherited from the dawn of civilization. This "cradle" represents the foundational beliefs and systems that have defined humanity, and it's these that the speaker feels compelled to question and disrupt.

"Truth ignites our generation to change what's been programmed inside the mind." Here, the speaker calls on a deep-seated truth, something that transcends the structures and systems around us. There's an acknowledgment that our minds have been "programmed," that we carry within us beliefs and behaviors shaped by forces outside our control—perhaps the influence of culture, education, and social expectations. The use of the word "programmed" paints these beliefs as artificial, a system that has been designed rather than one that's naturally grown. This perspective suggests that true freedom, true individuality, lies in recognizing and challenging this programming.

The line "Don't you turn a blind eye" is an emphatic plea against complacency. It urges us to stay alert and aware, to resist the temptation to ignore uncomfortable truths. There's a moral imperative here, a warning that turning a blind eye to reality is a form of complicity. The repeated phrase, "Change what's been programmed inside," reinforces this need to actively resist and rewire our own minds, to break free from inherited patterns and see the world through a lens of clarity and truth. The intensity of the music rises here, with powerful chords underscoring the urgency of the speaker's call, giving it the weight of a mission or mandate.

"Listen to me when I tell you, feel the passion in my breath," the speaker says, calling for immediate and heartfelt attention. There's a personal investment here—this isn't just a theoretical or philosophical musing, but a deeply felt truth the speaker wants to communicate. "Feel the passion in my breath" highlights the urgency and authenticity behind his words, as if he's sharing something fundamental to his own experience. The passion here is contagious, almost visceral, as if the listener is meant to feel the heat of conviction in each line, each breath.

"Stay on top if they let you, 'cause the change is permanent." This line introduces a cautious optimism, tempered by the reality of external resistance. The phrase "if they let you" hints at forces that may oppose change, systems or people invested in maintaining the status quo. The warning that "change is permanent" is both hopeful and intimidating—it suggests that once you step into this new way of thinking, there's no going back. This isn't a temporary shift; it's a lasting transformation. The music here takes on a heavier, more resolute tone, emphasizing the gravity of such a commitment to change.

The reference to "rudiments of interpersonal communication" shifts the focus to human connection, suggesting that change must start in the way we relate to one another. True transformation isn't isolated or abstract; it's something that manifests in how we communicate, how we share ideas, and how we challenge each other's beliefs. "Truth will uproot and bring war's devastation to light" is a powerful line, likening truth to a force that unearths hidden scars. By revealing the devastation wrought by lies, misunderstandings, and complacency, truth becomes both a weapon and a healer, capable of clearing the rubble of past conflicts to make way for a new foundation.

Once again, the refrain, "Don't you turn a blind eye," presses on the listener's conscience. This time, it feels even more urgent, carrying the weight of responsibility. There's a clear sense that ignoring reality is not only a personal failure but also a disservice to others, a refusal to engage with the truth that has the potential to liberate.

The bridge of the song, "Change starts in your mind, leave the past behind, forget everything you know," is where the lyrics become intensely introspective. This is an invitation to embrace a radical reset, to let go of preconceived notions and allow a new perspective to take root. The repetition of "leave the past behind" carries a liberating energy—it's a call to release the weight of history, to set aside old fears and limitations. The phrase "forget everything you know" is daunting; it challenges the listener to question even the most fundamental beliefs and to start anew, as if wiping the slate clean. The repetition of these lines becomes almost like a chant, a hypnotic mantra encouraging the listener to embrace change as a transformative journey.

The crescendo of "let go, let go, let go" becomes a climactic release. These words are liberating, urging a surrender of resistance, an acceptance of the unknown. The music swells in this section, mirroring the release of pent-up emotions, the freedom that comes from finally letting go. There's an emotional catharsis in this moment, as if by letting go, the speaker is not only shedding old beliefs but also stepping into a new, uncharted realm of possibilities.

As the song nears its conclusion, the refrain returns with renewed intensity, each repetition of "Listen to me when I tell you, feel the passion in my breath" serving as a final, impassioned reminder. The speaker's voice becomes almost prophetic, as if calling on the listener to embrace this transformation not just for themselves, but for the world at large. This passion is contagious, a fire that spreads with each breath, each note. The closing repetition of "Change is permanent" reinforces the finality of this shift. It's a message that leaves no room for doubt or hesitation—this is a path that, once taken, cannot be undone.

The final lines, "Leave the past behind, make a change, let go," echo like a parting wisdom. The repetition feels like an echo, lingering long after the music fades, as if the words themselves hold the power to inspire transformation. It's a message that demands reflection, encouraging the listener to not only internalize but also act on what they've heard. The song ends on this note of openness, a space where new growth can begin.

In "Fear," Creed creates an anthem for transformation, a reminder that true change is both difficult and necessary. The song challenges us to confront our programming, to examine the fears and limitations that have been instilled within us, and to choose a new path. Through impassioned lyrics and intense instrumentation, the song becomes a call to action—a personal and collective journey toward truth, liberation, and a commitment to evolve. It's a powerful reminder that while change may be permanent, it's also the doorway to a more authentic and meaningful life, if only we're willing to let go.

Application

In *"Fear,"* Creed crafts a powerful anthem of transformation, calling listeners to confront their deepest fears, question ingrained beliefs, and embrace a new mindset. Through urgent lyrics and driving instrumentals, the song conveys an unmistakable call to action—encouraging individuals to break free from mental programming and societal constraints. This isn't just about personal change; it's about reshaping collective perspectives, a push for cultural and intellectual evolution that reverberates with a raw sense of purpose.

The opening line, *"The cradle of civilization sparks my fascination,"* instantly places the song within a broad, historical context. This allusion to the origins of society suggests that the issues we face today are not recent but rooted in ancient structures that have shaped human behavior and thought for centuries. The "cradle" symbolizes foundational ideas and systems that have defined humanity, yet the speaker is drawn to question and disrupt these inherited norms. Musically, the initial notes have a contemplative quality, setting up a reflective but intense tone, as if diving into the very core of human consciousness.

The next line, *"Truth ignites our generation to change what's been programmed inside the mind,"* invokes truth as a catalyst for awakening. Here, the speaker acknowledges that minds have been "programmed," suggesting that much of human belief and behavior stems from societal expectations and cultural conditioning. By describing these ideas as "programmed," the speaker casts them as artificial structures that can—and should—be questioned. This perspective calls for a more genuine, liberated approach to life, and the music mirrors this call to action with escalating intensity, adding layers that underscore the urgency of breaking free.

The repeated phrase *"Don't you turn a blind eye"* serves as both a plea and a warning. It urges listeners to confront reality rather than ignore it, as turning away from the truth is a form of complicity. The insistence here adds a moral dimension to the call for change, reinforcing that personal transformation is not just about self-improvement but also about serving a greater good. The accompanying instrumentals grow sharper, almost like an alarm, creating a sense of heightened responsibility.

The line *"Listen to me when I tell you, feel the passion in my breath"* is personal and intense, as if the speaker is sharing a hard-won truth from his own experience. The phrase "feel the passion in my breath" communicates urgency and conviction, an invitation for the listener to connect with the fervor behind the words. It's not simply a call to listen but to engage deeply, to allow oneself to be moved. Musically, the piece swells here, amplifying the emotional weight and making it clear that this message is not abstract—it's immediate and heartfelt.

"Stay on top if they let you, 'cause the change is permanent" brings in a note of caution, recognizing the obstacles one might face when pursuing transformation. The phrase "if they let you" alludes to resistance from those who benefit from the status quo, implying that true change often meets opposition. The idea that "change is permanent" is both inspiring and intimidating, suggesting that once someone opens their mind to new perspectives, there's no turning back. The music here becomes heavier, mirroring the gravity of committing to change, reflecting that this is a choice that requires courage and resilience.

When the song shifts to *"rudiments of interpersonal communication,"* it zeroes in on the importance of human connection in effecting change. Transformation isn't an isolated experience; it's something that flows through relationships, conversations, and shared ideas. The line *"Truth will uproot and bring war's devastation to light"* further emphasizes truth's power to uncover hidden wounds and expose the lasting impact of past conflicts. By likening truth to a force that brings "devastation to light," the lyrics highlight that confronting reality is difficult and potentially painful but ultimately necessary for healing. Musically, there's a subtle yet powerful shift here, a more subdued yet poignant tone that underscores the dual nature of truth as both disruptor and healer.

The refrain *"Don't you turn a blind eye"* returns, intensifying the sense of responsibility. By this point, the message feels almost prophetic, challenging listeners to rise above apathy and engage with the world around them. The repetition drives home the moral weight of the speaker's call, reminding the audience that awareness is a duty. Each chord in this section reinforces the message, as if the music itself is urging listeners to wake up.

In the bridge, *"Change starts in your mind, leave the past behind, forget everything you know,"* the lyrics take on a more introspective tone. This is a profound call for self-examination, an invitation to let go of preconceived notions and create space for growth. The phrase "forget everything you know" challenges the listener to question the very foundations of their identity, which is both liberating and terrifying. The musical repetition here has a hypnotic effect, almost like a chant or mantra, pulling the listener into a state of reflection where they can consider what it truly means to leave behind past conditioning.

The repeated cry of *"let go, let go, let go"* becomes a powerful moment of release. These words are both an instruction and a cathartic invitation, urging listeners to surrender to change and embrace freedom from past limitations. The music crescendos in this section, capturing the liberating energy of releasing pent-up fears, doubts, and insecurities. It's a visceral moment of emotional catharsis, as if by letting go, the speaker and listener alike are stepping into a space of limitless potential.

As the song approaches its conclusion, the refrain returns with even greater intensity: *"Listen to me when I tell you, feel the passion in my breath."* By now, the speaker's plea has taken on an almost prophetic quality, urging the listener not just to hear but to internalize the message. Each repetition reinforces the permanence of the change being called for, pressing the listener to truly commit to this new way of thinking. The closing line, *"Change is permanent,"* leaves a lasting impression, asserting that this transformation is not temporary or fleeting—it's enduring.

The final echo of *"Leave the past behind, make a change, let go"* lingers, resonating long after the music fades. It feels like parting wisdom, a challenge to not only hear the message but to live it. The repetition invites a moment of introspection, as though the words themselves are planting seeds of transformation in the listener's mind. The song concludes on an open-ended note, allowing space for reflection and the possibility of real change.

In *"Fear,"* Creed delivers a powerful message of transformation, challenging us to break free from the limitations imposed by both society and our own minds. The song is a rallying cry for those who seek truth, urging listeners to confront the fears, doubts, and ingrained beliefs that keep them from growth. Through the impassioned lyrics and driving instrumentals, the song becomes a call to action—a personal and collective invitation to embrace the unknown, to let go of what holds us back, and to step into a new way of thinking. Ultimately, *"Fear"* is a reminder that while change may be daunting, it is also the doorway to a more authentic, liberated life, if we are brave enough to walk through.

CHAPTER 41
"On My Sleeve"

"On My Sleeve" by Creed captures a visceral struggle with vulnerability and resilience. The lyrics depict a speaker who is open and unguarded, emotionally raw, and wearing his heart "tattooed on his sleeve" for all to see. This openness, while courageous, brings him pain and exhaustion, as he finds himself surrounded by coldness and judgment that drain his spirit. The song speaks to the tension of being emotionally exposed in a world that often lacks compassion—a plea for connection in the midst of isolation.

The opening line, "The eyes around me are so cold," creates an immediate sense of alienation. There's a harshness in these "cold" eyes, a piercing detachment that the speaker feels deeply. This is a world where people observe from a distance, withholding warmth or understanding. The phrase "they steal my soul" captures the impact of such judgment and apathy—it doesn't just affect him superficially but reaches down to his very core, chipping away at his spirit. These cold eyes don't just ignore his struggles; they seem to strip him of his essence, making him feel exposed and defenseless.

The next lines, "So walk with me, talk with me, hold my hand," reveal a longing for companionship and understanding. Here, he reaches out in his vulnerability, hoping that someone will step alongside him. There's a quiet desperation in these words, as though he's calling for solace amidst a world that seems indifferent. The gesture of holding hands is intimate and grounding, a lifeline that he needs to keep himself steady. The music here reflects this yearning with a melody that is both delicate and intense, underlining the gravity of his appeal.

The phrase "I'm stumbling in consequence that buries me alive" suggests that he's weighed down by past mistakes or choices. "Stumbling" reflects an ongoing struggle, an inability to move forward smoothly, while "consequence" implies that he's shouldering the results of actions that cannot be undone. The consequences have become almost like a living grave, surrounding and suffocating him, keeping him trapped in the pain of regret. The music becomes heavier in this section, almost claustrophobic, mirroring the weight of his burden.

"Can you fix what's made to be broken? I can't fix what's made to be." This line introduces a sense of resignation and helplessness. The phrase "made to be broken" suggests an acceptance of certain imperfections, as though some aspects of his life or his heart were destined to be fractured. There's a fatalistic tone here, as if he's asking for help with something that may be beyond repair. It's not just that he feels broken; it's that he believes he was perhaps always meant to be this way. There's an inherent sadness in this, a recognition of limitations that he can't overcome on his own.

The refrain, "My heart is tattooed on my sleeve, I'm not hiding, no," is an assertion of his vulnerability. To have one's heart tattooed on their sleeve is to live openly, to allow others to see and understand his emotions without any pretense. This image is powerful; a tattoo is permanent, unerasable, a testament to the fact that he can't and won't hide who he is. There's strength in this openness, yet it comes with pain. The repetition of "It only hurts to breathe" conveys a sense of weariness, as if merely existing in this state of exposure is exhausting. His openness brings him no relief; instead, it magnifies his hurt.

The line "Standing now, I'm alone, I need answers, tell me everything you know" deepens his isolation. Despite his openness, he finds himself without the comfort or guidance he longs for. This request for answers reflects a search for meaning or understanding, a hope that someone can help make sense of his suffering. His loneliness is palpable here, standing in stark contrast to his previous call for connection. The music here is somber, almost hollow, accentuating his sense of emptiness.

"So heavy is the night, exhausted, whispers tend to crucify my mind" encapsulates the torment of sleepless nights filled with self-doubt and internal conflict. "Heavy is the night" suggests that darkness brings an oppressive weight, pressing down on him, amplifying his sense of isolation and despair. The whispers, perhaps self-criticisms or judgments from others, "crucify" his mind, nailing him to his fears and regrets. This language evokes an almost sacrificial image, as if he's being punished by his own thoughts. The music grows darker here, mirroring the mental anguish he endures in solitude.

In the next refrain, the repeated line "It only hurts, it only hurts to breathe" becomes more potent, embodying the relentlessness of his pain. Breathing, a basic act of survival, has become painful, a reminder of the burden he carries. His existence feels like an ongoing wound, a state of constant vulnerability that offers no respite.

As the song reaches a crescendo, he shouts, "Can you hear me? Mistakes have cost me years. Do they cost you? Are you like me?" This moment of raw confrontation suggests a deep need for empathy. He's calling out, desperate to know if anyone else feels the same pain, if anyone else has suffered for their mistakes as he has. There's a sense of self-doubt, wondering if he's alone in his experiences or if there are others who can relate. His question "Are you like me?" is a plea for understanding, a hope that someone else shares his struggles. The music here is intense, almost thunderous, amplifying the urgency of his cry.

The refrain returns, and this time, it feels even more resolved, almost defiant. "My heart is tattooed on my sleeve, I'm not hiding, no." He reaffirms his choice to live openly, embracing the pain that comes with such exposure. His repeated insistence on not hiding becomes a declaration of resilience. Despite the coldness around him, despite the whispers that crucify his mind, he refuses to retreat or close himself off. There's strength in his willingness to remain vulnerable, to continue showing his true self even when it leaves him wounded.

The song closes with a series of repeated lines, "It only hurts to breathe," each repetition sinking deeper into the listener's mind. This closing statement encapsulates the inescapable pain of his reality. The repetition feels like a heartbeat, a reminder of the endurance required to live with such intensity of feeling. There's a haunting quality to the way these words fade out, leaving the listener with a lingering sense of his isolation and exhaustion.

In "On My Sleeve," Creed offers a powerful meditation on vulnerability, pain, and resilience. The song is a testament to the courage it takes to live openly, to wear one's heart on one's sleeve in a world that can be cold and unforgiving. Through emotionally charged lyrics and a driving musical backdrop, the song explores the cost of such openness—the pain of being misunderstood, the weight of past mistakes, and the constant battle to remain true to oneself despite the hurt. Ultimately, the song leaves us with a sense of both sorrow and strength, a reminder that true authenticity often comes with a price, yet it's a price worth paying for the sake of integrity and self-acceptance.

Application

In *"On My Sleeve,"* Creed captures a raw, deeply introspective journey through vulnerability, resilience, and the relentless pursuit of authenticity in a world that often meets openness with cold indifference. The song's lyrics paint the picture of a speaker who wears his emotions on his sleeve, exposed and unguarded, even as it brings him immense pain. The haunting melody and intense instrumentation amplify the struggle of existing with such transparency and longing for connection amidst isolation.

The opening line, *"The eyes around me are so cold,"* establishes an immediate sense of alienation. These "cold" eyes represent a world that observes from a distance, withholding empathy or warmth, leaving the speaker feeling scrutinized and misunderstood. The line *"they steal my soul"* suggests that this judgment is more than superficial—it cuts to his core, stripping away pieces of his identity and leaving him feeling exposed. There's a defenselessness in his openness, a vulnerability that others seem to exploit rather than embrace.

The following lines, *"So walk with me, talk with me, hold my hand,"* reveal a quiet yet intense plea for companionship. Despite the coldness around him, the speaker reaches out, hoping that someone will stand beside him, share in his pain, and provide solace. The gesture of holding hands is intimate, a symbol of trust and comfort. His yearning for this connection is both simple and profound, a lifeline in a world that otherwise feels indifferent. The music echoes this appeal, with a melody that feels both delicate and intense, underscoring the gravity of his loneliness and need for support.

The line *"I'm stumbling in consequence that buries me alive"* hints at the weight of past mistakes or actions that have left him feeling trapped. *"Stumbling"* reflects an ongoing struggle to move forward, while *"consequence"* implies that he's burdened by the impact of choices that cannot be undone. These consequences have become almost like a living grave, suffocating him in regret and guilt. The music takes on a heavier, almost claustrophobic tone, mirroring his entrapment and conveying the gravity of his inner turmoil.

"Can you fix what's made to be broken? I can't fix what's made to be," introduces a sense of resignation. The phrase *"made to be broken"* suggests that certain aspects of his life or himself may be fundamentally flawed. There's a sense of acceptance here, a recognition of limitations that he believes are beyond his ability to repair. This line reveals the depth of his hopelessness, as if he feels doomed to live with this brokenness. The melancholy in the music underscores this realization, creating a somber, reflective space that mirrors his despair.

In the refrain, *"My heart is tattooed on my sleeve, I'm not hiding, no,"* the speaker asserts his vulnerability with defiant pride. To have one's heart tattooed on one's sleeve is to live openly and honestly, allowing others to see and understand his emotions without reservation. A tattoo is permanent, unchangeable—a testament to his commitment to authenticity. Yet, this openness brings pain, a constant reminder of the emotional toll that comes with such exposure. *"It only hurts to breathe"* encapsulates this burden, suggesting that his very existence in this state of vulnerability is exhausting. The music here swells with intensity, mirroring his exhaustion and struggle.

The line *"Standing now, I'm alone, I need answers, tell me everything you know"* deepens his sense of isolation. Despite his openness, he finds himself without the support or guidance he longs for, isolated in his search for understanding. His request for answers reflects a desperate need to make sense of his pain and the loneliness that surrounds him. The somber, almost hollow sound of the music at this point accentuates his feeling of emptiness, highlighting the distance between his desire for connection and the reality of his solitude.

"So heavy is the night, exhausted, whispers tend to crucify my mind" encapsulates the torment of sleepless nights filled with regret and

self-doubt. The night, heavy with solitude and inner conflict, feels oppressive, pressing down on him. The *"whispers"*—perhaps self-criticisms or memories of others' judgments— *"crucify"* his mind, pinning him to his fears and regrets. The use of crucifixion imagery suggests an intense psychological burden, as if he's being punished by his own thoughts. The music darkens here, mirroring his internal anguish and capturing the relentlessness of his mental battle.

In the next refrain, *"It only hurts, it only hurts to breathe,"* each repetition becomes more poignant, embodying the relentlessness of his suffering. The basic act of breathing has become painful, a reminder of the constant struggle to exist while feeling exposed and vulnerable. This repetition builds an almost hypnotic quality, drawing the listener deeper into his sense of exhaustion.

As the song crescendos, he shouts, *"Can you hear me? Mistakes have cost me years. Do they cost you? Are you like me?"* This raw, confrontational moment underscores his desperate need for empathy. He's reaching out, questioning whether anyone else has suffered in the same way, or if he's alone in his pain. The question *"Are you like me?"* is a plea for connection, a hope that someone else shares his struggles and understands his experiences. The music grows thunderous here, amplifying the urgency and rawness of his appeal.

The refrain returns with renewed intensity, *"My heart is tattooed on my sleeve, I'm not hiding, no,"* now feeling almost defiant. Despite the isolation, despite the pain, he reaffirms his choice to remain open. His repeated assertion of *"not hiding"* becomes a declaration of resilience. Though he's weary, he refuses to close himself off or retreat, embracing the strength required to remain true to himself. The music swells around this refrain, creating a powerful sense of determination.

The song closes with a series of repeated lines, *"It only hurts to breathe,"* each echoing with haunting finality. This line becomes a heartbeat of sorts, a rhythm that conveys the endurance required to continue living with such intensity of feeling. The repetition leaves the listener with a sense of his isolation and exhaustion, an almost tangible weight that lingers as the music fades.

In *"On My Sleeve,"* Creed offers a deeply reflective exploration of vulnerability, pain, and the resolve it takes to live authentically. Through emotionally charged lyrics and a stirring musical backdrop, the song examines the cost of openness—the ache of being misunderstood, the haunting whispers of past mistakes, and the constant battle to remain true to oneself. In the end, *"On My Sleeve"* stands as a powerful testament to the courage it takes to wear one's heart openly, a reminder that while such vulnerability often brings pain, it is also a mark of strength, resilience, and an unwavering commitment to self-acceptance.

CHAPTER 42
"Full Circle"

I n Creed's "Full Circle," we find a journey of hard-earned wisdom—a story of mistakes, regret, and ultimately, self-awareness. The lyrics weave through the disillusionment of choices made, friendships lost, and bridges burned. The tone is reflective, urging the listener to confront the consequences of past actions while realizing the irony of time's ability to both deepen and heal pain. The song is a meditation on reaching a point where one can look back, understanding the toll and recognizing the growth that only comes from confronting one's own errors.

The opening line, "Got your freedom now, boy. Who do you serve?" confronts the listener with a stark question about the purpose behind freedom. The "boy" here speaks to a younger self, one who has gained independence but lacks direction or purpose. This freedom is not a gift but a test—something that requires careful stewardship. The tone is almost reproachful, like a warning from someone who's seen the consequences of taking this freedom lightly. "Who do you serve?" demands introspection, urging the listener to consider the consequences of their allegiances and priorities.

"Took for granted what you should have preserved" brings to mind the recklessness of youth, the tendency to overlook what truly matters while pursuing fleeting thrills or material success. There's regret in this line, an acknowledgment of the short-sightedness that can lead to devastating losses. By the time the speaker realizes what they should have valued, it's too late—"No time left, no time left to make amends." The repetition of "no time left" underscores the finality, the impossibility of undoing certain actions. The listener is left with a sense of urgency and inevitability, as if the speaker is warning them of the cost of careless choices.

"Keep burning bridges while you're buying your new friends" speaks to the transient, superficial connections often pursued in place of authentic relationships. The act of "burning bridges" implies a destructive tendency, an inability or unwillingness to maintain meaningful connections. The image of "buying friends" suggests that these new relationships are hollow, built on convenience or gain rather than loyalty. This line speaks to the empty pursuit of validation, the tendency to surround oneself with people who offer temporary satisfaction but lack the substance of real friendship. The music here reflects this somber realization, its steady beat feeling almost like footsteps echoing down an empty hall, emphasizing the isolation that comes from choosing popularity over authenticity.

"A day of reflection hits; you're a shell, skin and bones, counting costs." This moment of reckoning is harsh and unyielding. The speaker sees themselves as a "shell," stripped down to the bare essentials, forced to confront the emptiness that years of misguided choices have left. "Counting costs" is an act of sober calculation, a painful assessment of what has been lost and sacrificed. It's a haunting image—reduced to the barest form, with nothing left but the consequences of past actions. The question "Is it worth your soul?" drives home the gravity of the choices made, suggesting that the price paid may be one's very identity, or even deeper, their integrity and inner peace.

The refrain "It's funny how times can change, rearrange, and distance makes the pain fade away" introduces a bittersweet reflection on time's ability to dull past hurts. There's irony in the word "funny," as if the speaker is marveling at how once-important moments lose their grip on us. The line captures the tension between time's ability to heal and its power to create regret, making once-significant people and events seem inconsequential. "So important then, doesn't matter now" speaks to this disconnection, the realization that what felt urgent and crucial eventually fades, often leaving a trail of unacknowledged or unresolved emotions.

The chorus, "Come full circle," marks a moment of realization, an acknowledgment that despite everything, he has returned to where he started, albeit with a deeper understanding. To come full circle is to revisit the same place, but with new eyes. This cyclical journey is one of growth—of revisiting past choices with the benefit of hindsight, of seeing the truth behind old illusions. The phrase "both feet on the ground" implies a newfound stability, a grounding that comes from experience. The music here is both triumphant and contemplative, as if celebrating this hard-won clarity while also mourning the path that led to it.

"No access granted now, boy; you've been denied. Jump a fence to see what's on the other side." Here, the speaker confronts the reality of being shut out of certain circles or opportunities, likely because of the very bridges he burned earlier. The image of jumping a fence suggests an undeterred curiosity, a lingering desire to see what was lost or missed. There's a subtle defiance here—he may have been denied, but he's still seeking, willing to go beyond the restrictions to understand what lies beyond. "Are you wanted, are you wanted?" is a haunting question about belonging and worth. It's not just about fitting in; it's a search for validation, for acceptance that runs deeper than surface-level interactions.

The line "Can second chances mean another impression?" introduces the idea of redemption and reinvention. The speaker wonders
if it's possible to remake oneself, to create a new identity in the wake
of past mistakes. There's a cautious hope here, a sense that while
some bridges may be burned, there's still a chance to find renewal or
forgiveness.

As the song progresses, "I got one foot stuck in heaven, yeah, one
boot stuck in hell" reveals the internal conflict of someone torn between past and future, between redemption and damnation. This image captures the speaker's divided state, his ambivalence about where
he truly belongs. The juxtaposition of "heaven" and "hell" suggests
that he's living in a moral gray area, not fully committed to either
path but hovering between them. It's a moment of self-awareness, an
admission of the struggle to reconcile past choices with the desire for
a better future.

"I looked at God, He winked at me; I made this mess myself" is both
humorous and humbling. The wink from God suggests a sense of
understanding, even forgiveness, as if the divine acknowledges human
frailty. There's a subtle humor here, a recognition that the speaker is
fully responsible for his predicament. By admitting "I made this mess
myself," he takes ownership, acknowledging that while he may seek
forgiveness, he must also take responsibility for his actions.

"Close the door and don't look back or you will fade away" signals a final farewell to the past. This line advises against dwelling on
past mistakes, emphasizing that moving forward requires letting go.
There's a cautionary tone here—the past, if clung to, has the power
to consume him, to erase the progress he's made. The music grows
solemn here, with a steady, resolute rhythm that feels like the steps of
someone walking away from an old life toward a new beginning.

The final refrain, "It's funny how times can change, rearrange, and distance makes the pain fade away," is repeated with a mix of acceptance and resignation. This line now feels less ironic and more reflective, as if the speaker has come to terms with the nature of time, loss, and healing. The phrase "both feet on the ground" returns with a sense of finality, marking the end of a tumultuous journey. "Come full circle" here feels conclusive, a statement that he has arrived at a place of understanding, if not peace.

In "Full Circle," Creed captures the journey of reckoning with one's past and the slow path toward self-acceptance. The song is a reminder that every action has a cost, that the bridges we burn can't always be rebuilt, but that growth is possible if we face the truth of our choices. Through poignant lyrics and a steady, contemplative melody, the song invites the listener to consider their own cycles, to question the things they've taken for granted, and to reflect on whether the paths they've chosen have led them closer to or further from who they want to be. It's a powerful reminder that coming full circle doesn't erase the past but allows us to carry forward the lessons we've learned, standing on solid ground, ready to move forward with clarity and resolve.

Application

In *"Full Circle,"* Creed explores the journey of reflection, regret, and self-awareness—a story of facing one's mistakes, grappling with the loss of friendships, and ultimately reaching a place of acceptance and growth. The lyrics navigate through the complexity of choices made, bridges burned, and the wisdom that emerges from learning hard lessons. The song is both a warning and a meditation, urging the listener to confront the consequences of their past while finding solace in the perspective that time and experience bring.

The opening line, *"Got your freedom now, boy. Who do you serve?"* confronts the listener with a sobering question about the purpose behind one's choices. The use of *"boy"* suggests a younger, perhaps more reckless version of oneself, someone who once saw freedom as limitless but lacked the wisdom to navigate it responsibly. This freedom is presented not as a gift but as a test, challenging the listener to examine their intentions and consider the true impact of their decisions. *"Who do you serve?"* presses for self-reflection, asking who or what ultimately holds influence over their life.

Took for granted what you should have preserved speaks to the impulsiveness of youth, the tendency to overlook what's genuinely valuable in favor of momentary pleasures or superficial gains. There's a poignant regret here, an acknowledgment that the speaker realizes, too late, the importance of what was lost. The repetition of *"no time left, no time left to make amends"* adds a sense of urgency and finality, reminding the listener of the irreversible nature of certain choices. The tone is almost a cautionary tale, warning against careless decisions and the failure to recognize the worth of enduring values.

"Keep burning bridges while you're buying your new friends" captures the hollow pursuit of transient relationships over authentic connections. *Burning bridges* implies a destructive path, one that severs meaningful ties, while *buying friends* suggests relationships based on convenience rather than loyalty or mutual respect. This line speaks to the futility of chasing superficial validation, leaving the listener with a sense of emptiness that such choices ultimately bring. The music here reflects this stark realization, with a steady, somber rhythm that echoes the isolation that comes from valuing popularity over substance.

The line *"A day of reflection hits; you're a shell, skin and bones, counting costs"* reveals a harsh moment of reckoning. The speaker sees himself as a *"shell,"* stripped to his core, forced to confront the emptiness left behind by years of misguided choices. *Counting costs* becomes an act of somber calculation, a painful review of what has been sacrificed. It's a haunting image of being reduced to one's mistakes and losses, questioning whether the pursuit of temporary gratification was worth the damage to one's soul. *"Is it worth your soul?"* brings gravity to this reflection, suggesting that the price of these choices may be one's very essence or integrity.

The refrain, *"It's funny how times can change, rearrange, and distance makes the pain fade away,"* brings a bittersweet observation about the way time reshapes perspective. There's an irony in *"funny,"* as if the speaker marvels at how past grievances that once felt all-consuming have lost their hold. This line captures the paradox of time's ability to dull pain while also creating distance, making former conflicts and passions seem less significant. *"So important then, doesn't matter now"* reflects this shift, acknowledging how what once seemed vital fades into the background with the passing years.

The chorus, *"Come full circle,"* signals a moment of realization, an acknowledgment that he has returned to where he started, but with new wisdom. To come full circle is to revisit a familiar place with a transformed perspective, finding clarity in the lessons of the past. The phrase *"both feet on the ground"* suggests a newfound stability and grounding, a sense of maturity that comes from hard-earned experience. The music in this section is both triumphant and introspective, capturing the sense of fulfillment that accompanies this revelation and the acceptance of the journey it took to get here.

"No access granted now, boy; you've been denied. Jump a fence to see what's on the other side" introduces the reality of facing the limitations imposed by past actions. The image of *jumping a fence* conveys a desire to break free from constraints, to seek answers despite being shut out. There's a defiance here, a refusal to be limited by past mistakes, and a

curiosity to explore what lies beyond. *"Are you wanted, are you want-ed?"* is a haunting question of worth and belonging, hinting at a search for validation and a sense of purpose that goes beyond surface-level acceptance.

The line *"Can second chances mean another impression?"* reflects a hopeful curiosity about redemption and reinvention. It suggests a desire to rebuild, to redefine oneself in the wake of past failures. There's a cautious optimism here, a sense that, despite mistakes, there may still be room for renewal or forgiveness, even if it requires a fresh start.

"I got one foot stuck in heaven, yeah, one boot stuck in hell" reveals the internal conflict of someone torn between past regrets and the hope for redemption. This image speaks to the speaker's divided state, his struggle to reconcile past actions with his desire for a better future. *Heaven* and *hell* represent the moral tug-of-war within, a tension be-tween light and darkness, between the desire for peace and the weight of his own failings. The juxtaposition of these two realms captures his sense of being caught between two worlds, unable to fully commit to either.

The line *"I looked at God, He winked at me; I made this mess myself"* is both humbling and humorous. The wink from God suggests an ac-knowledgment of human frailty, as if even the divine understands and forgives. The line, *"I made this mess myself,"* is a moment of account-ability, an admission that he is fully responsible for his predicament. This acceptance of responsibility is a key step toward redemption, a recognition that growth requires facing the consequences of one's actions with humility.

"Close the door and don't look back or you will fade away" signals a final farewell to the past. This line emphasizes the importance of mov-ing forward without being held back by old regrets. There's a sense

of caution here, a warning that dwelling too long on past mistakes can consume a person, making it impossible to grow. The music here is solemn and resolute, capturing the weight of this decision to leave behind the past and embrace a new beginning.

The closing refrain, *"It's funny how times can change, rearrange, and distance makes the pain fade away,"* returns with a tone of acceptance and understanding. This line now feels less ironic and more reflective, as if the speaker has found peace in the way time reshapes perspective. *"Come full circle"* feels conclusive, a testament that he has arrived at a place of wisdom, grounded in both the pain and growth of his experiences.

In *"Full Circle,"* Creed crafts a reflective narrative on confronting one's past and the journey toward self-acceptance. The song serves as both a reminder of the cost of certain choices and a meditation on the possibility of growth through accountability and reflection. With poignant lyrics and a steady, contemplative melody, *"Full Circle"* encourages the listener to reflect on their own cycles, to question what they've taken for granted, and to consider whether they're closer to becoming the person they truly want to be. It's a powerful reminder that coming full circle doesn't erase the past but provides the strength to move forward, grounded and wiser, ready for the future.

CHAPTER 43
"Time"

C reed's "Time" is an intimate confrontation with one of life's most unyielding forces. In this song, time isn't an abstract concept but a relentless adversary, something that the speaker resents, wrestles with, and ultimately cannot escape. The lyrics convey frustration, resignation, and a sense of betrayal, as time exposes wounds and failures, demanding movement and change even when he feels powerless to control his own life's trajectory.

The song opens with the line, "I can't explain, can't quite put my finger on it," which immediately sets the tone of confusion and helplessness. He's grappling with an ineffable feeling, a difference or dissonance that he can sense but not fully articulate. This undefined tension grows as he continues, "The difference that makes us so different." Here, he's acknowledging a divide, perhaps between who he is and who he wants to be, or between himself and the world around him. It's a feeling of alienation, of being out of sync, not just with others but with time itself—a theme that will echo throughout the song.

"We've said everything; our words only betrayed us. Nothing is left, nothing was left unsaid." This line hints at exhaustion and the failure of communication. It's as if he's tried to articulate his struggles and desires, but words have proven insufficient or even deceptive. His attempts to connect or resolve his inner turmoil have led nowhere, leaving him with nothing. The image of words betraying him suggests that language itself has limits, that the emotions and frustrations he's experiencing can't be fully captured or understood. It's a haunting moment of isolation, as though he's speaking into a void, unheard and unheeded.

"This time I have nothing left to lose; I'm stuck, the second hand won't move." These lines strike at the heart of his conflict with time. There's a sense of being frozen, as if he's trapped in a moment that refuses to pass. The second hand's stillness is a powerful metaphor for stagnation and powerlessness. He feels immobilized, unable to move forward or reclaim what he's lost. The phrase "nothing left to lose" suggests a breaking point; he's been stripped of hope, illusions, and the sense of progression. The music here deepens in tone, reflecting the gravity of this internal struggle, each beat resonating like the tick of a clock that refuses to budge.

"It's about time that I speak my mind, it's about time, about time I find pieces of me I have lost." This line carries both urgency and regret. He realizes that he can no longer stay silent or passive—he must reclaim his voice and his identity. The repetition of "it's about time" is laced with irony; it's as though he's taunting time itself, declaring that he will no longer be a passive bystander. He's ready to dig through the fragments of himself that have been scattered by time, to rediscover parts of his identity he's neglected or forgotten. The music swells here, emphasizing the sense of resolve, though there's still a hint of sorrow, a reminder of all that he's lost.

The refrain "Hey time, you're no friend of mine" feels like a personal indictment. Time here is personified as an antagonist, something that has not only failed him but actively worked against him. The resentment in these words is palpable; he blames time for the erosion of his life, for the opportunities and relationships that have slipped away. By calling time "no friend," he's vocalizing the bitterness that comes from realizing how swiftly it moves and how indifferent it is to his struggles.

"You cover yourself, you cover your skin; you cover yourself like you cover your sin." This line paints time as something deceitful, something that hides its true nature. The use of "cover" suggests layers, as if time conceals the toll it takes until it's too late to recover what's lost. The comparison to sin adds a layer of moral weight, as if time's effects are inherently harmful, leading him to guilt, regret, and loss. This portrayal of time as both an enemy and a judge is unsettling, reinforcing the idea that time is not just indifferent but actively punishing.

"Please untie my hands, I'm a sinner, I'm a man; I ask for one minute to make you understand." This plea is raw and humble. He acknowledges his flaws, his mistakes, and his humanity. In admitting he's a "sinner," he's taking responsibility for his own choices, but he's also begging for reprieve—a single minute to explain himself, to convey his pain. The phrase "untie my hands" captures his sense of helplessness, his inability to change the past or escape the binds that time has placed on him. There's a vulnerability here, a sense that he's baring his soul to something beyond his control.

"Will you be there to catch me when I stumble, when I fall?" This question is directed at time, a plea for mercy or understanding. He's asking whether time will be forgiving, whether it will offer him a second chance or let him fall into oblivion. But he knows the answer, as the next line reveals: "It's so very clear you left me when I had no one at all." This is a moment of profound betrayal, an acknowledgment that time, rather than being a guiding force, abandoned him when he needed it most. The repetition of "no one at all" underscores his isolation, his feeling of being utterly alone in his battle with time.

The repetition of the refrain "This time I have nothing left to lose; I'm stuck, the second hand won't move" returns, reinforcing his entrapment. It's as if he's locked in a cycle of loss and resignation, unable to break free. The phrase "nothing left to lose" now resonates even more deeply, as if he's slowly accepting that there may be no escape, no way to reclaim what's been lost.

"Time, you're no friend of mine" becomes his mantra, a final declaration of enmity against a force that's shaped his life yet denied him peace. The music intensifies here, reaching a crescendo that mirrors his emotional climax. The repetition of "you're no friend of mine" feels like an unyielding condemnation, a way of vocalizing the grief and frustration that have consumed him. He's not just lamenting time's passage; he's accusing it of betrayal, of taking without giving, of leaving him with fragments of a life he can't fully piece together.

The final lines, "The pieces of me I have lost; without any choice I move on," encapsulate the bittersweet nature of time's power. He acknowledges that moving forward is inevitable, even though it's not necessarily what he wants. The phrase "without any choice" is a resigned acceptance of time's dominion over him—despite his bitterness, he must keep going, even if he's left with only pieces of himself. Time may be his enemy, but it's also the only path forward.

In "Time," Creed presents a deeply introspective battle between acceptance and resistance, resignation and hope. The song is a poignant reflection on the ways in which time shapes, binds, and eventually defines us, whether we like it or not. Through stirring lyrics and a driving melody, "Time" becomes an anthem for those who feel trapped in the relentless march of days, those who have lost parts of themselves to moments they can't reclaim. Ultimately, the song leaves us with a sobering truth—that while time may not be a friend, it's an inescapable part of our journey, one that we must reckon with even as we mourn what it takes from us.

Application

In *"Time,"* Creed confronts life's most unyielding force with a powerful sense of frustration, resignation, and vulnerability. Time in this song is more than an abstract concept; it's a relentless adversary, a force that exposes wounds and unravels choices. The lyrics tell a story of feeling trapped, isolated, and ultimately resigned to the fact that time moves on, with or without us. The music reflects this inner battle, creating a landscape of intense reflection and emotion as the speaker grapples with his relationship to time, a force that demands change but offers no mercy.

The opening line, *"I can't explain, can't quite put my finger on it,"* immediately conveys a feeling of helplessness and confusion. The speaker is wrestling with something intangible, a sense of disconnection that he can feel but can't articulate. *"The difference that makes us so different"* hints at a divide—perhaps between himself and his past, or between who he is and who he wants to be. This sense of alienation suggests he feels out of sync not only with others but with the progression of his own life, as if he's struggling to keep up with time's relentless pace.

"We've said everything; our words only betrayed us. Nothing is left, nothing was left unsaid." This line captures a profound sense of disillusionment, as though all attempts to understand or communicate his feelings have led only to emptiness. Words, rather than bringing clarity or connection, have turned against him, leaving him with a haunting sense of isolation. It's as if every conversation, every attempt to reach out, has only deepened the divide, reinforcing the futility of trying to capture emotions that feel beyond words. The music here is sparse and haunting, mirroring the isolation he feels as he confronts

the inadequacy of language to bridge the gap between himself and others.

"This time I have nothing left to lose; I'm stuck, the second hand won't move." This line speaks to the heart of his struggle with time. The imagery of a "stuck" second hand evokes a sense of immobilization, of being frozen in a moment that refuses to pass. The phrase *"nothing left to lose"* suggests he's reached a point of despair, stripped of hope and illusions, left only with a sense of stagnation. There's a powerlessness here, as if time has abandoned him in a place of regret and longing, denying him the freedom to move forward or reclaim what's been lost. The music deepens in tone, each beat like a tick of a clock that's both unyielding and indifferent, adding to the sense of inevitability.

"It's about time that I speak my mind, it's about time, about time I find pieces of me I have lost." This line is both a declaration of intention and a reflection of regret. The repetition of *"it's about time"* feels ironic, as though he's challenging time itself to let him reclaim his voice and identity. He's no longer willing to stay silent; he wants to gather the fragments of himself that time has scattered. This realization brings a sense of resolve, though it's tinged with sorrow over all that he has already lost. The music swells, giving weight to this moment of self-assertion, as if he's trying to rise up against the force that's held him captive for so long.

The refrain *"Hey time, you're no friend of mine"* is a bitter indictment, personifying time as an antagonist. This line becomes a personal declaration of enmity, a way of vocalizing his resentment toward the force that has shaped his life, often to his detriment. By addressing time directly, he blames it for the erosion of his dreams and the relationships that have slipped away. *"You're no friend of mine"* captures a deep sense of betrayal, as though time itself has been an adversary, something that takes without ever giving.

"You cover yourself, you cover your skin; you cover yourself like you cover your sin." This line portrays time as something deceitful, a force that conceals its effects until it's too late. The use of *"cover"* suggests hidden layers, as if time cloaks its consequences, masking the toll it takes on life and on the soul. The comparison to sin adds a sense of gravity, portraying time's effects as inherently damaging, leading him down a path of regret and sorrow. Time is not just a neutral force here; it's something dark and punishing, a judge that exacts its toll without mercy.

"Please untie my hands, I'm a sinner, I'm a man; I ask for one minute to make you understand." This plea is deeply vulnerable, an acknowledgment of both his flaws and his desire for understanding. In admitting he's a *"sinner,"* he's taking responsibility for his choices, yet he's also begging for grace—a single minute to express himself, to explain his pain. The phrase *"untie my hands"* speaks to his sense of helplessness, as though he's bound by time, unable to change his past or free himself from the constraints it's placed on him. This line is a moment of humility, a raw appeal for a reprieve that he knows time will not grant.

"Will you be there to catch me when I stumble, when I fall?" is a plea for mercy, a question directed at time as if it could somehow be compassionate. He's asking if time will offer him a second chance, a soft place to land. But he already knows the answer, as the next line reveals: *"It's so very clear you left me when I had no one at all."* This admission cuts deep, exposing the bitterness he feels toward time for abandoning him when he was most vulnerable. The repetition of *"no one at all"* underscores his isolation, his awareness that time moves on regardless of human need or suffering.

The refrain *"This time I have nothing left to lose; I'm stuck, the second hand won't move"* returns, reinforcing his entrapment. Each repetition makes it clear that he's locked in a cycle of resignation, unable to move forward. The phrase *"nothing left to lose"* now carries a weight of finality, a reluctant acceptance that time's grip on him is unbreakable.

"Time, you're no friend of mine" becomes a mantra, his final declaration of defiance against a force that has shaped his life yet denied him peace. The music builds to a crescendo, echoing the intensity of his realization. The repetition of *"you're no friend of mine"* feels like an unyielding condemnation, a way of vocalizing the grief and frustration that have consumed him. He's not just lamenting time's passage; he's accusing it of betrayal, of taking without giving, of leaving him with fragments of a life he can't fully piece together.

The closing lines, *"The pieces of me I have lost; without any choice I move on,"* encapsulate the bittersweet nature of time's power. He acknowledges that moving forward is inevitable, even though it's not what he wants. The phrase *"without any choice"* is a resigned acceptance of time's dominion over him—despite his bitterness, he must keep going, even if he's left with only pieces of himself. Time may be his enemy, but it's also the only path forward.

In *"Time,"* Creed offers a raw reflection on the complex relationship we have with the past, present, and future. The song is an anthem for those who feel trapped in the relentless march of days, a testament to the reality that while time may not be a friend, it's an inescapable force that shapes our journey. Through stirring lyrics and a haunting melody, *"Time"* captures the inner battle between resistance and acceptance, offering a sobering reminder that we must reckon with time, even as we mourn what it takes from us.

CHAPTER 44
"Good Fight"

I n "Good Fight," Creed channels the relentless inner struggle between one's current self and the ideal of who they want to become. It's a song of perseverance, a call to press forward despite setbacks and doubts. Through powerful lyrics and a driving rhythm, the song explores the tension of striving to be better, to overcome what feels insurmountable, and to hold onto hope when the path is anything but clear. There's a raw honesty in the speaker's journey, a recognition that true growth requires not only courage but also an acceptance of one's flaws and limitations.

The opening lines, "I give my all, my everything, anything you want, I strive to be," set the tone of devotion and self-sacrifice. These words suggest someone willing to pour themselves out, to give all they have in pursuit of a higher purpose or a meaningful goal. Yet, the intensity of this striving hints at a deeper struggle—an unyielding push to meet expectations that may feel unreachable. The phrase "anything you want" implies an external standard, possibly a person or an ideal he's trying to live up to. The music here is steady and deliberate, emphasizing the commitment and weight behind this statement.

"I tried, God knows I tried," reveals a sense of exhaustion and vulnerability. The repetition of "I tried" feels almost like a confession, a plea to be seen and understood in his efforts. The invocation of "God" adds a spiritual weight, as though the speaker's struggles are not just personal but cosmic, part of a larger battle between light and darkness. There's a sense of humility in these words, an acknowledgment that despite his best efforts, he hasn't yet achieved what he longs for.

"Or am I stuck somewhere between who I am and who I hope to be?" This line is the heart of the song, encapsulating the tension between reality and aspiration. The speaker is caught in an in-between space, navigating the gap between his present self and the person he envisions. This question reflects the universal human struggle with growth—the feeling of being on the edge of transformation but not quite there. It's a moment of self-doubt, a recognition of the frustration that comes with striving yet feeling that progress is just out of reach. The music here mirrors this ambiguity, with a melody that rises and falls, like someone caught in an endless loop of self-reflection.

The refrain, "Keep pressing on, fight the good fight, fight what you know is wrong," serves as an anthem of perseverance. It's a mantra, a rallying cry to keep going even when the road feels steep and unforgiving. "Fight the good fight" is a phrase often associated with moral or spiritual battles, suggesting that the struggle isn't just against external obstacles but against internal weaknesses or doubts. There's an implicit call to integrity here, a reminder to hold onto what's right, even when it's difficult. The repetition of "keep pressing on" reinforces this determination, an encouragement to push forward no matter the cost.

The line "I've come so far to fall too fast" captures the fear of losing hard-won progress. It's a moment of realization that every step forward could be undone by a single misstep. This fear of falling "too fast" speaks to the fragility of growth and the lingering insecurity that the effort could be in vain. The phrase "eyes forward, I can't look back" highlights the resolve to stay focused on the future, to resist the pull of past failures or regrets. The decision to look forward is one of courage and determination, a conscious choice to believe that the path ahead holds promise.

The line "I shift my eyes to the sky, in the distance see the horizon line" introduces a moment of hope, a glimpse of something beyond the struggle. The horizon symbolizes possibility, a new beginning that lies just out of reach. This image of the horizon line reflects both his desire for change and the patience required to reach it. "She waits for me fighting the good fight" hints at a person or ideal that serves as his motivation, someone or something he's fighting for beyond himself. It's a reminder that his efforts are not solitary; there's a purpose or relationship that gives his struggle meaning.

The refrain returns with renewed intensity, as if each repetition strengthens his resolve. "Fight what you know is wrong" becomes more than just a call to action; it becomes a moral compass, a guiding principle that keeps him grounded. Each line reinforces the speaker's commitment to his values, even when the journey is difficult. The music here is urgent, almost relentless, mirroring the drive to keep moving forward no matter the cost.

The repetition of "Am I stuck somewhere between who I am and who I hope to be?" is a moment of introspection that brings the listener back to his internal struggle. This line feels heavier with each repetition, as though he's wrestling with the weight of his own expectations. He's acknowledging the discomfort of growth—the feeling of being in a constant state of becoming, without ever fully arriving. The refrain "fighting, I'm fighting" underscores this tension, capturing the ongoing, unfinished nature of his journey.

The verse "Remember that sometimes I fall in between the night's blue moon and the shadows it keeps" introduces a more introspective tone, evoking the imagery of a lonely, reflective night. The "blue moon" symbolizes something rare, a fleeting moment of clarity or beauty, while the "shadows" represent the fears and insecurities that haunt him. This line captures the duality of hope and doubt, light and darkness, that coexist in his life. He's acknowledging that even in moments of clarity, there's a shadow that lingers, a reminder of the challenges that persist.

The closing lines, "Fight on, fight the good fight, and I'll keep fighting the good fight," bring the song to a powerful conclusion. There's a sense of resilience in these words, a vow to continue despite the obstacles. The repetition of "fight on" is like a heartbeat, a steady rhythm that propels him forward. It's a promise to himself, a commitment to face whatever comes, grounded in the belief that his efforts are worthwhile.

In "Good Fight," Creed captures the universal experience of struggling to live up to one's ideals. The song is a powerful reminder of the courage required to keep pressing on, to fight for what's right, even when success feels uncertain. The lyrics and music work together to create a sense of urgency and resolve, urging the listener to embrace the struggle as a necessary part of growth. It's a call to hold onto hope, to find strength in moments of weakness, and to keep moving forward toward the horizon, knowing that the journey itself is a testament to one's character.

Application

In "Good Fight," Creed explores the relentless inner battle of striving to become a better version of oneself, grappling with both the hope and hardship that come with transformation. The lyrics reflect a deep commitment to growth and perseverance, while acknowledging the inevitable struggles and setbacks that test one's resolve. Through powerful, introspective lyrics and a driving melody, the song becomes a call to keep moving forward even when the path is unclear, to press on with integrity, and to embrace the journey of self-discovery.

The opening lines, *"I give my all, my everything, anything you want, I strive to be,"* set the stage for a story of devotion and sacrifice. These words suggest someone who is pouring everything they have into becoming better, willing to push themselves to meet a high standard. The phrase *"anything you want"* hints at an external influence or ideal, something or someone the speaker is working tirelessly to live up to. The steady, deliberate rhythm in the music underscores the weight of this commitment, reflecting the seriousness of the speaker's dedication.

The line *"I tried, God knows I tried,"* reveals a sense of exhaustion and vulnerability. Repeating *"I tried"* feels almost like a confession, a way of admitting that despite his best efforts, he hasn't yet reached his goal. The mention of *"God"* adds a spiritual dimension, suggesting that his journey is not just personal but part of a larger struggle between light and darkness. There's humility in these words, an acknowledgment of his limits and a plea for understanding.

"Or am I stuck somewhere between who I am and who I hope to be?" This line captures the essence of the song, reflecting the tension between his current reality and his aspirations. The speaker is caught in an in-between state, aware of who he wants to become but feeling unable to fully reach that potential. It's a moment of self-doubt, revealing the frustration that comes with striving but feeling that progress is always just out of reach. The melody mirrors this ambiguity, rising and falling as if caught in a cycle of hope and hesitation.

The refrain, *"Keep pressing on, fight the good fight, fight what you know is wrong,"* serves as a rallying cry for resilience. It's more than just a call to keep going; it's a commitment to uphold moral and spiritual values, even when the journey is difficult. *"Fight the good fight"* invokes the idea of a noble struggle, suggesting that the speaker's challenges are as much about internal battles as they are about external ones.

The repetition of *"keep pressing on"* reinforces the idea of perseverance, encouraging the listener to move forward despite any obstacles.

"I've come so far to fall too fast" reflects a fear of losing all the progress he's made. There's a recognition that growth is fragile, that a single mistake could undo everything he's worked for. The phrase *"eyes forward, I can't look back"* speaks to his resolve to stay focused on the future, resisting the temptation to dwell on past failures. Choosing to look forward is an act of courage, a conscious decision to believe in the possibility of change despite the risk of setbacks.

"I shift my eyes to the sky, in the distance see the horizon line" introduces a moment of hope, a vision of something greater that lies just beyond his reach. The horizon becomes a symbol of possibility, a reminder that while the journey is difficult, there is something worth striving for. The line *"She waits for me fighting the good fight"* hints at a person or ideal that serves as his motivation, a source of strength that makes his struggle meaningful. It's a reminder that his efforts aren't just for himself; there's a purpose or relationship that gives him hope.

As the refrain returns, *"Fight what you know is wrong"* becomes not just a mantra but a guiding principle. Each repetition strengthens his resolve, creating a rhythm that matches the steady beat of perseverance. The music here intensifies, reflecting the urgency of his commitment to keep moving forward no matter the challenges he faces.

The repetition of *"Am I stuck somewhere between who I am and who I hope to be?"* brings the listener back to his inner conflict. Each time he asks this question, it feels heavier, as though he's wrestling with the weight of his own expectations. There's an honesty in his uncertainty, an acknowledgment of the discomfort that comes with self-growth and the feeling of being in a state of continuous transformation. *"Fighting, I'm fighting"* becomes a raw declaration of this ongoing journey, underscoring the struggle to reconcile who he is with who he wants to be.

The verse *"Remember that sometimes I fall in between the night's blue moon and the shadows it keeps"* introduces a quieter, more introspective tone. The "blue moon" represents rare moments of clarity, while the "shadows" are the fears and insecurities that linger. This line captures the coexistence of light and darkness in his life, the realization that even in moments of understanding, doubt remains close. It's a reminder of the duality of hope and fear, of the challenge of finding peace amidst internal struggles.

The closing lines, *"Fight on, fight the good fight, and I'll keep fighting the good fight,"* create a powerful, defiant ending. There's a sense of resilience and commitment in these words, a vow to continue despite the obstacles. The repetition of *"fight on"* is like a heartbeat, steady and unyielding, representing his promise to face whatever comes his way. It's a reminder that growth is not a destination but a journey, one that requires constant effort and unwavering dedication.

In *"Good Fight,"* Creed captures the universal experience of striving to live up to one's ideals, facing the fear of failure, and the determination to persevere. The song is a testament to the courage required to keep moving forward, to fight for what's right even when the outcome is uncertain. Through stirring lyrics and an intense musical backdrop, the song inspires listeners to embrace their struggles as part of a meaningful journey, finding strength in moments of doubt and holding onto the hope that the journey itself is worthwhile.

CHAPTER 45
"The Song You Sing"

I n "The Song You Sing," Creed offers a meditation on purpose, influence, and the significance of our individual voices in a world that often feels chaotic and discouraging. The song serves as both a call to self-reflection and a reminder of the impact our words and actions have on those around us. Through a blend of introspective lyrics and resonant instrumentation, the song encourages us to look inward and ask if the life we lead and the message we share are meaningful enough to inspire others. It's a journey toward authenticity, one that urges us to embrace a purpose that not only uplifts us but resonates with the world around us.

The song opens with an intimate, reflective moment: "Woke up and had a face to face; guess my reflection had a lot to say." This line sets the stage for an introspective exploration, where the speaker is compelled to confront himself. There's a vulnerability in facing one's reflection, an act that forces him to look deeper, beyond surface appearances, and reckon with his inner thoughts and emotions. The reflection becomes a voice of reason, pushing him to question the life he's leading. The music here is soft and contemplative, as if holding space for this moment of self-examination, setting a reflective tone that permeates the rest of the song.

"Why let my worries steal my days? It just brings me down." This line expresses the universal struggle of allowing anxieties and doubts to consume us, robbing us of the present moment. It's a recognition of how easy it is to lose ourselves in fears and concerns, letting them overshadow the beauty of everyday life. The simplicity of this question belies its depth, inviting the listener to consider the ways in which worry and stress steal joy and purpose. There's a quiet resolve here, a sense that the speaker wants to rise above these worries and find something more meaningful.

The chorus, "Does the song you sing have enough meaning? Inspire us to sing along," is the heart of the song, posing a profound question about purpose and influence. The "song" symbolizes the life we live, the message we project to the world. It's not just about music; it's a metaphor for the values, actions, and choices that define us. The question of whether our "song" has enough meaning is a call to live intentionally, to ensure that what we stand for resonates deeply enough to inspire others. The repetition of "inspire us to sing along" is a plea for connection, a desire for a message that is not only personal but universally meaningful. The music swells during this refrain, adding weight to the question and emphasizing its importance.

"Does the song you sing keep echoing?" This line introduces the idea of legacy, the lasting impact of one's words and actions. An echo suggests something that lingers, a message that endures beyond the moment it's spoken. This question asks whether our lives leave a lasting impression, whether what we say and do continues to resonate with others long after we're gone. It's a powerful reminder of the responsibility we carry to live in a way that uplifts and inspires others. The music here takes on a resonant quality, almost as if creating an echo within the song itself, underscoring the idea of an enduring impact.

The next verse shifts outward: "What's wrong with the world today? Tell me what's all the talk about." Here, the speaker expands his focus from personal reflection to the world at large, questioning the current state of society. There's a sense of frustration, as though he's tired of the superficial conversations and noise that dominate public discourse. This question is more than a complaint; it's a yearning for depth and substance, a desire for people to focus on what truly matters. The music here grows more intense, capturing the speaker's urgency and his dissatisfaction with the distractions of modern life.

"Lately, I've been in a real bad place, can't let the world bring me down." This line reveals the speaker's struggle with maintaining hope and purpose amidst a challenging and often disheartening world. It's an acknowledgment of the difficulty of staying true to oneself in a society that often pulls us in multiple directions. Yet, there's resilience here, a commitment to not allow external negativity to define his outlook or actions. This line speaks to the importance of holding onto one's own values and message, even when the world feels bleak. The music here builds in strength, mirroring his resolve to rise above his circumstances.

In the bridge, the speaker expresses a wish: "I hope the words I wrote keep calling out, keep calling out." This line is deeply personal, a hope that the message he has created will continue to reach others, that his words will resonate long after they're spoken. The repetition of "keep calling out" emphasizes a desire for lasting influence, for words that have the power to inspire others to introspection and action. This sentiment is both hopeful and humble, recognizing that while he cannot control how others respond, he wishes for his voice to serve as a positive force.

"Forever let them sing that song you sing," he continues, expressing a wish for his message to endure and inspire future generations. The phrase "that song you sing" shifts from a personal message to something broader, perhaps a universal truth or value that transcends the individual. The speaker's hope is not just for his own message to endure but for a collective song—a truth that all can share and find meaning in. The music here swells with a sense of possibility, as if reaching toward something larger, something infinite.

As the song approaches its conclusion, the refrain returns with renewed poignancy. "Does the song you sing have enough meaning? Inspire us to sing along." By this point, the question has transformed from a challenge into an invitation. It's as if the speaker is no longer just asking himself this question but is extending it to the listener, urging them to consider the impact of their own "song." The repetition of "inspire us to sing the song you sing" reinforces the desire for unity, for each person to find a voice that is both true and meaningful.

In the closing lines, "It's the song you sing, it's the life you bring, that's why I sing the song you sing," the speaker expresses gratitude and solidarity. He acknowledges that the inspiration to live meaningfully comes not only from within but also from those around us who live with purpose. There's a sense of harmony here, an acknowledgment that we are all interconnected, that the lives others lead can inspire us to find our own purpose. This line underscores the idea that our "songs" are not isolated but part of a larger, collective chorus that shapes and uplifts.

The song fades out on this message of unity, leaving the listener with a powerful reminder of the importance of living with intention. "The Song You Sing" by Creed isn't just a reflection on one's own purpose; it's a call to action, a reminder that our lives have the potential to inspire others, to create echoes that last long after we're gone. Through introspective lyrics and a stirring melody, the song becomes a celebration of purpose, resilience, and the enduring power of a life well-lived. It's a reminder that each of us has a voice that can resonate, a "song" that, if sung with authenticity and meaning, has the potential to inspire others to sing along.

Application

In *"The Song You Sing,"* Creed offers a reflective journey into the power of purpose, the impact of our words, and the significance of our individual "songs" in a noisy world. Through introspective lyrics and resonant music, the song poses deep questions about the life we lead, encouraging us to consider if our "song"—our message, our actions, and our influence—is meaningful enough to inspire and uplift those around us. This is a call to live authentically and purposefully, with an awareness of how our voices can resonate and create lasting echoes.

The song opens with a scene of introspection: *"Woke up and had a face to face; guess my reflection had a lot to say."* This line sets a contemplative tone, with the speaker engaging in a moment of self-confrontation, an inward dialogue that invites honesty and vulnerability. Facing one's reflection is a powerful metaphor for self-evaluation, urging him to dig deeper than appearances and explore his intentions and actions. The music here is soft, allowing space for this moment of reflection, signaling a thoughtful mood that threads through the entire song.

"Why let my worries steal my days? It just brings me down," captures the universal struggle of allowing anxieties to rob us of joy and purpose. The question is simple yet profound, reminding the listener of how easily we let fears and concerns consume our thoughts. There's an underlying resolve in this line, a desire to rise above the weight of worry and focus on something more meaningful. The melody here remains gentle, almost meditative, as if urging the listener to pause and reflect on their own experiences with worry and distraction.

The chorus, *"Does the song you sing have enough meaning? Inspire us to sing along,"* serves as the thematic core of the song, challenging the listener to consider the impact of their life's message. The "song" here is a metaphor for the choices, values, and actions that define us. This question goes beyond surface-level existence; it calls for intentional living, for words and deeds that resonate deeply and inspire others. The repeated call to "inspire us to sing along" underscores a yearning for connection, a reminder that the most meaningful lives often spark unity and shared purpose. Musically, the refrain rises in intensity, adding weight to the question, signaling its importance.

"Does the song you sing keep echoing?" introduces the concept of legacy, asking if our lives and actions leave a lasting impression. An echo suggests something that lingers, that reverberates beyond the moment, impacting others long after it's first heard. This question speaks to the desire for a meaningful existence, one that leaves behind more than transient success or superficial accomplishments. The music takes on a fuller, more resonant quality, reflecting the concept of an enduring impact that continues to resonate over time.

In the verse *"What's wrong with the world today? Tell me what's all the talk about,"* the speaker shifts his focus outward, questioning the state of society. There's a sense of frustration here, a weariness with the trivial distractions that often dominate our attention. This line isn't just a complaint; it's a call for substance and authenticity, a wish for people to focus on what truly matters. The music here intensifies, mirroring the speaker's urgency and dissatisfaction, capturing the dissonance he feels with a world that often overlooks depth and meaning.

"Lately, I've been in a real bad place, can't let the world bring me down," reveals the speaker's struggle with maintaining hope in challenging times. He acknowledges the difficulty of staying true to his purpose amidst a world that feels overwhelming or discouraging. Yet, there's resilience in his words, a commitment to not let external negativity dictate his outlook. This line speaks to the importance of

holding onto one's values, even when the world seems bleak. The music builds in strength, reflecting his determination to rise above his surroundings.

In the bridge, *"I hope the words I wrote keep calling out, keep calling out,"* the speaker expresses a personal wish for his message to endure. This repetition emphasizes his desire for lasting influence, for words that resonate beyond the moment and inspire introspection or change in others. This hope is both humble and profound, recognizing that while he cannot control how others respond, he wishes for his voice to be a positive force. The music here is both hopeful and resonant, reflecting a sense of continuity and enduring impact.

"Forever let them sing that song you sing," broadens his message, expressing a wish for a collective song—a universal message that inspires everyone to find purpose and meaning. The speaker's hope is not just for his own message to endure but for a greater truth that all can embrace. The music swells, evoking a sense of possibility and shared purpose, as if reaching for something larger than the individual self, something timeless.

As the song approaches its conclusion, the refrain returns with renewed poignancy. *"Does the song you sing have enough meaning? Inspire us to sing along."* By this point, the question transforms from a personal reflection to an invitation for the listener. It urges each person to consider the influence of their own "song," to think about the legacy they're creating. The repeated call to "inspire us to sing the song you sing" becomes a celebration of unity, a reminder that each of our lives can contribute to a larger, harmonious chorus.

In the closing line, *"It's the song you sing, it's the life you bring, that's why I sing the song you sing,"* the speaker acknowledges the power of shared purpose and the influence of others. This line expresses gratitude for the lives of those who live with meaning, recognizing that their examples inspire him to find his own purpose. There's a sense of harmony and interconnection here, an acknowledgment that our "songs" are not isolated but part of a collective effort to uplift and inspire.

The song fades on this message of unity, leaving the listener with a powerful reminder of the importance of living with intention. *"The Song You Sing"* by Creed is not just a meditation on personal purpose but a call to action, a reminder that our lives can resonate with meaning and inspire those around us. Through introspective lyrics and a stirring melody, the song becomes a celebration of purpose, resilience, and the power of a life well-lived. It's a reminder that each of us has a voice, a "song" that, if sung with authenticity and depth, has the potential to inspire others to join in harmony.

CONCLUSION

CHAPTER 46
A Place With Golden Streets

The Testimony of Creed: A Journey from Darkness to Light

The story of Creed is not ultimately about music, fame, or even personal struggle. It is, at its core, a story of the human condition—marked by the sinfulness of man, the futility of worldly pursuits, and the desperate need for redemption through Jesus Christ. From their humble beginnings in the broken backdrop of Tallahassee's underground music scene to their ascent in the cultural mainstream of the late 1990s, Creed's path reveals a truth that Scripture makes plain: the things of this world cannot satisfy the soul.

Their success—by earthly standards—was rapid and overwhelming. Yet, behind the accolades and album sales was a deeper narrative: a band comprised of men wrestling not only with personal trials, but with eternal realities. Their music gave voice to the unrest that marks every fallen heart. Their lyrics echoed the questions asked by every man and woman since the Fall: Who am I? What is my purpose? Is there meaning beyond this life? And most importantly—where can peace be found?

They did not know, in those early years, the impact their words would have. But God's providence often uses the unlikely to bring clarity to the confused and conviction to the convicted. Creed's journey is not merely the story of musicians but of sinners confronted by the weight of truth, grappling with the emptiness of this world, and reaching—however imperfectly—for something eternal.

Confronting the Depravity of Man

Songs like *My Own Prison* and *Torn* portray the deep internal torment that results from sin. Whether intentional or not, these lyrics illustrate the biblical doctrine of total depravity. Man is not merely misguided or broken—he is dead in his trespasses and sins (Ephesians 2:1). The "prison" the band sang about was not a metaphor; it was the spiritual condition of every person apart from Christ: bound in guilt, enslaved to sin, alienated from God.

The band's first album brought these themes to the forefront. There was an authenticity to the lyrics that resonated with a generation numbed by superficiality. The pain expressed was not fictional—it was real, and it was familiar to anyone who has ever felt the weight of a guilty conscience. The Word of God tells us that the conscience bears witness to the law written on the heart (Romans 2:15), and in Creed's early work, that witness came through—loud and clear.

Human Clay, their follow-up, continued that exploration. Songs like *Higher* gave voice to a longing that all men know: the desire to be lifted from despair. The question, "Can you take me higher?" is not ultimately about success or escapism; it is the cry of a soul seeking deliverance. Man was made to worship God, and when he does not, he will look for substitutes—career, relationships, recognition—but none of these satisfy. Only Christ can save. Only Christ can transform.

In *With Arms Wide Open*, a picture is drawn of fatherhood, responsibility, and hope. It is a moment of tenderness, but also of weight. The desire to protect, to bless, and to lead a new life rightly echoes the biblical role of the father as both provider and spiritual guide. But apart from the gospel, these longings remain unfulfilled.

Creed's sincerity in expressing them reveals the law of God at work in the conscience—but sincerity alone does not save. It must be joined to truth.

From Brokenness to Redemption

The world is not lacking in emotional expression. It is lacking in truth. Creed's music, in its best moments, exposed the reality of sin and the burden of guilt. But only the gospel provides the remedy. And it is in God's providence that these themes led many listeners to seek answers beyond the lyrics—some to the Word of God itself.

Creed's transparency about their personal battles—Scott Stapp's public spiral into addiction and mental anguish, the internal strife within the band—made clear that worldly success cannot insulate anyone from the consequences of sin. Fame is fleeting. But God, in His mercy, uses even our lowest points to humble us. Trials are not wasted when they bring us to the end of ourselves.

Mark Tremonti, Scott Phillips, and Brian Marshall, like Stapp, faced their own valleys. But the message that emerged was not one of human strength—it was the necessity of grace. And this is biblical. God resists the proud but gives grace to the humble (James 4:6). Through difficulty, the Lord often brings clarity. He shows us our need, strips away our pride, and calls us to repentance.

Their story reflects this: broken men, used by God—not because of their talent, but despite it. The honesty of their struggle opened the door for listeners to face their own. It reminded many that sanctification begins with recognition of sin and continues by the power of the Holy Spirit, not the will of man.

Grace That Transforms

The central theme in Creed's music—particularly in songs like *One Last Breath*—is the possibility of restoration. "Hold me now, I'm six feet from the edge and I'm thinking maybe six feet ain't so far down."

This is not just poetic—it is theological. Man is always closer to death than he realizes, and only the grace of God can intervene in time.

Biblical grace is not sentiment. It is power. It is the unmerited favor of God shown to undeserving sinners. It is through grace that we are saved (Ephesians 2:8), not through effort, not through emotional appeal, and certainly not through art. Creed's lyrics hint at grace, long for it, and sometimes point to it—but grace must be defined biblically. It is not merely God's kindness; it is His divine intervention to redeem and regenerate the heart of stone.

Creed's audience—many of whom were in seasons of darkness—heard in these songs a cry for something real. And God, in His sovereign wisdom, often uses such cries to lead people to truth. The Bible teaches that none seek after God unless God first draws them (John 6:44). When we hear longing in music or see it in culture, it reminds us that all creation groans for redemption (Romans 8:22). But the answer is not art—it is the gospel of Jesus Christ.

Faith That Endures

As Creed's journey continued, so too did the development of their message. Though not always explicit, the undercurrent was clear: human achievement is insufficient. What man builds will fall. What man seeks will fade. The only lasting foundation is Christ (1 Corinthians 3:11).

Their later work, particularly the album *Weathered*, speaks to this endurance. It presents a soul that has been battered but not broken, refined but not destroyed. This perseverance is the mark of true faith. The believer is not exempt from suffering. On the contrary, suffering is often the means by which faith is strengthened (1 Peter 1:6–7). Creed's music acknowledged the storm—and pointed, however faintly, to the Rock.

Their evolving message serves as a challenge to every listener: where is your hope placed? On what do you build your life? Is it fame, comfort, popularity—or the person and work of Christ? Everything else is shifting sand.

The Narrow Way

As we come to the end of Creed's story, there must be a final word—one that transcends the music. It is a call to serious reflection. Following Christ is not a cultural gesture. It is not a lifestyle addition. It is death to self and life in Him. Jesus said, "If anyone wishes to come after Me, he must deny himself, and take up his cross and follow Me" (Matthew 16:24). That is not optional. That is the cost.

To follow Christ may mean losing friends, promotions, status, comfort—even your life. But the true disciple counts that cost gladly, because what he gains is of infinite worth. Our Lord never courted the masses with easy messages. He never lowered the standard. He never said, "Come, and keep your life as it is." He said, "Come, and die."

So I urge you—consider your soul. Examine your life. Christ does not ask for part of you. He demands all of you. Not as a tyrant, but as Lord. And He has the right, because He bought you with His blood (1 Corinthians 6:20). To receive the free gift of salvation is to submit fully to His authority. Anything less is not saving faith.

If today you hear His voice, do not harden your heart. Repent. Believe. Surrender. Salvation is not earned by works, but it demands a response. It is not a fleeting emotion, but a permanent transformation. Jesus said, "You must be born again" (John 3:3). That is the only way to enter the kingdom of God.

Creed's music may have opened your ears—but only Christ can open your heart. If through their journey you've seen your need for grace, don't wait. Come to Him now. The path is narrow. The way is hard. But it leads to life. And at the end of it—by God's mercy—you will find a place where the streets are indeed golden, and the blind see, and the broken are whole.

www.ingramcontent.com/pod-product-compliance
Lightning Source LLC
Chambersburg PA
CBHW021603120626
46545CB00001B/40